THE
HOME CRAFTSMAN

BANNER PRESS
NEW YORK, NEW YORK

Managing Editor: Linda Timko Gonzalez
Art Director: Maureen Marsh

CONTENTS

CANOPY BED

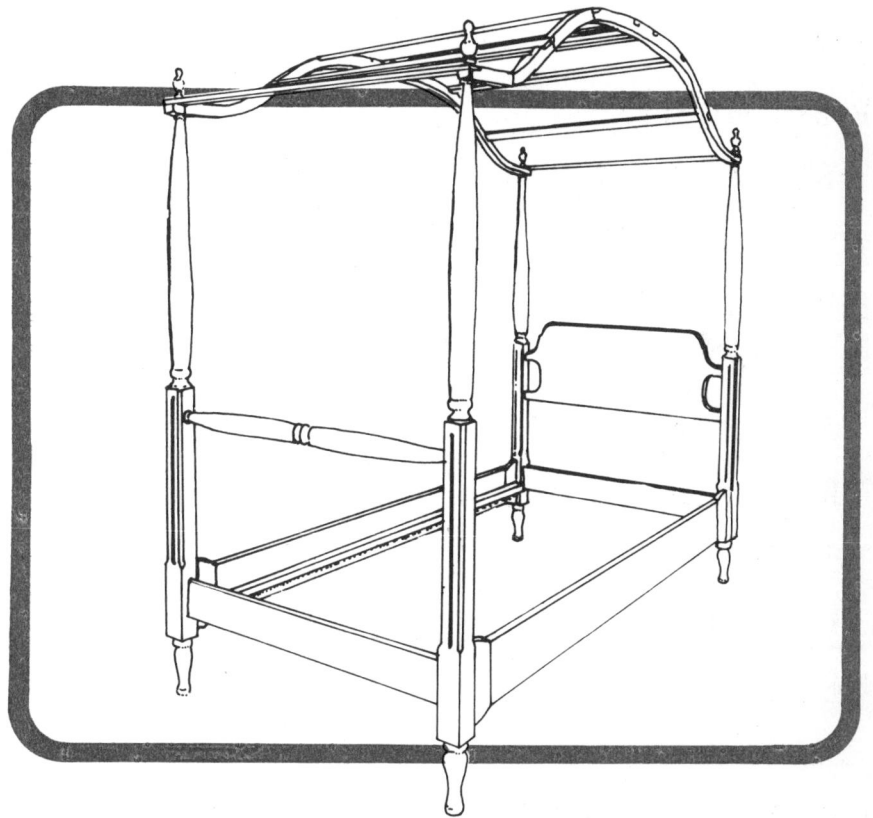

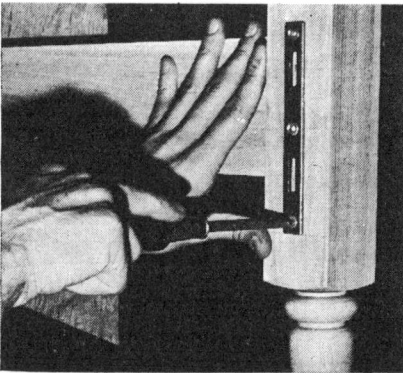

Bed irons are screwed to corner posts; joining pieces are on side rails.

Sections of corner-post turnings are joined with dowels. Using this method permits shorter sections to be turned.

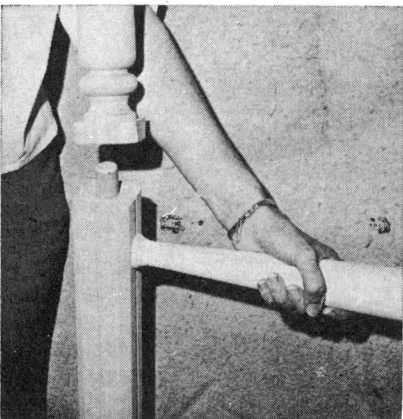

There really is no "standard" size for beds, as they vary considerably in size and shape. Even the box springs and mattresses are only relatively standard, as they can vary an inch or two in length and width, depending on the manufacturer. For these reasons it is strongly recommended you first get the spring and mattress before starting construction of this bed, and make it to suit the size of the units you get.

Start construction by turning the four corner posts, which are all identical. They are designed to be made in sections and doweled together, so the sections can be turned in a standard 36-inch lathe. An optional feature are the four "feet." If the bed seems too high when they are added, simply put casters under the ends of the lower sections of the corner posts. Spherical casters, which seem to roll the easiest, permit easy moving for cleaning under the bed and making it up.

The side rails of the bed have extra pieces splined to them at the ends. This provides edge-grain, instead of end-grain for driving the screws that hold the bed irons. When installing the male and female sections of the bed irons, be sure to align the rails vertically so there is no twist in the wood when the bed is assembled. It will be necessary to chisel recesses behind the female ends of the bed irons that fit on the corner posts, to allow the hooks in the male portions to fit.

The canopy frame is made as indicated, with a splined joint at the center. Assemble the two arches, one on top of the other, with waxed paper or plastic food wrap at the joints to prevent gluing them together. This will assure that both arches are the same.

Turn the spacer for the foot of the bed, using a pattern made by enlarging the squared drawing, then make patterns for the head and footboard panels by enlarging the squared drawings of these parts. These various parts as well as the straight end rails are doweled and glued to the corner posts.

Assemble the canopy frame, using half-laps for the crosspieces, as indicated. Holes in the frame ends accept the dowels on the finials that slip down through the frame and into holes in the tops of the posts. Do not glue the finials in the holes, as their removal permits taking off the canopy frame when the bed is dissambled.

White enamel, or other finish of your choice, completes the project.

Spline for center joint of canopy frame is cut on length of stock, which permits using it to both join and clamp sections.

BED ASSEMBLY

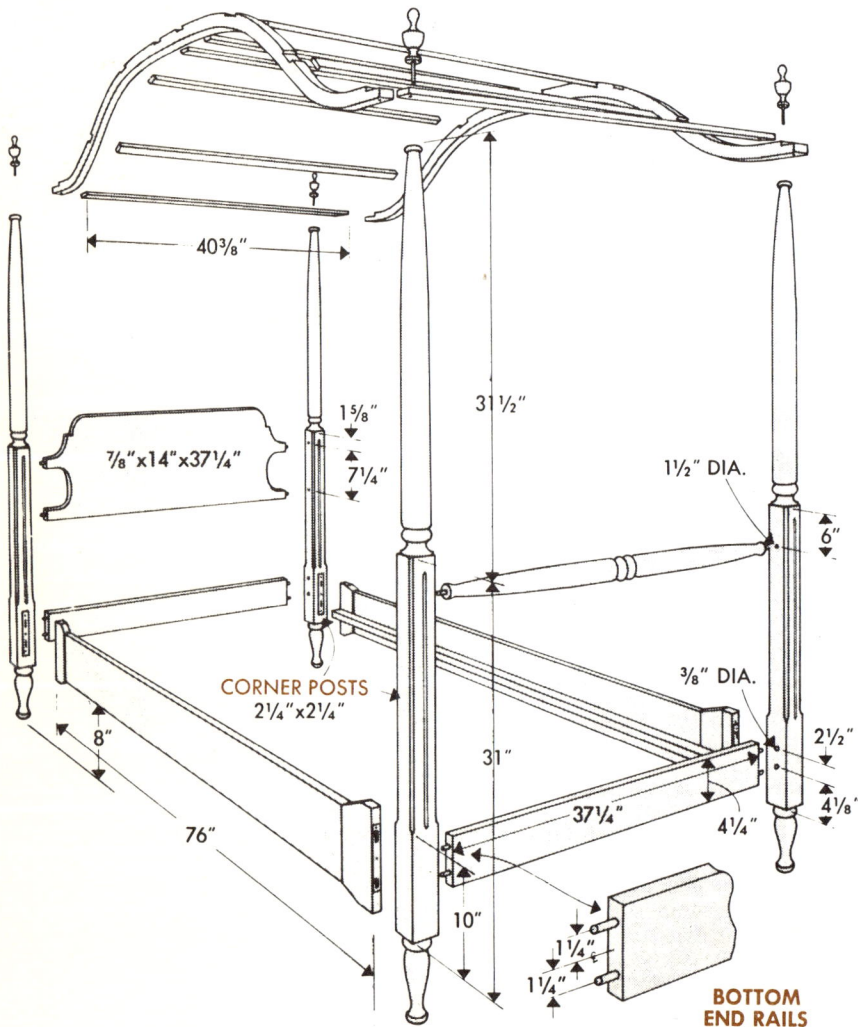

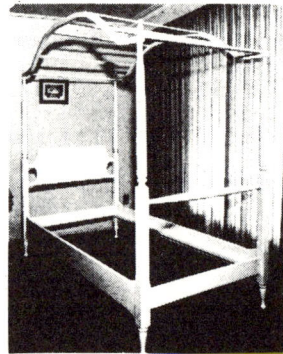

40⅜″

31½″

1½″ DIA.

1⅝″

7¼″

6″

⅞″x14″x37¼″

CORNER POSTS
2¼″x2¼″

⅜″ DIA.

2½″

8″

31″

4⅛″

76″

37¼″

4¼″

10″

1¼″

1¼″

**BOTTOM
END RAILS**

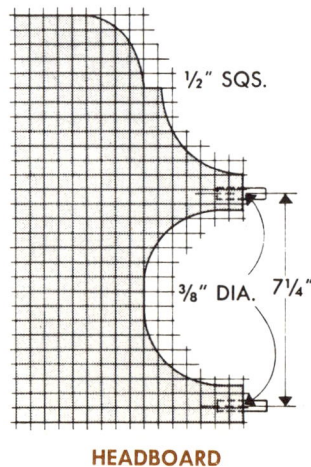

½″ SQS.

⅜″ DIA.　7¼″

HEADBOARD

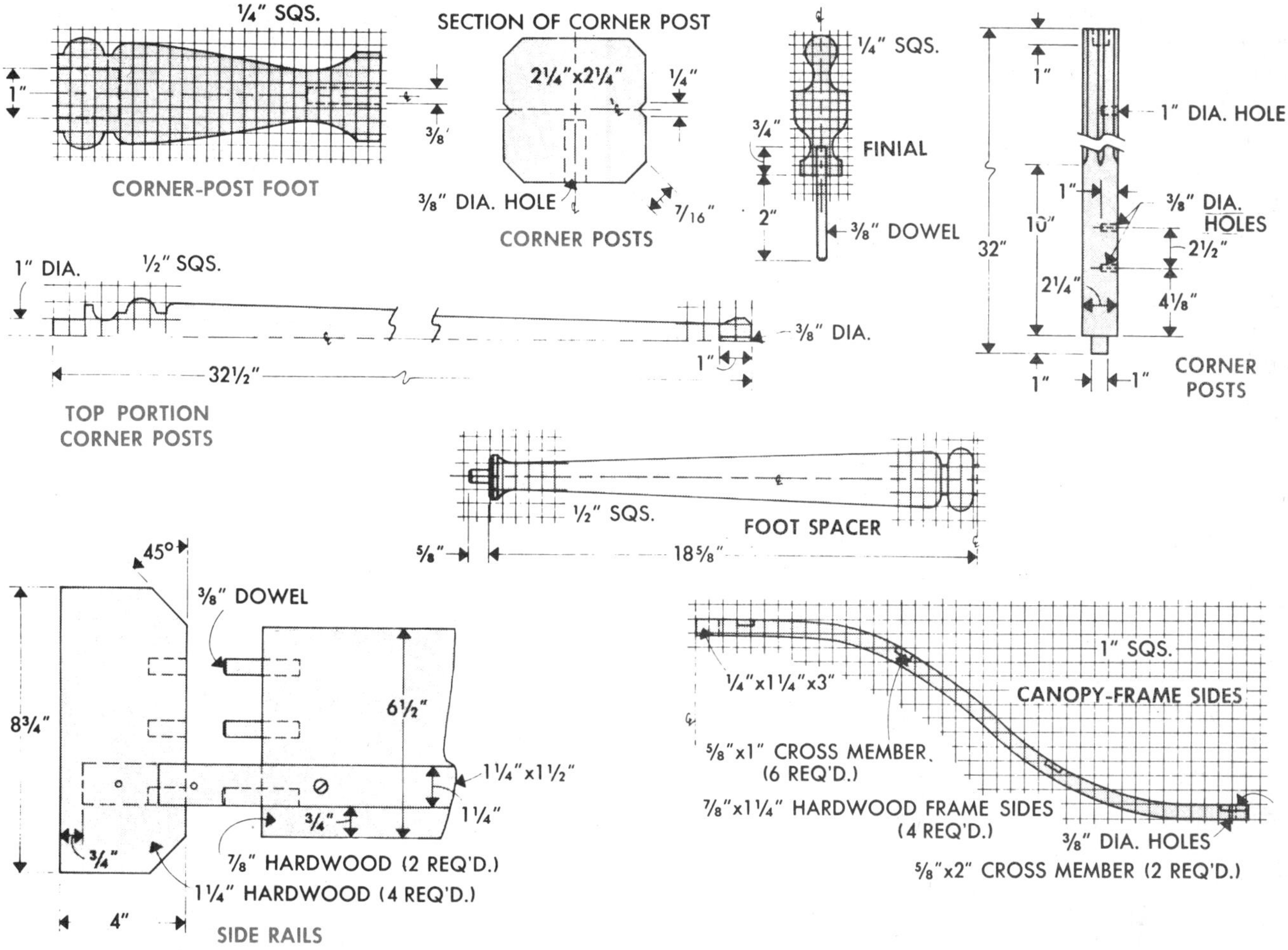

¼" SQS.
1"
⅜"
CORNER-POST FOOT
SECTION OF CORNER POST
2¼"x2¼"
¼"
⅜" DIA. HOLE
7/16"
CORNER POSTS
¼" SQS.
¾"
FINIAL
2"
⅜" DOWEL
1"
1" DIA. HOLE
1"
⅜" DIA. HOLES
10"
32"
2½"
2¼"
4⅛"
1"
1"
CORNER POSTS
1" DIA.
½" SQS.
⅜" DIA.
1"
32½"
TOP PORTION CORNER POSTS
½" SQS.
FOOT SPACER
⅝"
18⅝"
45°
⅜" DOWEL
8¾"
6½"
1¼"x1½"
1¼"
¾"
¾"
⅞" HARDWOOD (2 REQ'D.)
1¼" HARDWOOD (4 REQ'D.)
4"
SIDE RAILS
1" SQS.
¼"x1¼"x3"
CANOPY-FRAME SIDES
⅝"x1" CROSS MEMBER
(6 REQ'D.)
⅞"x1¼" HARDWOOD FRAME SIDES
(4 REQ'D.)
⅜" DIA. HOLES
⅝"x2" CROSS MEMBER (2 REQ'D.)

SHERATON FIELD BED

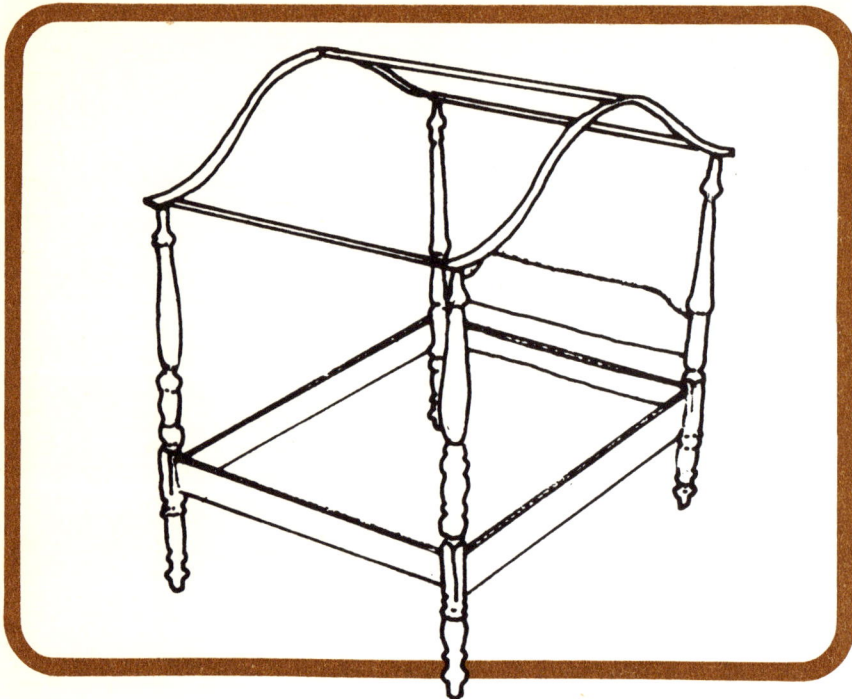

This elegant four-poster is of Sheraton style but also exhibits a touch of the approaching Federal Period.

The posts have been designed in short sections to be doweled together, so that they can be turned on the average home lathe that has 30 inches between centers. Note that four "A" sections are required; this portion of each post is identical.

The side rails will vary somewhat in lenth, depending on the bed fasteners used, but should create the 72¾-inch distance between the posts. The arched canopy supports (which make the "field" in the name) are cut from three 1 x 8s face-glued to produce the 2¼-inch width of stock. The center brace is butted inside the half-lap joints and reinforced with dowels.

Maple was used for the original, with the headboard of pine. Use a close-grained hardwood for the posts for cleaner turning.

The choice of finish is up to the builder, whether a light contemporary color or dark antique.

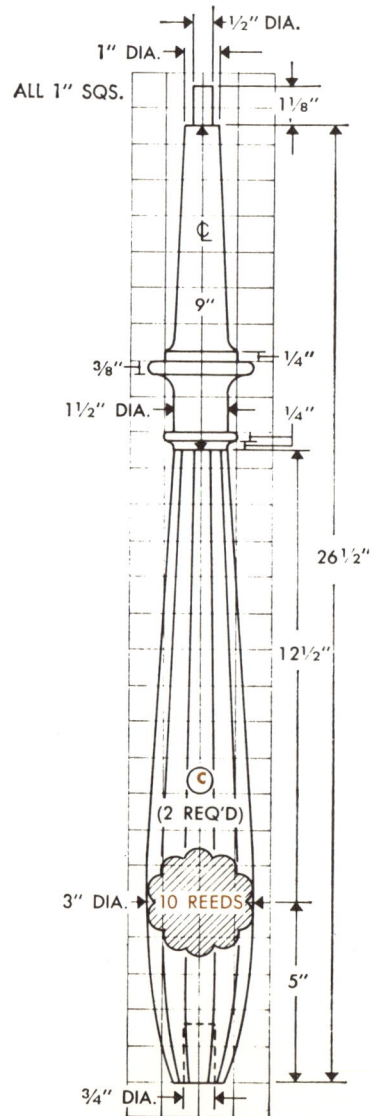

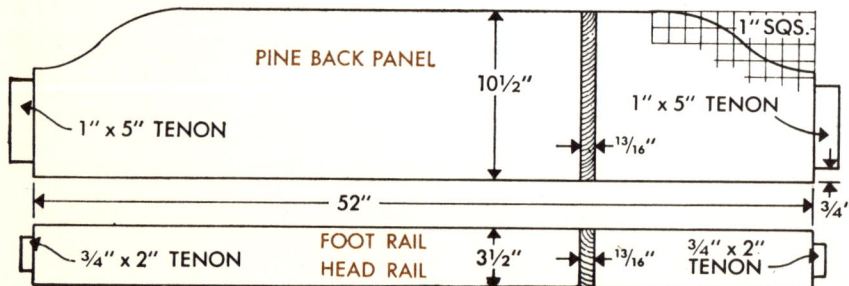

PINE BACK PANEL

1" x 5" TENON

10½"

1" SQS.

1" x 5" TENON

13/16"

52"

¾"

¾" x 2" TENON

FOOT RAIL
HEAD RAIL

3½"

13/16"

¾" x 2" TENON

½" DIA.

1" DIA.

ALL 1" SQS.

1⅛"

℄

9"

⅜"

1½" DIA.

¼"

¼"

26½"

12½"

C
(2 REQ'D)

3" DIA.

10 REEDS

5"

¾" DIA.

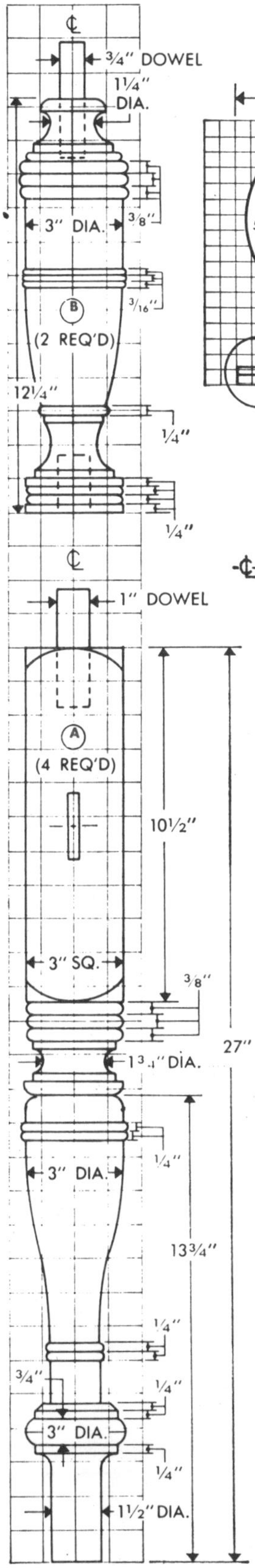
¾″ DOWEL
1¼″ DIA.
3″ DIA.
3/8″
B
(2 REQ'D)
3/16″
12¼″
¼″
¼″
1″ DOWEL
A
(4 REQ'D)
10½″
3″ SQ.
3/8″
27″
1¾″ DIA.
3″ DIA.
¼″
13¾″
¼″
¾″
¼″
3″ DIA.
¼″
1½″ DIA.

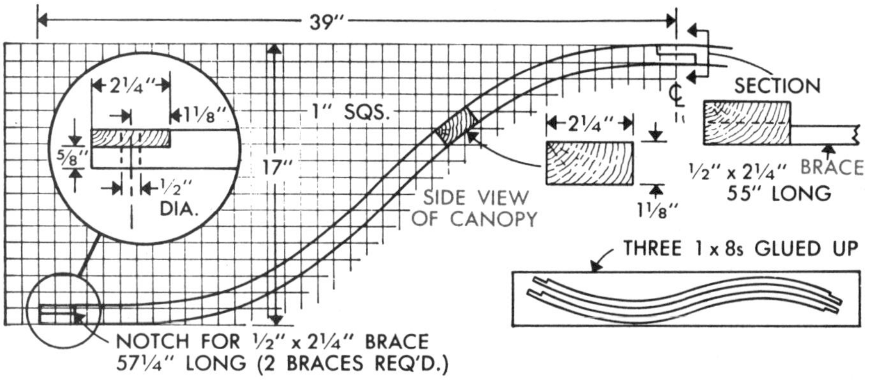
39″
2¼″
1⅛″
1″ SQS.
5/8″
17″
½″ DIA.
SIDE VIEW OF CANOPY
2¼″
1⅛″
SECTION
½″ x 2¼″ BRACE
55″ LONG
THREE 1 x 8s GLUED UP
NOTCH FOR ½″ x 2¼″ BRACE
57¼″ LONG (2 BRACES REQ'D.)

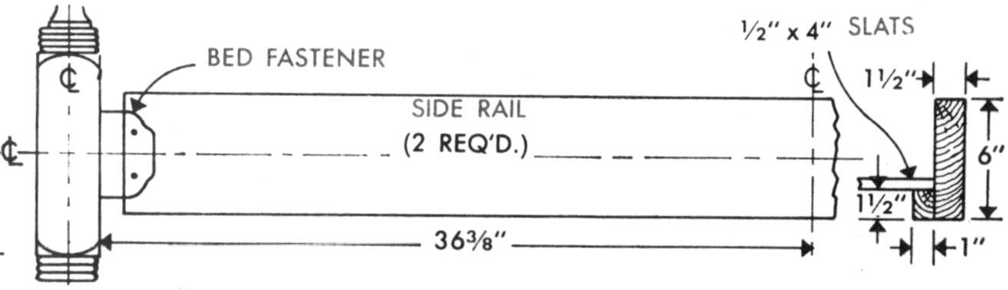
BED FASTENER
SIDE RAIL
(2 REQ'D.)
36⅜″
½″ x 4″ SLATS
1½″
6″
1½″
1″

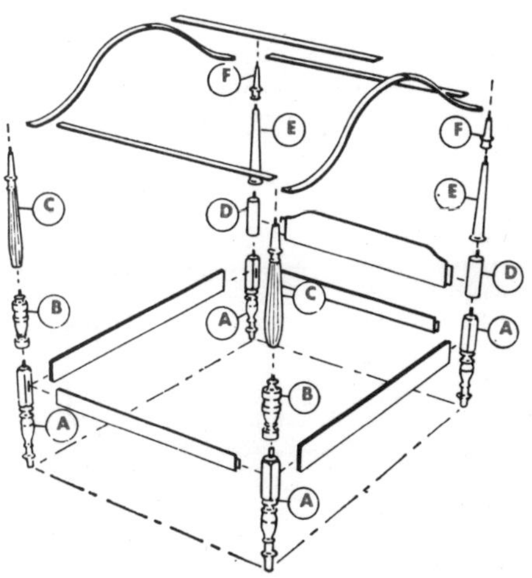
F
E
C
D
B
A

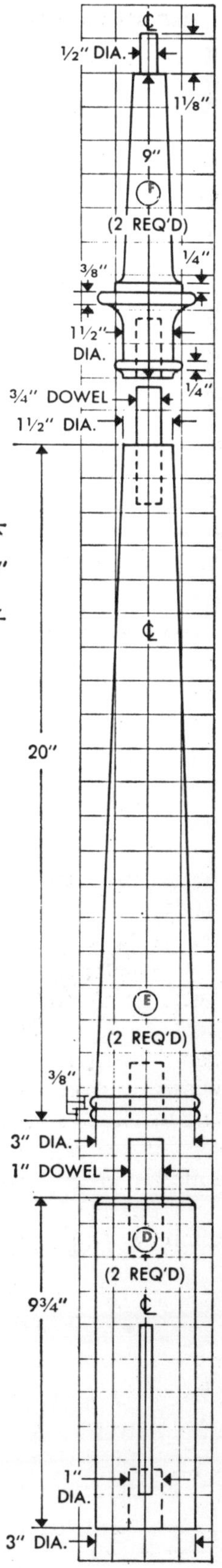
½″ DIA.
1⅛″
9″
F
(2 REQ'D)
¼″
3/8″
1½″ DIA.
¼″
¾″ DOWEL
1½″ DIA.
20″
E
(2 REQ'D)
3/8″
3″ DIA.
1″ DOWEL
D
(2 REQ'D)
9¾″
1″ DIA.
3″ DIA.

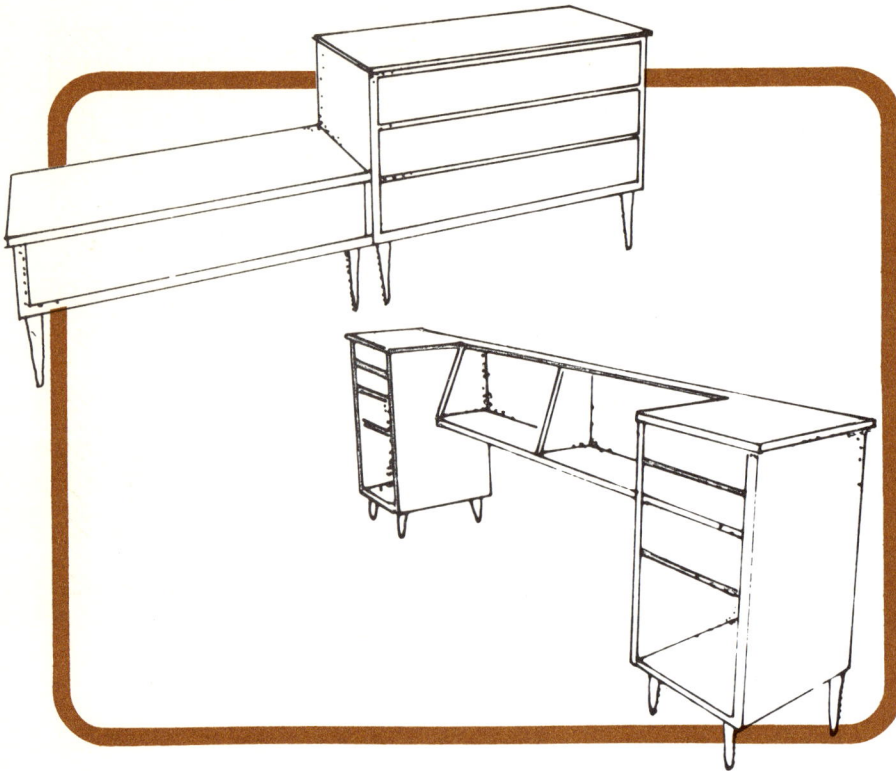

CONTEMPO-RARY BEDROOM SET

Contemporary in design, yet conservative enough in styling to be in fashion for many years, this bedroom set offers many extra conveniences as well as ample storage. The headboard-bookcase is a three-piece unit that quickly disassembles for easy transport to another room or another house. The dresser-chest unit shown is bolted together, but also is readily separated into two pieces for easy moving. If space is restricted, the dresser and chest can be kept separate and located in different parts of the room. For more storage, make two of the dressers; double the length, keeping the drawers the same height, for a massive unit that will easily store clothes for two people.

Construction has been kept simple, and just two sheets of ¾-inch hardwood-plywood and one sheet of fir plywood are required for most of the construction. Additional strips of hardwood are needed for some framing, and hardboard and perforated hardboard also are used, for the backs of the units. The legs on the original furniture are ready-made items. You may wish to make your own, or use a different type to change the styling.

Start construction by laying out the various pieces on the plywood sheets (figures 1 and 6). These can be cut slightly oversize, then squared up on the saw when they are of convenient size. Lumber-core plywood is suggested for this furniture.

Before assembling the various units, fit the adjacent sides of the chest and dresser and drill through for the Tee-Nuts. Do the same for the headboard and its bookcases. Figure 7 illustrates how the Tee-Nuts hold the bookcases and headboard together. Figure 11 indicates how the Tee-Nuts are tapped into predrilled holes.

Figure 1

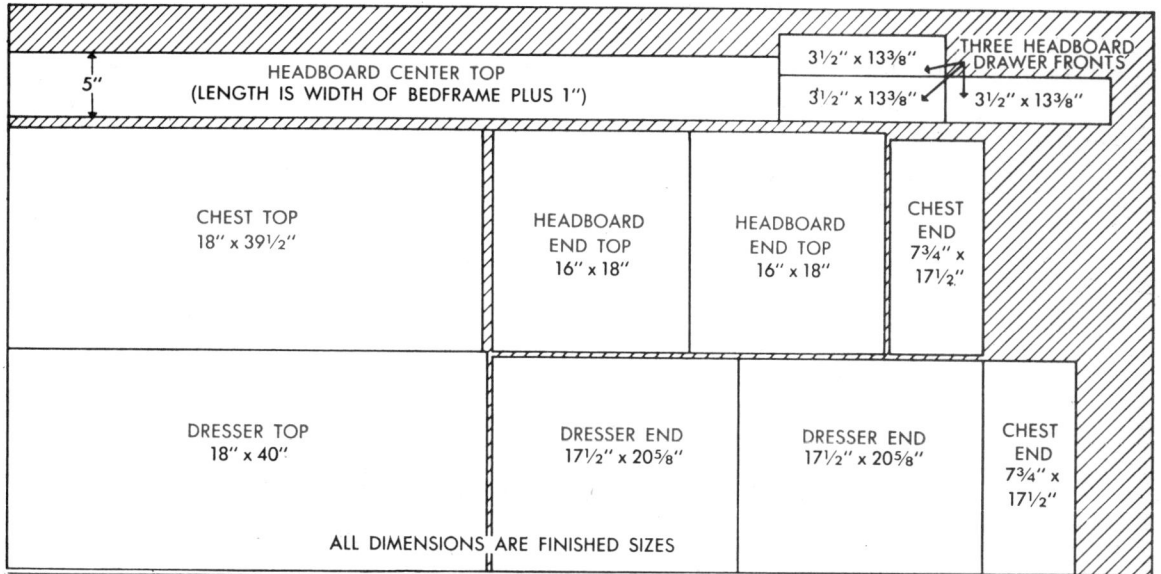

HEADBOARD CENTER TOP
(LENGTH IS WIDTH OF BEDFRAME PLUS 1")

5"

$3\frac{1}{2}$" x $13\frac{3}{8}$"

$3\frac{1}{2}$" x $13\frac{3}{8}$" $3\frac{1}{2}$" x $13\frac{3}{8}$"

THREE HEADBOARD DRAWER FRONTS

CHEST TOP
18" x $39\frac{1}{2}$"

HEADBOARD END TOP
16" x 18"

HEADBOARD END TOP
16" x 18"

CHEST END
$7\frac{3}{4}$" x $17\frac{1}{2}$"

DRESSER TOP
18" x 40"

DRESSER END
$17\frac{1}{2}$" x $20\frac{5}{8}$"

DRESSER END
$17\frac{1}{2}$" x $20\frac{5}{8}$"

CHEST END
$7\frac{3}{4}$" x $17\frac{1}{2}$"

ALL DIMENSIONS ARE FINISHED SIZES

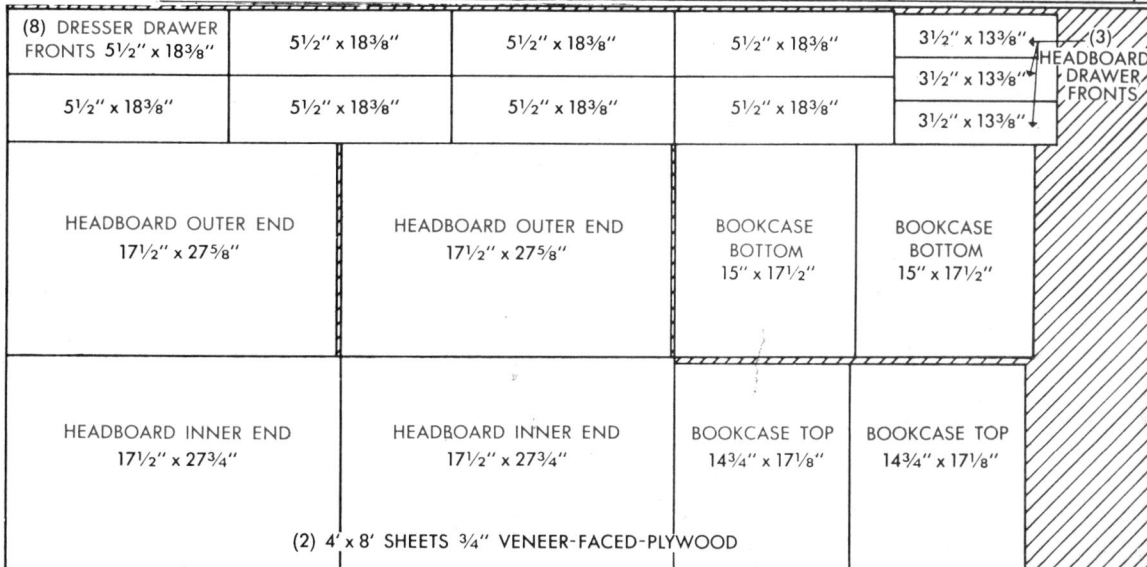

(8) DRESSER DRAWER FRONTS $5\frac{1}{2}$" x $18\frac{3}{8}$"

$5\frac{1}{2}$" x $18\frac{3}{8}$" $5\frac{1}{2}$" x $18\frac{3}{8}$" $5\frac{1}{2}$" x $18\frac{3}{8}$"

$3\frac{1}{2}$" x $13\frac{3}{8}$"   (3) HEADBOARD DRAWER FRONTS

$5\frac{1}{2}$" x $18\frac{3}{8}$" $5\frac{1}{2}$" x $18\frac{3}{8}$" $5\frac{1}{2}$" x $18\frac{3}{8}$" $5\frac{1}{2}$" x $18\frac{3}{8}$"

$3\frac{1}{2}$" x $13\frac{3}{8}$"

$3\frac{1}{2}$" x $13\frac{3}{8}$"

HEADBOARD OUTER END
$17\frac{1}{2}$" x $27\frac{5}{8}$"

HEADBOARD OUTER END
$17\frac{1}{2}$" x $27\frac{5}{8}$"

BOOKCASE BOTTOM
15" x $17\frac{1}{2}$"

BOOKCASE BOTTOM
15" x $17\frac{1}{2}$"

HEADBOARD INNER END
$17\frac{1}{2}$" x $27\frac{3}{4}$"

HEADBOARD INNER END
$17\frac{1}{2}$" x $27\frac{3}{4}$"

BOOKCASE TOP
$14\frac{3}{4}$" x $17\frac{1}{8}$"

BOOKCASE TOP
$14\frac{3}{4}$" x $17\frac{1}{8}$"

(2) 4' x 8' SHEETS $\frac{3}{4}$" VENEER-FACED-PLYWOOD

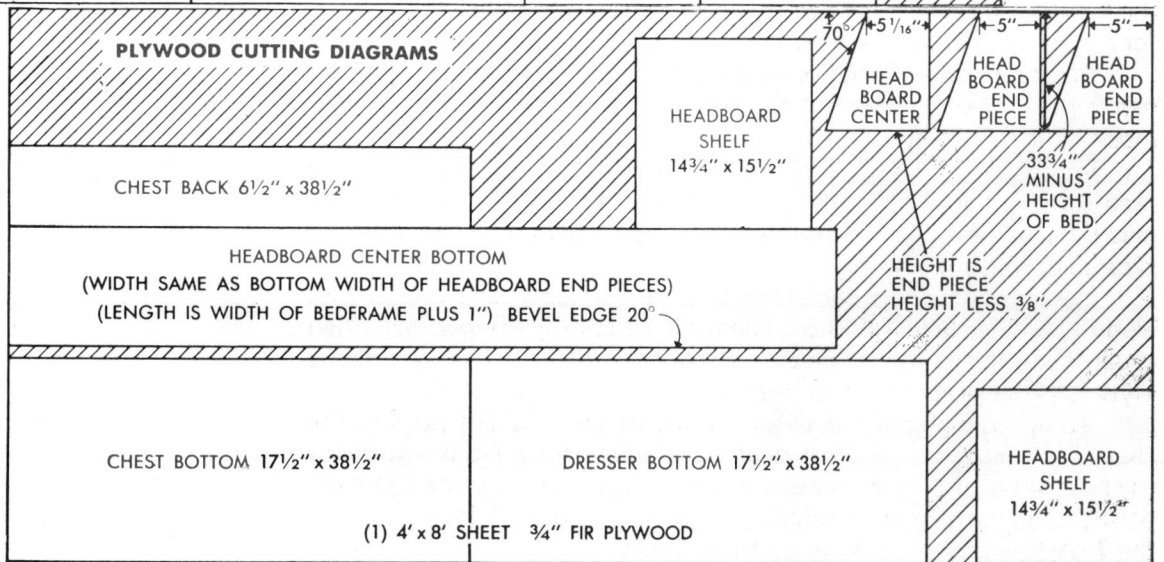

PLYWOOD CUTTING DIAGRAMS

CHEST BACK $6\frac{1}{2}$" x $38\frac{1}{2}$"

HEADBOARD SHELF
$14\frac{3}{4}$" x $15\frac{1}{2}$"

70° $5\frac{1}{16}$"   5"   5"

HEAD BOARD CENTER

HEAD BOARD END PIECE

HEAD BOARD END PIECE

$33\frac{3}{4}$" MINUS HEIGHT OF BED

HEADBOARD CENTER BOTTOM
(WIDTH SAME AS BOTTOM WIDTH OF HEADBOARD END PIECES)
(LENGTH IS WIDTH OF BEDFRAME PLUS 1") BEVEL EDGE 20°

HEIGHT IS END PIECE HEIGHT LESS $\frac{3}{8}$"

CHEST BOTTOM $17\frac{1}{2}$" x $38\frac{1}{2}$"

DRESSER BOTTOM $17\frac{1}{2}$" x $38\frac{1}{2}$"

HEADBOARD SHELF
$14\frac{3}{4}$" x $15\frac{1}{2}$"

(1) 4' x 8' SHEET $\frac{3}{4}$" FIR PLYWOOD

Width and height of the backrest portion of the headboard will vary with bed size. The width should be 1 inch more than the bed frame to allow the bed to fit easily between the bookcase units, including the bedding. Make up the bed carefully and measure the distance from the floor to the top of the covers. Subtract this from 33¾ inches to determine the height of the headboard. If the height of legs is changed, the dimensions will have to be altered to suit. The headboard bookcase shown is designed to be 34 inches high.

The above procedure allows the head of the bed to be positioned just under the edge of the backrest frames. If the bed rolls easily on casters you may need stops on the inside surfaces of the bookcases to prevent the bed rolling too far back. A hook can be attached to the bed to fit a screweye on the bookcases to prevent the bed rolling away from the headboard.

Machine the various parts for the chest and dresser (figure 5) cutting the necessary dadoes and rabbets. Drawer construction is detailed in figure 15. Use screws whenever possible, to strengthen joints. White glue is fine for assembly, but be sure to immediately wipe away an excess that appears on any of the surfaces. Glue will not allow stain or finish to penetrate the wood properly. On the original chest unit the inside was lined with aromatic red-cedar veneer (figures 4 and 13) but this is an optional feature. The framing for the dresser (figure 15) also includes drawer guides. Note that the front frame (figure 12) is recessed for better appearance. Walnut-veneer plywood was used for the case of the original, with a light-color hardwood for the framing. You may wish to reverse this, as "fruitwoods" and other light-colored hardwoods are now popular. The framing then would be of a darker wood for contrast. Before taping and the installation of the framing the chest-dresser assembly will appear as in figure 8.

An optional, wall-hung mirror is detailed in figure 5. The frame is styled to match the furniture, and a plate glass mirror of the proper size will have to be purchased to fit the frame. Double-check your own measurements so if they vary slightly from those given you can

2. Bedside conveniences include bookshelves, phone, writing or snack shelf, clock-radio and a comfortable backrest.

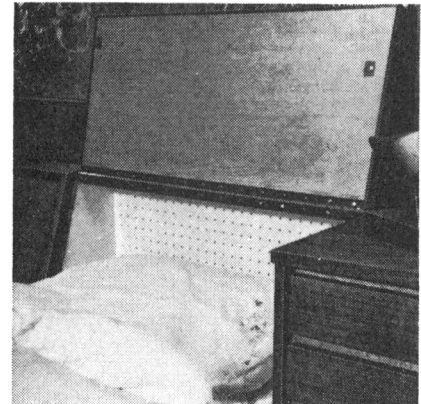

3. Cushioned headboard pivots up to provide storage for pillows and speed the daily chore of making the bed.

4. Low-chest portion of chest-dresser assembly is cedar-lined, with lift-up lid for easy storage of blankets.

Figure 5   DRESSER-CHEST UNIT

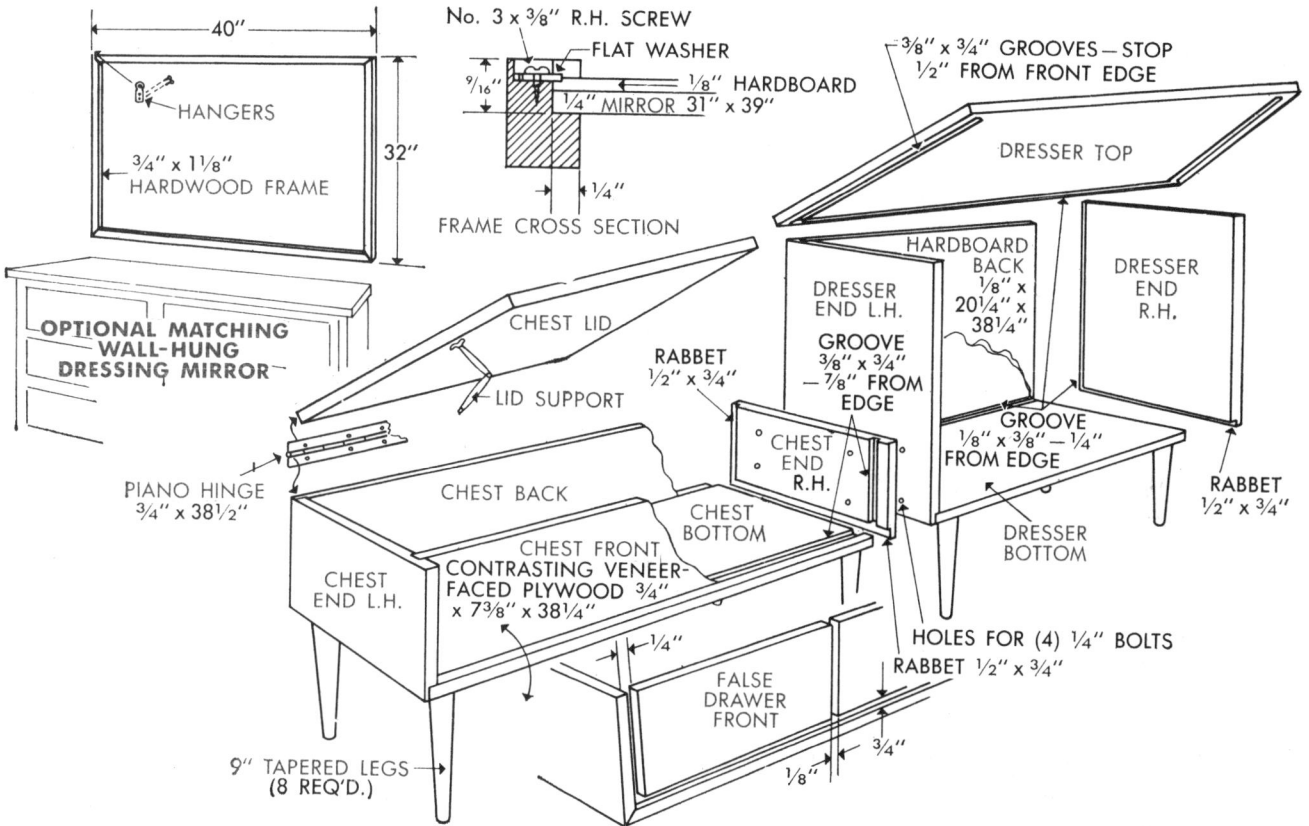

change the dimensions of the mirror to fit your own frame.

Figure 9 details all the parts for the bookcase and headboard. Note that the upper shelf in each bookcase is notched to accommodate the hinge. This type hinge is called a "concealed pivot-type cabinet hinge" and is used on some kitchen cabinets, as the only portion visible is the edge of each leaf. They are available at hardware stores and at mail-order houses. Notches also are cut in the partitions in the head-

6. All parts are drawn on hardwood-plywood according to cutting schedule; sizes allow for finish squaring.

7. Headboard-bookcase assembly before edge-taping and addition of doors on headboard, drawers in cases.

8. "Take-apart" chest-dresser unit is shown before drawers are installed in dresser, edge-taping on the plywood.

Figure 9   BOOKCASE-HEADBOARD UNIT

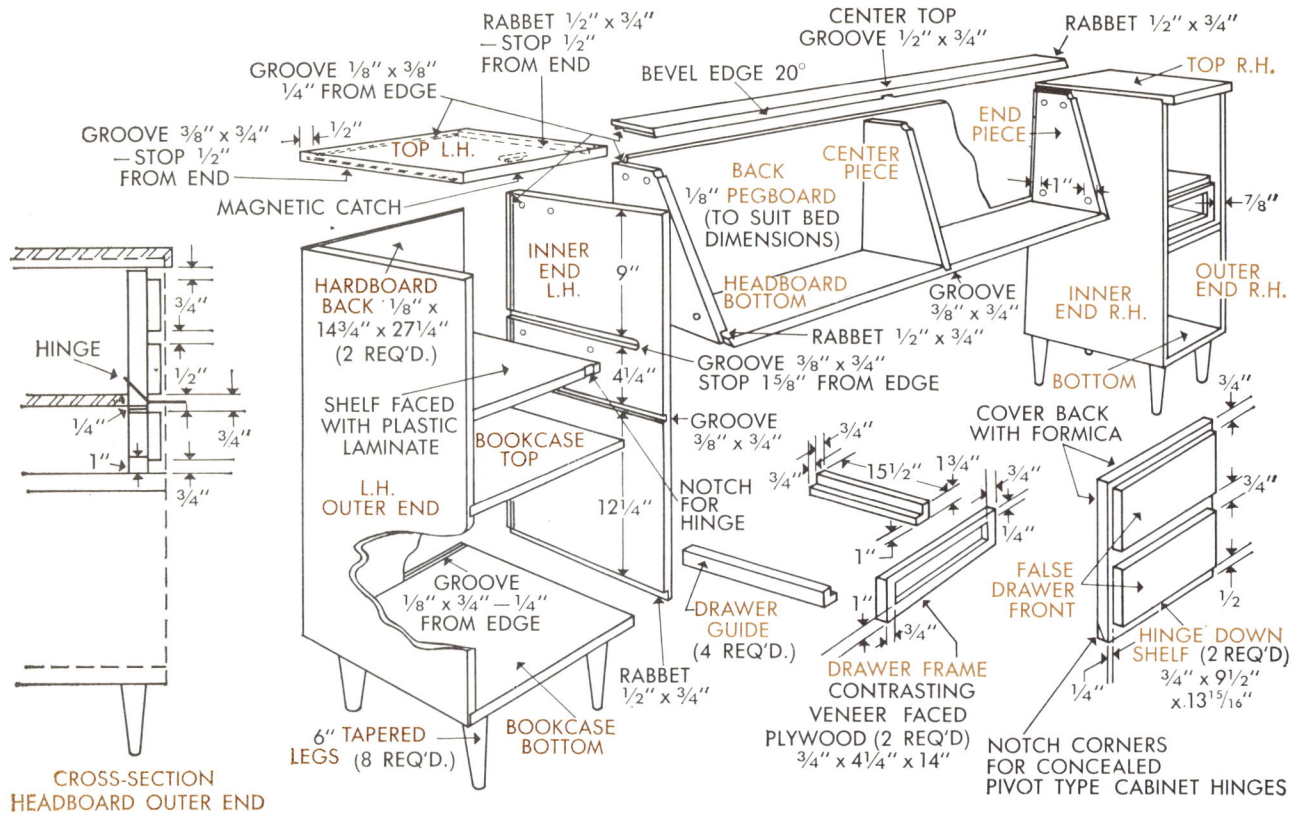

board cabinet to accommodate the piano hinge; the notches should be about 3/16 x ¾ inch for a ¾-inch hinge.

The optional clock-radio can be installed in one of the bookcases. For this an opening is cut as indicated, first covering the area with masking tape to prevent damage to the veneer from the saw (figure 14).

All exposed edges of the chest-dresser and the bookcase-headboard are covered with veneer tape. Projecting lips of fir plywood in both assemblies also are covered with the tape (figure 10). This tape sometimes is available as a self-adhering material from which a paper

10. Veneer tape is applied to projecting lips of fir-plywood dresser and chest, as well as to plywood edges.

11. Tee-Nuts are driven into holes in dresser end, bolts from chest unit hold the two pieces together.

12. Drawer frame of contrasting hardwood in dresser is recessed 7/8" from front for appearance.

13. Aromatic red cedar veneer, 1/20"-thick, is glued inside chest used for storing woolens.

14. Opening for optional clock-radio is marked on masking tape that protects surface from saw.

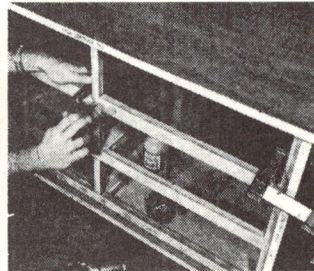
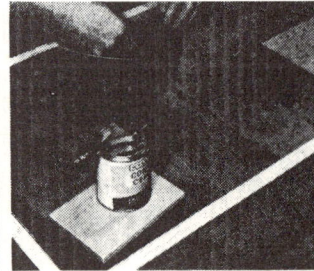
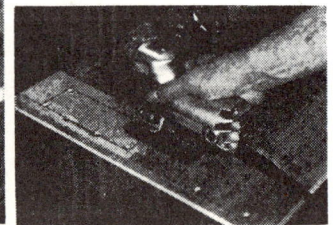
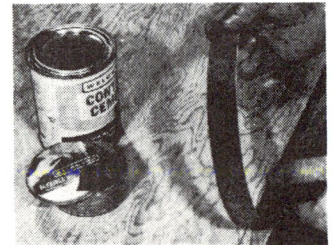

Figure 15   HEADBOARD BACKREST DETAILS

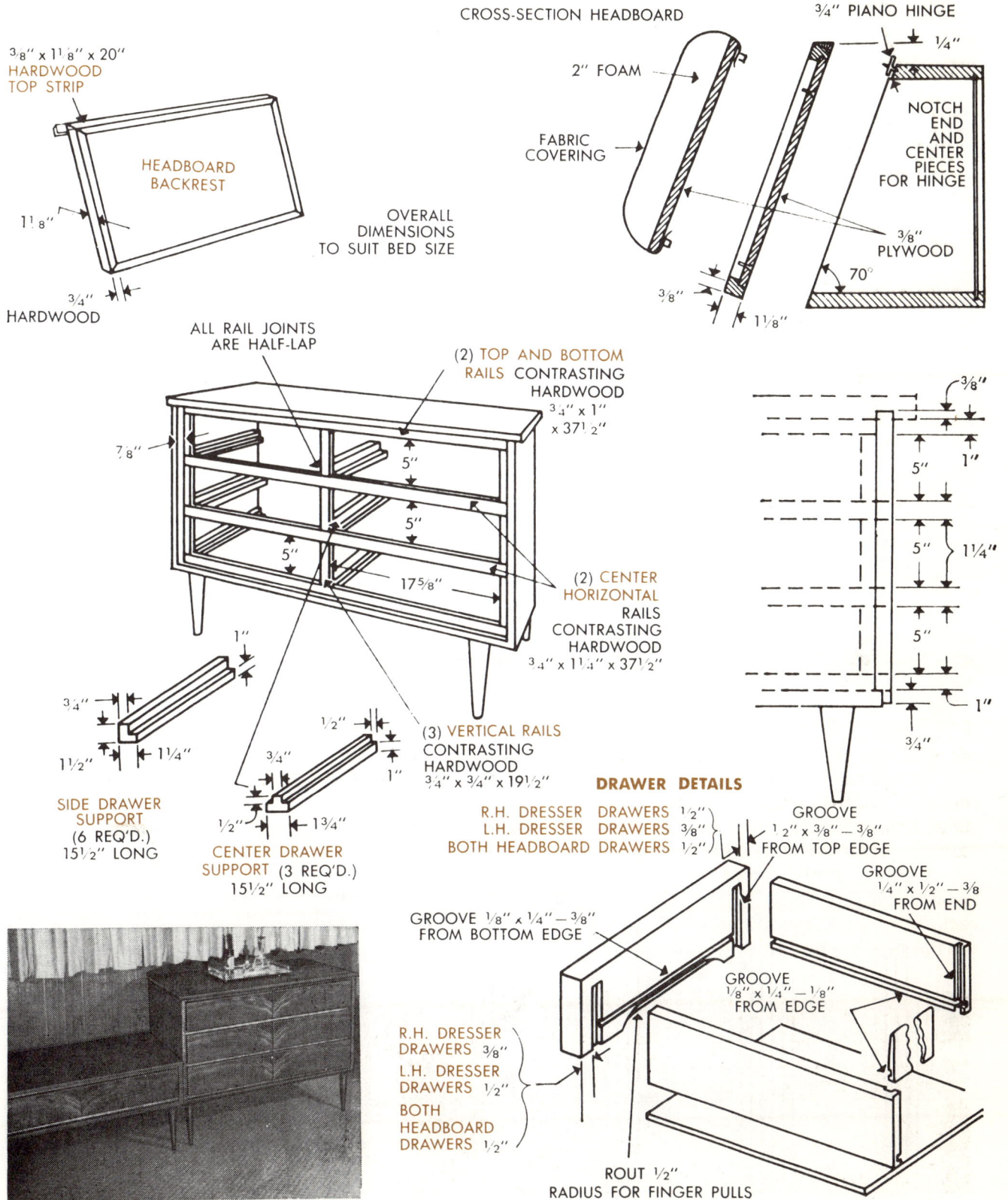

$3/8'' \times 1\frac{1}{8}'' \times 20''$
HARDWOOD
TOP STRIP

HEADBOARD
BACKREST

$1\frac{1}{8}''$

$3/4''$
HARDWOOD

OVERALL
DIMENSIONS
TO SUIT BED SIZE

CROSS-SECTION HEADBOARD

$3/4''$ PIANO HINGE

$1/4''$

2'' FOAM

FABRIC
COVERING

NOTCH
END
AND
CENTER
PIECES
FOR HINGE

$3/8''$
PLYWOOD

$70°$

$3/8''$

$1\frac{1}{8}''$

ALL RAIL JOINTS
ARE HALF-LAP

(2) TOP AND BOTTOM
RAILS CONTRASTING
HARDWOOD
$3/4'' \times 1''$
$\times 37\frac{1}{2}''$

$7/8''$

5''

5''

5''

$17\frac{5}{8}''$

(2) CENTER
HORIZONTAL
RAILS
CONTRASTING
HARDWOOD
$3/4'' \times 1\frac{1}{4}'' \times 37\frac{1}{2}''$

$3/8''$

1''

5''

5'' $1\frac{1}{4}''$

5''

1''

$3/4''$

1''

$3/4''$

$1\frac{1}{2}''$ $1\frac{1}{4}''$

SIDE DRAWER
SUPPORT
(6 REQ'D.)
$15\frac{1}{2}''$ LONG

$1/2''$

$3/4''$

$1/2''$ $1\frac{3}{4}''$

1''

CENTER DRAWER
SUPPORT (3 REQ'D.)
$15\frac{1}{2}''$ LONG

(3) VERTICAL RAILS
CONTRASTING
HARDWOOD
$3/4'' \times 3/4'' \times 19\frac{1}{2}''$

DRAWER DETAILS

R.H. DRESSER DRAWERS $1/2''$
L.H. DRESSER DRAWERS $3/8''$
BOTH HEADBOARD DRAWERS $1/2''$

GROOVE
$1/2'' \times 3/8'' - 3/8''$
FROM TOP EDGE

GROOVE
$1/4'' \times 1/2'' - 3/8$
FROM END

GROOVE $1/8'' \times 1/4'' - 3/8''$
FROM BOTTOM EDGE

GROOVE
$1/8'' \times 1/4'' - 1/8''$
FROM EDGE

R.H. DRESSER
DRAWERS $3/8''$

L.H. DRESSER
DRAWERS $1/2''$

BOTH
HEADBOARD
DRAWERS $1/2''$

ROUT $1/2''$
RADIUS FOR FINGER PULLS

backing is peeled, but the better method is to get the plain kind that can be glued as needed. Contact adhesive is the best for this operation, as the tape is tapped into firm contact with the stock, then trimmed with a razor blade or X-Acto knife to be flush with the edges of the stock. It is stained and finished the same as the veneered plywood.

Grain patterns typical of high-grade veneered plywood are illustrated in the photos, with one exception. The plywood on the dress- and chest drawer fronts has been overlaid with matching walnut crotch veneer to attain a desired symmetrical appearance.

The hinged shelves (figure 2) require no shelf supports, as they rest on the edges of the false drawers below. Figure 2 also illustrates the several conveniences built into each bookcase. It will be necessary, of course, to cut holes in the hardboard backs of the cases to permit passage of the cords and wires for the clock and telephone if they are included.

The cushioned backrest of the headboard (figures 3 and 15) is two hinged sections, one for each side of the bed. Perforated hardboard is used for the backs of this assembly to allow ventilation for the pillows that are stored inside during the day. The plywood cushion backs (figure 15) are cut about 1/8 inch shy of fitting the openings in the frames. Generously round the edges to prevent damage to the upholstery.

Position the foam-rubber cushions on the backs, then stretch a quality upholstery material over the foam and staple it to the back of the plywood. The material can match the bedspread or curtain material in the room. Fasten the cushions to the frames with wood screws. The material can be changed whenever room decor is changed.

Sand and smooth the various pieces during assembly. The pre-sanded hardwood-plywood should require very little work. A natural, oiled finish looks best on this style of furniture. Try one of the materials that looks "hand-rubbed" when applied, or a satin-finish varnish.

On the bedroom set shown no pulls were used, finger grooves being routed on the bottom edge of each drawer. If pulls are used, of course, then this operation can be eliminated. Magnetic latches are used on the lids of the headboard backrest and the doors of the book cases. The inner surfaces of the lids, as well as the upper compartments in the bookcases are lined with a plastic laminate for easy cleaning. The laminate also makes a fine writing surface.

Lights and other accessories will be up to the individual. Be sure to allow for receptacles for the lights, wiring them into the headboard backrest or bookcases, but not both, so there is no problem with wires when separating the units.

BUNK BEDS

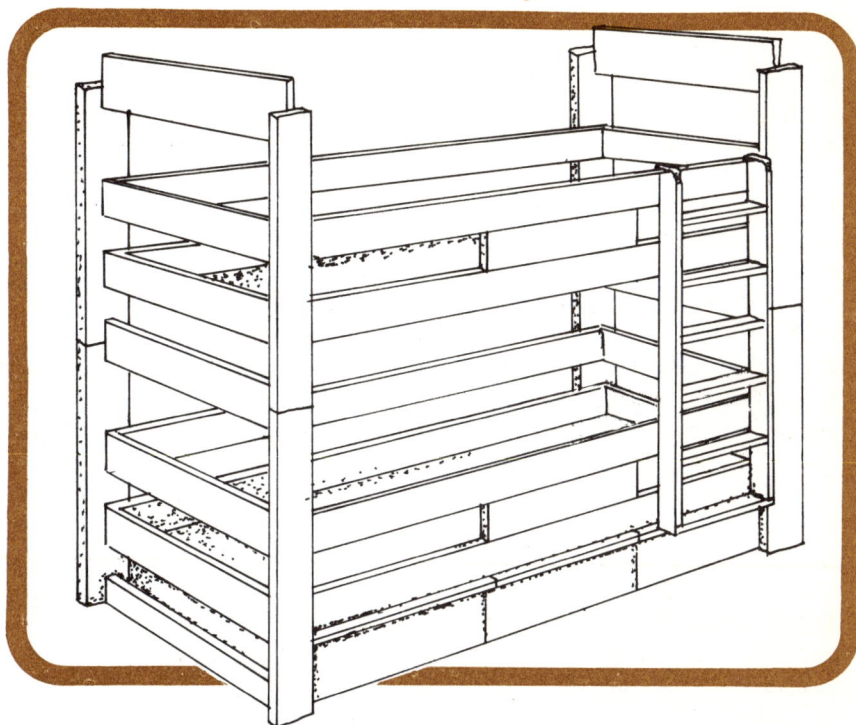

These beds can be used as matching single units or stacked as bunks to save floor space. Roll-out drawers under the bottom bed provide generous storage for blankets, sheets, and even the paraphernalia that youngsters seem to gather. If the beds are used as singles, you can make drawers for both beds.

The mattress-and-frame set is designed for a standard 29 x 75-inch size, but get the mattress before you start construction, just to make sure the size of your unit does not require some modification to accept it.

All assemblies are relatively easy to build, as standard board widths are utilized where possible, to minimize the need for ripping stock. Clear white pine is suggested for the stock, and it can be stained and finished in a number of ways. There is no reason, of course, that hardwood cannot be used and some builders will prefer it. Be sure any stock you use is well seasoned or kiln-dried, and that it is flat, straight-grained and free of knots, splits and checks.

Shop-made wheels are shown to be used under the storage drawers, but you can substitute casters. The plate type that can be screwed to the underside of the drawers is a good choice. Make the drawer bottoms without the notches, and eliminate the boxes that are designed to cover the wheels. If your casters project more than the wheels shown, reduce the overall height of the drawers to suit. Allow ample clearance; a bouncing youngster can reduce that clearance to zero with only moderate effort.

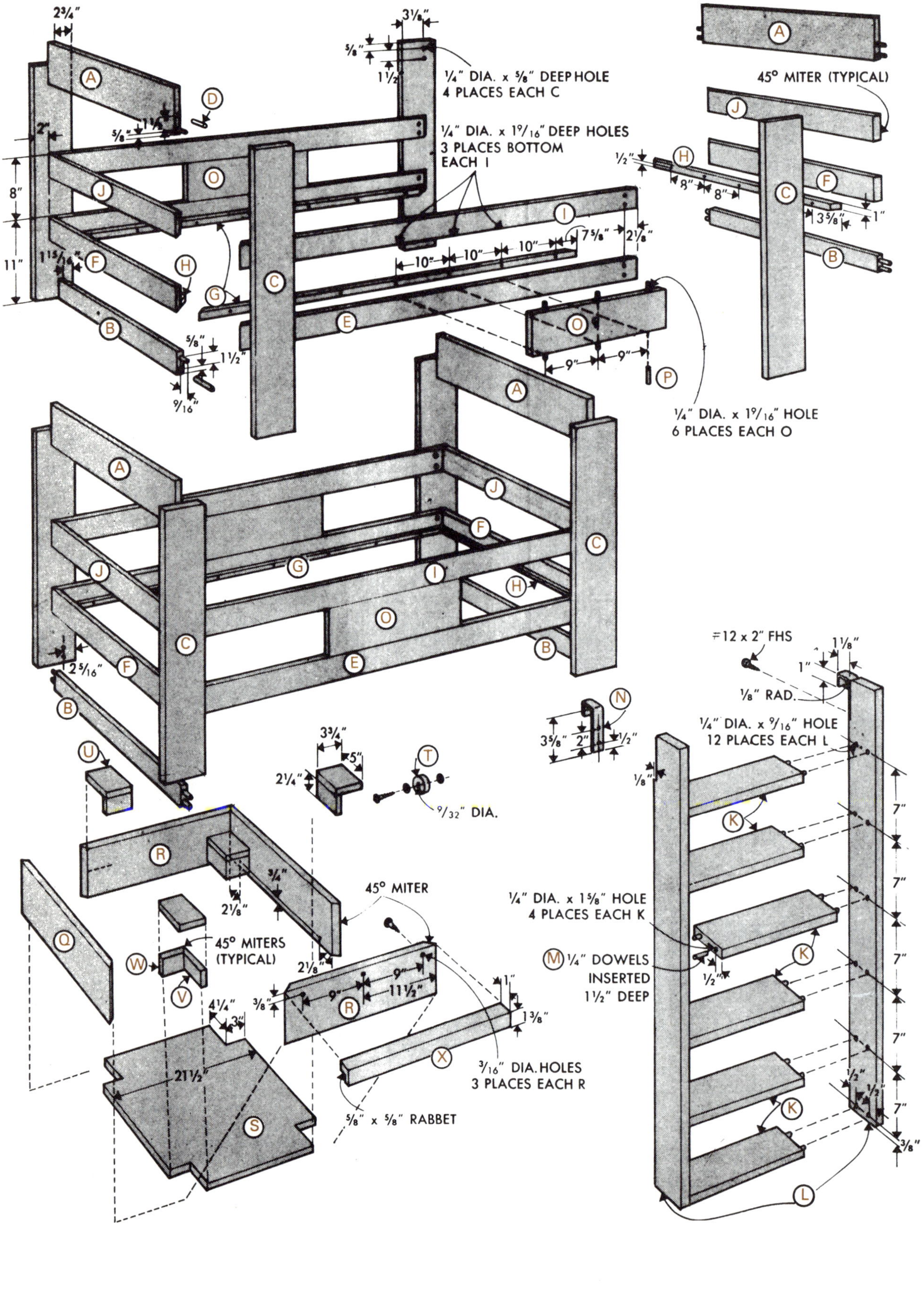

2¾"

3⅛"

⅝"

1½"

¼" DIA. x ⅝" DEEP HOLE
4 PLACES EACH C

¼" DIA. x 1⁹⁄₁₆" DEEP HOLES
3 PLACES BOTTOM
EACH I

2"

⅝" 1½"

8"

11"

1¹⁵⁄₁₆"

⅝" 1½"

9⁄₁₆"

A

D

J

O

C

H

G

F

B

E

I

O

10" 10" 10" 7⅝" 2½"

9" 9"

P

¼" DIA. x 1⁹⁄₁₆" HOLE
6 PLACES EACH O

45° MITER (TYPICAL)

A

J

H

½"

8" 8"

C

F

3⅝" 1"

B

A

J

F

G

C

F

I

H

O

E

B

2⁵⁄₁₆"

B

U

R

¾"

2⅛"

45° MITERS
(TYPICAL)

W

V

4¼" 3"

⅜"

9" 11½" 1"

21½"

S

Q

R

X

3⅛"

45° MITER

¾16" DIA. HOLES
3 PLACES EACH R

⅝" x ⅝" RABBET

3¾"

5"

2¼"

T

9⁄₃₂" DIA.

N

3⅝" 2" ½"

#12 x 2" FHS

1⅛"

1"

⅛" RAD.

¼" DIA. x ⁹⁄₁₆" HOLE
12 PLACES EACH L

⅛"

K

7"

7"

¼" DIA. x 1⅝" HOLE
4 PLACES EACH K

K

7"

M ¼" DOWELS
INSERTED
1½" DEEP

½"

K

7"

½" ½"

K

7"

⅜"

L

MATERIALS LIST

A. Top Cross
   Member: 1x6x40¾" (4)
B. Bottom Cross
   Member: ¾"x2¾"x40¾" (4)
C. Leg: 1x6x30" (8)
D. Dowels: ¼"x2-9/16" (32)
E. Side Frame: 1x4x76¾" (4)
F. End Frame 1x4x40¾" (4)
G. Cleat: ¾"x1"x75¼" (4)
H. Cleat: ¾"x1"x39¼" (4)
I. Guard Rail: 1x4x76¾" (4)
J. Guard Rail: 1x4x40¾" (4)
K. Ladder Step: 1x3x12" (6)
L. Ladder Rail: 1x3x41-5/8" (2)

M. Dowel: ¼"x2" (24)
N. Ladder Hooks: 1/8"x¾"x5¾" aluminum bar stock (2)
O. Spacer: ¾"x4½"x23" (4)
P. Dowels: ¼"x3" (24)
Q. Box Side: ¾"x6¾"x39¾" (6)
R. Box End: ¾"x6¾"x23" (6)
S. Box Base: 21½"x38¼" ¾"-plywood (3)
T. Wheel: ¾"x2½"-diameter (12)
U. Wheel-Cover Top: ¾"x3¾"x5" (12)

V. Wheel-Cover Side: ¾"x2¼"x5" (12)
W. Wheel-Cover End: ¾"x2¼"x3¾" (12)
X. Box Pull: 1"x1-3/8"x23" (3)

Miscellaneous

Bunk-bed mattress and spring (2)
White glue (8 oz.)
No. 10 x 1½" RH wood screws (48)
No. 12 x 2" FH wood screws (4)
No. 12 x 1¼" FH wood screws (16)
4d finishing nails
Wood putty
No. 8 x 1½" RH wood screws (9)
¼" x 1½" lag screws (12)
ID steel washers (24)

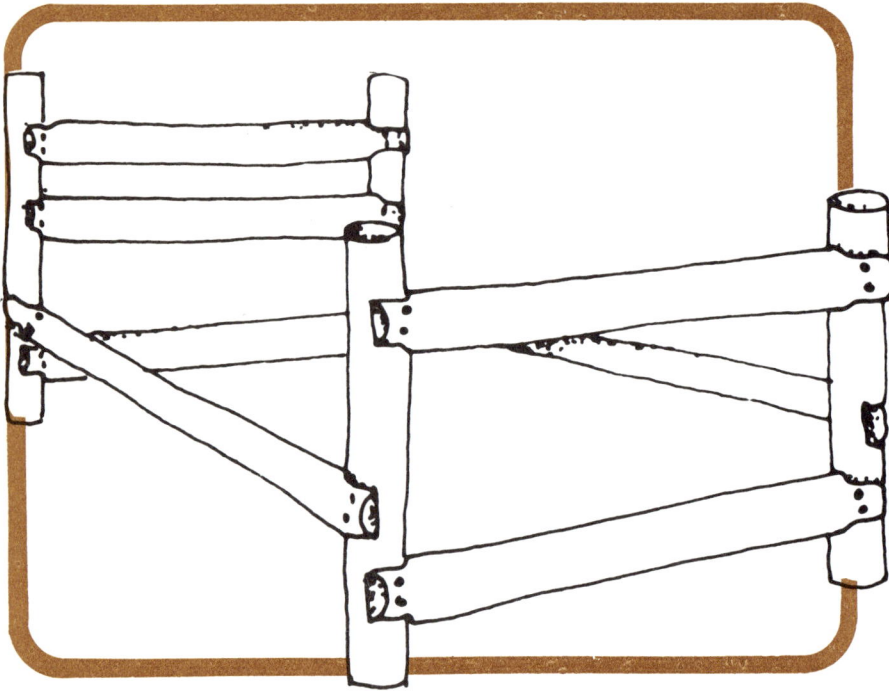

RANCH BEDS

If you have been searching for well-built, rustic-style beds for the children, summer cabin or hunting lodge here is the solution.

The springs used are the flat type and may be purchased second-hand. If you use new springs the cost will be somewhat higher.

Your building material is cedar fence posts which are used for the frames and legs. Two posts 7 feet long with a 4-inch diameter at the small end are used for the legs; three 7-foot posts with a 3-inch diameter at the small end are used for the side and end rails.

Each post used for the side and end rails is ripped in half lengthwise. If the posts, which usually are naturally checked or split lengthwise, are carefully selected, they can easily be split lengthwise without the need for sawing.

As indicated in the detail, the ends of the cross rails are half-lapped to fit in notches in the vertical members. Holes are bored at the joints and 3/8 x 4½-inch carriage bolts used to hold the joints. This method of assembly permits tightening the joints as wear takes place. Use washers under the nuts to prevent them digging into the wood. The square shoulder under the head of each carriage bolt will prevent it turning and assure a snug fit.

To support the springs 8-inch lengths of 1½ x 1½-inch angle irons are bolted inside the frame. The height of the angles would be determined by the height of the springs, but should be centered on the side members when possible, to assure maximum thickness for the bolts.

When the bed frames have been assembled, sand all surfaces thoroughly. The beds may be shellacked, but the posts could also be stained and then finished with a penetrating sealer or a quality resin-

base varnish, whichever you prefer.

If the springs are second-hand, wire-brush all surfaces and apply a good rust-inhibiting paint, over which any metal enamel can be applied.

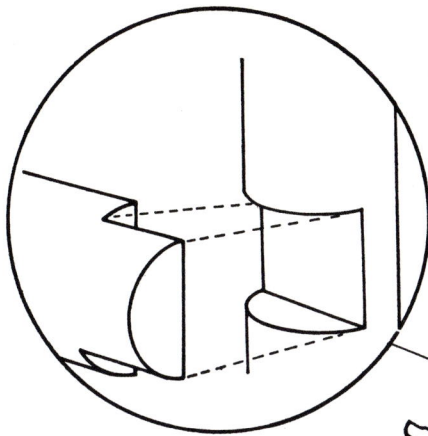

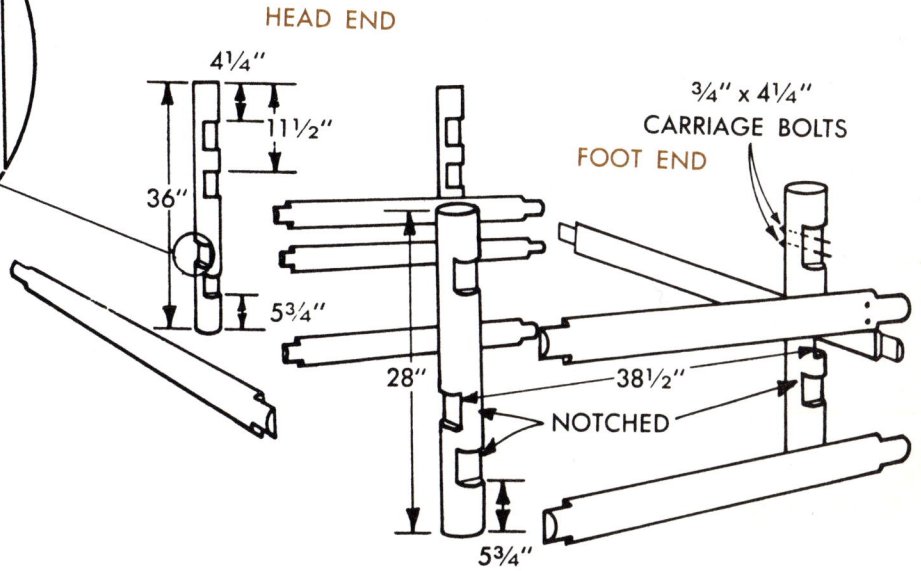

HEAD END

4¼"

11½"

36"

5¾"

¾" x 4¼" CARRIAGE BOLTS

FOOT END

28"   38½"

NOTCHED

5¾"

MEXICAN TILE BENCH

Utilizing beautifully hand-decorated tiles as the decorative motif, this handsome bench is Spanish in style. It is perfect for the front porch of a ranch-style home, will add graciousness to the foyer or seating space in the recreation room or kitchen.

The bench is made of 2 x 12 white pine or clear fir with good solid knots. The ends are two pieces glued together, then cut out to the pattern shown. The feet are 2 x 4s with the sides set in dadoes cut in their tops. The back, seat and stretcher are held in the ends by glued mortise-and-tenon joints. For extra rigidity you might wish to drive screws in from the ends, covering them with wooden plugs.

The seat, back and sides are routed the depth of the tiles and the tiles glued in place flush with the surfaces, then grouted to fill the cracks. Actual gluing and grouting of the tiles should be done after the finish has been applied to the bench.

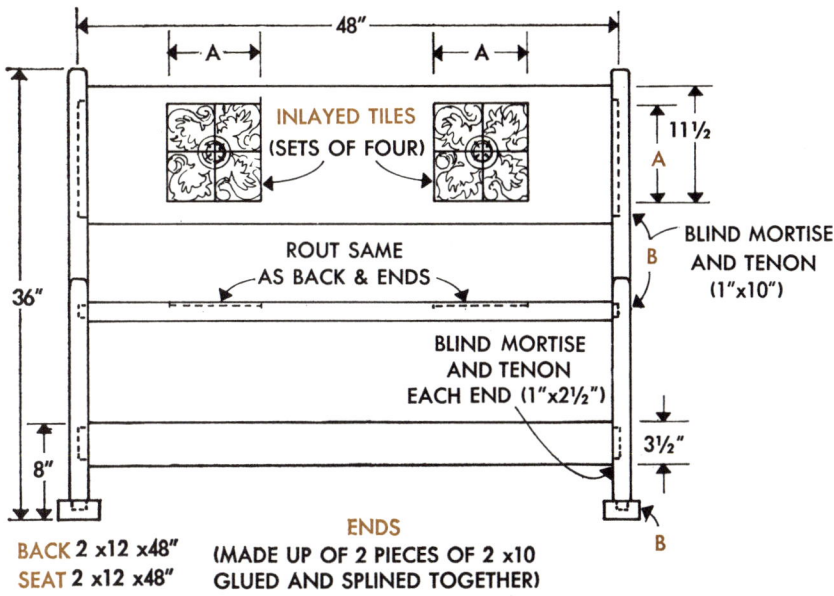

INLAYED TILES
(SETS OF FOUR)

ROUT SAME
AS BACK & ENDS

48"

A   A

36"

8"

11½

BLIND MORTISE
AND TENON
(1"x10")

B

BLIND MORTISE
AND TENON
EACH END (1"x2½")

3½"

B

ENDS
(MADE UP OF 2 PIECES OF 2 x10
GLUED AND SPLINED TOGETHER)

BACK 2 x12 x48"
SEAT 2 x12 x48"

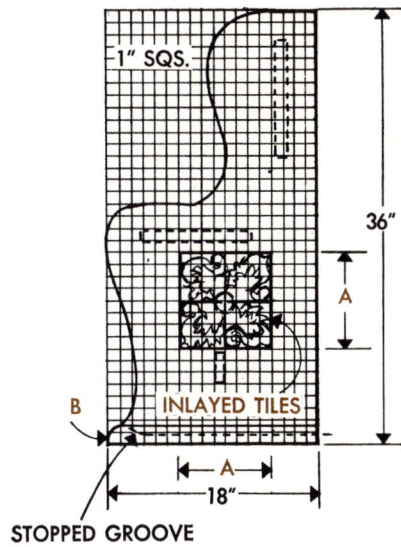

1" SQS.

36"

A

INLAYED TILES

B

A

18"

STOPPED GROOVE

TELEPHONE BENCH

Patterned after a colonial deacon's bench, this modern adaptation will fit in any modern home with early American decor and provide a conversation corner for the ever-present telephone. A handy shelf at the end accommodates the telephone with space beneath for telephone books and note pads. While the telephone shelf is at the left in the bench shown, some builders may wish to reverse the pattern and put it on the right of the user.

To create the wide stock necessary for the seat and telephone shelf, edge glue lengths of 1½-inch maple using dowels for reinforcement. Clamp the assembly and when the glue has set, cut the back rest, seat, phone shelf and armrest to the sizes indicated in the drawings. The seat depression is roughed out with a gouge or flexible disk sander, then finished with sandpaper. All the larger radii are cut with a band, coping or jig saw, and all edges and corners rounded using a block plane, rasp and sandpaper. Take your time on this operation and frequently check to see that the edges are kept straight as you round them. After cutting and shaping all members, drill the holes that accept the back, shelf and arm spindles and the holes for the legs. Bore the holes for the legs and spindles using the drill-press setup, or hand-drill jig detailed. Be sure not to drill completely through the seat and shelf. Spindles for the back and sides are ¾-inch dowels with their ends shouldered to ½ inch. Shoulders of the spindles for the back rest are angled to meet the seat. The legs are turned on a lathe to the tapers indicated.

To assemble the bench, position the legs and weight the seat to hold them in place while the glue sets. To assure the legs will splay out

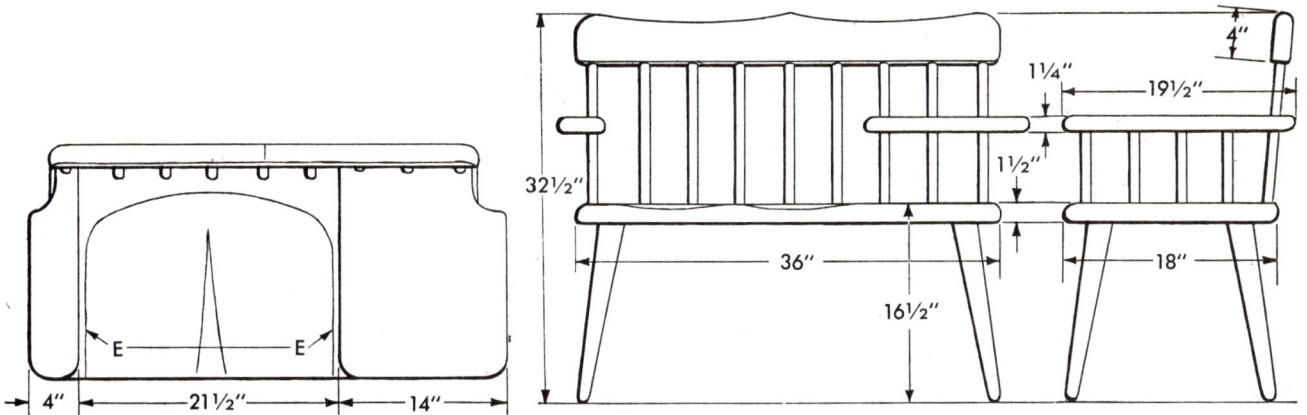

from the bench at equal angles and that it will set level, make a frame of 1 x 2s with an inside measurement of 18 x 36 inches. Set the frame on the floor and position the ends of the legs in the corners. When the glue has dried, assemble the rest of the bench using liberal amounts of glue. Clamps or weights are used to hold the back rest, spindles and telephone shelf while the glue sets. Sand all surfaces, stain, and finish with clear lacquer.

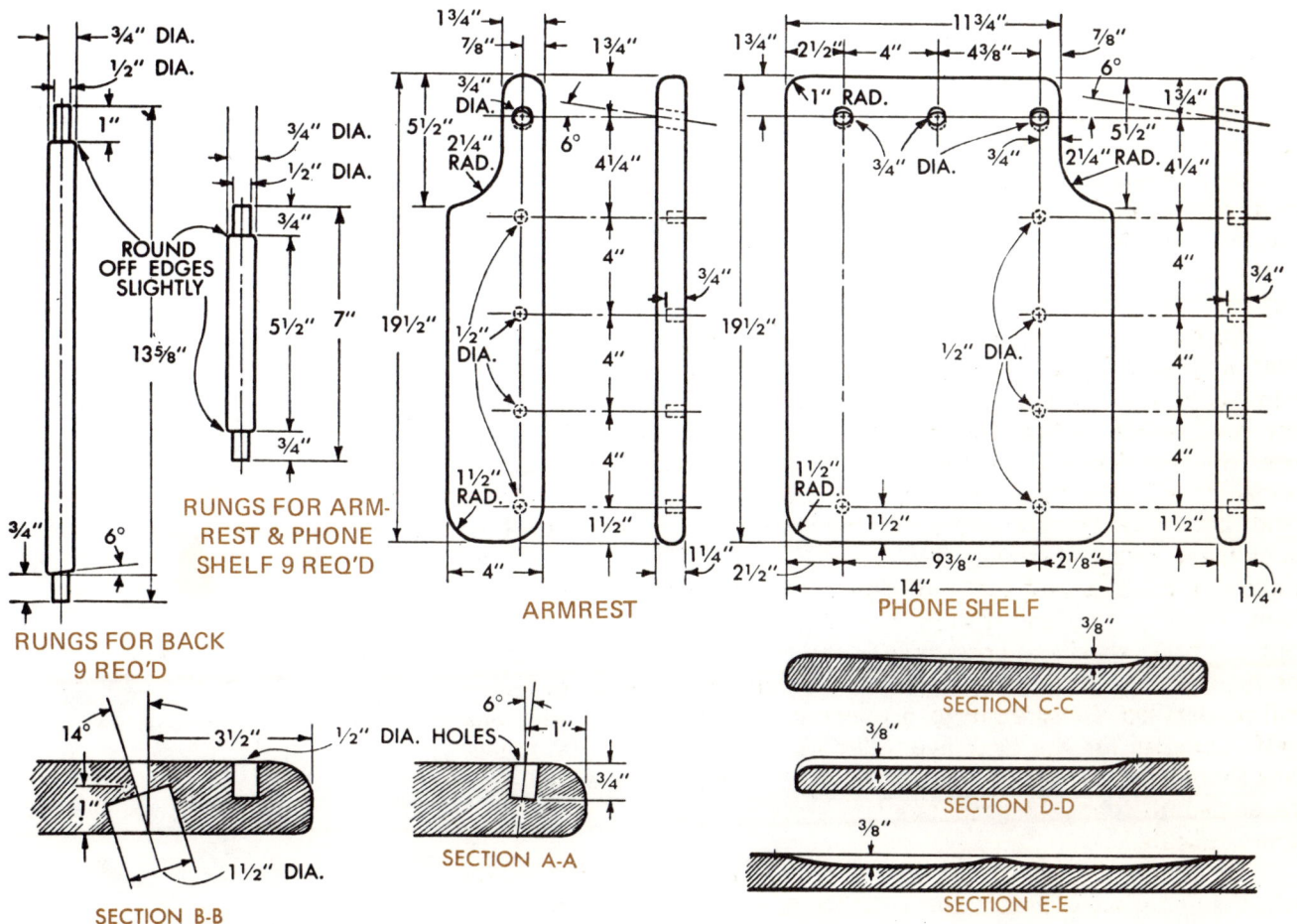

RUNGS FOR BACK 9 REQ'D

RUNGS FOR ARMREST & PHONE SHELF 9 REQ'D

ARMREST

PHONE SHELF

SECTION B-B

SECTION A-A

SECTION C-C

SECTION D-D

SECTION E-E

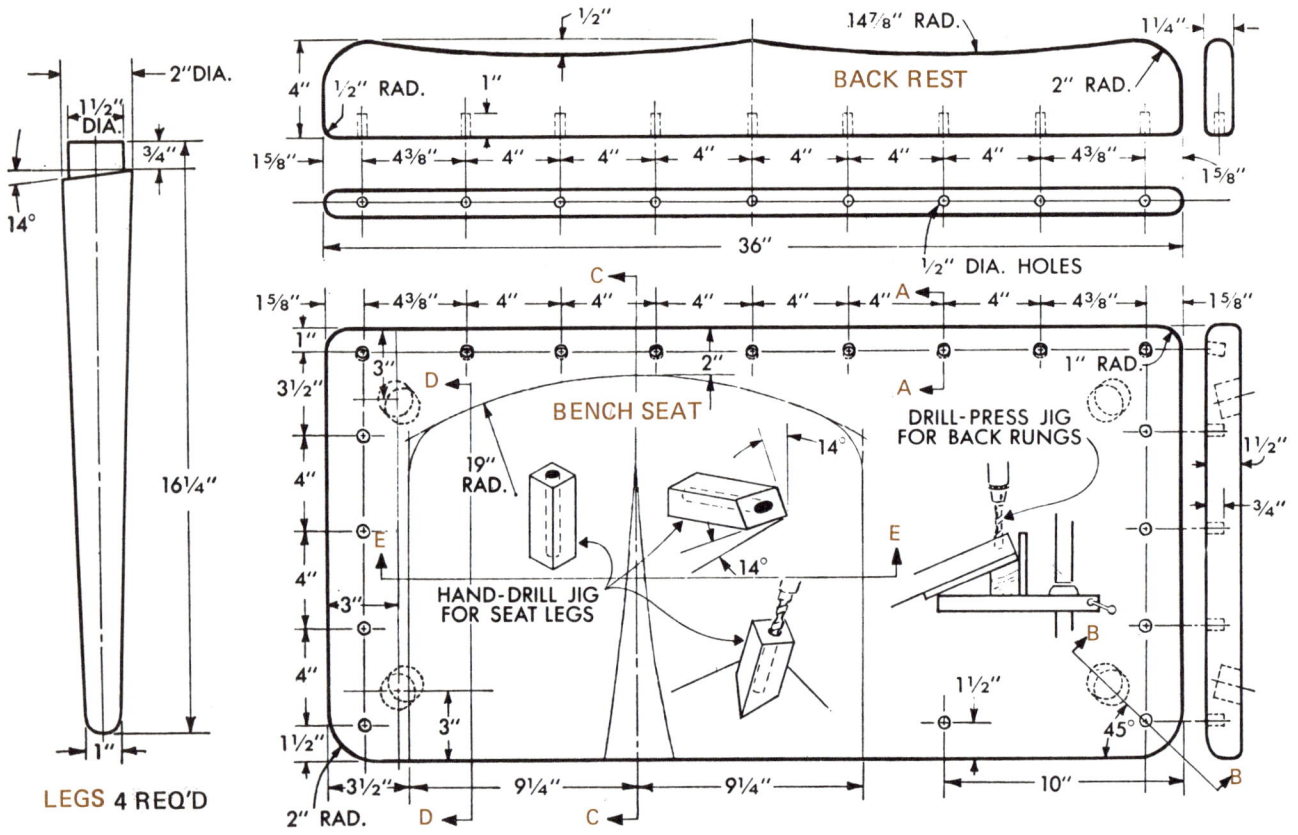

LEGS 4 REQ'D

BIRD FEEDER

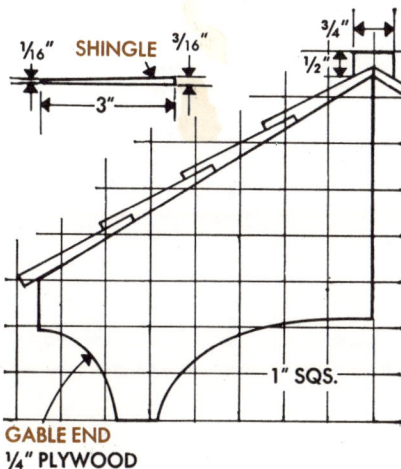

SHINGLE 1/16" 3/16" 3" 3/4" 1/2"

1" SQS.

GABLE END
1/4" PLYWOOD

Modeled after the covered bridges of New England, this bird feeder has the same quiet charm and look of ageless serenity those structures have.

Start construction by making rectangular frames for the sides from ¾ x ¾-inch strips (cut from 1-inch stock which is ¾ inch nominal). A 15-inch length is nailed to the tops of two 8-inch posts. The lower part of each frame is joined by a panel of ¼-inch plywood.

The six X-frames (trusses) are cut and assembled next, from the same ¾ x ¾-inch stock. The half-lap joints are held by waterproof glue and are clamped firmly while the glue sets.

With the trusses set aside temporarily, cut and assemble the two-piece floor/base by driving nails up through the base into the posts, and also using waterproof glue. Double-check to make sure the side frames are square, then install the trusses, using glue and finishing nails driven up through the base, and down through the top plate.

Four joists now are cut to length and glued and nailed to the tops of the plates. Space them as shown, one being located on the ends above the posts, the other two located above the joints between the trusses.

Hopper ends are cut next; note that the inner glass of each hopper touches the floor, the two outer glasses are 1/8 inch above the floor. Attach the hopper ends inside the trusses. Cut single-strength glass to fit the grooves.

Eight rafters are cut and installed, then covered with panels of ¼-inch plywood. Shape the gable ends and nail them in place. "Shingles" are ripped to the profile shown, cut the full length of the roof and nailed in place. A V-groove is cut in a strip of ¾-inch stock and nailed to the ridge of the roof.

Finish with white paint on the floor and side panels and stain on the trusses and the roof.

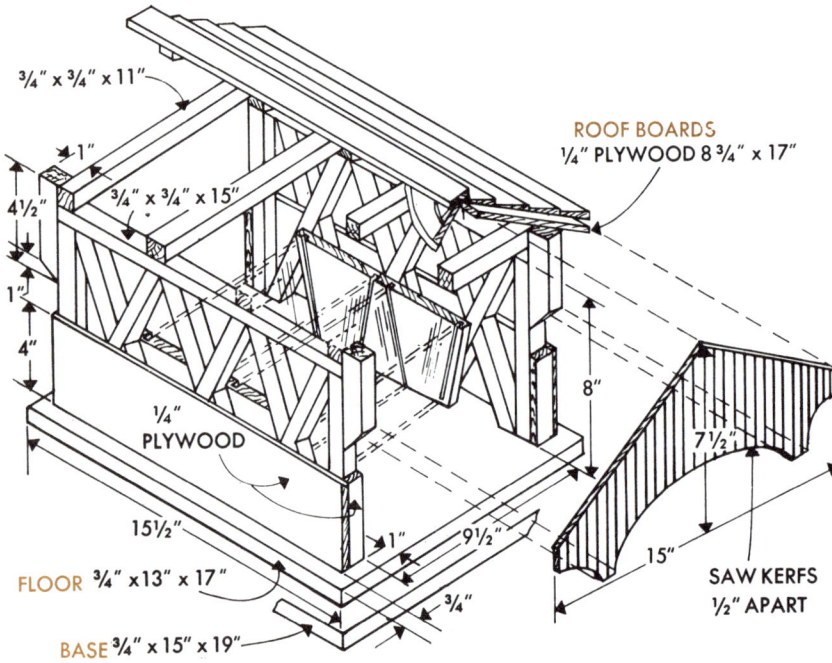

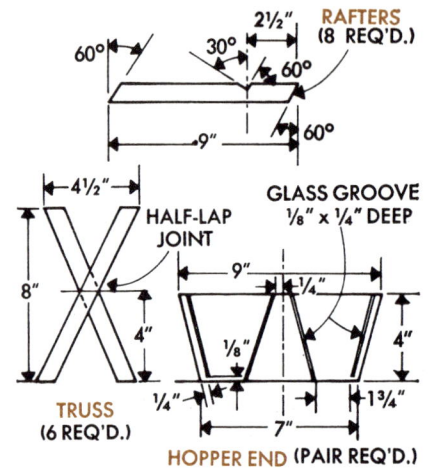

3/4" x 3/4" x 11"

1"

4½"

1"

4"

3/4" x 3/4" x 15"

ROOF BOARDS
1/4" PLYWOOD 8 3/4" x 17"

8"

7½"

¼"
PLYWOOD

15½"

9½"

1"

15"

SAW KERFS
½" APART

FLOOR ¾" x 13" x 17"

3/4"

BASE ¾" x 15" x 19"

60°

30°

2½"

60°

60°

RAFTERS
(8 REQ'D.)

9"

4½"

HALF-LAP
JOINT

GLASS GROOVE
1/8" x 1/4" DEEP

8"

4"

9"

¼"

1/8"

4"

TRUSS
(6 REQ'D.)

¼"

7"

1¾"

HOPPER END (PAIR REQ'D.)

BOBSLED

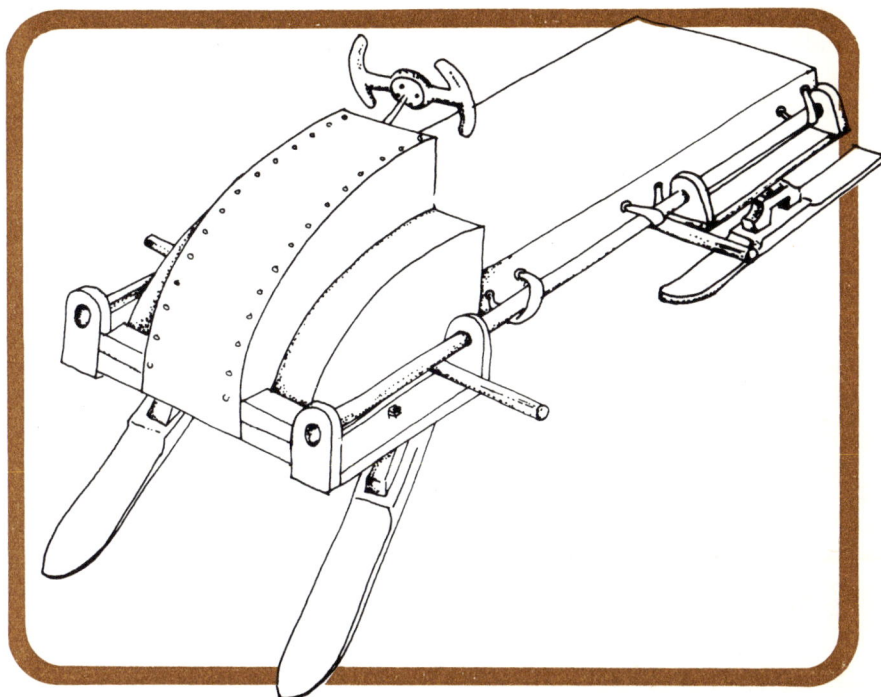

1. Riding platform is "grid" of hardwood strips and spacers. Holes in cross members are for hand grips.

2. Underneath view of steering mechanism shows position of column extension in bolts on tie rod.

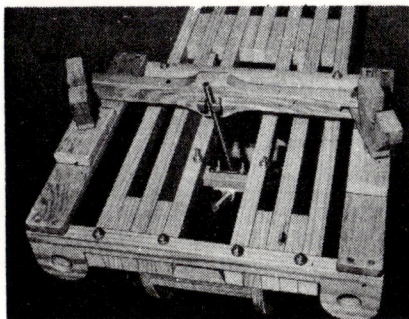

With quick-action "auto-type" steering, sleek styling and light weight, this bobsled will be in a class by itself as you go skimming down the slopes. It's sure to be a hit with the youngsters, and can provide plenty of fun for the young-in-heart of any age. The unique "skeletonized" riding platform is a light, yet strong and rigid structure.

Begin construction of the sled with the riding platform. Assemble it from strips (A-1, A-2) and spacers (A-3) with waterproof glue and screws. Cut the body cross members (B-1, B-2) and drill 1-3/8-inch holes in the ends as shown (figure 1). Fasten the cross members to the runner supports (C-1, C-2) then fasten both runner assemblies to the body platform with bolts, washers and nuts. (Note that front assembly is ¼-inch wider than the platform to accommodate the hood-side panels.) At this point, you may wish to give the platform several coats of clear marine varnish, as parts of it will be hard to get at later.

Attach the four die-cast shaft bearings to the back assembly as shown (figure 7).

Make the runners (G, H) from a good quality, springy stock such as ash, making sure it is straightgrained and clear. After the runners are rough-cut to shape, lay out the front and back radii, and saw them to shape (figure 8). Cut a shallow groove in the bottom of each runner and sand smooth to final shape. Apply several coats of marine varnish, sanding between coats of bees wax. Make the runner mounts (E) and attach to each back runner (figure 10). The back runner mounts also have a bearing for the axle as shown. Cut and shape the tie rod (F) and the front runner mounts and extensions (D-1, D-2) and fasten together (figure 9). A 2-inch bolt will have to be passed up through them before they are attached to the runners. Position the two bolts in the center of the tie rod, that locates the steering rod and position the tie rod and mounts together in their pivots with bolts, washers and nuts.

To make the "cowling" or front hood, enlarge the squared drawings of L and M, make patterns, and saw the curved frames from ½-inch stock. You will need four small and two large frames. Attach a 5-inch spacer (Z) at the center (figure 3) and glue and screw the large frame pieces to the spacer. Fasten the vertical supports (N) to the platform and to the top ends of the frames. These joints are reinforced with plywood gussets (P). Cut the two inside panels (X) and fasten in place with glue and screws. Attach the two smaller hood frames (M) next to the hood panels. Add spacers (ZZ) and attach the last two outside frames. These frames are also positioned with vertical supports and gussets.

At this point, construct and install the steering mechanism. If you don't own a welder, you will have to have a friend assemble this portion. Make sure before welding on the steering wheel flange plate and the column extension that you have one of the die-cast bearings on the column.

The exact position of the upper and lower steering column brackets (J, K) will be determined by the height you intend to have the steering wheel. After you have worked this out, cut out the brackets

3. Spacer positions hood frames. Supports and frame are held with gussets. Note bolts for cross members.

STEERING BRACKET DETAIL

STEERING WHEEL DETAIL

TIE ROD DETAIL

RUNNER MOUNT DETAIL

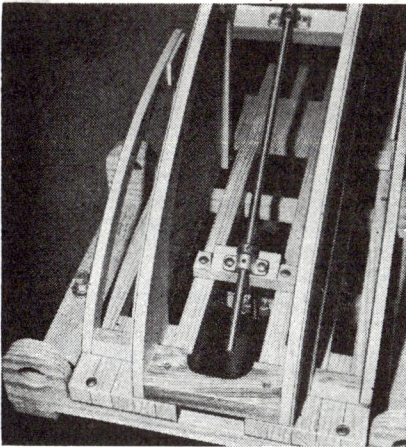

4. Steering wheel height is determined, assembly is welded, fastened in place with brackets and collars.

5. Center hood covering is attached with glue, screws, and finishing washers. Sides are glued, then clamped.

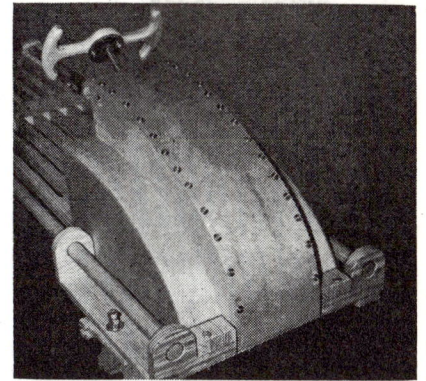

6. Outside hood panels are extended to lower edge of platform, between platform and crosspiece.

7. Four die-cast bearings are fastened on runner-mount assemblies to accept back axle and runners.

8. Runners are rough-cut from clear, straight-grained stock such as ash, shaped with rasp and sandpaper.

MATERIALS LIST

A-1.	Longitudinals:	1-1/8"x1-1/8"x6'-6" ash (6)
A-2.	Longitudinal:	1-1/8"x1-1/8"x56" ash (1)
A-3.	Spacers:	1-1/8"x1-1/8"x5" ash (22)
B-1.	Cross Members:	1"x4½"x21¾" ash (2)
B-2.	Cross Members:	1"x4½"x22" ash (2)
C-1.	Back Runner Support:	¾"x3½"x23" ash (2)
C-2.	Front Runner Support:	¾"x2½"x18" ash (2)
D-1.	Front Runner Mount:	1-1/8"x3"x5" ash (2)
D-2.	Mount Extension:	½"x1-1/8"x6" maple (2)
E.	Back Runner Mount:	1¼"x3¼"x8" ash (2)
F.	Tie Rod:	1"x3"x21" ash (1)
G.	Front Runner:	1½"x3½"x36" ash (2)
H.	Back Runner:	1½"x3½"x36" ash (2)
I-1.	Steering Wheel:	¼"x2¼"x7" ash (4)
I-2.	Steering Wheel:	1"x3¾"x12" ash (1)
I-3.	Steering Wheel:	½"x1-5/8"x2¼" ash (4)
J.	Upper Steering Column Bracket:	1¼"x1½"x6-3/8" ash (1)
K.	Lower Steering Column Bracket:	1¼"x1½"x5-5/8" ash (1)
L.	Hood Frame:	½"x8"x26" ash (2)
M.	Hood Frame:	½"x4"x22" ash (4)
N.	Frame Support:	½"x1¼"x12-7/8" ash (2)
O.	Frame Support:	½"x1¼"x6" ash (2)
P.	Hood Frame Gusset:	¼"x2½"x4" plywood (6)
Q.	Lower Hood Covering:	1/8"x3-3/8"x23" plywood (2)
R.	Upper Hood Covering:	1/8"x7-7/8"x28" plywood (1)
S.	Footrests:	1-5/16"-diameter x 36" fir dowels (2)
T.	Hand Grips:	1-5/16"-diameter x 6'-6" fir dowels (2)
U.	Steering Column:	½"-diameter x 23" C.R.S. (1)
V.	Steering Wheel Flange:	¼"x3"-diameter steel plate (1)
W.	Column Ext:	½"-diameter x 9" C.R.S. (1)
X.	**Inside Hood Side Panels:**	1/8"x13"x22" hardboard (2)
Y.	**Outside Hood Side Panels:**	1/8"x8"x20" hardboard (2)

and secure in place with bolts and screws. Position the steering column and fasten all collars (figure 4). Figure 2 shows the lower steering mechanism from the underside.

With the steering-column assembly in place and secured, attach the 1/8-inch plywood covering (R) to the center hood frame, using glue, screws and finishing washers. Cut the side hood coverings (Q) apply glue and fasten in place, clamping with blocks of wood (figure 5). Smooth off all sharp edges and attach the outer side panels (Y) with glue and small screws. The outer side panels extend down to the lower edges of the platform members.

Glue-up the laminated steering wheel as shown, rough-cut to shape (figure 11) and finish with rasp and sandpaper. Attach the completed wheel to the flange, using 1/4-inch carriage bolts. Fit the "closet-pole" footrests (S) on the underside of the platform and fasten with screws. Slide the hand grips (T) through the holes in the cross members and fasten with glue and screws.

Paint the steering wheel and footrests black. For a sporty look, paint the hood and hand grips in a bright color and follow with one of the "candy" colors in an aerosol can, (used on model cars). Make sure you apply enamel over lacquer, not lacquer over enamel. Of course, you should make a test run before turning it over to the younger set.

9. Tie rod and runner-mount assembly is bolted to front runners after inserting bolts in mounts.

10. Finish as you go. Platform and runners are finished natural, mounts black. Note bearings on mounts.

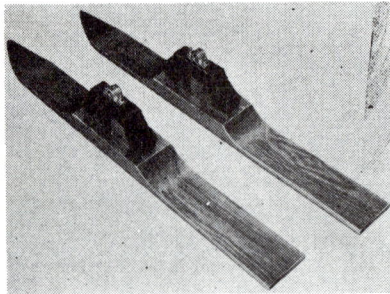

11. Steering wheel is laminated from hardwood, rough-sawn to shape then finished with rasp and sandpaper.

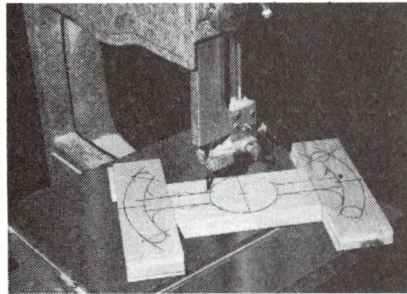

EARLY AMERICAN BOOKCASE

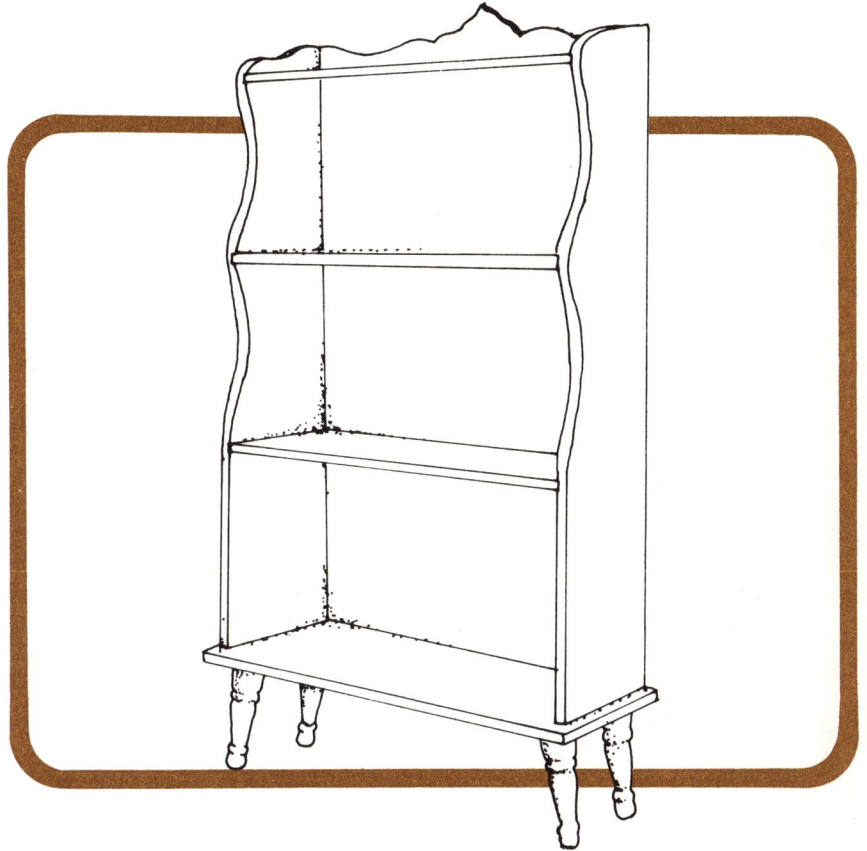

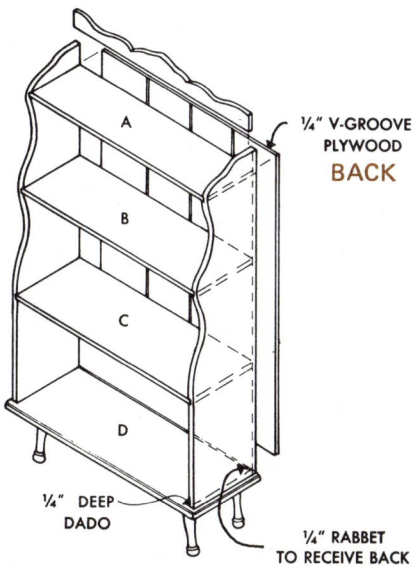

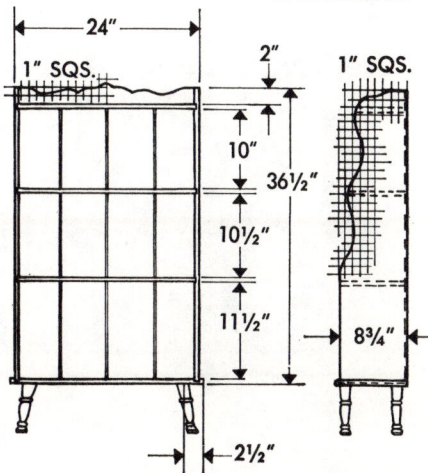

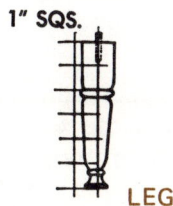

¼" V-GROOVE
PLYWOOD
BACK

A

B

C

D

¼" DEEP
DADO

¼" RABBET
TO RECEIVE BACK

It will take only a few evenings to complete this attractive book case. You can use a jig, saber or band saw to shape the two sides, while a table or radial-arm saw is used to cut the dadoes in the sides into which the shelves are fitted.

To start, make paper patterns from the squared drawings of the sides. If your particular saw has the capacity, tack-nail the pieces together and cut both sides at once to assure they are identical. Next, cut the shelf dadoes, holding the straight edges of the sides against the fence or miter gauge, depending on the type saw that is used. Cut rabbets on the rear, inner edges of the sides to accept the back.

Make the bottom of the case (Part D) and cut shallow dadoes as indicated, stopping short of the front and squaring the dadoes with a chisel. Cut the rabbet for the back.

Assemble the sides and shelves with glue and clamp square. You can use a couple of finishing nails in each shelf, driving them through the sides. Glue and brad the back in place, then the top trim piece that first is cut to shape.

Finally, install the stock and readymade 6 inch legs. Stain and finish to suit.

24"

1" SQS.

2"

10"

36½"

10½"

11½"

2½"

1" SQS.

8¾"

1" SQS.

LEG

SPANISH-STYLE BOOKCASE

Originally conceived as a book case, the design of this project has been modified so it is suitable for a number of functions. Dishes can be stored in the upper cabinet, with linens in the drawer below, or installing racks in the upper part, rather than shelves, makes it ideal as a gun cabinet. Shells and other gear can be stored in the drawers. Locks must be fitted to doors and drawers in the latter usage.

Structural design is such that the project is a pretty straightforward table-saw job, even though there is much detail work. The raised-panel assemblies, for example, if put together as described, can be assembled without clamps.

Because the project should have a hand-crafted look, some "careless craftsmanship" is in order. All corners should be rounded off, even drawer and door edges, and the frames in which they fit. All surfaces should be velvet-smooth, but a slight dent here and there adds to the feeling. One way to do this, after assembly, is to whack it in some areas with a light chain. Another touch is to be careless when wiping off excess glue; this will create lighter spots when you apply stain. Don't overdo it; too much is worse than none at all.

Most of the project calls for solid pine and we suggest you use edgeglued ponderosa pine boards available in most lumberyards. Seven pieces of this stock 24 inches wide and 72 inches long should just about do it.

Figure 1 gives the details of construction for the upper cabinet. Start by cutting the top and bottom to size, then running the ¾-inch wide dadoes parallel to each end. Be careful when cutting the stiles and rails for the side panels; dimensions in the Materials List are exact.

Molding is standard "scalloped edge" which is available at lumberyards. You may wish to choose a different style.

Shoulders on panels butt against inside edges of frame members. It is important to be accurate when making cuts.

Figure 1   CABINET ASSEMBLY

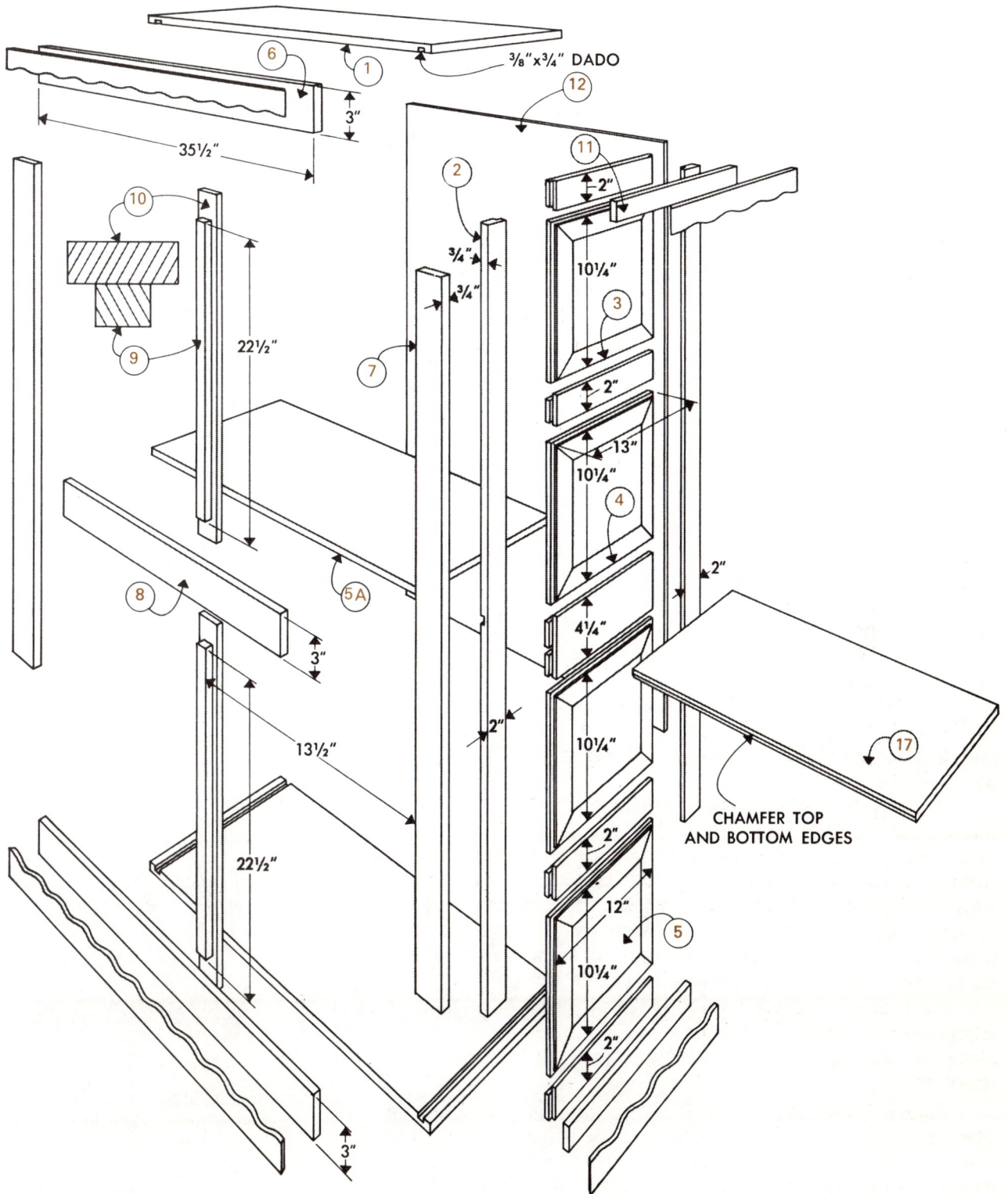

3/8" x 3/4" DADO

35 1/2"

3"

22 1/2"

3/4"

3/4"

2"

10 1/4"

2"

13"

10 1/4"

2"

4 1/4"

2"

10 1/4"

2"

12"

10 1/4"

2"

13 1/2"

22 1/2"

3"

3"

CHAMFER TOP
AND BOTTOM EDGES

Figure 2   PANEL DETAILS

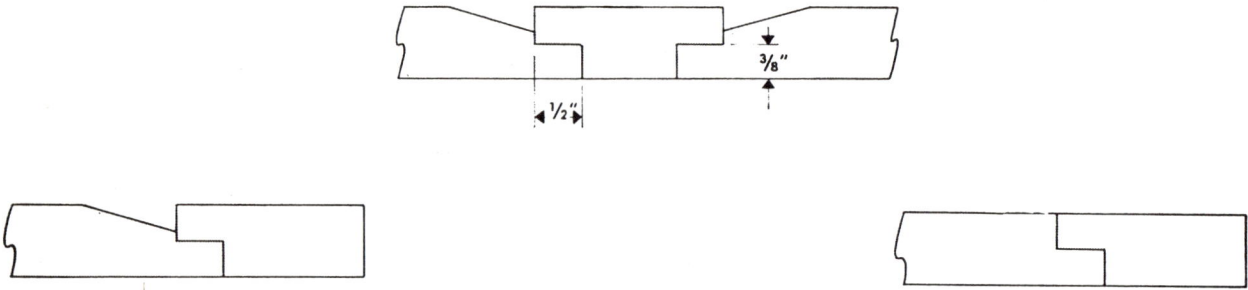

Figure 3   BASE ASSEMBLY

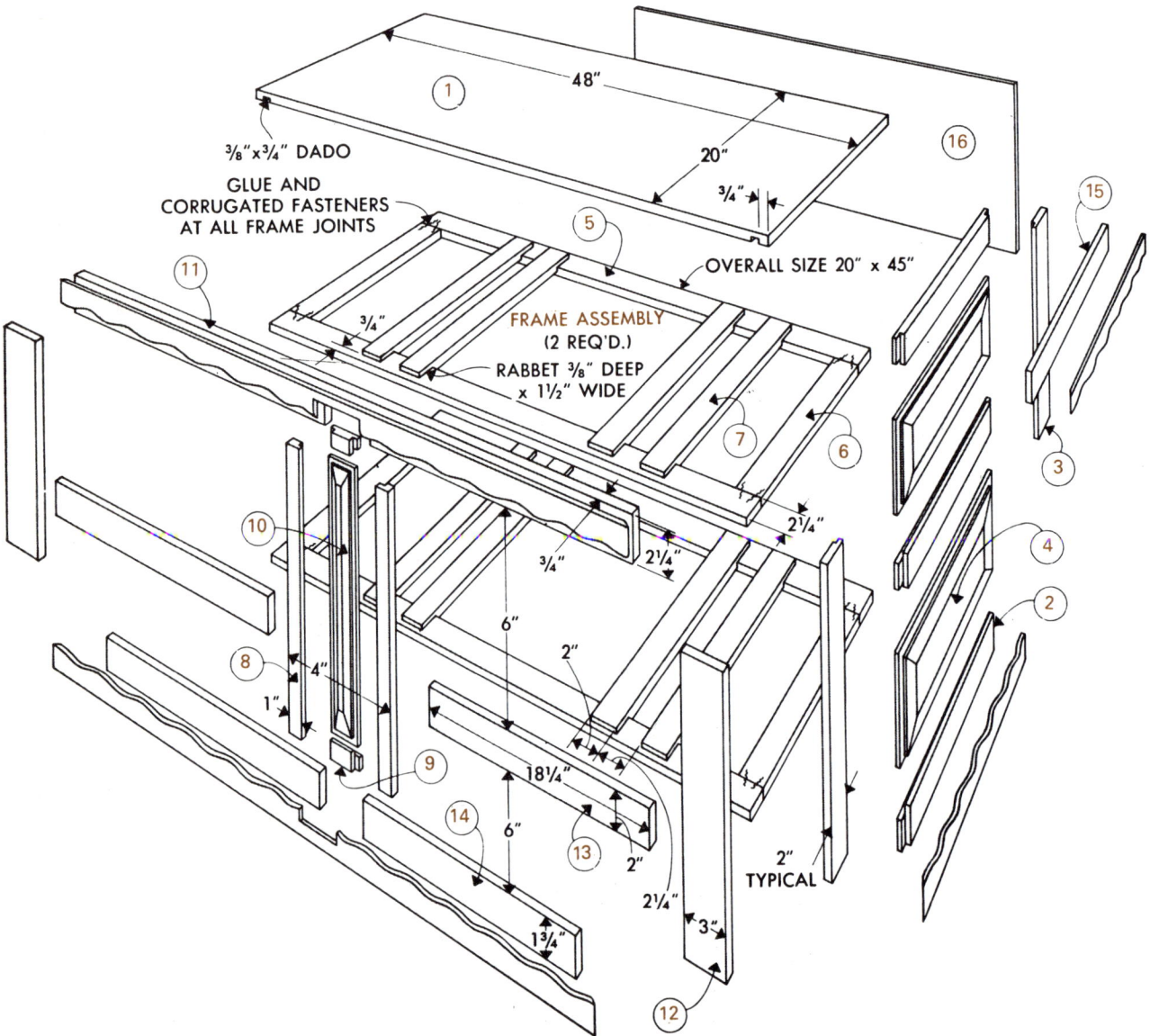

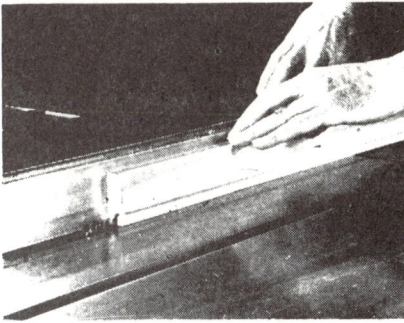

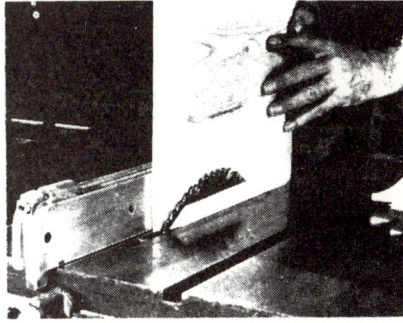

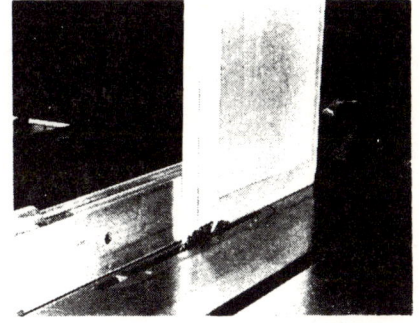

These photographs show how raised panels are cut on a table saw. Instructions are given in the text.

Spindles and spindle supports are put together as assembly before being inserted in door frames. Glue and brad.

Like the drawers, complete door assembly must not be a tight fit in the frame openings. Have 1/16" clearance.

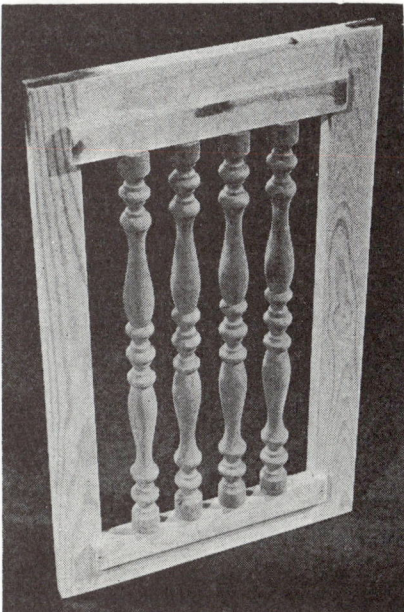

Rabbets are required on the inside edges of the stiles, both the edges and ends of the middle rails and the inside edges and ends of the top and bottom rail. You can do this with a dado blade, or several passes of a regular blade.

Next, cut the eight panel pieces (part 5) to size so the grain runs the long way. Set the saw blade to an angle of 15 degrees and the rip fence to leave a 3/8-inch thick solid edge. Make bevel cuts on all four edges of each panel, as shown in the photos. Return the saw blade to vertical and adjust it to project exactly ½ inch. Set the rip fence 3/8 inch from the blade and run the panels through on all four edges to create a small shoulder that butts against the stiles and rails.

To assemble, place the pieces face down on a bench top and coat mating surfaces with glue as you go along. Use ¾-inch brads to hold the parts, but don't set them or they'll project through the front. A good procedure to follow is: start with the top rail and a stile. Add a panel, then a rail and a panel and so on. Finally, add the opposite stile. Check with a square as you assemble.

Cut front facing strips, starting with the top and bottom pieces. Attach these with glue and finishing nails, then cut the vertical ones (part 7) for a tight fit. Finally, add the center one. Cut the divider (part 9) and glue and nail it to the divider support. Add this to the case with glue and nails driven through from the back. Attach the fillers and the molding.

Door details are shown in figure 4. Make and assemble the stiles and rails using end-lap joints in each corner, joining with glue and ¾-inch brads. Shape the spindle supports as indicated and drill the ½-inch holes at least ½ inch deep. The spindles are purchased ready-made; measuring about 1¼ inches in diameter and 17 inches long, exclusive of the tenons. Assemble them to the supports with glue and attach to the door frame as shown in the photo. To get a smooth-working door, trim 1/16 inch from the top, bottom and edge opposite the hinge side.

Make four shelves (part 17) and support them with standard shelf strips and clips. Four 4-foot pieces of shelf strip were cut in half to get the eight pieces needed. The last thing to do is nail on the plywood back.

The base cabinet requires much the same construction procedure as for the top cabinet. Details are shown in figure 3. Start by making

MATERIALS LIST

Base Cabinet

1. Top:	¾"x20"x48" (1)
2. Rail:	¾"x2"x17" (6)
3. Stile:	¾"x2"x17-5/8" (4)
4. Panel:	¾"x6-13/16"x17" (4)
5. Frame Side:	¾"x2¼"x45" (4)
6. Frame Ends:	¾"x2¼"x15½" (8)
7. Drawer Guides:	¾"x2"x18½" (8)
8. Front Stiles:	¾"x1"x17-5/8" (2)
9. Front Rails:	¾"x1"x3" (2)
10. Panel:	¾"x3"x16-5/8" (1)
11. Top Facing:	¾"x2¼"x48" (1)
12. Side Facing:	¾"x3"x15¾" (2)
13. Middle Facing:	¾"x2"x18¼" (2)
14. Bottom Facing:	¾"x1¾"x18¼" (2)
15. Filler:	¾"x1½"x20" (2)
16. Back:	¼"x17¼"x45¾" plywood (1)
17. Drawer Front:	¾"x6"x18¼" (4)
18. Drawer Side:	½"x6"x18¾" plywood (8)
19. Drawer Bottom:	3/8"x17¾"x18¾" plywood (4)
20. Drawer Back:	½"x5"x16¾" plywood (4)
21. Drawer Slide:	½"x2¼"x18¾" (4)

Top Cabinet

1. Top, Bottom:	¾"x16"x35½" (1 each)
2. Stiles:	¾"x2"x53¼" (4)
3. Rails:	¾"x2"x13" (8)
4. Middle Rail:	¾"x4¼"x13" (2)
5. Panel:	¾"x11¼"x13" (8)
5A. Divider:	¾"x16"x33¼" (1)
6. Top, Bottom Facing:	¾"x3"x35½" (2)
7. Front-Side Facing:	¾"x3"x48" (2)
8. Front-Middle Facing:	¾"x3"x28" (8)
9. Divider:	¾"x1"x22½" (2)
10. Divider Support:	¾"x2"x25½" (2)
11. Filler:	¾"x1½"x16" (4)
12. Back:	¼"x33¼"x53¼" plywood (1)
13. Door Stiles:	¾"x2"x22½" (8)
14. Door Rail:	¾"x2"x13½" (8)
15. Spindle Supports:	¾"x1½"x10½" (8)
16. Spindles:	1¼"-diameter x 17" ready-made (16)
17. Shelf:	¾"x14"x32¼" (4)

Figure 4

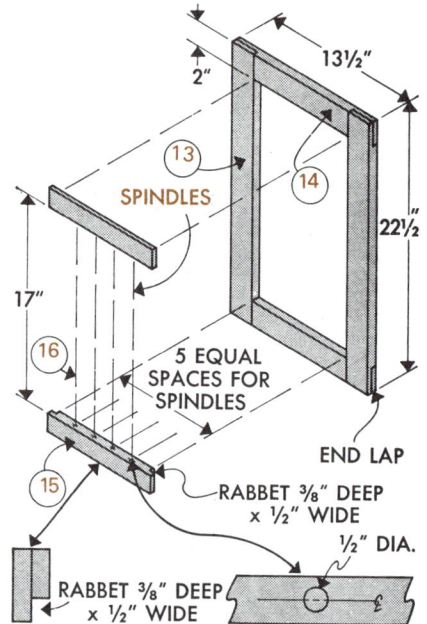

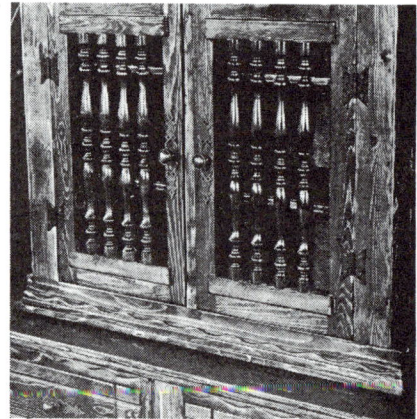

Choose hardware that is in keeping with the design of the project. There is a wide selection of styles available.

Size the drawer slide to move smoothly between the drawer guides. Front edges of drawer guides act as stop.

the top, then the side panels. Follow the details in figure 3, and the procedure outlined for the panels you made for the top cabinet.

Make the two shelf frames, then assemble them with the top and the side panels. Make the center, front panel (parts 8, 9 and 10) and attach to the assembly. Add the facing members, making sure the top edges of parts 13 and 14 are flush with the top surface of the frames. Add the fillers and the molding. Note that the front molding must be cut to fit around the front, raised panel. Round off the edges of the U-cuts you make.

Drawer details are shown in figure 5. Start by making the fronts and cutting the dadoes as shown. The V-cuts are shown in the detail, but set up to cut on some scrap stock before you do the actual fronts. Cut and dado the sides and assemble these to the front by using glue and finishing nails. Then size the bottoms and add to the assembly. Finally, cut the backs to fit then glue and nail in place. Cut the drawer slides (part 21) so they move smoothly between the drawer guides. If you cut these to fit snugly, the drawers may stick. Place these guides carefully on the drawer bottoms and attach with glue and nails.

Figure 5

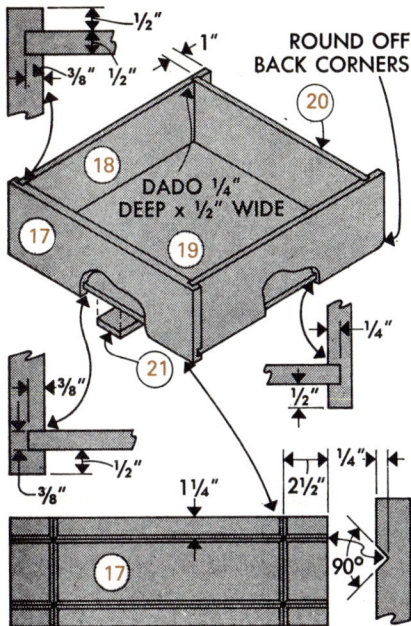

ROUND OFF
BACK CORNERS

DADO 1/4"
DEEP x 1/2" WIDE

If you find that the drawer fronts fit too tightly in the openings, work on them with sandpaper. Actually, a spacing of 1/16 inch between frame and drawer front is not out of line. The last step is to install the plywood back.

There is much available today in the way of hardware to fit this kind of project. In the book case shown, butterfly hinges with matching square screw heads, and similar pulls on the doors and drawers were used. Choose something with a dull, dark-gray finish. Attach all hardware, then remove it for the final finishing.

Be sure all nail heads are set, then use walnut paste filler in all holes. Use a pad sander with fine paper to smooth all surfaces. Don't be afraid to round off all edges, including drawer and door fronts and the frame edges against which they butt.

Stain can be applied heavily; let it set for about one-half hour before wiping off with a lint-free cloth. Don't attempt to clean out inside corners; the stain should settle more heavily there than on surfaces and outside corners. Let the stain dry 24 hours. If you prefer a darker finish, repeat the stain application.

After the stain is dry, smooth all surfaces with fine steel wool. Dust thoroughly—a tack rag is best—and apply the finish.

Any satin-finish material will do. The finish may be brushed on, just heavy enough not to run. The material is available also in an aerosol container. If you brush on the finish you may elect to spray areas which can be a problem with a brush, such as the spindles.

When the first application is dry, repeat the steel-wool procedure. Make sure every exposed surface is smoothed; any spots not worked over will show up even more in contrast to those areas that are properly finished. Apply another coat of finish. On the book case shown, three coats were used, with vigorous steelwooling between coats to create a really "hand-rubbed" look that gives the appearance of the patina of age.

RAILROAD BOOK ENDS

Representing a train passing through a tunnel of books, these **unique** bookends will appeal to railroad buffs, but will be appreciated **by** anyone liking the unusual.

Like the recipe for the chicken soup that says, "first get a chick**en**," you will need the train parts. Most railroad hobbyists will have **discarded** shells around, and even toy boxes can be a source of supply **for** no-longer-operating trains whose engine and caboose can be cut in half and used. The bookends shown have a diesel engine, but a steam **locomotive** would do just as well.

Cut the bases and uprights of the bookends, then the arches for the tunnels. Assemble with glue and nails. Paint the inside of the tunnel, also the bases, black, with the outside of the arches a gray that simulates concrete. For the tracks, you can buy rails with wooden ties, but you can also strip the metal ties from standard track and substitute shop-made wooden ones. Brush on a coat of glue around the tracks, then pour on model-train gravel. When the glue has set, brush away the excess.

Cut the locomotive and caboose any length you wish, then cut blocks of wood to fit inside the cut ends. Drill the shells for brads to hold the blocks. Wood screws through the bookends into these blocks hold the shells of the caboose and locomotive. The latter should be painted before attaching.

More ideas for bookends: How about the halves of cars, sail boats, steam ships?

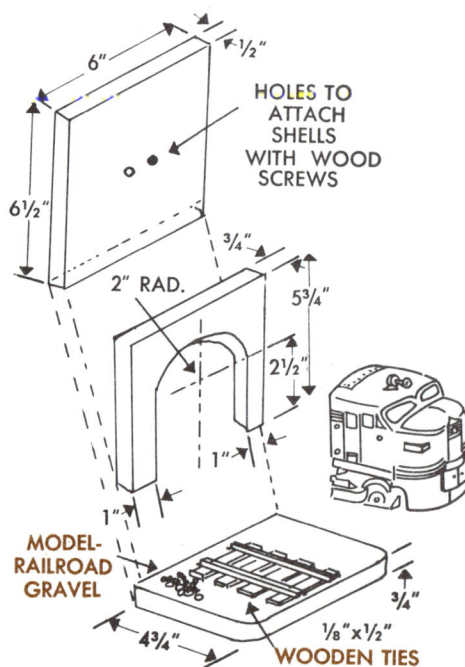

SPANISH BUFFET AND MIRROR

Deeply sculptured moldings, an unusual decorator finish, and antiqued-brass hardware on this buffet create the charm and elegance of Spanish styling. Although the ornate decorations suggest countless hours spent in carving, they really are ready-made moldings available in a variety of patterns. These plastic moldings are not to be confused with the pressed wood moldings on the market. The buffet is actually a simple box made elegant with the moldings. The finish and color of the buffet result in an unusual "old-world" antique appearance. It is a bright red overlaid with a transparent black walnut Danish oil finish. The woods used are birch plywood and solid stock. The "wild-grained" side of the plywood was used for more accent of the finish. Any lightcolored hardwood, with a definite grain pattern, such as ash, oak or pecan could be used.

Begin construction of the buffet by cutting the various hardwood plywood pieces to size as shown in the cutting diagram. Cut on the heavy lines first for access to the other lines. You will have to make one cut, as shown, with a saber or handsaw. Also required is a piece of ¼-inch hardboard (16¼ x 69 inches) for the back, and 1 piece of ¾-inch fir plywood (15¾ x 68½ inches) for the bottom. Rabbet the back edges of the top and sides ¼ x ¼ inch for the hardboard back. Start the assembly by fastening the two dividers to the cabinet bottom, using glue and No. 8 finishing nails. Note that the dividers are ¼-inch narrower than the buffet bottom and sides. Keep the dividers flush with the front edge of the bottom. Attach the sides, positioning the upper surface of the cabinet bottom three inches up from the lower edges of the sides. Cut the 3-inch facing strip of solid stock; nail it in

BUFFET

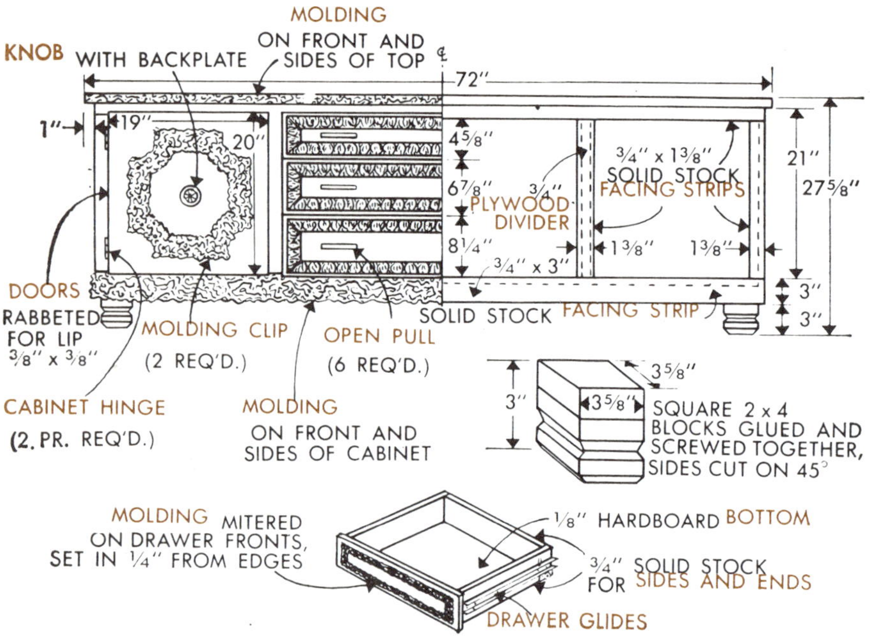
MOLDING ON FRONT AND SIDES OF TOP
KNOB WITH BACKPLATE
72″
1″
19″
20″
4⅝″
6⅞″
8¼″
¾″ PLYWOOD DIVIDER
¾″ x 3″
¾″ x 1⅜″ SOLID STOCK FACING STRIPS
1⅜″
1⅜″
21″
27⅝″
3″
3″
DOORS RABBETED FOR LIP ⅜″ x ⅜″
MOLDING CLIP (2 REQ'D.)
OPEN PULL (6 REQ'D.)
SOLID STOCK FACING STRIP
CABINET HINGE (2. PR. REQ'D.)
MOLDING ON FRONT AND SIDES OF CABINET
3″
3⅝″
3⅝″
SQUARE 2 x 4 BLOCKS GLUED AND SCREWED TOGETHER, SIDES CUT ON 45°
MOLDING MITERED ON DRAWER FRONTS, SET IN ¼″ FROM EDGES
⅛″ HARDBOARD BOTTOM
¾″ SOLID STOCK FOR SIDES AND ENDS
DRAWER GLIDES

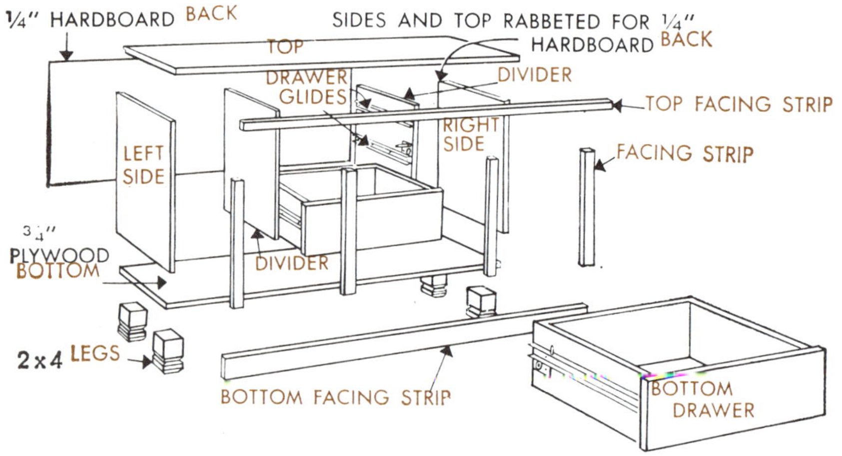
¼″ HARDBOARD BACK
SIDES AND TOP RABBETED FOR ¼″ HARDBOARD BACK
TOP
DRAWER GLIDES
DIVIDER
TOP FACING STRIP
RIGHT SIDE
LEFT SIDE
FACING STRIP
¾″ PLYWOOD BOTTOM
DIVIDER
2 x 4 LEGS
BOTTOM FACING STRIP
BOTTOM DRAWER

CUTTING DIAGRAM

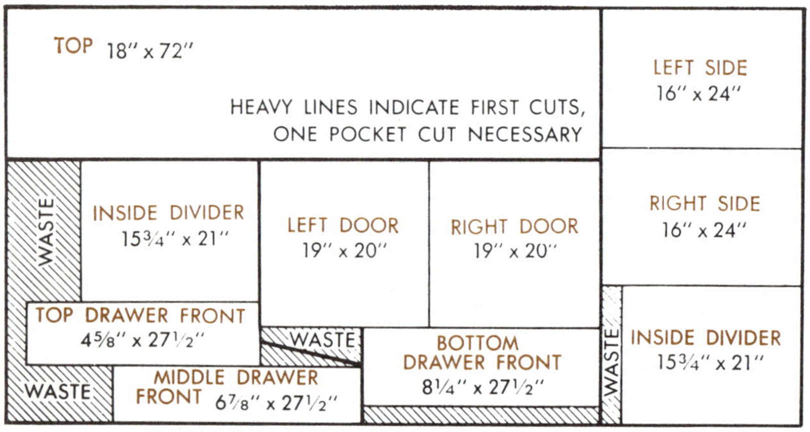
TOP 18″ x 72″
HEAVY LINES INDICATE FIRST CUTS, ONE POCKET CUT NECESSARY
LEFT SIDE 16″ x 24″
WASTE
INSIDE DIVIDER 15¾″ x 21″
LEFT DOOR 19″ x 20″
RIGHT DOOR 19″ x 20″
RIGHT SIDE 16″ x 24″
TOP DRAWER FRONT 4⅝″ x 27½″
WASTE
BOTTOM DRAWER FRONT 8¼″ x 27½″
WASTE
INSIDE DIVIDER 15¾″ x 21″
WASTE
MIDDLE DRAWER FRONT 6⅞″ x 27½″

Buffet consists of hardwood-plywood ends, top, dividers, doors and drawer fronts, fir plywood bottom.

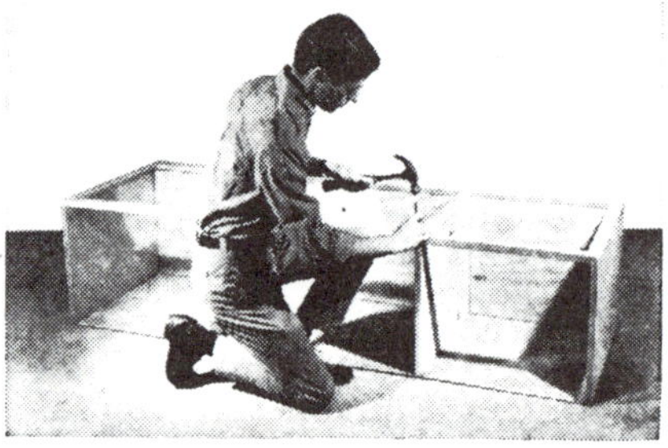

Hardboard back is set in rabbets in sides. Dividers are narrower than sides to accept back. All nails set, covered.

Front of facing strips are rough-sanded, then entire buffet, including doors and drawer fronts, is sanded with finer grits.

Short legs are made up of stacks of blocks cut from 2x4s. Three blocks per leg. Blocks are squared up, beveled.

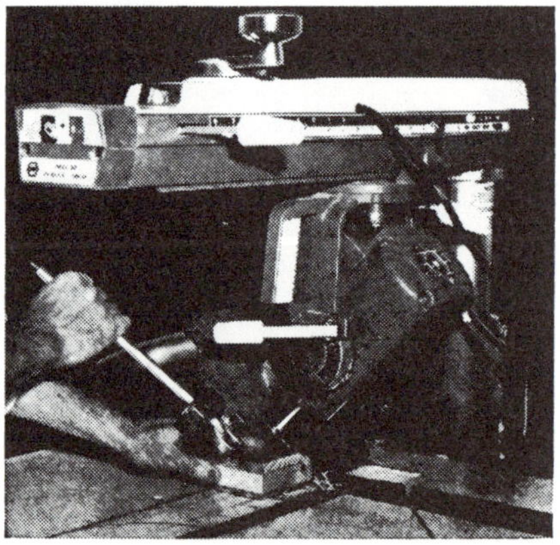

place on the lower front of the cabinet. Use predrilled holes to keep the solid stock from splitting. Cut the top facer strip and nail and glue to both ends. Fasten to the dividers, making sure they are vertical. Cut the facers for the sides and dividers and glue and nail in place. Cut the ¼-inch hardboard back to size and fit into the rabbets in the sides. Glue and nail in place. Set all nails and fill the holes with wood putty. Sand the entire buffet with progressively finer grits of sandpaper.

The legs are made of 2 x 4 stock cut to simulate hand-carved work. First step is to cut the 2 x 4s into 3-5/8-inch square blocks, (3 for each leg). Two of the blocks for each leg then have their edges cut at a 45-degree angle as shown. Glue and screw the three blocks together to form the legs. Smear their tops with glue and fasten in place using screws driven from inside the buffet.

Drill countersunk holes from the underneath side in the top facing strip. Place the buffet top in position and drive screws up through the facer into the top, making sure you do not penetrate the top. You may wish to use glue blocks in each end of the buffet to hold the top more strongly in place. Fasten the hardboard back into the rabbets in the top using small cement-coated nails.

Cut the doors and drawer fronts to the sizes shown, making 3/8 x 3/8-inch rabbets around the back edges of each. Drawer sides and backs are cut from solid stock with 1/8 x ¼-inch rabbets for a 1/8-inch hardboard bottom. Assemble the drawers and install the drawer slides to the cabinet and drawers.

The finishing details are done in a series of steps. After the buffet is sanded smooth, flood the entire surface with the bright red stain. In 45 minutes, lightly wipe over the stain with a soft cloth, going with the grain of the wood. (Even with a finely sanded surface some hardwoods will have a certain amount of raised grain, causing snagging of the cloth if rubbed against the grain. The second finishing step involves flooding over the red stain with a black walnut Danish oil-penetrating finish. This will almost obliterate the red, and should be flowed on until the wood will stop absorbing it. When the wood stops absorbing the oil, rub off the excess with a soft cloth or cheesecloth, wiping with the grain. (It has to be wiped off within one hour.) Careful wiping and some experimenting will result in a transparent finish of unusual brilliance and clarity. In some small areas, where the grain is weak, you may wish to use the cloth as a "graining device," to give the area an artificial grain to match surrounding areas. Note, when beginning to wipe off any stain or finish such as this, first load the wiping cloth with the finish or stain, squeezing out the excess. In this way the cloth will not stick when first applied, and will not leave "start and stop" marks.

The plastic molding is then stained (before cutting and placing on the buffet). The process of staining the molding is the complete reverse of staining the wood. A first application is flowed on the molding. This stain actually etches the surface of the plastic. Oil-base stains are not compatible with the molding as they just bead up and roll off. Should you wish to have a darker base color for the molding apply a second coat after the first dries. After the dark brown stain has dried, flow on a coat of red wood stain. Let this set for about an hour, then lightly wipe the top of the molding, giving the color on the carvings a

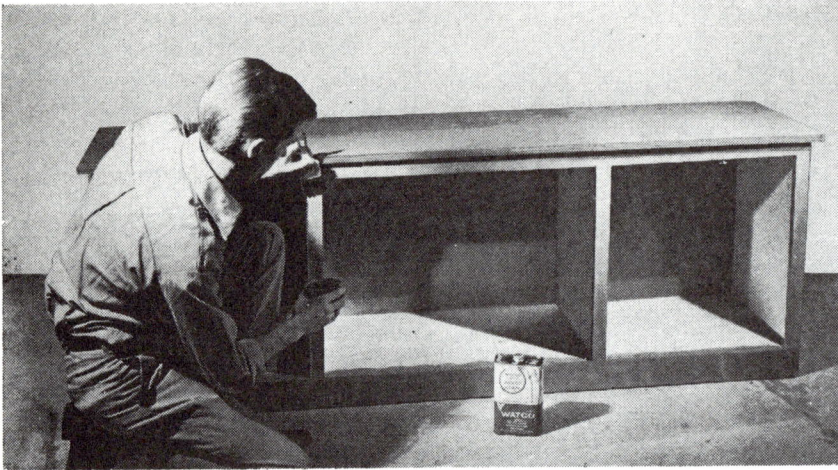

Bright-red stain is flowed over buffet, including doors and drawer fronts. Stain is left to set for about an hour, then wiped off.

Dark stain-finish is flowed over red stain. Flood the surface with the finish until the wood will not absorb any more, then wipe off.

The finish must be wiped off within one hour or it will become tacky. In some areas of weak grain you may wish to use a stain-soaked cloth to create a "grained" effect.

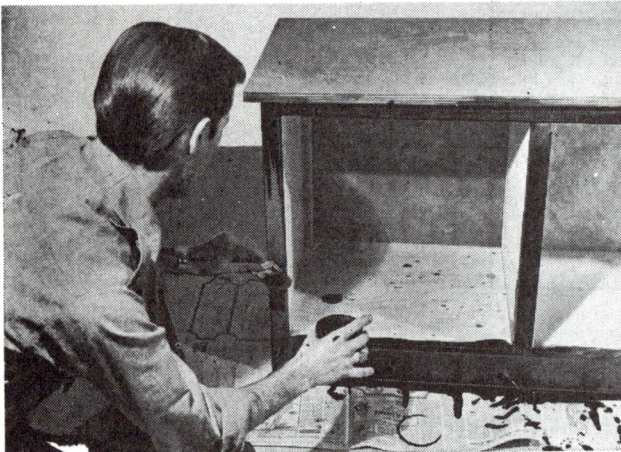

Plastic molding is first stained with the dark brown and then the red stain.

Plastic molding is applied to buffet with glue and brads in predrilled holes, after buffet and molding are stained.

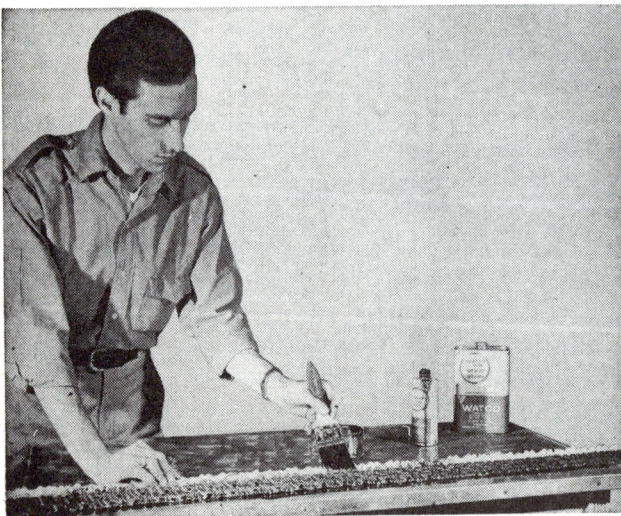

Mirror frame and molding are finished in the same manner as the buffet. Molding has a tendency to split unless predrilled holes are used for brads.

sort of "patina". After the molding has dried for a couple of days, wipe off any excess stain (it will appear shiny) with a soft cloth and touch up and white spots.

(You also can apply a base coat and glaze on the molding to create an "antique" finish.)

Cut the molding to fit the edges of the top, using butt joints. In places where you have to join shorter pieces of molding together to look like one long piece, such as the one on the front edge of the top, cut around the various carvings to match them together. The molding cuts easily with a coping or back saw, but can be cut with a sharp pocket knife or chisel when warm. Using white glue and small brads in predrilled holes in the molding fasten the molding in place. Attach the lower molding strips using the same procedures. The doors feature a preshaped "clip", molding No. 8-15, that is simply positioned in the center of the door and held in place with glue and brads. The molding on the drawer fronts is mitered. If you don't have a miter box, make a small U-shaped box of scrap wood. Use a combination square to find a 45-degree mark and make a slot on this mark. Lay the molding down in the box, and cut in the slot using a hacksaw for cutting the molding. One caution, the molding is brittle and will break if cold; when warm it can be bent almost into a circle. Attach the moldings on the drawers and touch up the corners and any white spots with stain. Install the hardware.

To give the penetrating-oil finish a sheen, apply several coats of a quality paste wax, using very fine steel wool to burnish it in. After the last coat, use a soft cloth to buff the project. Touch up all nail holes in the molding with stain, or fill with putty of a color to match the stain.

The mirror frame is made of ¾ x 3-inch solid stock with stopped rabbets on the back edges for the mirror. The top is one piece, the round edge being shaped to fit a "clip" cut off as indicated. The mirror is held in the frame by a 1/8-inch hardboard backing screwed to the frame. Finish the mirror the same as the buffet.

MIRROR FRAME

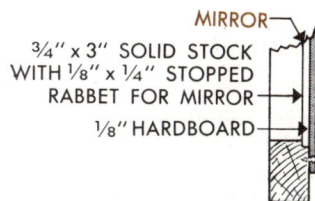

MIRROR

¾" x 3" SOLID STOCK WITH 1/8" x ¼" STOPPED RABBET FOR MIRROR

1/8" HARDBOARD

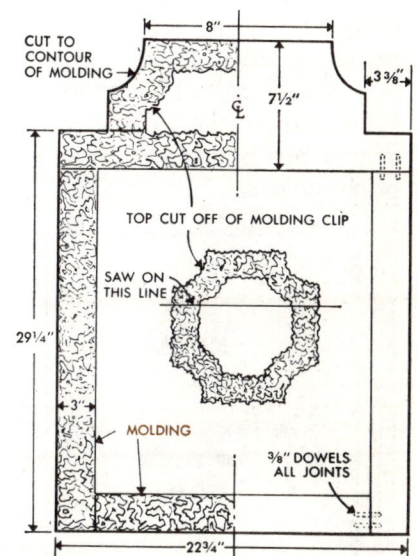

CUT TO CONTOUR OF MOLDING

8"

3 3/8"

7½"

TOP CUT OFF OF MOLDING CLIP

SAW ON THIS LINE

29¼"

3"

MOLDING

3/8" DOWELS ALL JOINTS

22¾"

TOY BUILDING BLOCKS

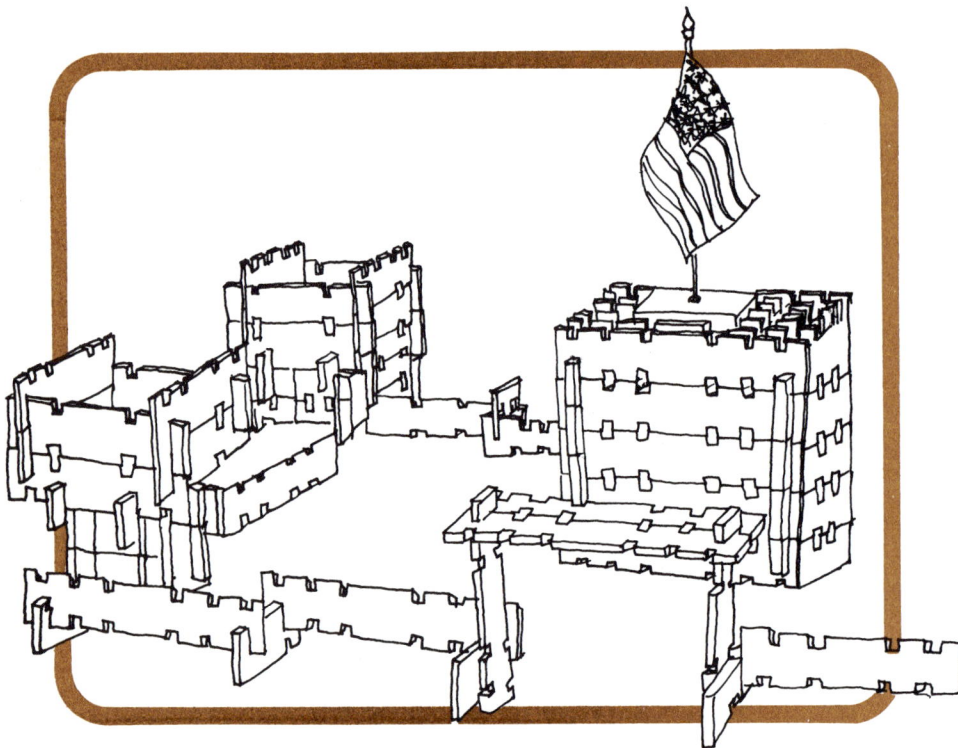

Children will have hours of fun building houses, forts and skyscrapers with these simple blocks.

Oak can be used to make these blocks; this tough material lasts longer than most woods, but maple or other close-grained hardwood can be substituted. Start by ripping the stock into ¼ x 1¾-inch strips. Cut the blocks to length before cutting the notches. A dado blade set at 5/16-inch will simplify cutting the notches. Saw the notches marked No. 1 in all blocks first; these locate the remaining notches.

A hole is drilled in the top piece for a flag pole. The flag is the type used on a bicycle and can be obtained at many hardware and novelty stores.

Knock off all the sharp edges on the blocks with sandpaper, then stain them a light oak over which varnish is applied. You also can enamel the blocks in various colors if a particular child is intrigued by bright colors.

50 BLOCKS EACH SIZE

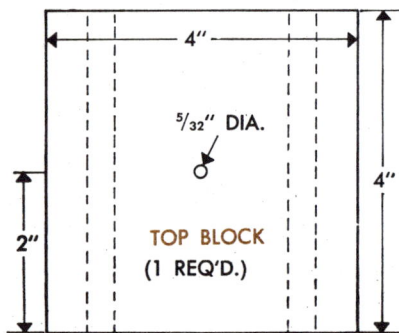

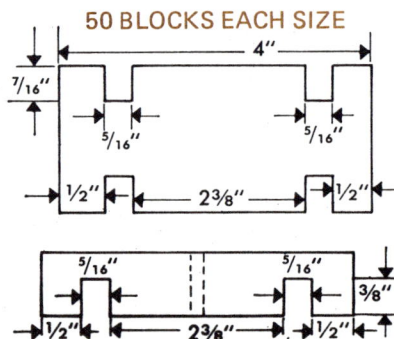

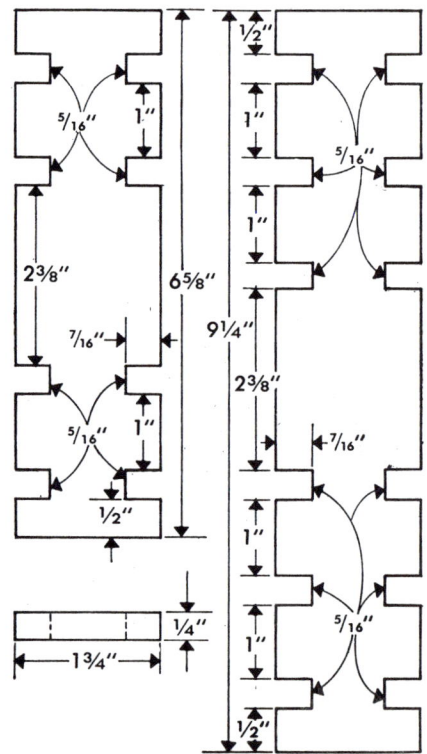

TOP BLOCK (1 REQ'D.)

50 BLOCKS EACH SIZE

CORNER CABINET

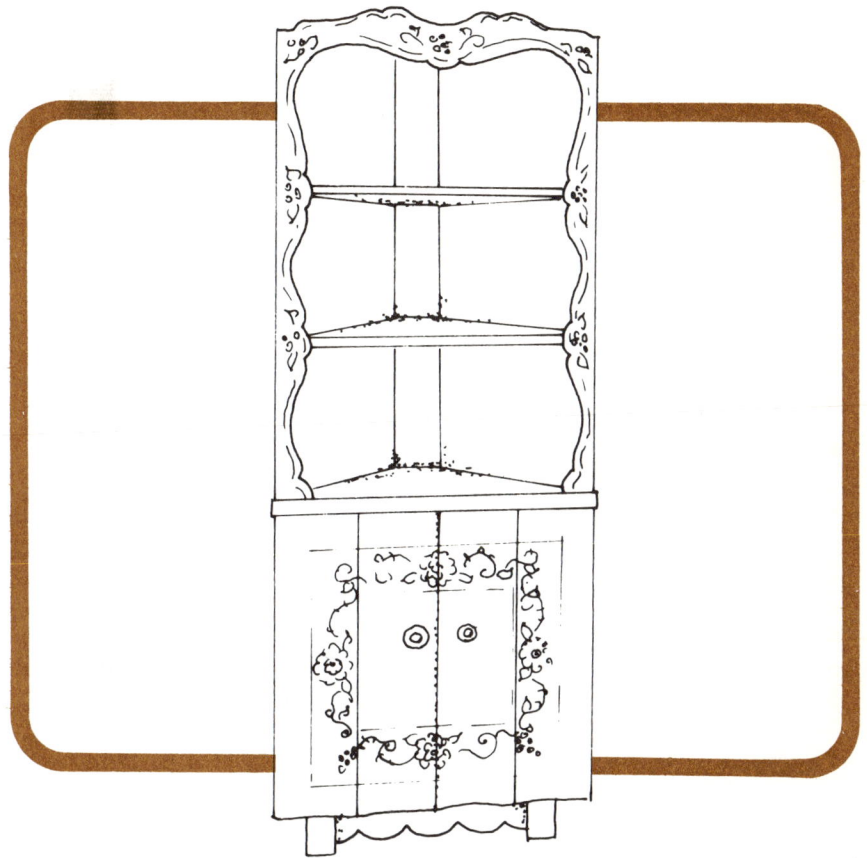

Besides being extremely attractive, this compact corner cabinet takes very little floor space, yet provides a generous amount of display-shelf space, plus a two-shelf, closed storage area. By varying the wood used (the original is in birch with painted stencils) the cabinet can be made to suit the decor of almost any room in the home.

The face of the cabinet is cut from ¾-inch hardwood-plywood, as is the back, while the two side panels are ¼-inch material. Shelves are shaped from ¾-inch plywood, with the front edges covered with veneer tape to hide the laminations.

Dadoes to accept and support the edges of the shelves are cut in the back (A) and the sides (B). Be sure to make the B pieces as a pair. One method is to cut the dadoes first, then the 45-degree angles on the edges. You still must cut the side pieces to be a pair, when cutting the 45-degree angles.

Plate grooves, on one or more shelves, are created by shallow saw kerfs, or they can be grooved with a narrow gouge. Check to be sure that the location and number of these plate grooves will accommodate the items to be displayed. Alternately, tack thin strips to the shelves to hold plates, platters and trays. Doors at the bottom of the cabinet can be edged-glued and splined solid stock, or plywood can be kerfed to create a plank effect.

The choice of finish is up to the builder. If a "Pennsylvania-Dutch" look is desired, first apply several coats of clear lacquer (or antiquing), then locate the stenciled figures.

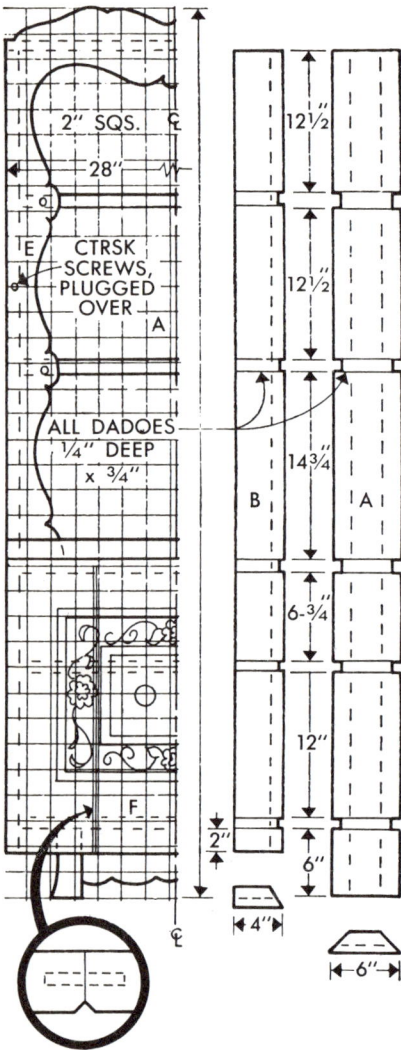

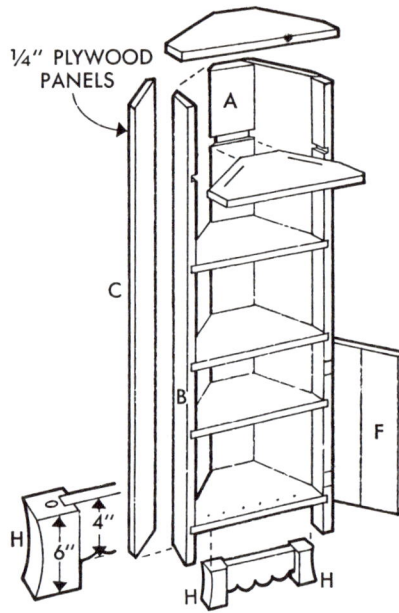

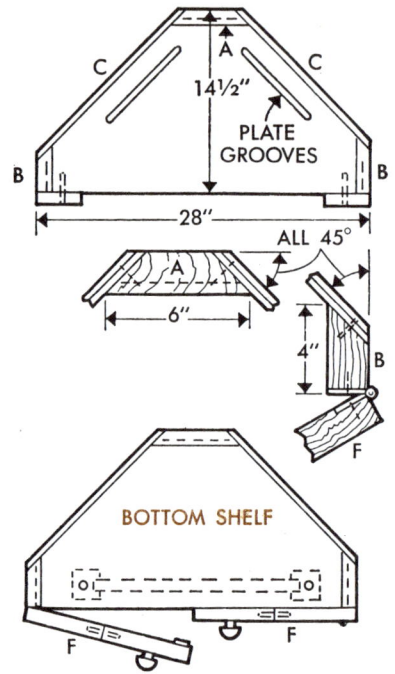

2" SQS.

28"

CTRSK SCREWS, PLUGGED OVER

E

A

ALL DADOES 1/4" DEEP x 3/4"

F

2"

12½"

12½"

14¾"

6-¾"

12"

6"

B

A

4"

6"

¼" PLYWOOD PANELS

A

C

B

F

H

4"

6"

H   H

A

C   C

14½"

PLATE GROOVES

B   B

28"

A

6"

ALL 45°

B

4"

B

F

BOTTOM SHELF

F   F

DECORATOR CABINET

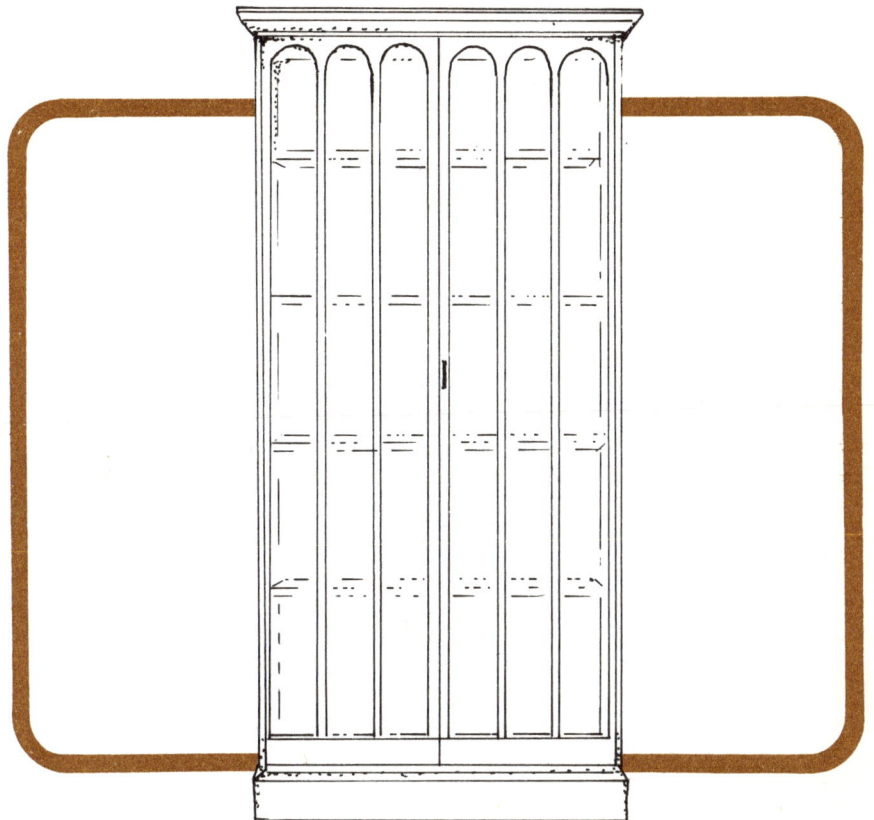

Making this wall cabinet is a real challenge to your craftsmanship, as it involves a high degree of accuracy. Inside width permits setting four 10-inch plates on edge on one or more of the shelves. In height the cabinet reaches up to 6 inches from the usual 8-foot room height. Soft illumination emitted from a tubular lamp pervades the inside from top to bottom, passing through glass shelves that are positioned directly behind the horizontal crosspieces of the door grilles. Satin-finish black for the outside of the cabinet produces an exquisite effect, although you can have the richness of natural or stained wood finished to a soft sheen.

Construction details of the cabinet body are shown in the drawing. The sides are rabbeted for the plywood back, and are held edge-wise on horses or a floor for attachment of the rails and trim at top and bottom. Note that the upper-front rail has a door stop glued and bradded to it. The stop fits between the sides, but the rail comes over the edges. Both the floor and rear upper rail come flush with the bottoms of the rabbets.

The back goes on next, being glued and nailed to the sides, floor and top rail to produce the needed rigidity to keep the case square. When nailing the back to the top rail be sure to support the rail against impact, which might move it out of position—or use ¾-inch flathead screws to attach it, eliminating impact.

The base and top-trim now are added, the parts being mitered at the corners. The base pieces are glued and clamped in place to assure over-all adhesion, and the corners are joined with finishing nails. The quarter-round molding is applied after the glue has set. The crown

ASSEMBLY OF CABINET BODY

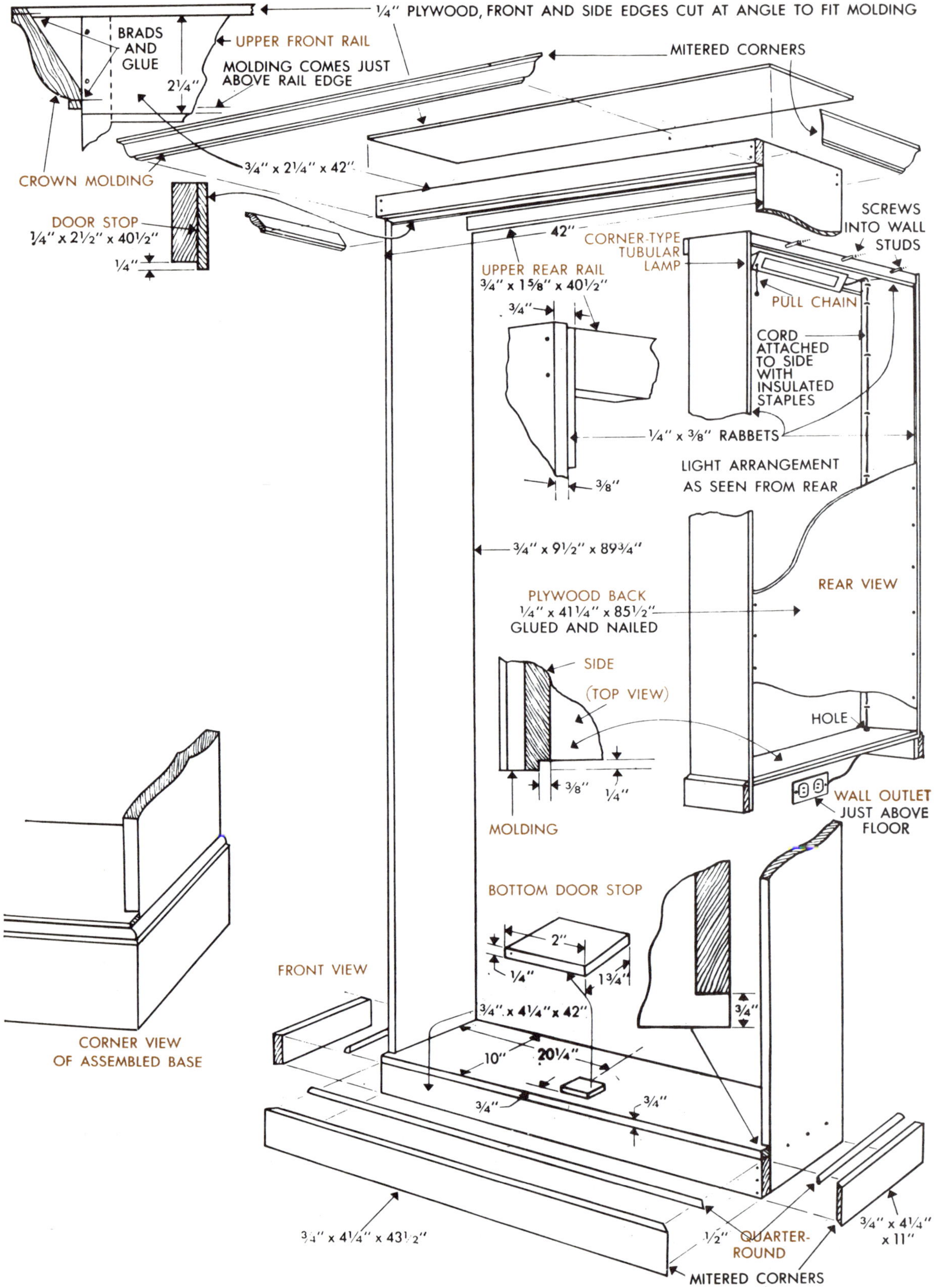

¼" PLYWOOD, FRONT AND SIDE EDGES CUT AT ANGLE TO FIT MOLDING
BRADS AND GLUE
2¼"
UPPER FRONT RAIL
MOLDING COMES JUST ABOVE RAIL EDGE
MITERED CORNERS
¾" x 2¼" x 42"
CROWN MOLDING
DOOR STOP
¼" x 2½" x 40½"
¼"
42"
CORNER-TYPE TUBULAR LAMP
SCREWS INTO WALL STUDS
UPPER REAR RAIL
¾" x 1⅝" x 40½"
¾"
PULL CHAIN
CORD ATTACHED TO SIDE WITH INSULATED STAPLES
¼" x ⅜" RABBETS
⅜"
LIGHT ARRANGEMENT AS SEEN FROM REAR
¾" x 9½" x 89¾"
PLYWOOD BACK
¼" x 41¼" x 85½"
GLUED AND NAILED
REAR VIEW
SIDE
(TOP VIEW)
HOLE
⅜"
¼"
MOLDING
WALL OUTLET JUST ABOVE FLOOR
BOTTOM DOOR STOP
2"
¼"
1¾"
¾"
FRONT VIEW
¾" x 4¼" x 42"
10"
20¼"
¾"
¾"
CORNER VIEW OF ASSEMBLED BASE
¾" x 4¼" x 43½"
½" QUARTER-ROUND
MITERED CORNERS
¾" x 4¼" x 11"

molding at the upper end is nailed in place temporarily to extend ¼ inch above the cabinet so you can determine the exact size of the plywood top. Side and front edges of the top are cut at an angle to fit against the inside of the molding. Then the molding is attached permanently with glue and nails. Edges of the top are glue-coated and the top placed in position, nailed to the rails, and the molding nailed to it. The size and shape of the molding you can get locally may vary somewhat from that shown, but this variation is not important as long as the molding comes a little above the lower edge of the front rail, and thus cannot interfere with movement of the doors. Last item of the cabinet-body assembly is the lower door stop, a small block glued and bradded to the cabinet floor so the lower, inside rails of the doors will contact it. The side and rear edges of the stop may be beveled or rounded for easier cleaning of the floor.

It is important to use close-grain hardwood for the frames of the two duplicate doors, as a maximum strength is required. The stiles are doweled and glued to the top and bottom rails. Be sure to use a doweling jig so the blind holes in stiles and rails are aligned. For simplicity of construction each door frame is fitted with two panes of glass separated by a cross rail. The grillework gives the appearance of many small panes. The height of the door is greater than the largest stock size of ordinary window glass available in hardware stores.

Inside edges of the doors have ¼-inch rabbets ½ inch deep. Rabbets of the stiles are stopped 2 inches from the top ends, and 2½ inches from the bottom ends. If rabbets are cut the entire length of the stiles, glue in small strips of wood at the ends as detailed, to get the same result.

The most exacting part of the entire job is making the top rail. The ¼-inch thick portion in which the arches are cut is susceptible to breakage at the slender ends during the process of sawing, or when the rail is being joined to the stiles. Should the ends break off a little, you can use wood putty to smooth out the curvature after the rail has been glued in place. Use epoxy glue for all joints of the doors, as utmost strength is essential. Apply pressure with bar clamps at both ends uniformly to keep the stiles parallel while drawing them together on the rails. Before leaving the work, check for squareness at the corners. Allow the glue to set for 24 hours before installing the inside rail, which is flued and toenailed in place. Note how the ends of this rail extend to fit into the rabbets of the stiles. Before attempting to toenail the rail, drill pilot holes for the brads to prevent splitting the wood. Drive the brads with a nailset or punch to avoid hammer marks on the wood. This method is used also when installing the grille pieces.

As the door frames can be handled most easily before installing the glass and grille, it is advisable to first cut the hinge and strike mortises, and also to plane slight bevels on the inside stiles. You can use four 2-inch ball-tipped butt hinges as shown, or other less-visible cabinet hinges. The grille work consists of ¼ x ¾-inch strips. Cut eight horizontal ones identically, and drill pilot holes at the ends for toenailing with small brads. Install the strips so the notches for the half-lap joints face the front of the doors, applying epoxy glue before toenailing them. Check the crosspieces for squareness while applying light clamping pressure on the stiles. The pilot holes in the crosspieces are

DETAILS OF DOORS, 2 REQ'D. (CLOSE-GRAINED HARDWOOD)

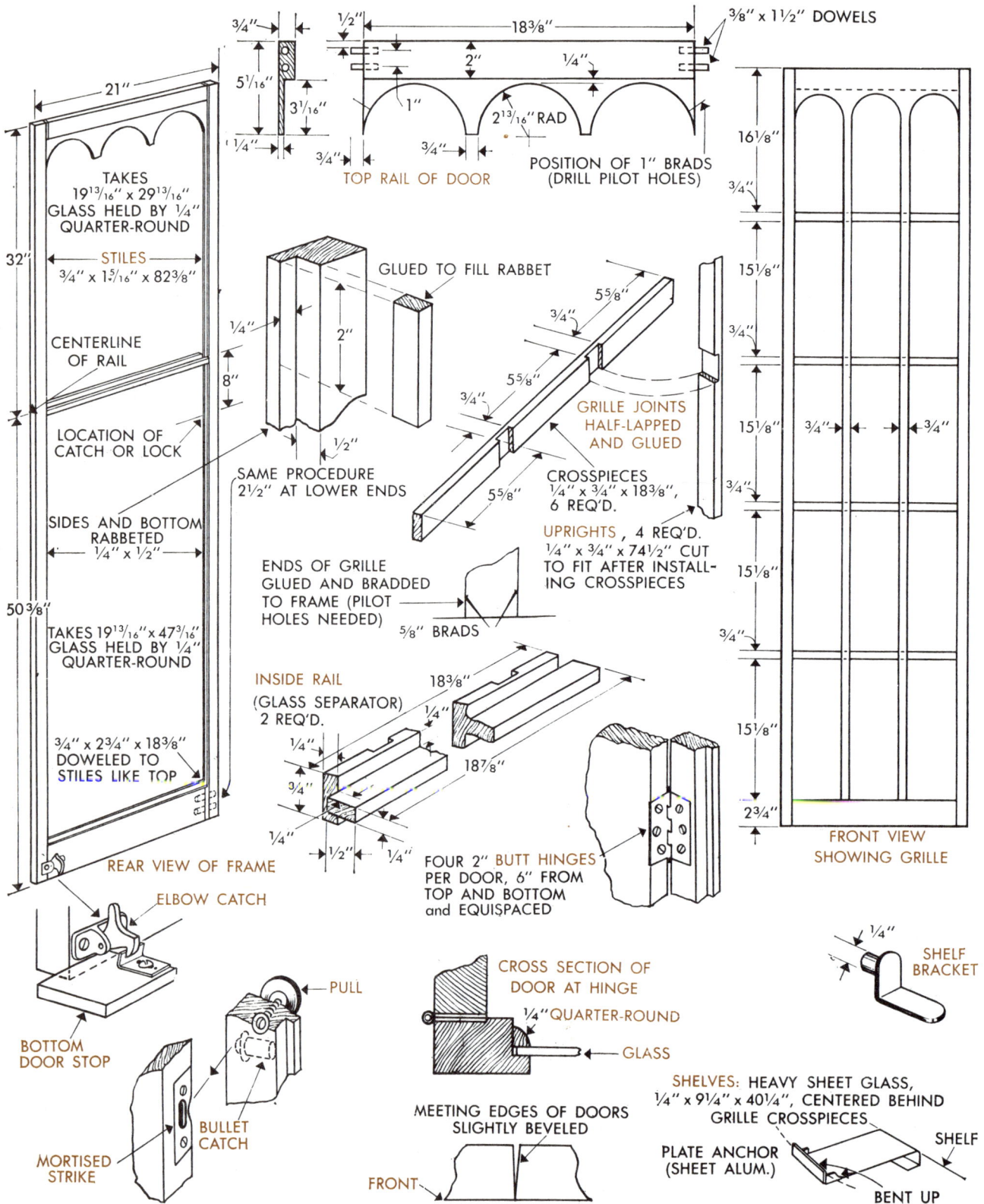

3/4"

1/2"

18 3/8"

3/8" x 1 1/2" DOWELS

5 1/16"

3 1/16"

2"

1/4"

1 1/4"

3/4"

1"

3/4"

2 13/16" RAD

POSITION OF 1" BRADS (DRILL PILOT HOLES)

TOP RAIL OF DOOR

21"

16 1/8"

3/4"

TAKES
19 13/16" x 29 13/16"
GLASS HELD BY 1/4"
QUARTER-ROUND

15 1/8"

3/4"

32"

STILES
3/4" x 1 5/16" x 82 3/8"

1/4"

2"

GLUED TO FILL RABBET

5 5/8"

3/4"

CENTERLINE
OF RAIL

8"

5 5/8"

15 1/8"

3/4"

3/4"

LOCATION OF
CATCH OR LOCK

1/2"

3/4"

SAME PROCEDURE
2 1/2" AT LOWER ENDS

5 5/8"

GRILLE JOINTS
HALF-LAPPED
AND GLUED

3/4"

3/4"

SIDES AND BOTTOM
RABBETED
1/4" x 1/2"

CROSSPIECES
1/4" x 3/4" x 18 3/8",
6 REQ'D.

15 1/8"

ENDS OF GRILLE
GLUED AND BRADDED
TO FRAME (PILOT
HOLES NEEDED)

5/8" BRADS

UPRIGHTS, 4 REQ'D.
1/4" x 3/4" x 74 1/2" CUT
TO FIT AFTER INSTALL-
ING CROSSPIECES

3/4"

50 3/8"

15 1/8"

TAKES 19 13/16" x 47 3/16"
GLASS HELD BY 1/4"
QUARTER-ROUND

INSIDE RAIL
(GLASS SEPARATOR)
2 REQ'D.

18 3/8"

1/4"

3/4" x 2 3/4" x 18 3/8"
DOWELED TO
STILES LIKE TOP

1/4"

3/4"

18 7/8"

1/4"

2 3/4"

1/2"

1/4"

REAR VIEW OF FRAME

FOUR 2" BUTT HINGES
PER DOOR, 6" FROM
TOP AND BOTTOM
and EQUISPACED

**FRONT VIEW
SHOWING GRILLE**

ELBOW CATCH

1/4"

SHELF
BRACKET

BOTTOM
DOOR STOP

PULL

CROSS SECTION OF
DOOR AT HINGE

1/4" QUARTER-ROUND

GLASS

MORTISED
STRIKE

BULLET
CATCH

MEETING EDGES OF DOORS
SLIGHTLY BEVELED

FRONT

SHELVES: HEAVY SHEET GLASS,
1/4" x 9 1/4" x 40 1/4", CENTERED BEHIND
GRILLE CROSSPIECES

PLATE ANCHOR
(SHEET ALUM.)

SHELF

BENT UP

continued into the stiles. The uprights of the grilles should be slightly longer than required so they can be cut to an exact fit between upper and lower rails. The upper ends are glued only, the lower ends are toe-nailed and glued.

Hang the doors next, then add the elbow and bullet catches, strike plate and knob. You can substitute a cabinet lock for the bullet catch. Some of these small locks are screwed to the back surface of a door and need no mortise that would weaken the narrow stile. The panes of glass are 1/16 inch smaller than the openings in which they fit. The panes are held by ¼-inch quarterround molding mitered at corners and bradded in place. Inside surfaces of the cabinet and doors may be enameled a light color, or the back and sides can be covered with felt-surfaced (flocked) wallpaper.

A corner-type tubular lamp having a pull chain is attached to the top or the upper-front rail. To control the lamp from outside you can extend the pull chain with a black cord threaded through a hole in the side. The electric cord runs down vertically, about ½ inch from the front edge of one side, goes through a hole in the cabinet floor and extends to a wall outlet installed just above floor level. Installation of the outlet will require chiseling out part of the wall floor plate to house the receptable box, or the outlet can be installed in the floor under the cabinet. The location is determined before the cabinet is set up. Long screws that go into the wall studs should be used for fastening the upper-rear rail. Holes for the shelf brackets are drilled so the shelves will center behind the grille crosspieces and rails. To prevent slipping of plates, use simple anchors made of sheet aluminum that hook over the rear edges of the shelves, as detailed.

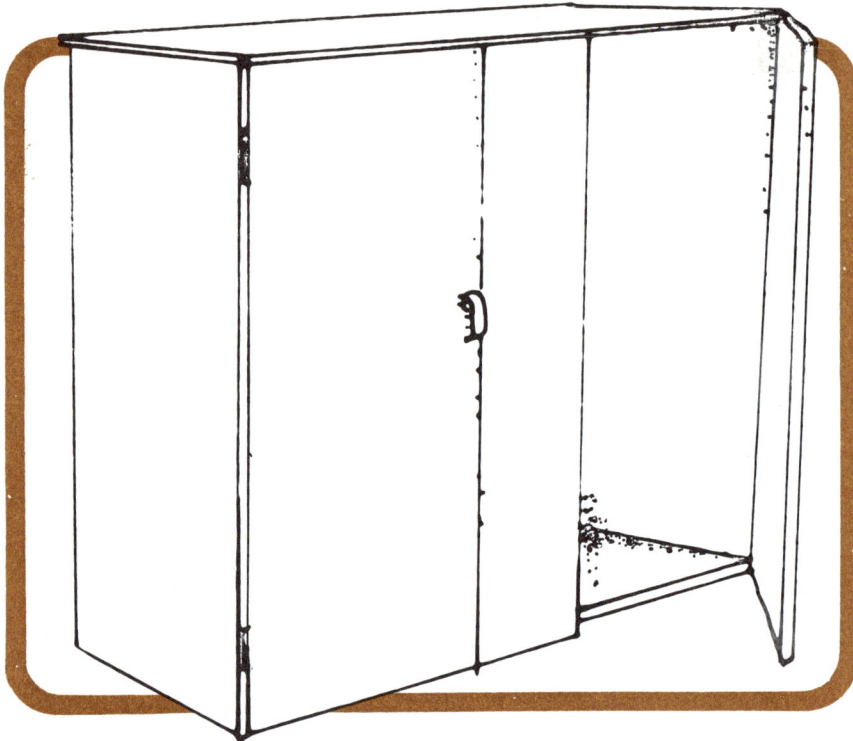

ROOM-DIVIDER CABINET

Despite the popularity of synthetic materials everyone has a favorite wool sweater, jacket, ski pants or blanket that needs to be stored in a safe place for the summer, and this cedar-lined closet that doubles as a room divider is the perfect place.

Designed as a free-standing storage unit for any room of a home or apartment, the divider is small and light enough to be moved easily. It could even be fitted with casters. The shell is of ¾-inch hardwood-plywood and has false "doors" on the back, to duplicate the front.

A clothes pole extends the full length of the interior and a removable shelf is in one half. It can be used as a combination storage for blankets, small items and clothing, or for clothing alone by removing the shelf. It is lined with tongue-and-groove aromatic red cedar closet lining available at lumberyards, or building supply stores.

Two and a half 4 x 8-foot sheets of hardwood-plywood are needed to construct the basic shell, and the cutting diagram shows how the pieces are cut so the grain runs lengthwise on all parts except the front and back center panels. The cross grain on these adds interest to the front and back of the unit.

Cut out the basic pieces and lay the three back pieces, false doors and center panel, side by side on the floor. Cut the top and bottom framing strips (¾ x ¾ x 57½ inches), and glue and screw them to the back assembly, flush with the top and bottom edges and ¾ inch in from each end. Then attach the end strips (¾ x ¾ x 46½ inches) in the same manner.

Cut the side panels to size (21½ x 48 inches), and add the bottom framing strip (¾ x ¾ x 20 inches). Glue and screw both sides to

CUTTING DIAGRAM

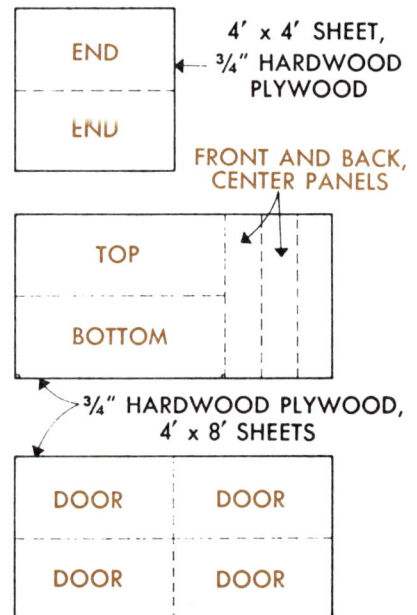

4' x 4' SHEET, ¾" HARDWOOD PLYWOOD

END

END

FRONT AND BACK, CENTER PANELS

TOP

BOTTOM

¾" HARDWOOD PLYWOOD, 4' x 8' SHEETS

DOOR	DOOR
DOOR	DOOR

the back, being sure it is squared up. Attach the top framing strips, 1¼ inches from each end on the top, and the same distance from the front edge to allow for the proper overhang. Then set the top on the back and sides and secure it with wood screws and glue.

Cut the bottom to fit inside the back and sides, with a ¾-inch notch at each back corner. Center the front panel support under the front edge, then screw the bottom in place.

Line the interior with aromatic red cedar closet lining, nailing it in position with 7/8-inch brads. Stagger each board as you line up the top and back horizontally. The side boards are placed vertically. These boards are all the same length, but the board at the front edge is notched where the hinges are located. Line the bottom last, butting the ends against the sides for a tight fit. Stagger adjoining boards.

After the interior is lined, fasten the front center panel and secure the catch strips on the edges. Line the panel and then screw the shelf support cleats to the front and back. Then fasten the shelf support board to the cleats and the shelf support to the left side.

Cut out and locate the clothespole supports, fasten to the cedar lining and add the pole. Line the shelf with cedar and place it on the rests, but do not fasten it down. Line the doors, but be sure to allow clearance at the edges so the doors will fit flush. Hang them with semi-concealed hinges, attach catches and handles to the front doors and handles to the back "doors." Weatherstripping can be added to the doors to increase airtightness.

Tape all exposed plywood edges and finish as desired.

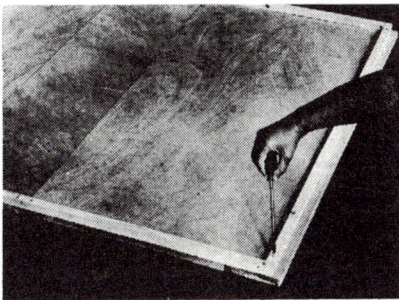

Lay back panels on floor and attach top and bottom framing strips with glue and screws. Then add end strips.

Locate strips on ends, then glue and screw both ends to the back, making sure it is squared up. Allow to dry.

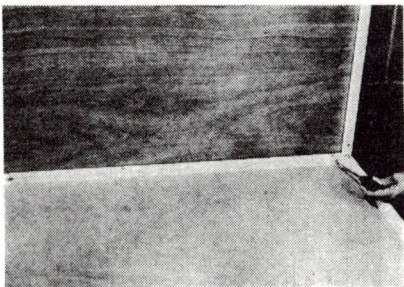

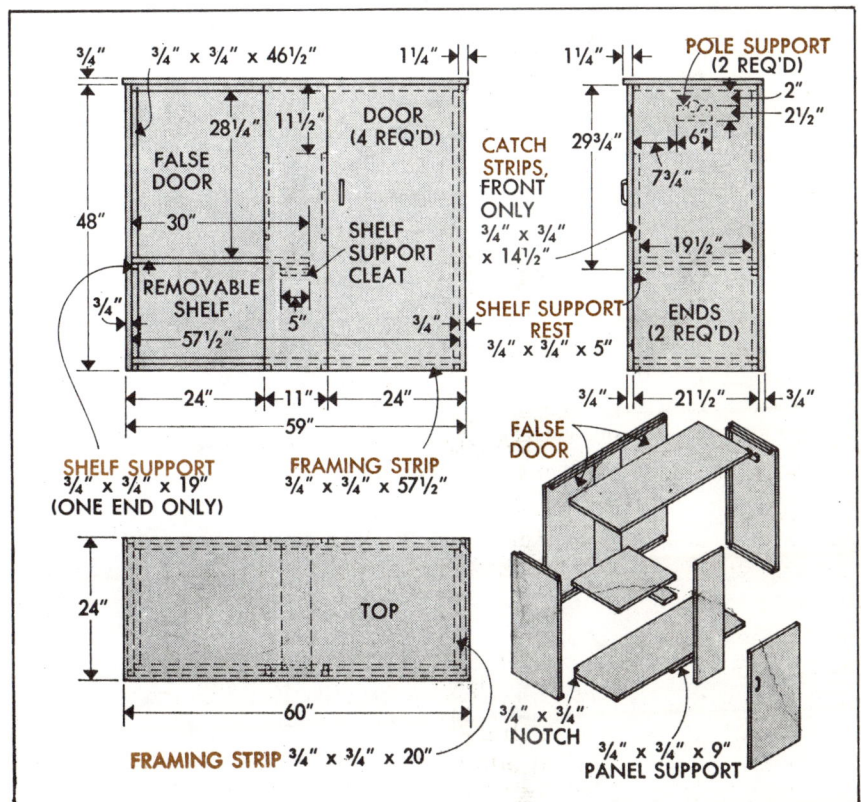

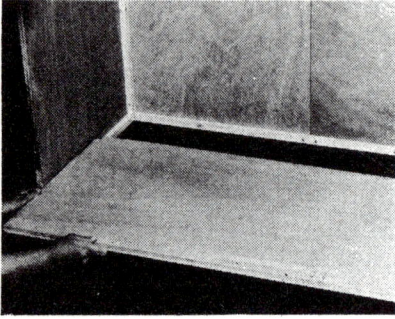

Top is attached first, the bottom is notched at back, front panel support added and bottom fitted in place.

Tongue and groove lining is next, top and back runs horizontally, sides vertically. Bottom fits snug against sides.

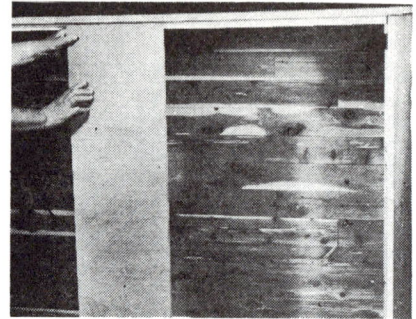

Locate front center panel, line with red cedar, then attach shelf support cleats to the panel and the back.

Cut and locate clothes pole supports, attach with wood screws and cut pole to fit. Note notches in lining for hinges.

Line shelf and place on supports, but do not fasten it down. Doors are fitted, lined and weatherstripped. Add handles.

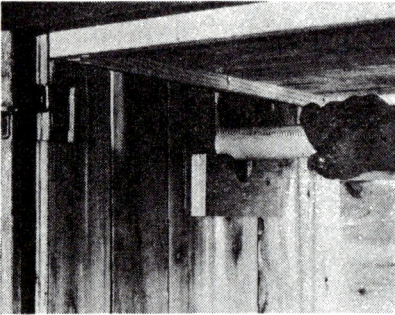

SLIDE-PROJECTOR CABINET

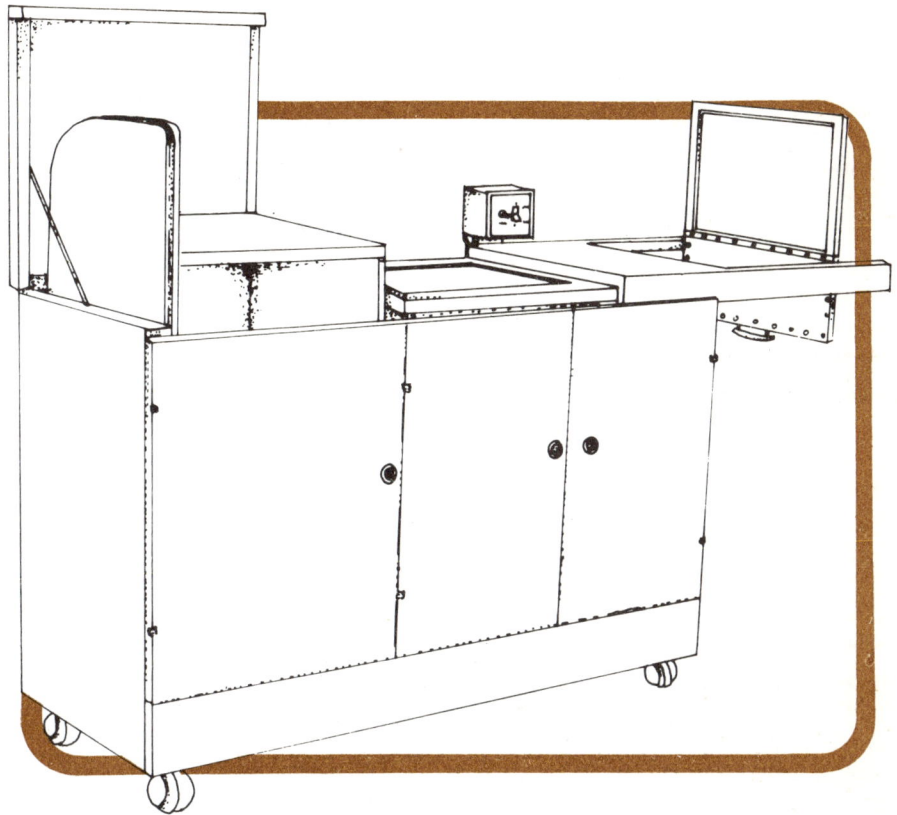

1. Slide trays store on shelf above power head. Upper shelf provides more storage for slides and other related equipment.

2. Projector sets on shelf in "lift" that is raised by cords. Projecting side of lift raises lid, here raised manually.

At the flip of a switch the slide projector stored in this cabinet rises to the level of the top for easy operation. Sliding the top panel to the left causes a small projection screen to lift to a vertical position for quick viewing of slides. For previewing slides there is a glass-top illuminated surface also under the top.

The basic cabinet (figures 1 and 6) is quite simple; any problems will come from adjusting the electro-mechanical system that raises and lowers the lift on which the slide (or movie) projector sets. When you get the cabinet with the mechanism installed, as in figure 6, all adjustments to the system should be made so it works right before finishing the cabinet.

Start construction by assembling the base of the cabinet, the ends, back and partition.

The electric motor should be as low as possible in the cabinet, so an opening is cut in the base and the motor is mounted on a piece of ¾-inch plywood that then is fastened to the underside of the base. The center line of the motor shaft should be about 2½ inches above the base. The motor should be a ¼ HP split-phase unit (figure 4). This type motor has two sets of windings, one for starting, the other for running. One lead from the starting winding is combined with one from the running winding to make an electrical circuit. Rotation of the motor is reversed by switching the starting windings.

The power head (figure 3 and drawing) consists of a steel angle bolted to a steel flat to clamp a ½-inch nut that is turned on a length of threaded rod as indicated. This assembly is fitted on a spacer block and a shaped piece of plywood that contacts the limit switches to stop the power head at each end of its travel.

The lift (figures 2 and 6 and drawing) is made next and positioned in the cabinet. The cables are 3/16-inch sash cord that run from the power head and over the pulleys in the lift section. These pulleys are nylon, the type used in drapery rods. Use short lengths of ¼-inch brass tubing as bushings for the pulleys, holding them with No. 8 wood screws. Locate the lower pulleys so the cords run parallel to the threaded rod (figure 5). Note that the lift sets on the lift supports, and is not actually attached to anything in the cabinet. This permits it to easily be removed for access to the motor and cables. The lift "floats" on the supports, sliding against the cabinet back, and against the front strips. Hardwood cleats are glued to the front edges of the lift, and rabbets in the cleats slide against the front strips. Wax the strips and rabbets for easier operation.

One end of the "flip-up" screen is weighted so it drops down and raises the screen. The upper side of the weight cavity is formed by the plywood top, while sheet metal is used on the underside. Pieces of lead, scrap iron or whatever you have on hand can be used for the weight. Make it just heavy enough to pivot the screen; additional weight simply makes the screen more difficult to raise in position when the top is to be slid back over the cabinet.

The viewing table has a piece of opal glass fitted in the frame over the light box. On the original a set of Christmas-tree lights were used. The "pin" sockets were moved closer together and the wire shortened. You can, of course, use one or two small fluorescent lamps instead. A separate switch is used for these lights. A cord long enough to move up and down with the lift is used for the receptacle in the lift.

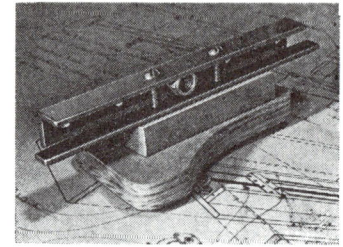

3. Power head consists of steel angle bolted to steel flat to clamp ½" nut between in which threaded rod turns.

4. Cabinet before lift is installed, showing motor, left cords and pulleys. Note weight and cord to pull down lid.

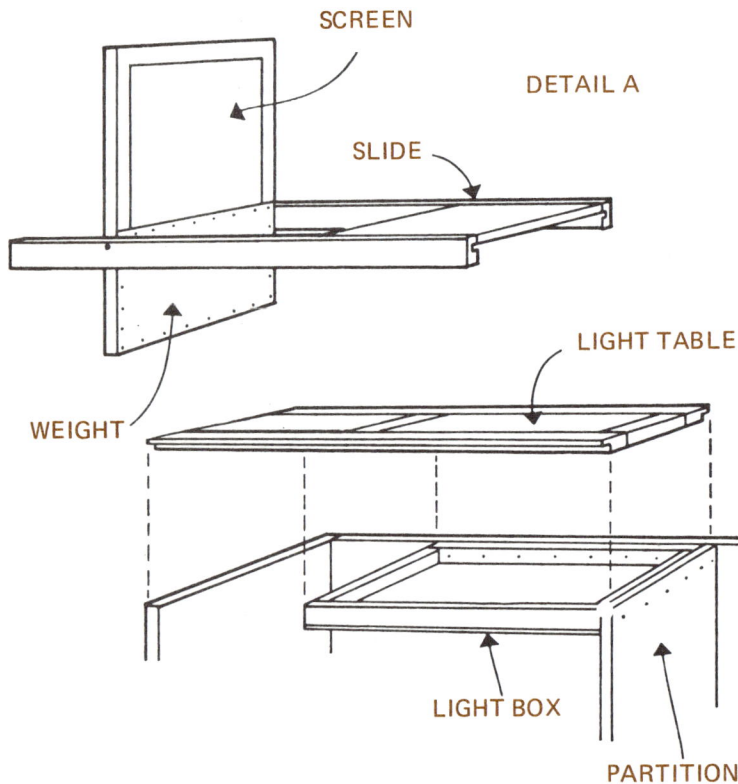

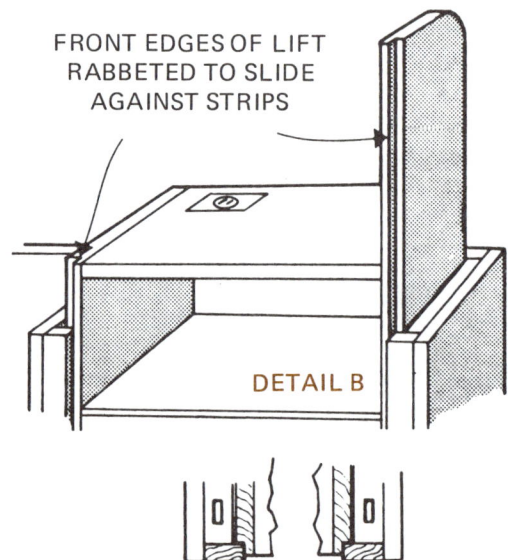

SCREEN
DETAIL A
SLIDE
WEIGHT
LIGHT TABLE
LIGHT BOX
PARTITION
FRONT EDGES OF LIFT RABBETED TO SLIDE AGAINST STRIPS
DETAIL B

SWITCH 1, DPDT WITH CENTER
POSITION "OFF" SWITCH 2, 3PDT
WITH CENTER POSITION "OFF"
SWITCHES 3 AND
4, NORMALLY
CLOSED SPST

OUTLET ON
PROJECTOR
LIFT

SWITCH 2

SWITCH 1
PROJECTOR

P2   S1   S2

R1P1

P2

P2

JUMPER
WIRES

P1

LIGHT
BOX

S1
S2

R2

R1

MOTOR

SWITCH 3

P2

SWITCH 4

R2

PLUG

P2

P2

P2

WIRING DIAGRAM

S1 and S2 ARE STARTER WINDINGS.
R1 AND R2 ARE RUNNING WINDINGS.

OUTLET FOR PROJECTOR
WIRED FROM SWITCH
NO. 1 IN SWITCH BOX

LID

18"

16½"

1½"

18"

2"

17¼"

DRAWERS IN THIS
SPACE IF DESIRED

PIANO
HINGE

RABBET TO FIT
GUIDES IN CABINET

¾" x ¾"
SOLID STOCK

6" RAD.

SEE
DETAIL
B

27"

1"
DIA.

8"

3"

1"

2"

SHEET METAL
ATTACHED WITH
FLATHEAD
WOOD SCREWS

½" x ¾"
FRAMING

¼" SQ.

FILL CAVITY
WITH LEAD FOR
COUNTERBALANCE

¾" x ¾"
SOLID STOCK

15½"

4¼"

14½"

14½"

¼" PLYWOOD

15¾" x 26½"

¾" x 2"
FRAMING

HOLE AT BACK
FOR ELECTRICAL
CORD

¼"
PLYWOOD

SCREEN

FLIP-UP
SCREEN

16"

15"

9"

16½"

SWITCH
BOX

6"

2½"

2"

15

¾"
PLYWOOD

7¾"

2"

3⁄8"

15¾"

1½"

1¼"

28"

16¼"

½"

¼"

¾"

2"

¼"

B

SEE DETAIL A

SINGLE-STRENGTH
GLASS

1½"

1½"

1¼"

¾"

1"

¾"

A

28"

15¾"

¾" DIA. HOLE FOR
CORDS TO SWITCH BOX

DIA. PULLEYS

¾"

4 4½"

¾"
A

7⁄8"

5⁄16"

½"

¾"
B

1½"

5⁄16"

1⁄16"

DOOR

BACK

CLAMP BULB HOLDERS
BETWEEN
THESE PIECES

7-WATT LAMPS

3⁄8" STOCK

4"

LINE LIGHT BOX
WITH METAL FOIL

1¾"

15¾"

19¼"

LIGHT BOX

LIGHT BOX

14"

14"

18"

22½"

22½"

22½"

26½"

½"

1"

27¼"

27¼"

4¼"

46"

26½"

15¾"

44½"

CORD AND
WEIGHT RETAINS
LID

¼"
PLYWOOD   SHELVES

LOWER PULLEYS

2½" DIA.
CASTERS
(4 REQ'D.)

16½"

LOWER PULLEY
ASSEMBLY
(2 REQ'D.)

¾" DIA.
NYLON PULLEYS

¼" DIA.
CARRIAGE
BOLT

¾"

2"

3⁄8"

3⁄8"

7⁄8"

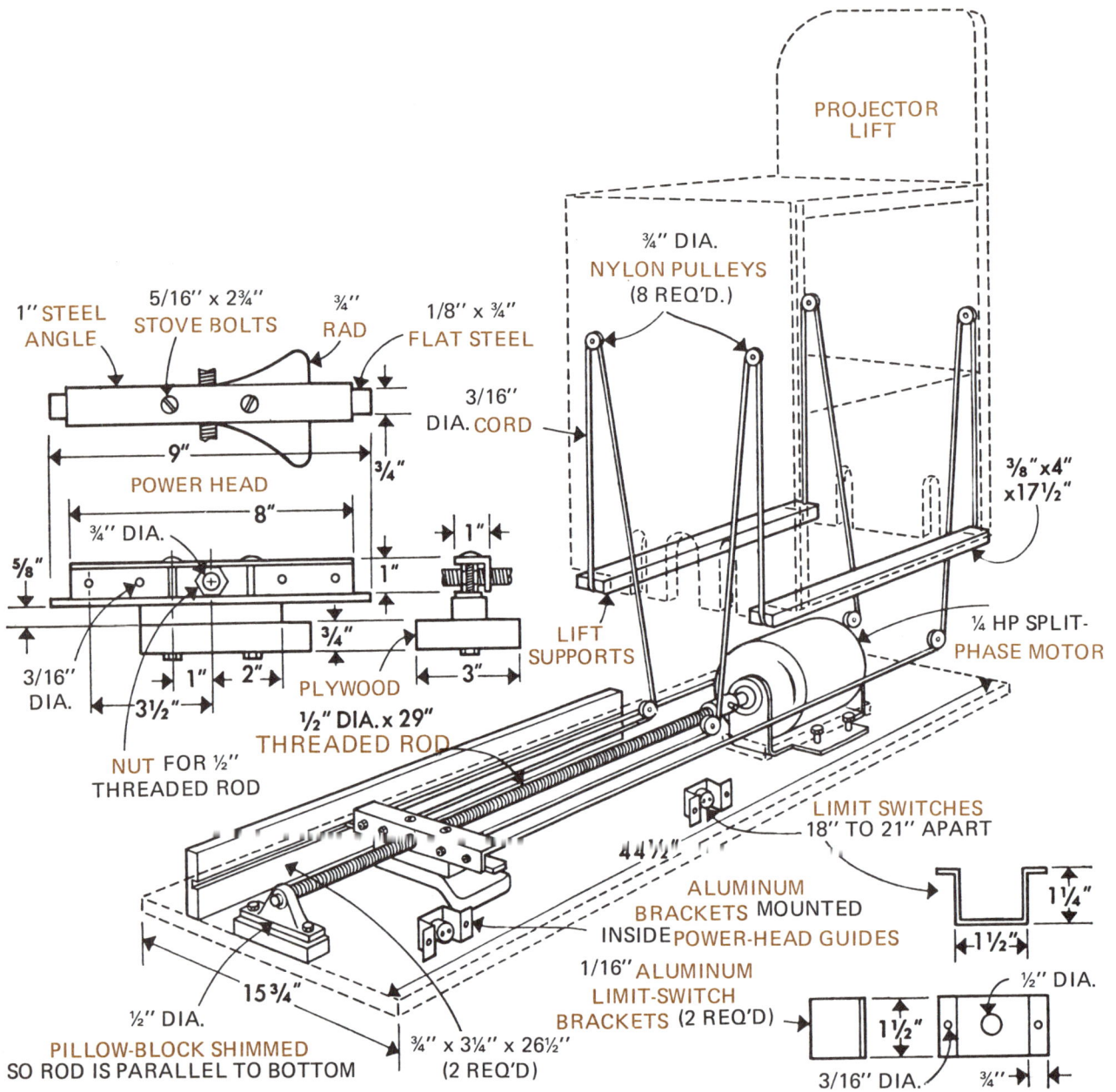

PROJECTOR LIFT

1" STEEL ANGLE

5/16" x 2¾" STOVE BOLTS

¾" RAD

1/8" x ¾" FLAT STEEL

¾" DIA. NYLON PULLEYS (8 REQ'D.)

3/16" DIA. CORD

9"

¾"

POWER HEAD

8"

5/8"

¾" DIA.

1"

1"

3/8" x 4" x 17½"

3/16" DIA.

¾"

3½"

1"   2"

PLYWOOD

3"

LIFT SUPPORTS

¼ HP SPLIT-PHASE MOTOR

NUT FOR ½" THREADED ROD

½" DIA. x 29" THREADED ROD

44½"

LIMIT SWITCHES 18" TO 21" APART

1¼"

1½"

ALUMINUM BRACKETS MOUNTED INSIDE POWER-HEAD GUIDES

1/16" ALUMINUM LIMIT-SWITCH BRACKETS (2 REQ'D)

½" DIA.

15¾"

½" DIA.

PILLOW-BLOCK SHIMMED SO ROD IS PARALLEL TO BOTTOM

¾" x 3¼" x 26½" (2 REQ'D)

1½"

3/16" DIA.   ¾"

5. Power head at end of threaded rod, opposite motor location. Cords are attached to head, run through pulleys.

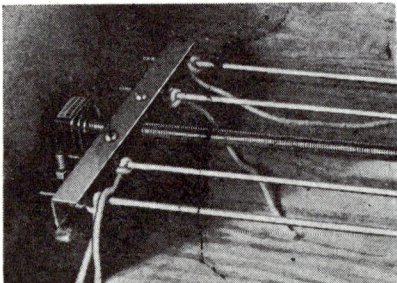

6. Basic cabinet with base, ends, back and partition of ¾" plywood, with power unit and lift installed.

STEREO CABINET

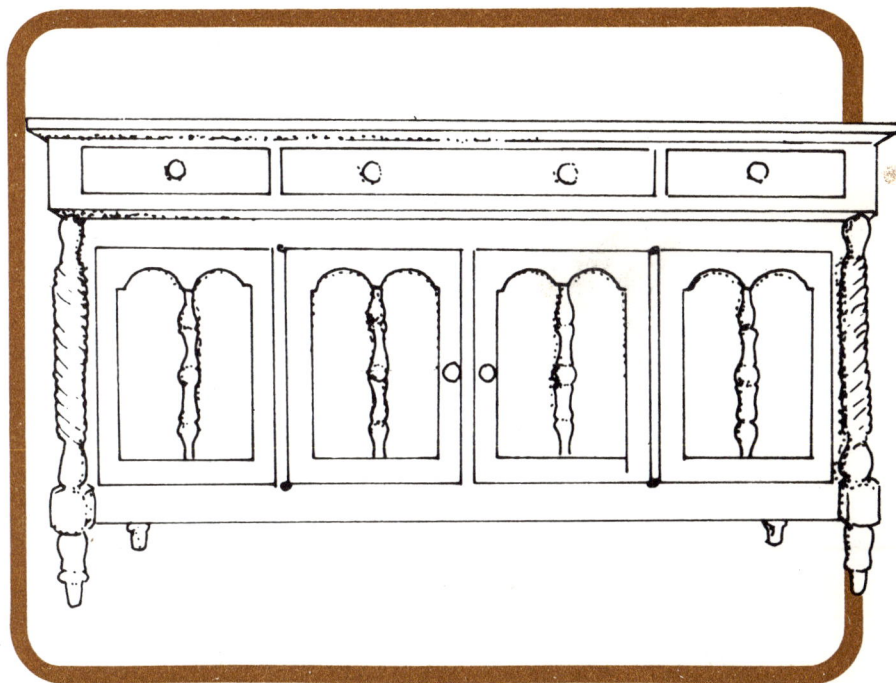

The classic design of this cabinet makes it compatible with period, early American or modern Mediterranean furniture. It is basically a box that is given styling by the hardware, the shape of the door panels and the added turnings.

When used as a stereo unit, the drawers are false and two of the doors are fixed and act as speaker grilles. To change the unit to a buffet you simply hinge the end doors and build drawers to fit. The top then is fixed in place as one piece.

Note that the partitions are L-shape to create an opening between drawers and doors for sound passage and for cooling the turntable and radio.

The front legs are spiraled by first wrapping tape around them as a pattern, then holding each one firmly against the miter gauge clamped to the saw table at an angle. The leg is rotated against the turning blade to create a shallow groove. A finishing nail next is tapped into the wooden facing of the gauge. It acts as a guide to rotate the leg in a spiral fashion against the blade. Advance the leg a little at a time, clamping the gauge to the table each time, until you have made the spiral groove the correct depth. Note that the spirals on the two legs are angled opposite each other.

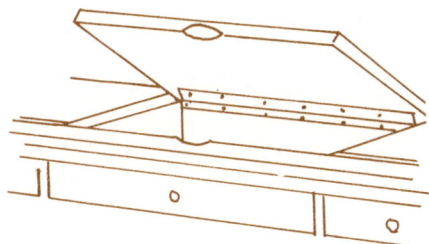

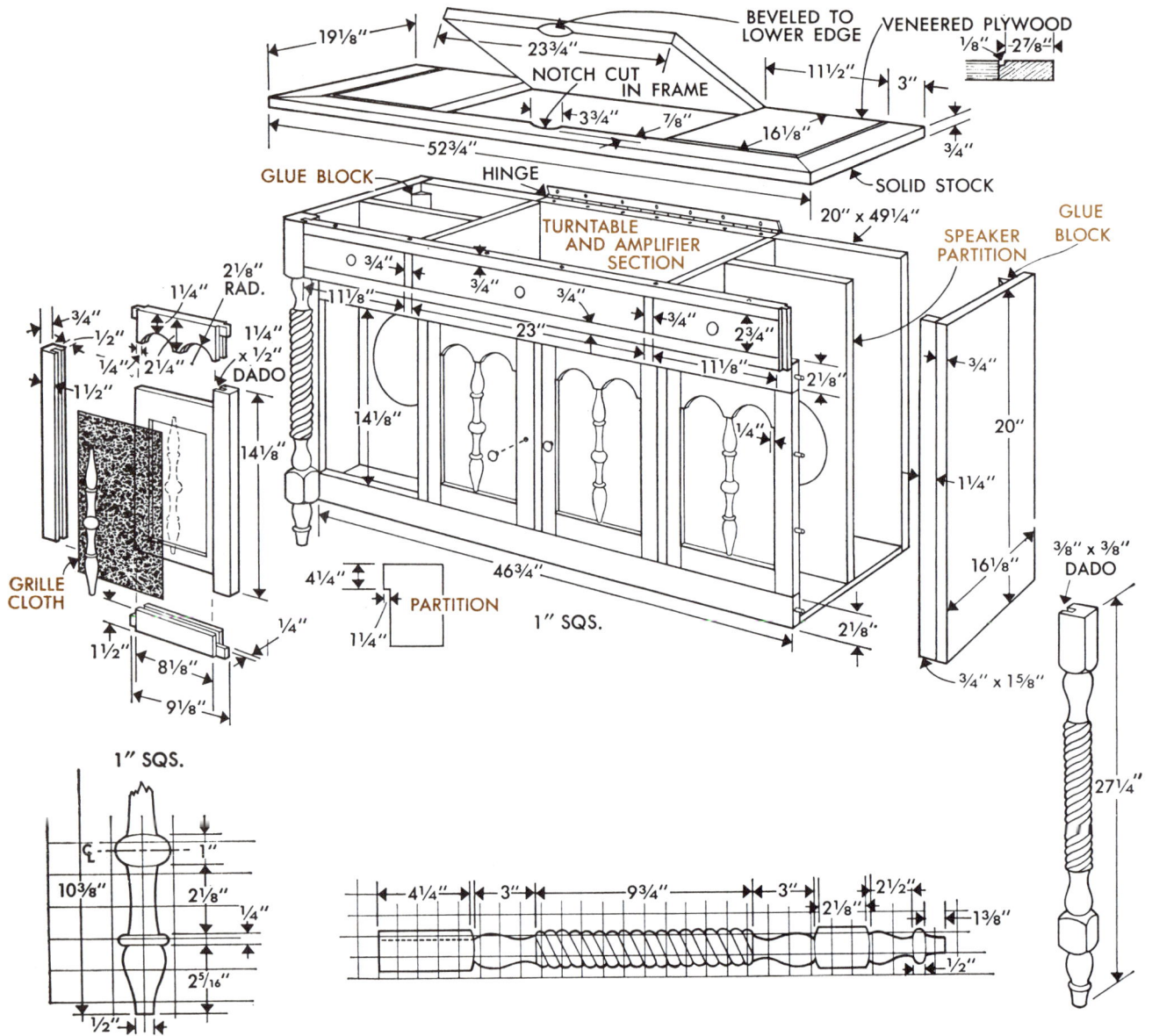

BEVELED TO LOWER EDGE

VENEERED PLYWOOD

1/8" 2 7/8"

19 1/8"

23 3/4"

NOTCH CUT IN FRAME

11 1/2"

3"

3 3/4"

7/8"

16 1/8"

52 3/4"

3/4"

SOLID STOCK

GLUE BLOCK

HINGE

20" x 49 1/4"

GLUE BLOCK

TURNTABLE AND AMPLIFIER SECTION

SPEAKER PARTITION

2 1/8" RAD.

1 1/4"

3/4"

1/2"

1 1/4" x 1/2" DADO

11 1/8"

3/4"

3/4"

3/4"

3/4"

1/4" 2 1/4"

3/4"

1 1/2"

23"

2 3/4"

11 1/8"

2 1/8"

14 1/8"

1/4"

1 1/4"

20"

GRILLE CLOTH

4 1/4"

46 3/4"

16 1/8"

3/8" x 3/8" DADO

PARTITION

1 1/4"

1" SQS.

2 1/8"

1 1/2"

8 1/8"

1/4"

3/4" x 1 5/8"

9 1/8"

27 1/4"

1" SQS.

1"

10 3/8"

2 1/8"

1/4"

2 5/16"

1/2"

4 1/4"

3"

9 3/4"

3"

2 1/2"

2 1/8"

1 3/8"

1/2"

CANDLE ARRANGER

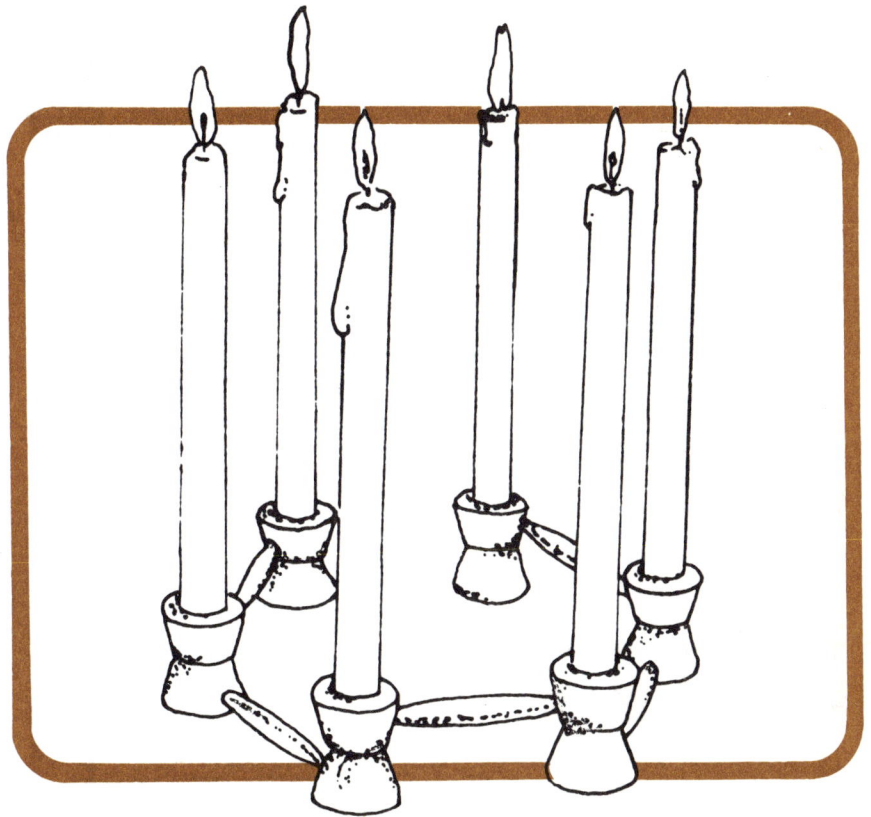

Beautiful as a centerpiece, mantle decoration or a touch of glamour for a buffet, this candle arranger can be used in countless ways.

Walnut was used for turning the original, but any good hardwood will do. Turn the six candle holders to an "hour-glass" shape as indicated in the dimensioned drawing. Clamp the turning square in the jaws of a lathe chuck with the other end held by the tailstock and turn the outside. Then, back off the tailstock and turn the cup in the exposed end.

Turn five connecting sticks to the dimensions given. Next, drill a pilot hole in each candle holder for a No. 7 x 1-inch flathead screw. Run the hole 1 inch below the bottom of the cup, then countersink it as detailed. Place each candle holder in a V-block and drill ¼-inch

Drill screw pilot hole at center to about 1 inch below the cup in turning. Candle holder is placed on its side in V-block, holes drilled for sticks. Two parts of candle cup are sawed apart at the center line, as shown.

holes centered 5/16 inch from the edges. Note that four holders have holes top and bottom, two have them in the top only.

Saw the candle cups apart at the center, then reassemble them with screws and washers so the upper and lower parts rotate. Join the cups together by gluing the sticks between them. Before the glue sets, push the assembly together so the cups are side by side in two sets of three. Clamp them between two pieces of plywood as illustrated to assure the tops and bottoms are parallel and in alignment.

Finish the candle arranger with your favorite method.

Two halves of the candle holder are assembled with flathead screw and washer betwen so halves rotate.

Candle arranger is assembled by gluing sticks into upper and lower halves of individual holders to form zigzag.

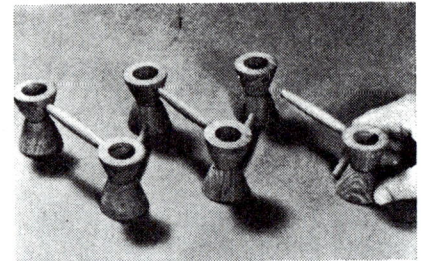

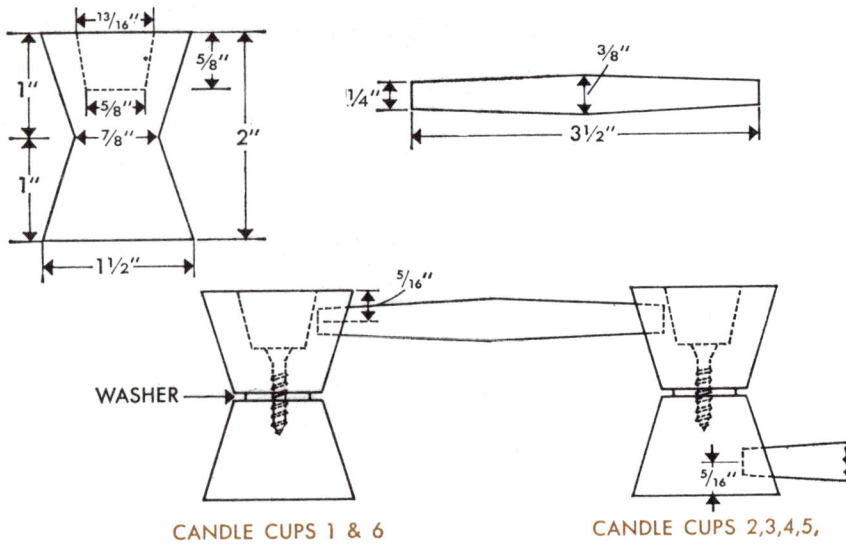

CANDLE CUPS 1 & 6   CANDLE CUPS 2,3,4,5,

Assembled candle cups and sticks are clamped between pieces of plywood to assure alignment of tops and bottoms.

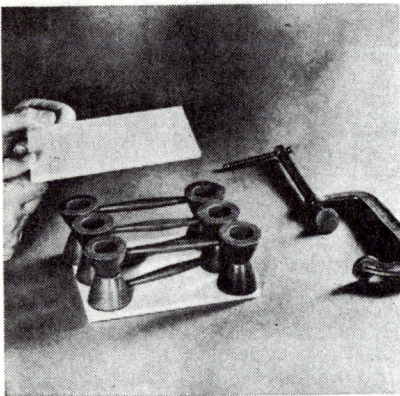

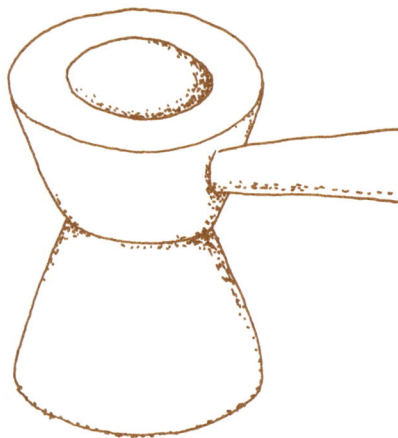

SERVING CART

Cut bucket staves, dado them and assemble with 1/8" splines and lots of glue. Clamp tightly with rope.

Attractive and functional, this trim serving cart with its authentic Colonial styling is a nice addition to the living room, besides being useful on the patio or near the pool area. Buckets on each end will hold magazines or sewing needs, or if lined with aluminum or copper, they could hold ice or even plants. The 14-inch rubber-tired tea-cart wheels make the cart easy to move from room to room.

Made from hardwoods selected to complement existing decor, the cart can be easily constructed with hand or power tools. The only problem might involve turning the back legs, handle and the buckets. The legs and handle can be purchased, and the buckets can be left rough or sanded smooth with a power sander.

Start with the buckets first, by cutting the required angle of 11¼ degrees on the 16 staves. It might be a good idea to practice a bit, as a slight error in angle can result in one or more of the joints being open. Make the staves a little longer than 10 inches as they can be trimmed on the lathe. You might also make a couple of extra staves in case one or two do not fit properly. Cut dadoes along the length of the staves to hold the 1/8-inch splines.

Carefully assemble all the staves into a circle and check for misalignment. Then use generous amounts of glue and assemble the bucket as shown in the photograph. Clamp the staves, using a strong rope and the "tourniquet" method.

The bucket can be turned on a lathe using a jig as shown in the photograph. To make the jig, cut two pieces of stock 2 inches wide and 2 inches shorter than the staves and screw them to the inside of the bucket on opposing staves. Attach two other pieces to the ends of

1½" BUTT HINGES MORTISED

¾" BRASS BANDING

BUCKET LID
(2 REQ'D.)

6¼" RAD.

1¼"

7" RAD.

7½"

14½"

14" DIA. RUBBER-TIRED
TEA-CART WHEELS

13"

13"

17"

BOTTOM
¾"
HARDWOOD

7" RAD.

18½"

9"

6½"

1½"

85°

BRACE

11"

2" DIA.
SPHERICAL
CASTERS

ENDS ¾" STOCK
(PR. REQ'D.)

½" SQS.

12¾"

¾" STOCK

5° ANGLE

1½"

2"

14"

BRACE

CHAMFER

9"

AXLE SUPPORT
1" HARDWOOD (1 REQ'D.)

5"

6"

2"

1½"

3½"

2½"

4" RAD.

3½"

2¼"

9½"

2¼"

½"
DIA.

1¼"

HARDWOOD HANDLE (1 REQ'D.)

14"

LEGS HARDWOOD
(PR. REQ'D.)

1½" DIA.

1" DIA.

1¼" DIA.

10"

1½"

7⁄8" DIA.

1⁄8"

3⁄8" DIA. x 1½"
FOR CASTER STEM

1⁄8"

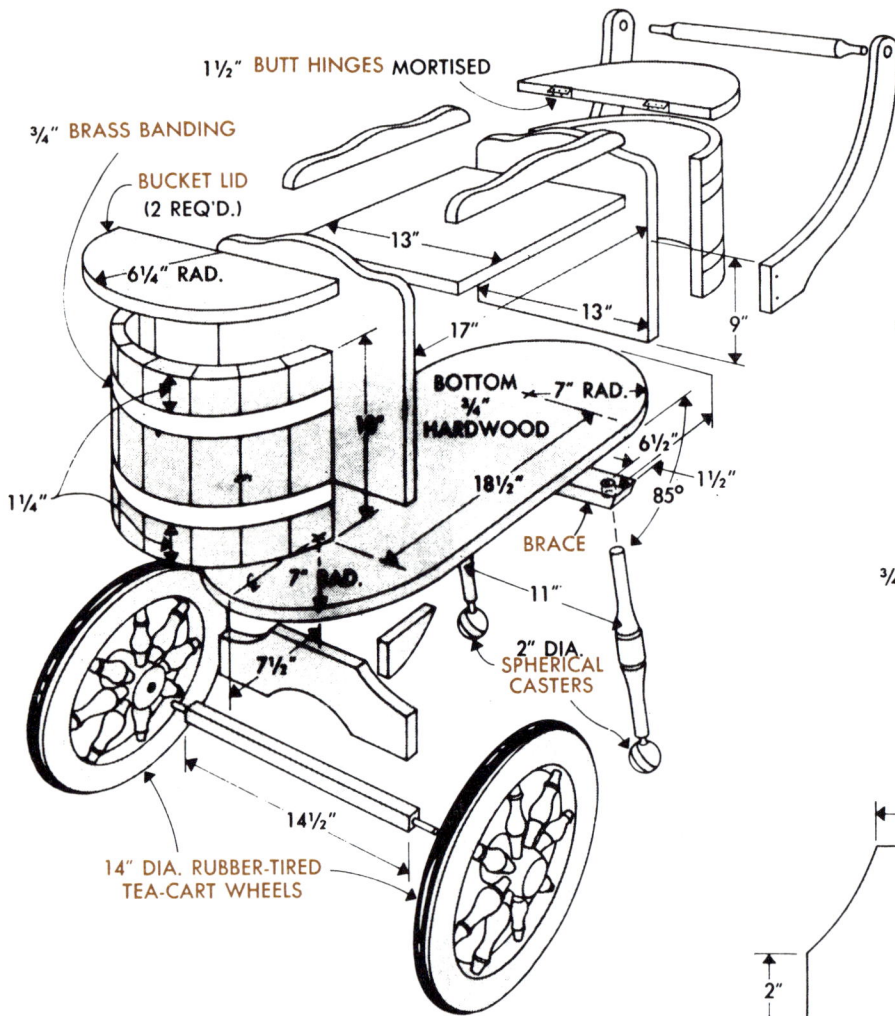

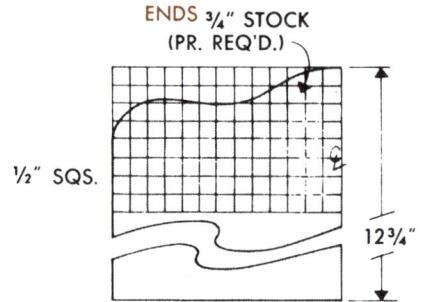

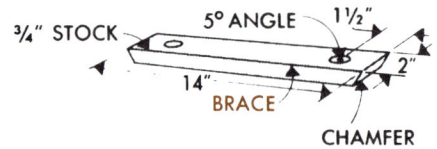

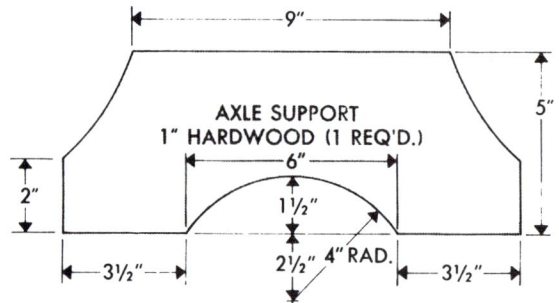

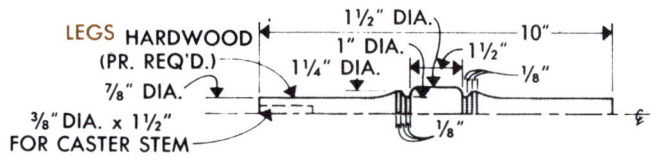

SHELF TRIM ½" STOCK (PR. REQ'D.)

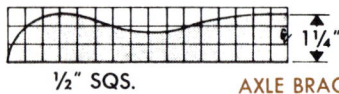

1¼"

½" SQS.

AXLE BRACKET
(PR. REQ'D.)
¾" STOCK

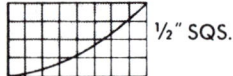

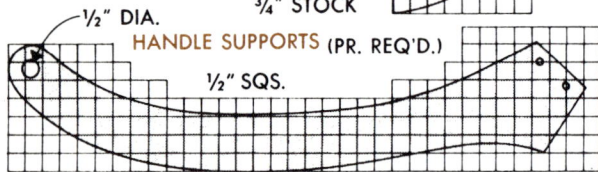

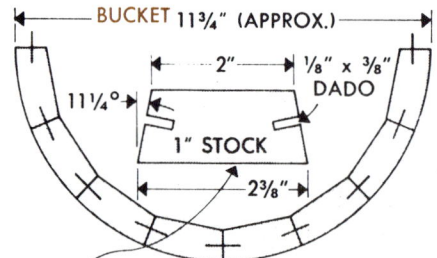

½" SQS.

½" DIA.

HANDLE SUPPORTS (PR. REQ'D.)

½" SQS.

½" STOCK

BUCKET 11¾" (APPROX.)

2"

1⁄8" x 3⁄8"
DADO

11¼°

1" STOCK

2⅜"

10" FINISHED LENGTH

BUCKET "STAVE"
(16 REQ'D.)

Bucket is turned to lathe with aid of simple jig screwed to inside of bucket. Bar clamp provides tool rest.

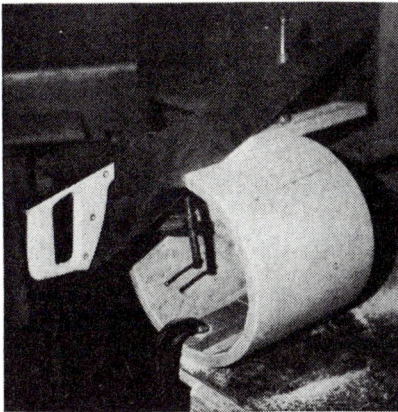

After bucket is turned smooth, cut it in half along opposing joints using a fine-toothed saw and guide strip.

Bucket lids are attached with 1½" butt hinges. The spherical casters are fitted into the turned back legs.

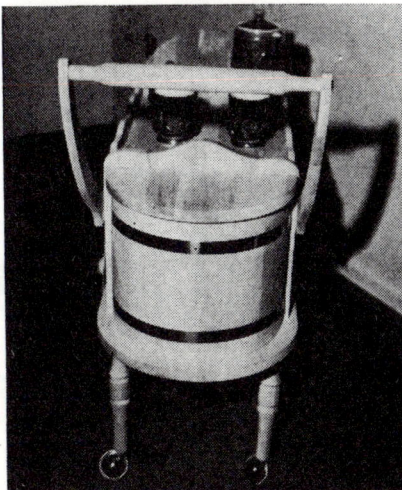

these strips and make the center of each. Attach to the faceplate and the tailstock of the lathe and you are in business. If you don't have a lathe, sand the bucket round or leave it rough.

After turning, cut the bucket in half along opposing joints, using a piece of scrap stock as a guide for a fine-toothed saw. Sand the rough edges smooth for a tight fit against the ends of the cart.

The legs and handle are simple turnings, or they can be purchased items cut to the correct length with a similar shape filed in them.

Cut the bottom and ends of the cart to the proper shape, using the squared drawings. Assemble them using glue and No. 10 x 2-inch FH wood screws through the bottom. The shelf is secured to the sides by glue and two No. 6 x 1½-inch FH screws. The screws are concealed under the hinges on the lids.

Attach the buckets to the bottom and sides with No. 10 x 1½-inch FH screws, driving the screws through the sides and up through the bottom. The screws in the sides can be concealed with plugs, or left exposed. If exposed, use chrome-plated roundhead screws and finishing washers.

Drill 3/8-inch holes in one end of the two back legs to take the caster sleeves. Then press the legs into holes bored in the bottom brace. Drill holes at a 5-degree angle.

The axle support is attached to the bottom with glue and held firmly by two quarter-round brackets.

The bucket lids are fitted in place with 1½-inch butt hinges, mortised into the edges.

Using a coping or a band saw, cut the scalloped shelf edges and the handle arms from ½-inch stock. Glue the former in place. The handle arms are attached to the outer edge of the sides using glue and 1½-inch RH chrome screws and finishing washers. First, press the turned handle into the ½-inch holes and glue and screw them. They can be held in place with tiny brads from underneath, but the screws and finishing washerw will give a uniform appearance to the cart.

You can make your own axle assembly or purchase one. If you do purchase one you will have to cut several inches from the middle.

After a good sanding, apply the finish of your choice. Then add the metal banding to the buckets, the back casters and the rubber-tired wheels for mobility.

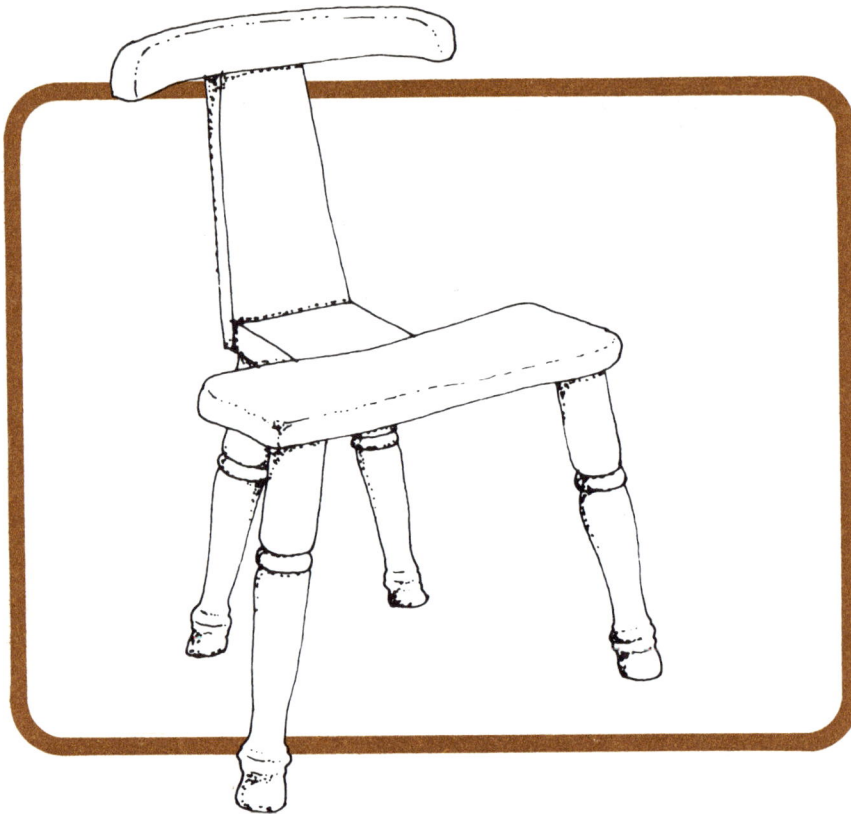

ANTIQUE PINE CHAIR

Rough structural lumber is employed in making this chair. Pine, or fir, 2 x 8 is used for the seat parts and the back. The "arm" takes a piece of stock 3 x 8 inches in cross section, and 17¼ inches long. The legs are turned from 20-inch lengths of stock 2½ inches square. Straight-grained pine can be used, or a hardwood. If the legs vary slightly in profile, don't worry about it; it will just add to the quality of "handmade antique" quality of the chair.

The "arm" is best cut with a band saw, but a little patience and a saber or jig saw also can be used.

A lap-joint is used to join the two parts of the seat together. Power tools save time; a dado blade on a table or radial-arm saw will make quick work of the lap-joint, but a sharp wood chisel can be employed to produce the same effect. The two pieces of the seat are attached with glue and four No. 12 wood screws.

The back of the chair is fastened to the seat with glue and two 3/8 x 4-inch lag screws. A flat washer is used under each lag bolt to prevent the head digging into the wood.

Three dowels, ½ x 5-inch, are used to hold the "arm" securely to the back. Flathead wood screws can be substituted, but they should be set in counterbored holes into which wood plugs are fitted.

The four legs are turned to the profile shown, then a saw kerf is made in the upper end, at right angles to the grain to avoid splitting when a wedge is driven into the kerf, from the top of the seat after the legs are inserted.

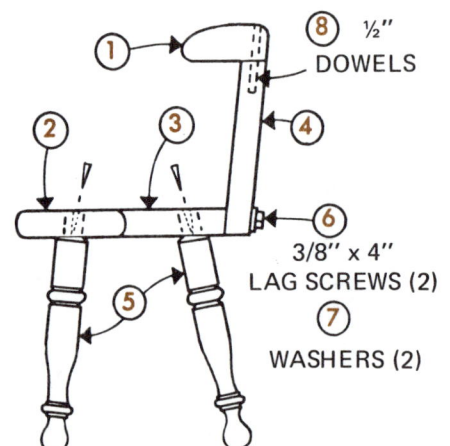

⑧ ½" DOWELS

3/8" x 4" LAG SCREWS (2)

WASHERS (2)

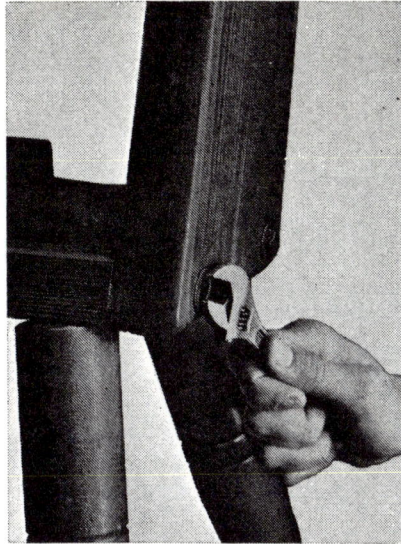

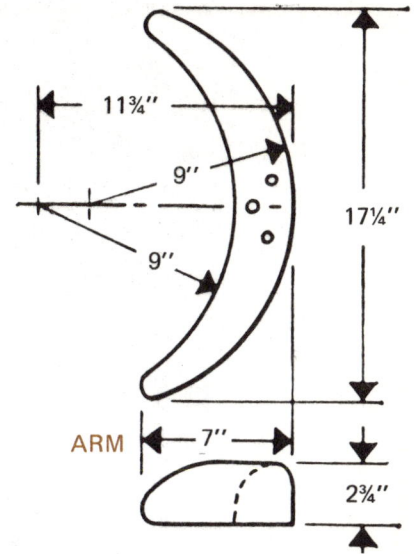

ARM

11¾''   9''   9''   17¼''   7''   2¾''

The two-part seat is assembled with glue and four countersunk flathead wood screws; additional screws can be used.

Lag screws are used to attach the seat back to the chair. After several months, tighten to compensate for drying wood.

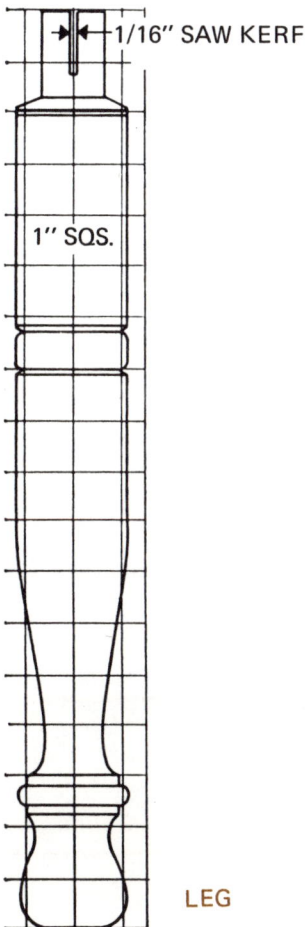

1/16'' SAW KERF

1'' SQS.

LEG

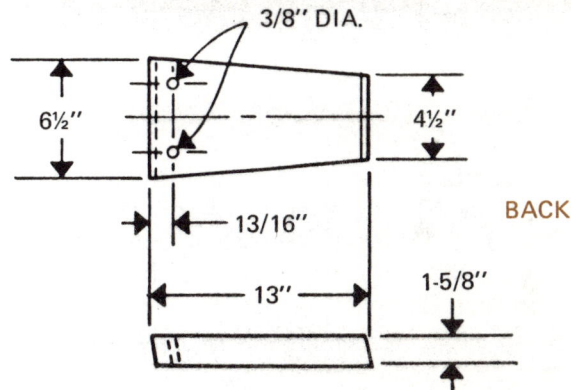

3/8'' DIA.

6½''   4½''

13/16''

BACK

13''   1-5/8''

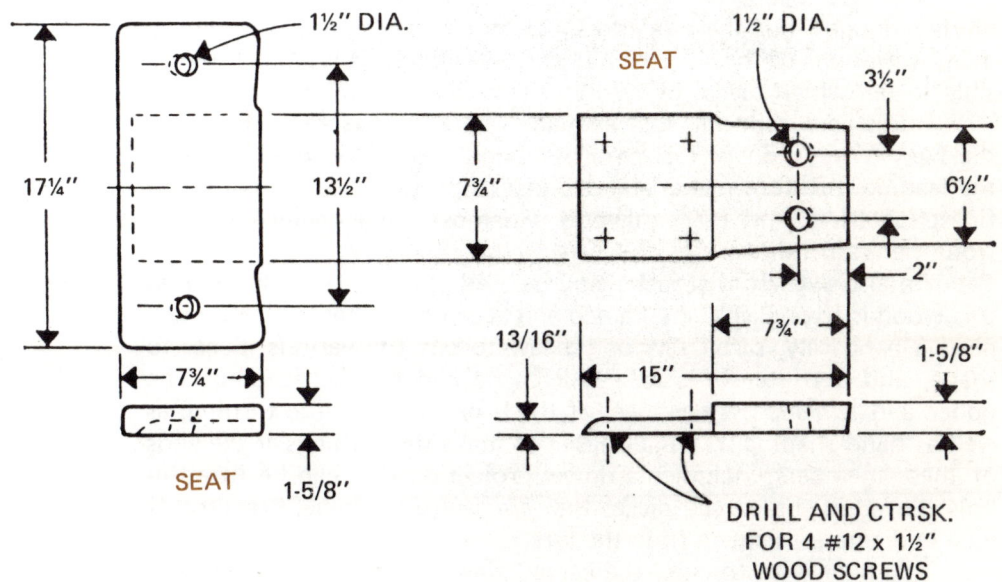

1½'' DIA.

SEAT

1½'' DIA.

3½''

17¼''   13½''   7¾''   6½''

2''

7¾''

7¾''   1-5/8''

13/16''

15''

SEAT

7¾''   1-5/8''

SEAT

DRILL AND CTRSK. FOR 4 #12 x 1½'' WOOD SCREWS

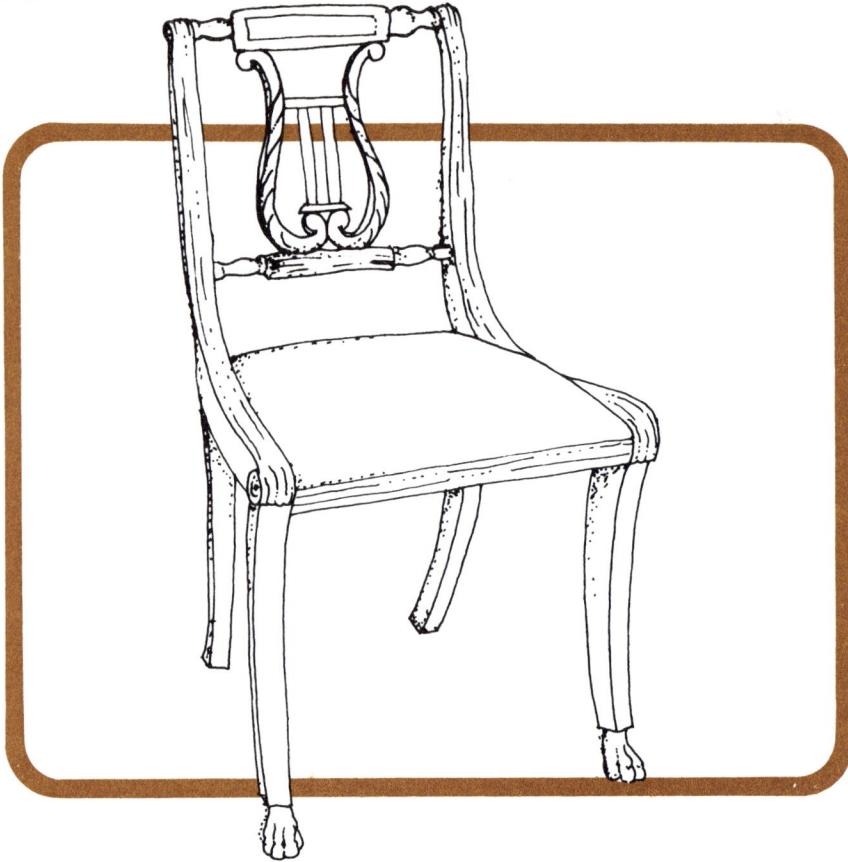

DUNCAN PHYFE SIDE CHAIR

This is an outstanding example of a side chair from the school of Duncan Phyfe, circa 1810. The term "school" is used because Duncan Phyfe (he spelled it "Fife" in the usual Scottish manner until he became successful) did not create a style of furniture, as did Hepplewhite, Sheraton and Chippendale. Rather, he made refinements and added embellishments to existing styles, adding to their grace and elegance.

The lyre back, curved legs and reeding are characteristic of Phyfe's designs, but these features were not new with him. Because so many variations of the side chair shown were made, it is almost impossible to tell which pieces of furniture actually were made in his shop.

It has been reported that as many as 100 men were employed in the New York shop of Duncan Phyfe, and there is no doubt he was the leading furniture maker and designer of his time. He used only the finest materials, and the hardwood was mostly mahogany imported from the West Indies.

We also suggest that mahogany be used for your reproduction, as this wood is strong, straight-grained and accepts finishes well. You will need a band saw, scroll saw or jig saw to cut the various pieces to shape, and a router or shaper will be needed for the reeding. The upper and lower cross members of the back require lathe turning, as well as hand shaping. It will be easier to make the turnings at the ends of these members, including a dowel projection that can be fitted in holes bored in the curved pieces that are sawed to shape. Brass rod ¼ inch in diameter is cut to fit in the lyre.

You may wish to copy the carved claw feet of the chair shown, but the alternate leg shown in the drawing is possibly more typical of the Duncan Phyfe designs.

The seat is upholstered by wrapping material over a 2-inch thick foam rubber cushion and stapling or tacking it to a piece of ¼-inch plywood. While the plastic leatherette on the chair shown simulates the glove leather used on chairs of that period, a brocade would be more in keeping with the elegance of the chair. Only a small amount of material will be required so even the very best upholstery material should not be too expensive.

The finish on the original is the dark color fashionable at the time the chair was made, but a lighter "fruitwood" would be more in keeping with modern decor.

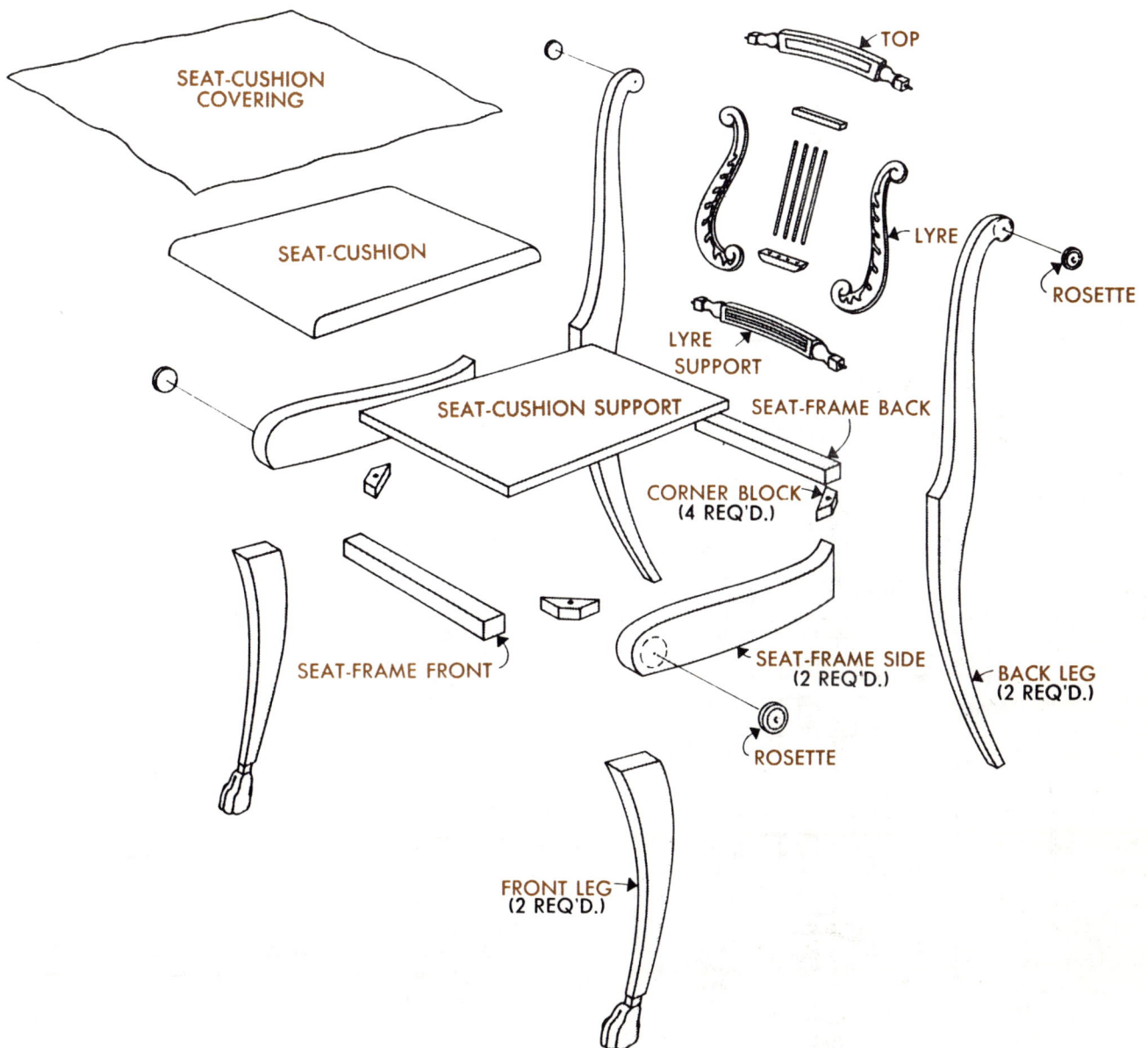

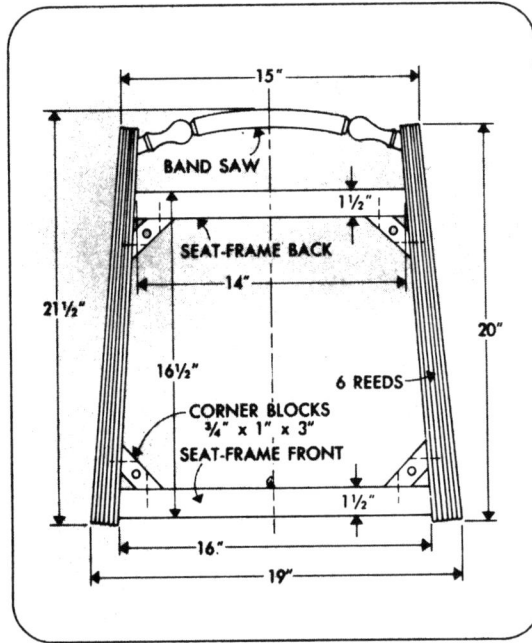

Top view (seat frame plan):
- 15″
- BAND SAW
- 1½″
- SEAT-FRAME BACK
- 14″
- 21½″
- 20″
- 16½″
- 6 REEDS
- CORNER BLOCKS ¾″ x 1″ x 3″
- SEAT-FRAME FRONT
- 1½″
- 16.″
- 19″

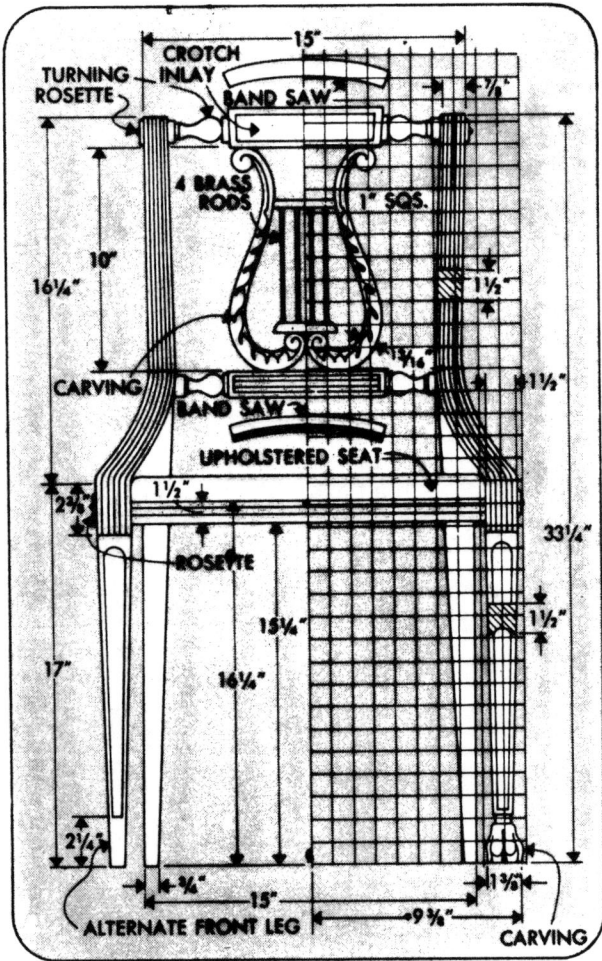

Front elevation:
- TURNING ROSETTE
- CROTCH INLAY
- 15″
- BAND SAW
- ⅞″
- 4 BRASS RODS
- 1″ SQS.
- 10″
- 16¼″
- 1½″
- CARVING
- BAND SAW
- 1¾₁₆″
- 1½″
- UPHOLSTERED SEAT
- 1½″
- 2½″
- ROSETTE
- 33¼″
- 1½″
- 15¼″
- 17″
- 16¼″
- 2¼″
- ¾″
- 15″
- 9¾″
- 1⅜″
- ALTERNATE FRONT LEG
- CARVING

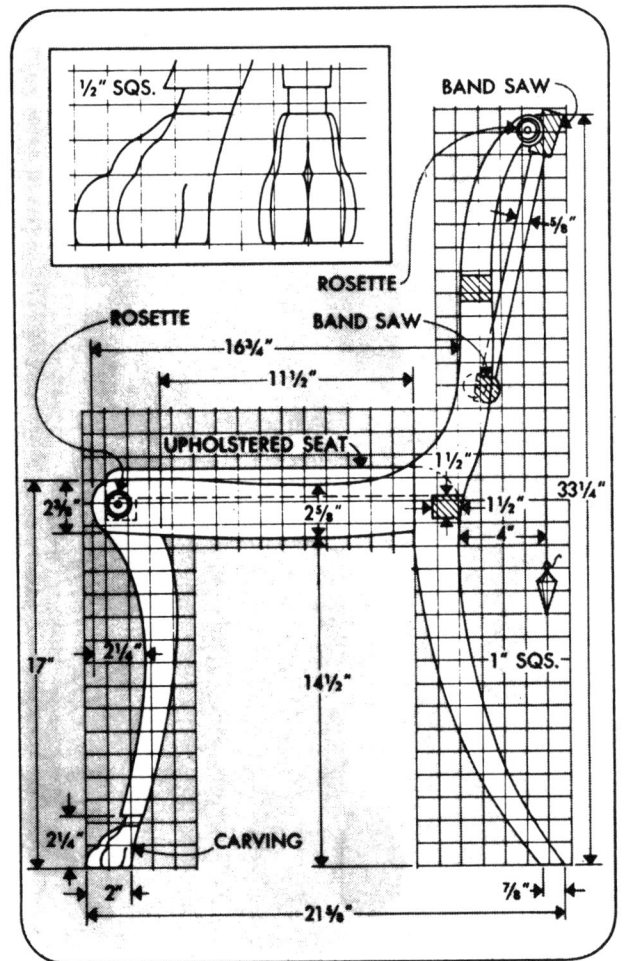

Side elevation:
- ½″ SQS.
- BAND SAW
- ROSETTE
- ⅝″
- ROSETTE
- BAND SAW
- 16¾″
- 11½″
- UPHOLSTERED SEAT
- 1½″
- 2½″
- 2⅝″
- 1½″
- 33¼″
- 4″
- 17″
- 2¼″
- 14½″
- 1″ SQS.
- CARVING
- 2″
- 21⅝″
- ⅞″

EARLY AMERICAN ROCKING CHAIR

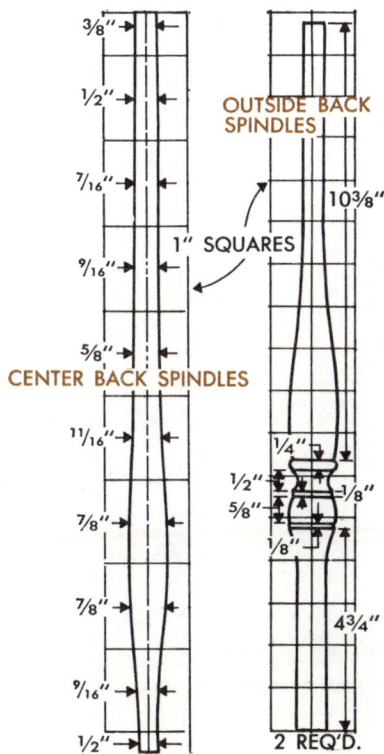

3/8"

1/2"

7/16"

1" SQUARES

9/16"

5/8"

CENTER BACK SPINDLES

11/16"

7/8"

7/8"

9/16"

1/2"

OUTSIDE BACK SPINDLES

10 3/8"

1/4"

1/2"   1/8"

5/8"

1/8"

4 3/4"

2 REQ'D.

This handsome Boston rocker is an ideal project for the lathe enthusiast, requiring many hours to turn the various spindles, legs and stretchers.

A hard, dense wood such as birch or maple should be used for the rocker, as the strains induced by the rocking require strong wood and tight constructions. Start construction by making the saddle seat, edgegluing stock 1-1/8 inches thick, also using dowels to reinforce the joints. Locate the dowels near the lower surface of the glued-up plank, so they will not be exposed when you cut into the plank to create the seat depression. This depression is about ½ inch and is produced with gouge or chisel after cutting the plank to the seat outline. Rough out the depression, then smooth it up with a flexible disc sander. The type that chucks in an electric drill will do. Start with coarse grit and use progressively finer paper until final hand sanding finishes the job, feathering the depression at the edges.

The splayed legs and slanted back require accurate drilling of the holes for these members. If you do not have a drill press, templates can be made to permit using a hand or power drill. An optional feature on the seat is a groove cut around the spindle holes. This is created with a 1/8-inch veining bit in a portable router, cutting the groove 1/8 inch deep. Edges of the seat should be rounded, simulating the wear an antique will have received over the years.

The back is cut from a piece of solid or glued-up stock 2½ x 4½ inches. Cut the back to shape, including the projecting, rounded ends, then use a band saw to cut the front and back arcs. The edges of the back also are rounded to appear worn. The back must be drilled carefully to accept the upper ends of the back spindles.

Rockers are cut from 1-1/8-inch stock, then sanded smooth. Be sure there are no flat spots on the underside of the rockers, assuring smooth rocking.

The legs are turned from stock 1½ inches square, the lower portion being kept square and tapered to 1-1/8 inch to match the width of the rockers. A dowel is either turned on the lower ends of the legs, or a separate dowel can be used. Note that the back legs are shorter than the front, and that an angle is cut on the lower ends of the legs to match the curve of the rockers at the points where they join. Be sure that the pairs of legs are exactly the same length; this is to make sure the chair will sit square and true after assembly.

Spindles for the chair back must also all be the same length. A steady-rest is required in the lathe for the spindles, as these slender turnings will whip if not properly supported. Although the two outside back spindles are somewhat larger than the center spindles, they still will require additional support at the center when being turned.

The front and side stretchers are of the same design, but vary in length. Again, it is important that pairs of these stretchers be exactly the same length to maintain a square and true assembly.

For the final assembly the legs and stretchers are joined first, using a good quality glue. The two stretchers between the front legs are installed first, then the stretcher on each side between the front and back legs. A single stretcher, cut from a 1-inch dowel is used between the two back legs. Be particular about squaring the four legs with each other and clamp the assembly either with a strap clamp or wind heavy cord around them and tighten with a "Spanish windlass," inserting a dowel between the turns of the cord and twisting with the aid of the leverage provided by the dowel.

After the glue has dried thoroughly in the leg assembly, fit and

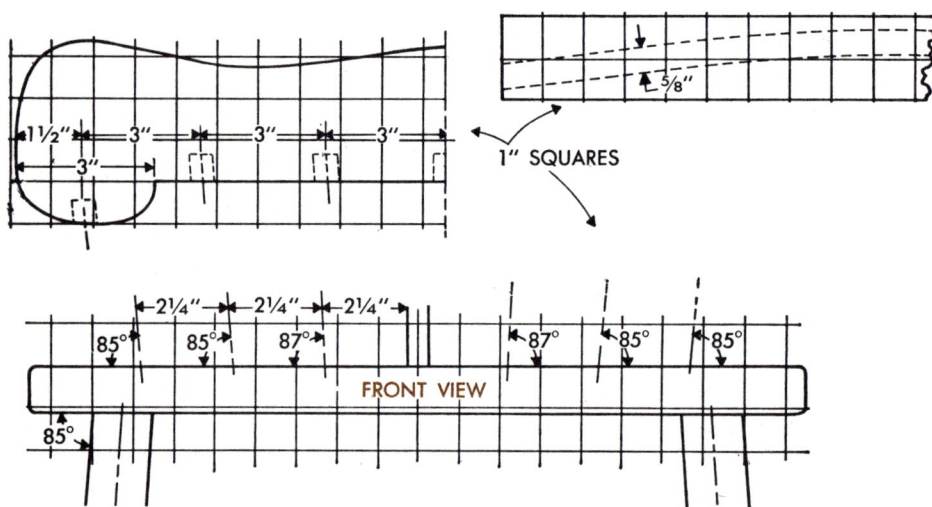

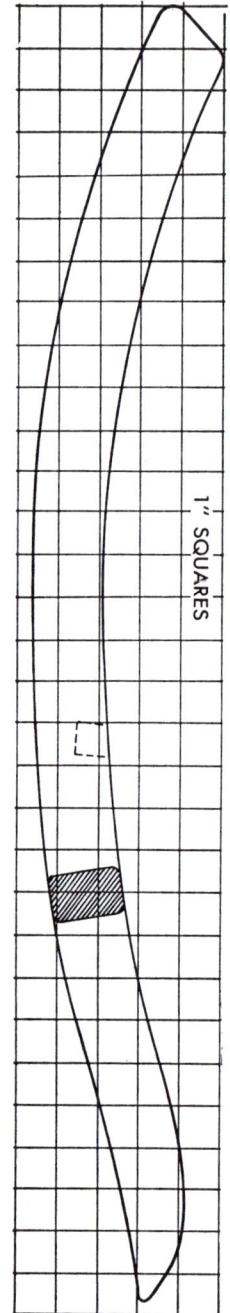

1" SQUARES

1½" 3" 3" 3"
3"

5⁄8"
1" SQUARES

2¼" 2¼" 2¼"
85° 85° 87° 87° 85° 85°
FRONT VIEW
85°

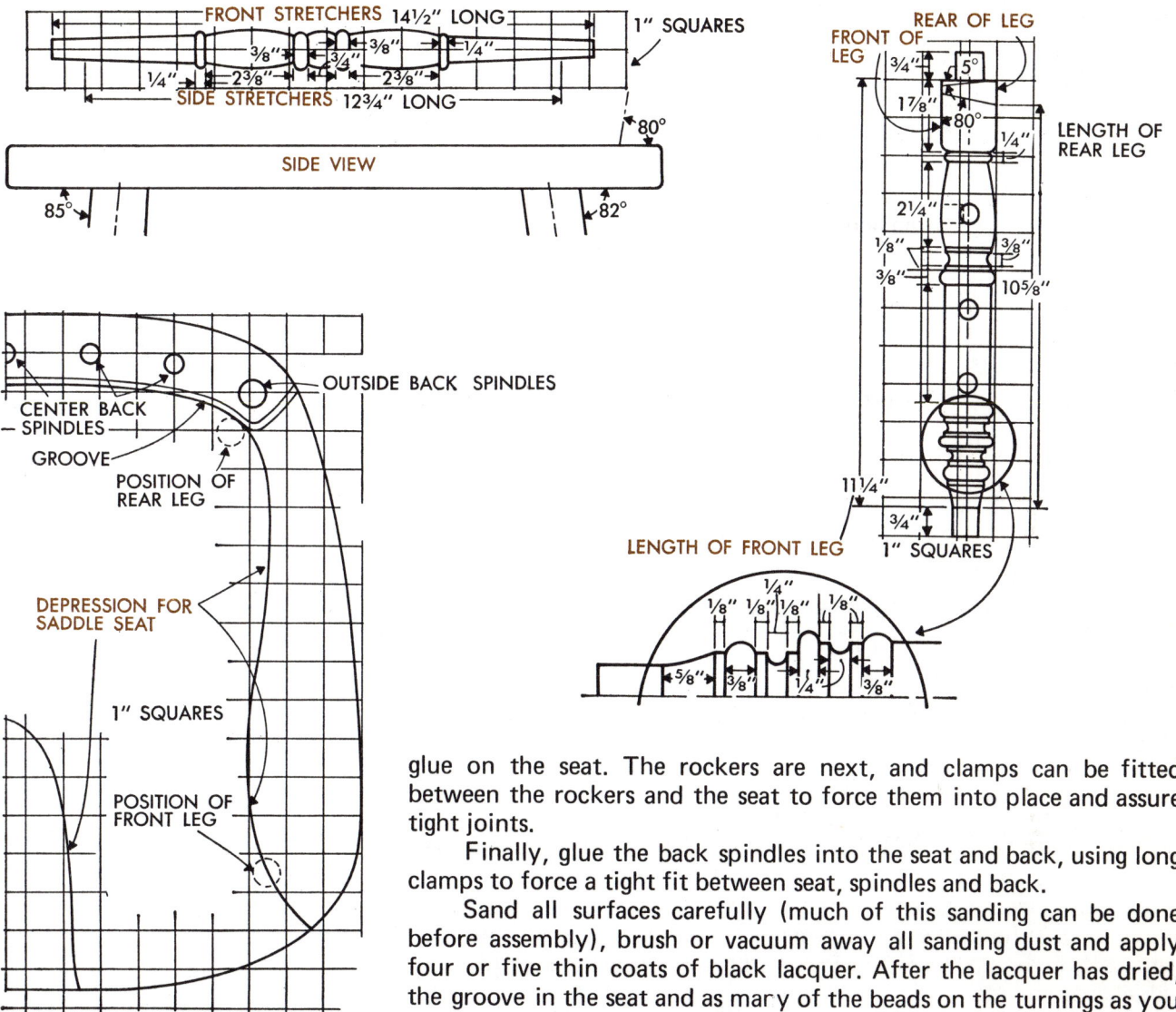

FRONT STRETCHERS 14½" LONG

SIDE STRETCHERS 12¾" LONG

SIDE VIEW

REAR OF LEG

FRONT OF LEG

LENGTH OF REAR LEG

LENGTH OF FRONT LEG

1" SQUARES

OUTSIDE BACK SPINDLES

CENTER BACK SPINDLES

GROOVE

POSITION OF REAR LEG

DEPRESSION FOR SADDLE SEAT

1" SQUARES

POSITION OF FRONT LEG

glue on the seat. The rockers are next, and clamps can be fitted between the rockers and the seat to force them into place and assure tight joints.

Finally, glue the back spindles into the seat and back, using long clamps to force a tight fit between seat, spindles and back.

Sand all surfaces carefully (much of this sanding can be done before assembly), brush or vacuum away all sanding dust and apply four or five thin coats of black lacquer. After the lacquer has dried, the groove in the seat and as many of the beads on the turnings as you wish can be trimmed with gold paint.

If you have an artistic flair, you can paint your own patterns on the face of the back, using gold paint (bronzing lacquer) and designs of your own. Decals may be used if you prefer.

During assembly be sure to wipe away any excess glue that is forced out of the joints as the various parts are clamped together. Although the glue will not show as much as on a piece of furniture that is stained and varnished or finished with clear lacquer, the glue will show through the opaque finish on close examination. For real craftsmanship, such minor flaws are not acceptable and should be eliminated.

For the same reason, be sure you have a steady hand when doing the striping on the beads. A slight amount of irregularity is expected here, but the less the better.

Over the years the chair will gather value and may some day be a real antique; burn or stamp your name and the date on the bottom to help authenticate it for some descendant.

VICTORIAN CHAIR

Diverse design elements in this charming little chair would indicate that the antique from which it was copied was made in someone's home shop.

Squared patterns are given for the turned front legs and stretchers, while the side stretchers are simply straight dowels. The seat frame is assembled from segments, and a groove is cut as indicated to accept the spline that holds the machine-made caning. If you weave your own cane seat, holes also will have to be drilled in the groove for the individual cane strands.

The arms (actually braces) are cut to shape and the profile cut with a router or shaper. The back legs, splat and the two crosspieces are cut to shape from the patterns made by enlarging the squared drawings. If you use dowels for assembling these pieces measure between the legs to get the correct length and angle. For a mortise-and-tenon joint, allow extra material at the ends of the pieces. Be sure to cut the angles on the ends to match those of the legs.

The small decorative piece on the upper edge of the top crosspiece can be eliminated, or changed in design to suit. This also is true of the inlays in the splat and top crosspiece.

The curved decoration on the underside of the front edge of the seat is another design element that can be eliminated, but it does add a little something to the charm of the design, and provides a bit of bracing under the front of the seat frame.

Cherry was used for the chair shown, but you can use any straightgrained hardwood. Finish to suit, and add glides on the bottoms of the legs.

Assembly jig to keep parts aligned is piece of plywood with "stop" of 1 x 4 and 2 x 4 on one end.

CHAIR ASSEMBLY

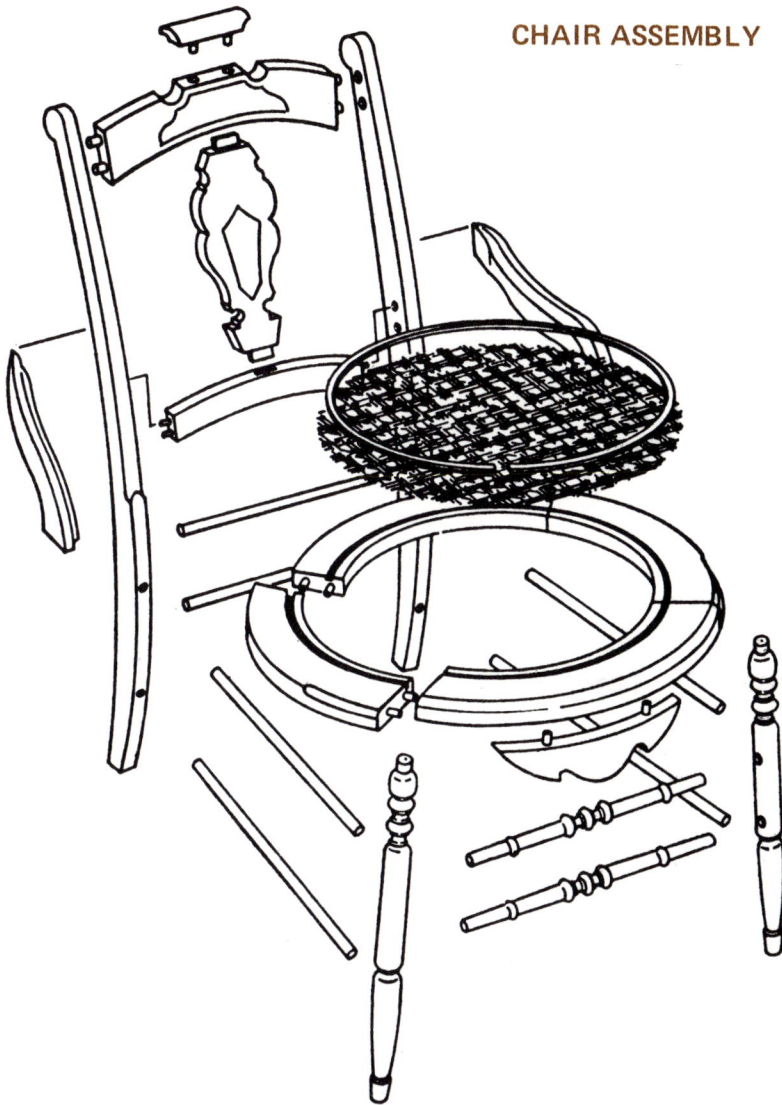

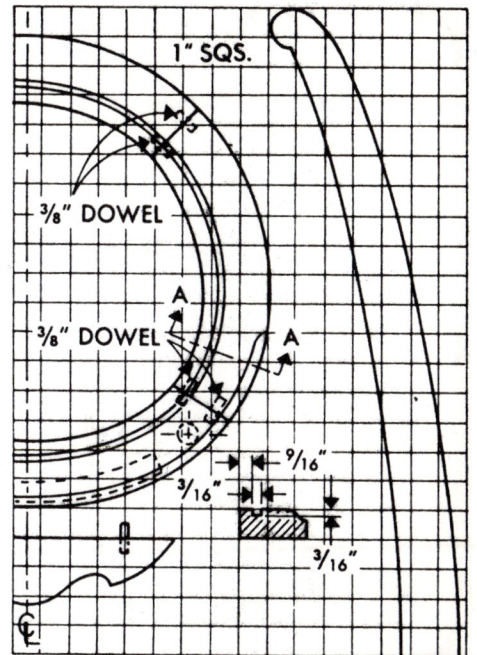

1" SQS.

³⁄₈" DOWEL

³⁄₈" DOWEL

A

A

⁹⁄₁₆"

³⁄₁₆"

³⁄₁₆"

LEG (2 REQ'D.)

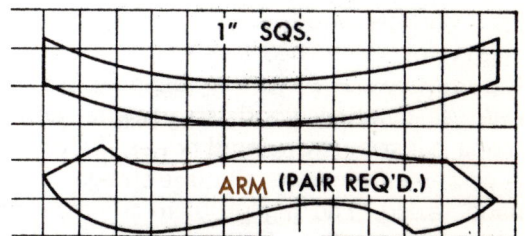

1" SQS.

ARM (PAIR REQ'D.)

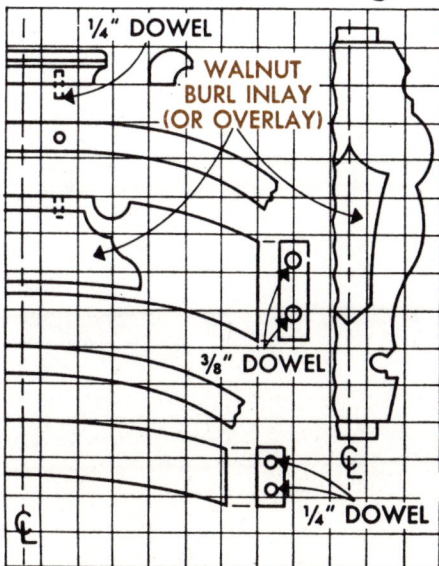

¼" DOWEL

WALNUT
BURL INLAY
(OR OVERLAY)

³⁄₈" DOWEL

¼" DOWEL

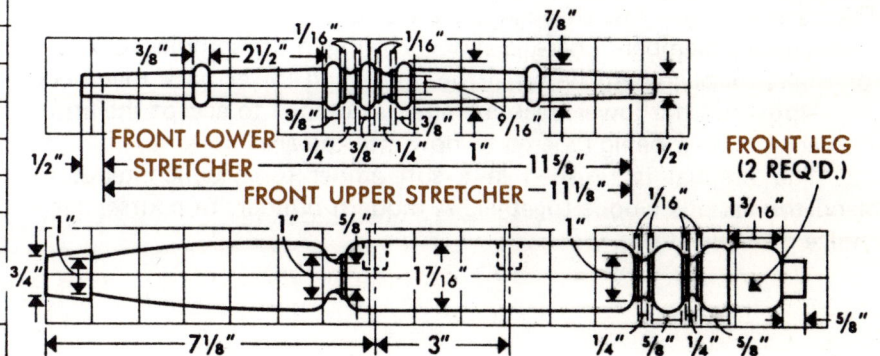

³⁄₈"   2½"   ¹⁄₁₆"   ¹⁄₁₆"   ⁷⁄₈"

³⁄₈"   ³⁄₈"   ⁹⁄₁₆"

FRONT LOWER
STRETCHER

¼" ³⁄₈" ¼"   1"   ½"

½"   11⁵⁄₈"

FRONT UPPER STRETCHER — 11⅛"

1"   1"   ⁵⁄₈"   1"

FRONT LEG
(2 REQ'D.)

¹⁄₁₆"   1³⁄₁₆"

¾"   1⁷⁄₁₆"

7⅛"   3"   ¼" ⁵⁄₈" ¼" ⁵⁄₈"

⁵⁄₈"

HIGH-BACK WINDSOR CHAIR

Although Windsor chairs are supposed to have originated in the little town of Windsor, England, the American interpretations are far superior in workmanship and character.

At the time of the making of this particular chair almost every home in America had at least one, including Washington's home, Mt. Vernon, although the styling may have varied; there were fan-backs, comb and loop backs.

Various woods were used in the original; oak for a strong seat, cherry for the turned legs and arm supports, with maple used for the top rail because of its easy bending. We show a laminated block, however, as bending wood is somewhat complicated and a band sawed shape is just as strong, and not as likely to spring out of shape.

The turnings are all quite straight forward, as are the shapes to be band sawed. The big problem comes in boring the holes for the legs and back spindles. The legs go through the seat for added strength. The back spindles pass through the lower back brace and are inserted in the upper member. There is enough spring in the spindles to adjust for slight misalignment between the upper and lower back members.

Note that the lower back member is notched to accept the arms; the back member being tapered to flow into the arm.

The original is finished in a soft amber tone, which tends to blend the various woods together. A modern builder, of course, has a choice of many stains.

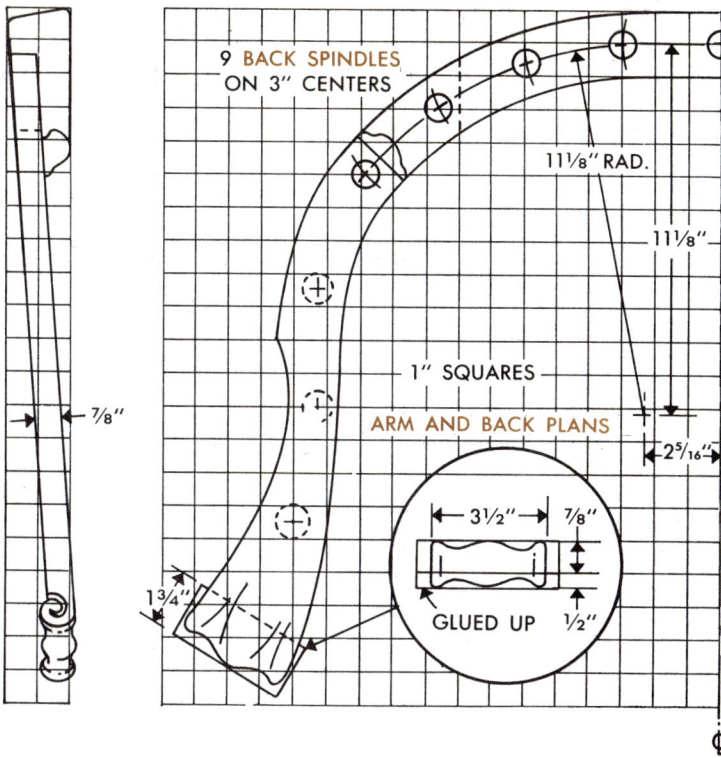

9 BACK SPINDLES ON 3" CENTERS

11⅛" RAD.

11⅛"

1" SQUARES

ARM AND BACK PLANS

7/8"

2 5/16"

1¾"

3½"   7/8"

GLUED UP   ½"

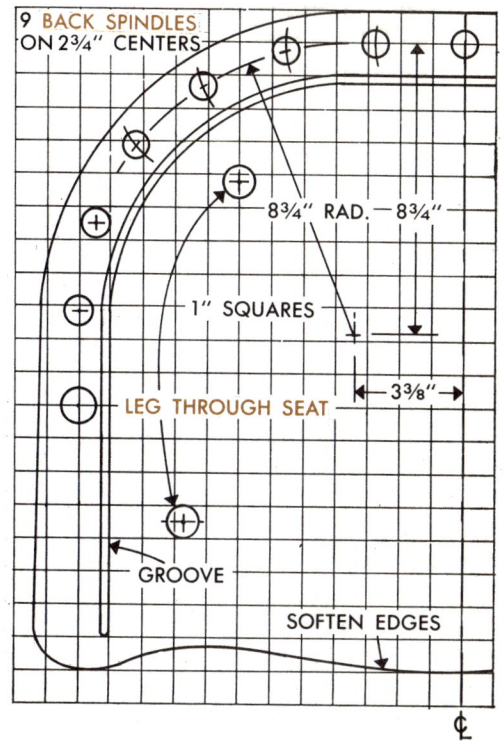

9 BACK SPINDLES ON 2¾" CENTERS

8¾" RAD. — 8¾"

1" SQUARES

LEG THROUGH SEAT

3⅜"

← **GROOVE**

SOFTEN EDGES

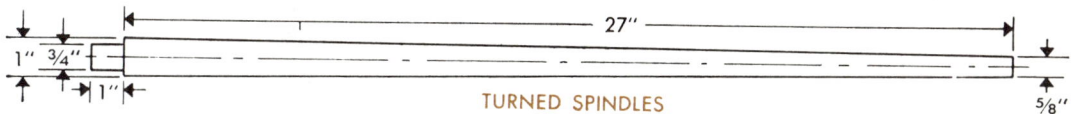

27"

1"   ¾"

1"

TURNED SPINDLES

5/8"

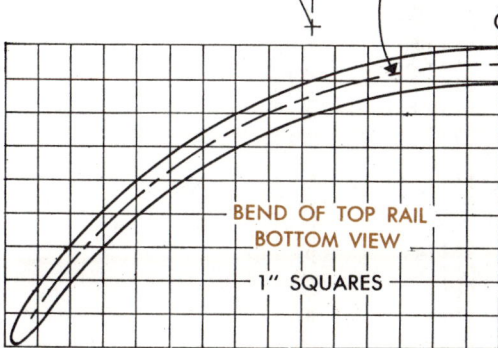

17" RAD.

TWO PCS CABINET LUMBER 1¾" x 9½" x 36"

CENTERLINE OF BACK SPINDLES

BEND OF TOP RAIL BOTTOM VIEW
1" SQUARES

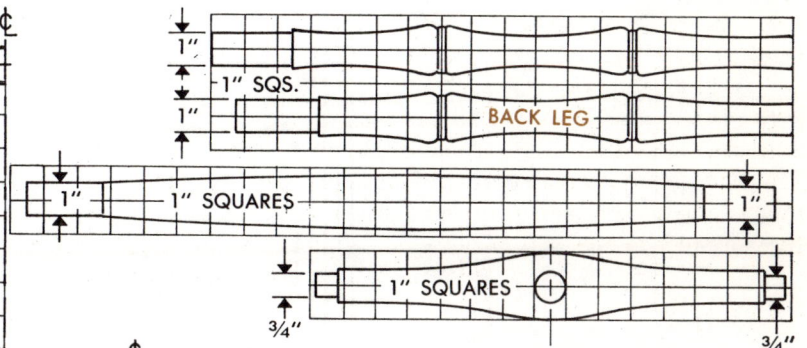

¾"   7/8"

1" SQUARES

¾"   7/8"

1"

1" SQS.

1"

BACK LEG

1"   1" SQUARES   1"

1" SQUARES

¾"   ¾"

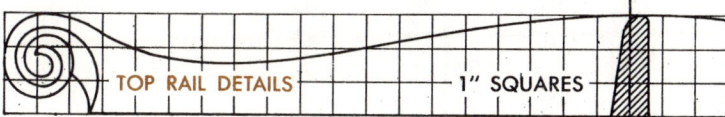

TOP RAIL DETAILS   1" SQUARES

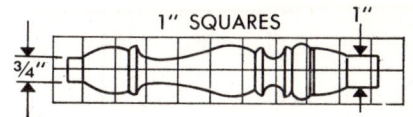

1" SQUARES   1"

¾"

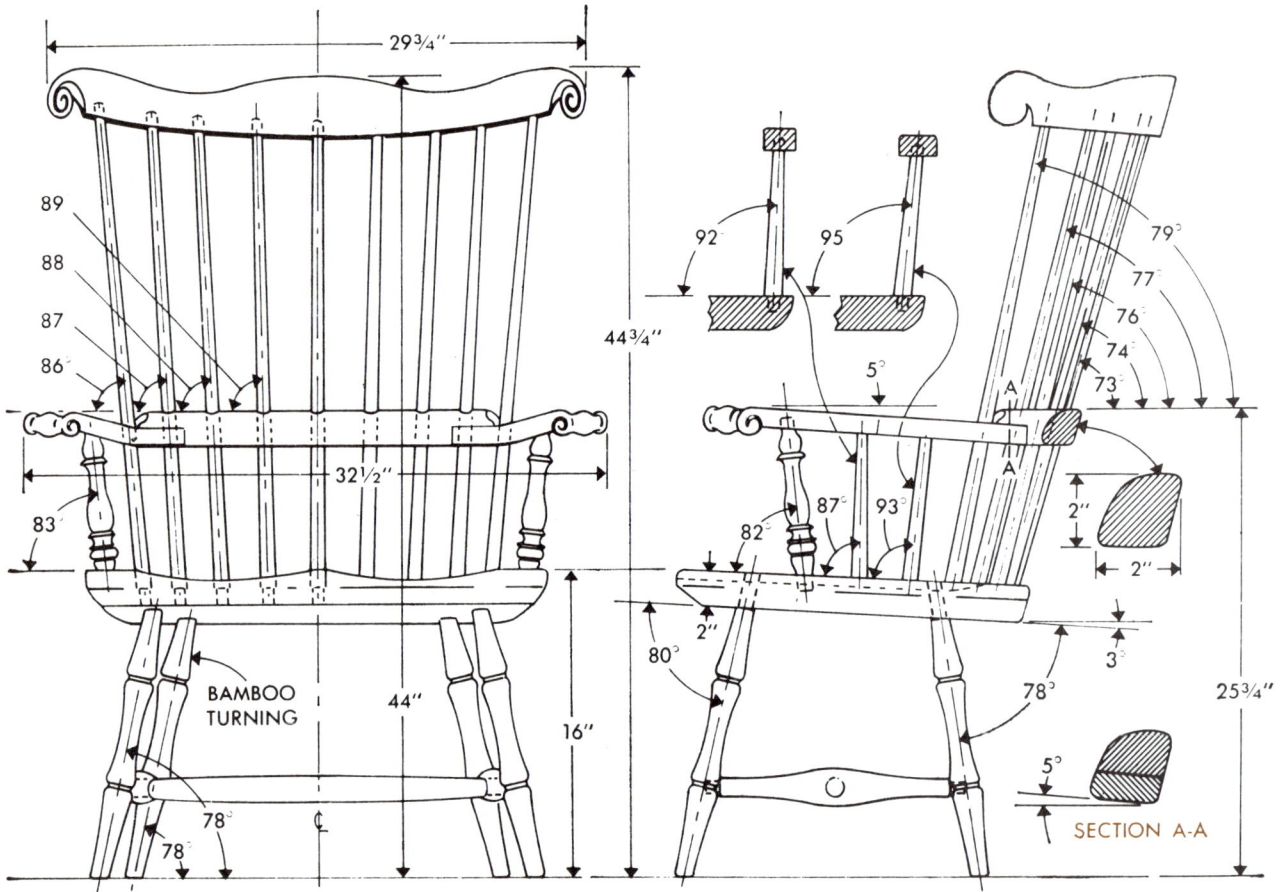

29¾"

44¾"

89
88
87
86

32½"

83

BAMBOO
TURNING

44"

16"

℄

78°
78°

92   95

5°

87°   93°

82

2"

80°

78°

79°
77
76
74
73

2"
2"

3"

25¾"

5°

SECTION A-A

AMERICAN WING CHAIR

One of the most attractive and comfortable of all styles, the wing-back chair originally was designed to protect the sitter from drafts, which were common in old-time houses heated with fireplaces. In a modern home the wings provide a feeling of privacy, and help create a bit of quiet when you read or just relax.

The chair is not large, and so will fit in almost any room. It is light enough to be moved about easily, but heavy enough so it does not shift when you change position in it.

Start construction by making patterns of the various pieces from the squared drawings. The original chair has square, tapered legs, but two alternate styles are shown: a cabriole and a turned, "early American" type. Note that some of the stretchers are simply lengths of stock, but that the angles on the ends are required to assure a close fit. All joints are held with dowels and glue. Because the chair frame is covered with upholstery (except for the "show wood" that includes the legs, stretchers, etc.) you can clamp the pieces together and drill through one member into another and insert lengths of dowel. When the glue has set, you saw off the dowel if it projects, and lightly sand the cut end. This makes for simpler and faster assembly.

Because every builder will vary his assembly slightly, it's best to cut and fit the stretchers and other members that run from one piece to another. This also is true of the angle cuts; they may vary slightly according to your assembly, so check them with the stretcher in place.

The first subassembly is the four legs, the side, back and front seat-frame members and the stretchers. A strap clamp is handy to hold this assembly. Be sure to assemble it on a flat surface so all four legs

1. First subassembly made consists of the four legs, side, back and front seat-frame members and the three stretchers.

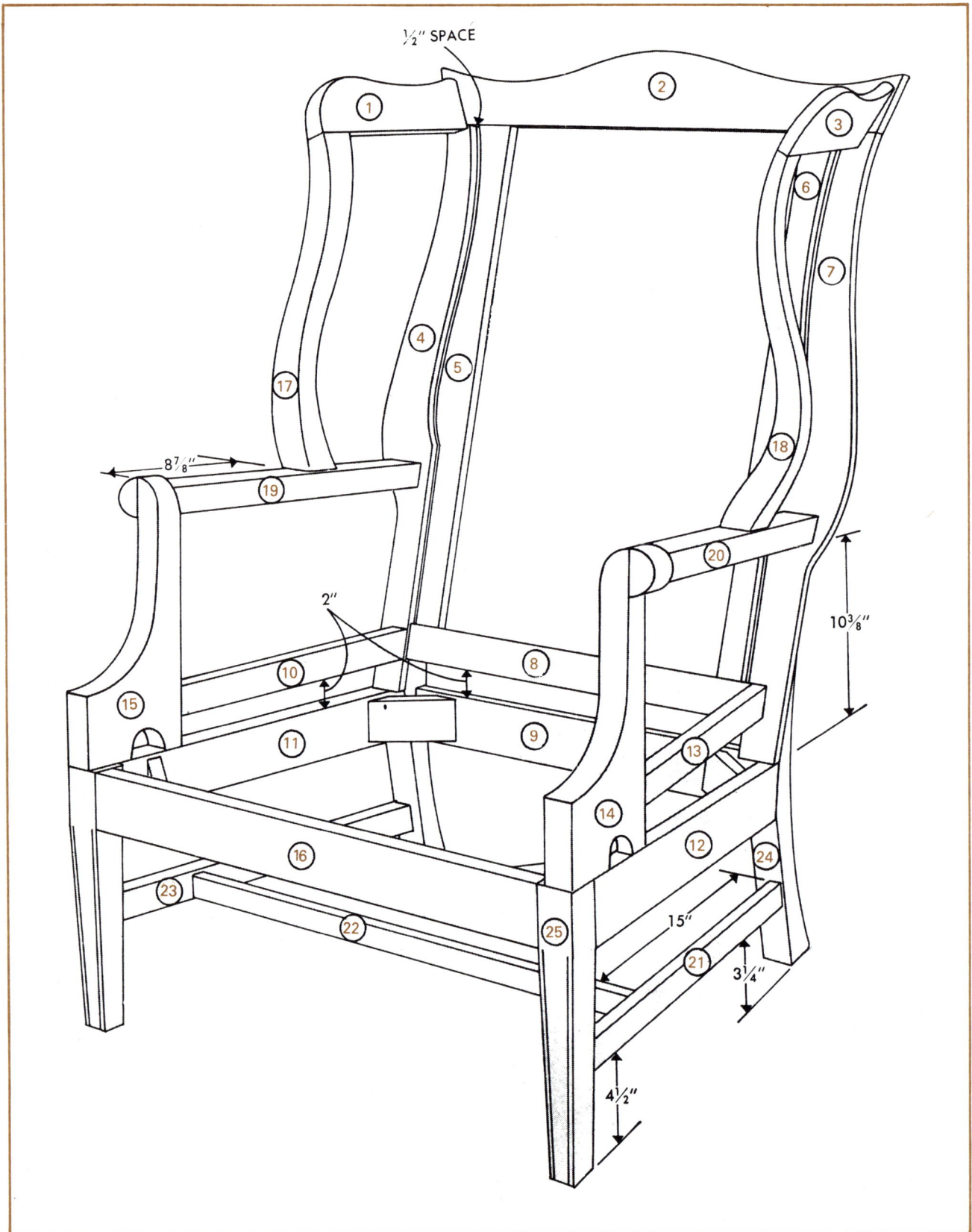

½" SPACE

8⅞"

2"

10⅜"

15"

3¼"

4½"

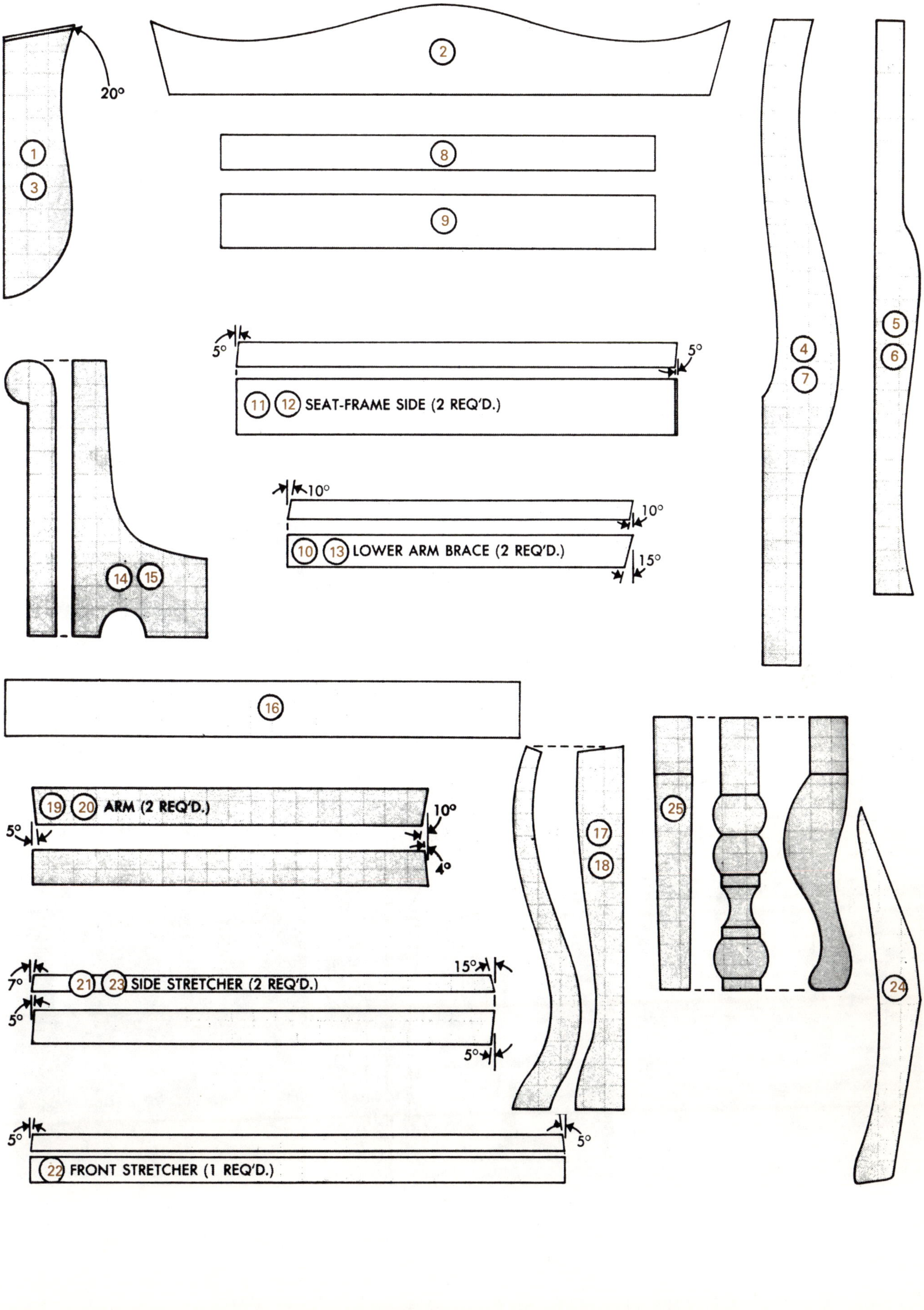

20°

① ③

②

⑧

⑨

⑤ ⑥

④ ⑦

5°   5°

⑪ ⑫ SEAT-FRAME SIDE (2 REQ'D.)

10°   10°

⑩ ⑬ LOWER ARM BRACE (2 REQ'D.)   15°

⑭ ⑮

⑯

⑲ ⑳ ARM (2 REQ'D.)   10°

5°   4°

15°

7° ㉑ ㉓ SIDE STRETCHER (2 REQ'D.)

5°   5°

⑰ ⑱

㉕

㉔

5°   5°

㉒ FRONT STRETCHER (1 REQ'D.)

The back is made next, being assembled on a flat surface so it is all in one plane. Note in the photo and drawings that the various pieces are numbered for easy selection of the right shape for the specific location. Clamp the back to the back legs, then drill for dowels and wood screws to attach the back to the legs.

The next subassembly. is the arm and wing. In this operation it is best to apply glue and assemble the various pieces with dowels, then immediately position the subassembly on the chair and clamp it in place. This permits moving the various pieces slightly before the glue sets up. As indicated in the photo, this requires a number of bar clamps and wood screws (wooden clamps), as well as C-clamps. Be sure to wipe off any excess glue that squeezes out of the clamped joints. This is especially important where the glue runs onto the "show wood."

Upholstering the chair will take time, but with our step-by-step photos you should have no problem.

MATERIALS LIST

No.	Part	Dimensions
1,3.	Wings	¾"x3¼"x12¼" (2)
2.	Back Top Crosspiece:	¾"x4"x26½" (1)
4,7.	Back Outside Verticals:	¾"x(see drawing) (2)
5,6.	Back Inside Verticals:	¾"x(see drawing) (2)
8.	Back Stretcher:	1"x(see drawing) (1)
9.	Back Seat Frame:	1-1/8"x2½"x19¾" (1)
10,13.	Side Braces:	7/8"x1½"x15-11/16" (2)
11,12.	Side Seat Frame:	1-1/8"x2½"x20" (2)
14,15.	Arm Support:	(see drawing) (2)
16.	Front Seat Frame:	1½"x2½"x23-5/16" (1)
17,18.	Wing Supports:	(see drawing) (2)
19,20.	Arms:	1½"x1¾"x17¾" (2)
21,23.	Side Stretchers:	¾"x1½"x21-1/8" (2)
22.	Center Stretcher:	¾"x1-1/8"x24-5/16" (1)
24.	Back Leg:	1¾" x (see drawing) (2)
25.	Front Leg:	1¾"x1¾"x12" (2)

2.   The back is assembled on a flat surface, then attached to the back legs with dowels and wood screws.

3.   Arm-wing subassembly is somewhat complex; clamp it to the chair before the glue sets.

4.   Clamping wing-arm assembly to the chair takes a number of clamps; you may need someone to assist.

5.   Finished frame is strong and solid, made so upholstery materials can be pulled around the various parts.

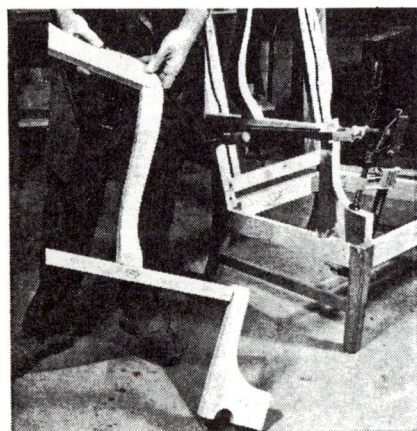

UPHOLSTERING

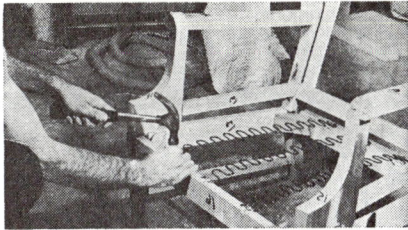

1.

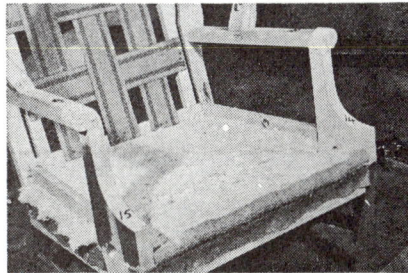

4.

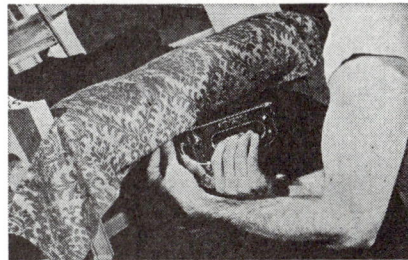

6.

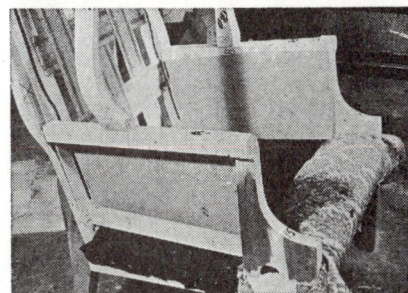

8.

11.

1.   Zig-zag steel webbing forms base for seat upholstery. Is cut to length, held in place by steel clips.

2.   Burlap is applied over steel webbing, 1½" edge roll tacked on top of front seat-frame member.

3.   Jute webbing is tacked and woven to form base for back upholstery of chair, provide "springing."

4.   Cotton batting is applied over burlap to chair seat. Batting is split across about 6" from the front of seat.

5.   A short piece of upholstery material is sewn to inexpensive material, then stitched to burlap through slit in cotton.

6.   Front piece is split to go around arm supports, brought under front frame and stapled from center outwards.

7.   Material is cut around back legs, stapled to side and back frame pieces, stretched taut and smooth.

8.   Lightweight cardboard is cut to fit on inside of arms and stapled in place, provides reinforcement.

9.   Small ½" edge roll is stapled to outside edge of front of arm support, to build up and pad front of arm.

10. Cotton batting is fitted to arm around wing post and stapled in position. Cotton should be torn, not cut.

11. Cotton is smoothed in place, fitted under lower stretcher, shaped to front of arm support.

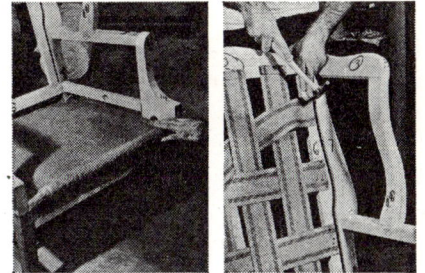

2. 3.

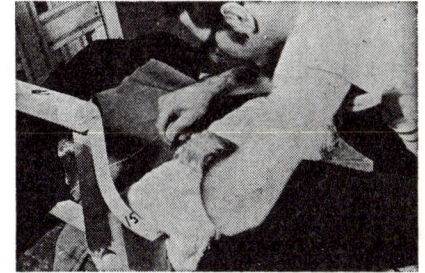

5.

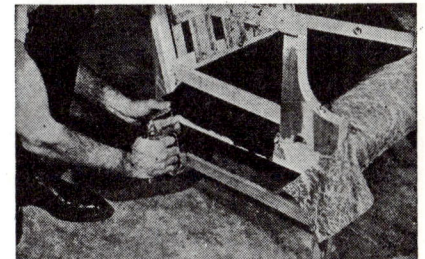

7.

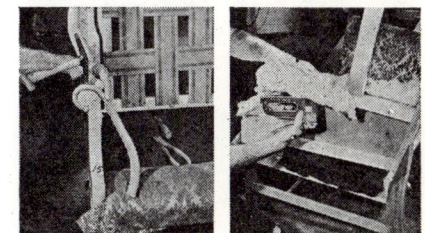

9. 10.

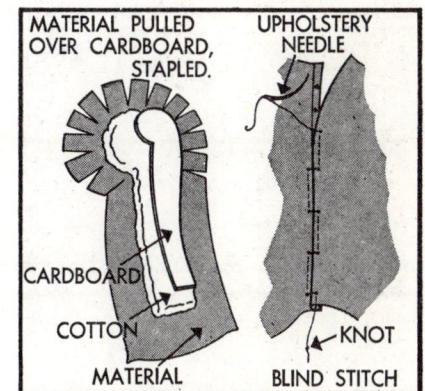

MATERIAL PULLED OVER CARDBOARD, STAPLED.

UPHOLSTERY NEEDLE

CARDBOARD

COTTON

MATERIAL

KNOT

BLIND STITCH

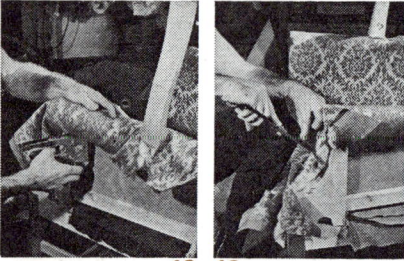

12. 13.

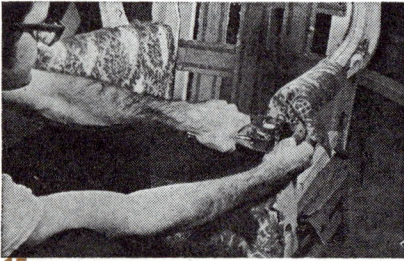

15.

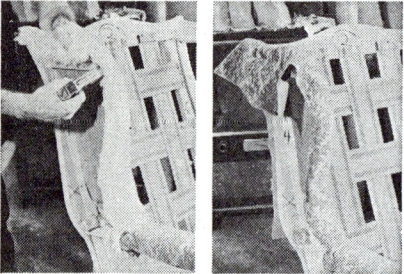

17. 18.

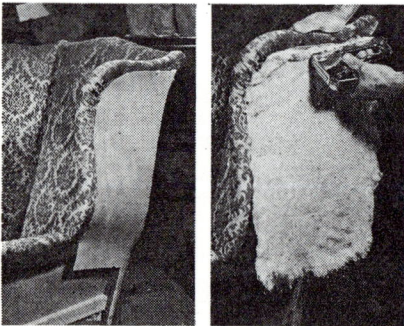

23.

20. 21.

12. Inside-arm material is cut to fit around wing support, smoothed in place, and stapled to underside of arm.

13. Material is pulled tightly to remove wrinkles, slits cut in portion that "rounds" front of arm and stapled.

14. Lower-front material covering of arm front is slipped under front-seat material, smoothed, both tacked.

15. Wrinkles are carefully pulled out of material covering upper portion of arm front, material stapled-in place.

16. Burlap is stapled to inside of wings, trimmed to fit. For best results fit staples to job; short ones here.

17. Cotton padding is fitted over burlap, smoothed out and stapled on outside surface of outer wing surface.

18. Material is stapled to outside surface of wing, carefully removing all wrinkles and bumps as you go.

19. Inside lower edge is folded under, "blind stitched" to inside arm material with heavy thread and upholstery needle.

20. Fasten lightweight cardboard to outside of wing, shaping it to fit wing contours. Use staples.

21. Staple one layer of cotton padding over cardboard wing form. Smooth it as it is fastened.

22. Using a cardboard tacking strip, fasten top of outside wing material from wrong side, as shown.

23. Pull material down in place and fasten to underside of arm with tacks or staples, pull out wrinkles as you go.

24. Cut front edge to rough shape of wing, leaving about 1" extra protruding, fold under and blind-stitch to wing.

25. Cut burlap to fit seat back and fasten in place on back side of chair. Cut off excess at front side.

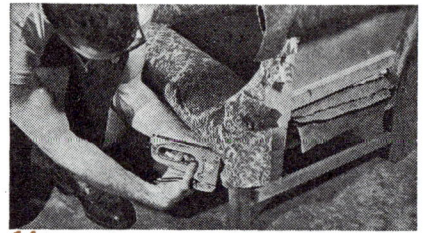

14.

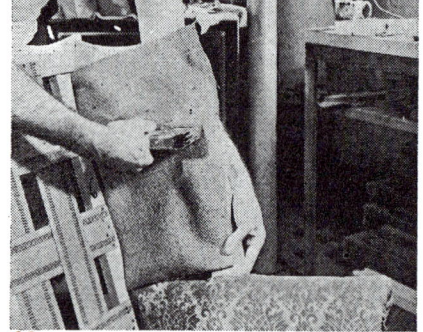

16.

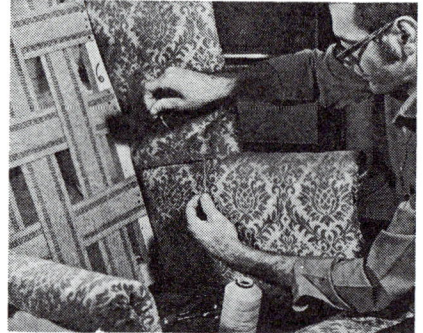

19.

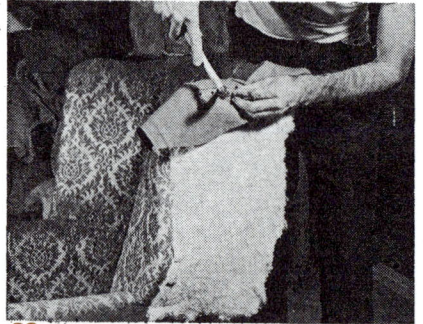

22.   24. 25.

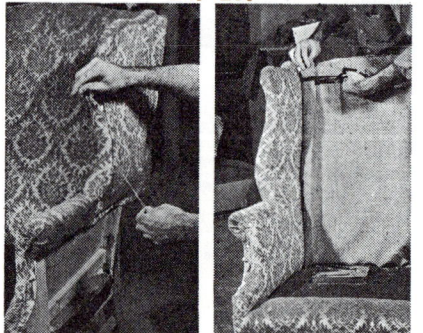

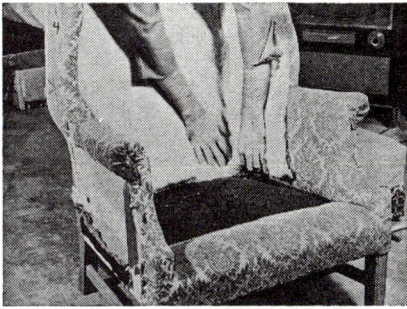

26.

28.

26. Pad back with cotton batting, tearing to outline of inside of back. Shape to back with your hands.

27. Place inside back material in position, tack upper edge on back side of top rail, push side and bottom out.

28. Fasten inside back material with staples or tacks on back side. Smooth corners and remove wrinkles as you go.

29. Fasten top of backpiece with tacking strip, fold under sides, temporarily tack then blind stitch sides to finish.

30. Make front panel. Fasten with brads driven deep into cardboard, through material. Pull material out over brads.

31. Cut dust cover to fit and fasten in place with staples. Make cushion to fit seat of chair.

27.

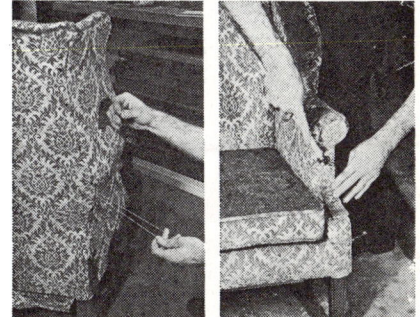

29. 30.

31.

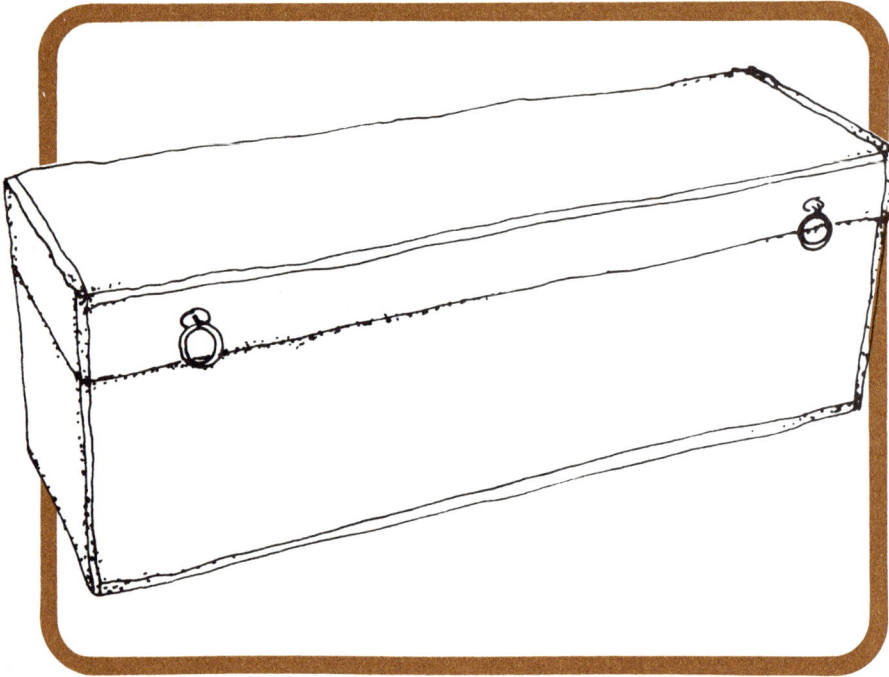

COLONIAL SEA CHEST

In the colonial days every sailor that went to sea had a sea chest in which he kept his clothes and other gear that he needed for living aboard ship. The chests were of simple construction, many of them being built by the ship's carpenter who was basically not a cabinet-maker but a rough carpenter whose main job was to keep the wooden ship afloat and operating.

Our reproduction of the chest is made from lengths of common pine or fir with butt joints used throughout. Flathead steel wood screws 2 inches long, plus waterproof glue are used for all joints, and the screws are driven into counterbored holes.

Start construction by cutting the various pieces of 1 x 10 lumber to the legnths indicated in the drawing. Assemble the top, bottom and sides, squaring the corners as you go along. Be sure the end pieces are cut true and square, and when you add these, you can recheck the squareness of the corners of the rest of the assembly.

When you have made the chest completely, and the glue has set, cut the box apart to create the lid. Saw along a line 4 inches down from the top. A table saw makes this operation a simple one, but even a handsaw can be used. Even if your cut is not exactly true, the lid and box will still fit together tightly, as the irregularities will match.

Before cutting the box apart you can add ''age'' and ''wear'' by first using a drawknife or rasp to round all edges, as shown in the photos. These first cuts should be between the screws, then you next can run a rasp over the screw heads, being careful not to go to the bottom of the counterbores to hit the screw heads. A gouge is used next to make marks that would be produced from many years of dragging

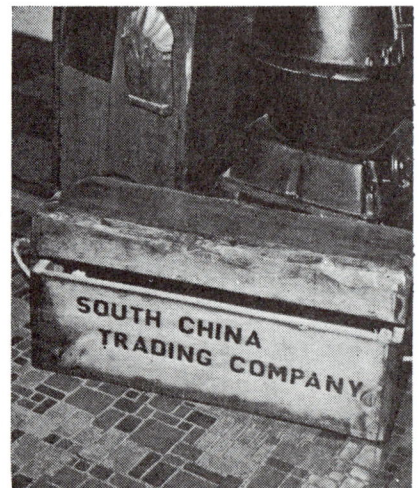

the chest over rough surfaces. This is done on all faces of the chest. Walnut stain now is applied, allowed to set 15 minutes, then wiped off. Thinned black paint is rubbed along the edges, allowed to set, then wiped off. This creates the "soil" of years of handling.

When the stains have dried, apply a coat or two of penetrating sealer. You can partition the inside of the chest to suit the purpose for which it will be used: toy box, sewing cabinet, linen or china storage.

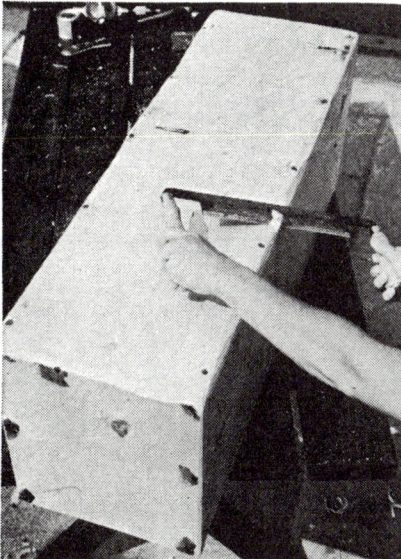

Drawknife or rasp is used to round edges between screws. You also can round edges over screw heads.

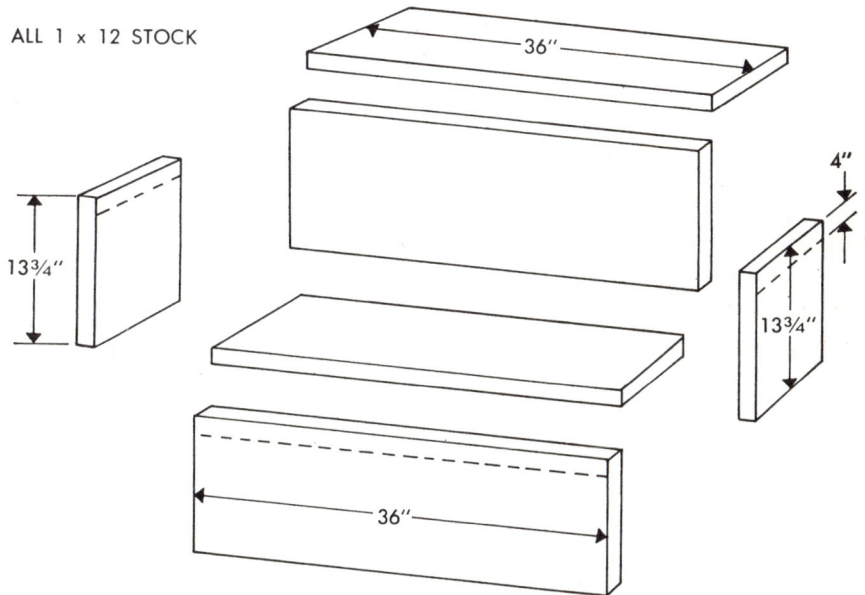

ALL 1 x 12 STOCK

Screw heads are covered with wood putty, then walnut stain is applied and black paint is wiped along edges.

Gouge is used to "distress" surfaces, add "age" and effects of rough treatment that chest would receive.

Top, Bottom, two sides and ends are joined, then top is cut free to assure an absolutely accurate fit for the lid.

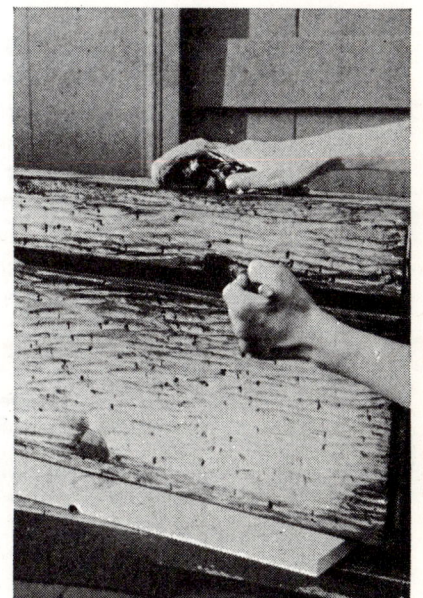

JEWEL CHEST

This charming little jewel chest is a miniature version of an antique chest of drawers and will grace the bedroom of any woman who has need for storage of jewelry where it is handy for selection at any time. The chest is just 10 inches deep, 12 inches high and 15 inches long, but there is a generous amount of space in the four drawers. In keeping with the styling, the pulls shown are of antique design. When purchasing the hardware remember that it must be small to maintain the scale of the miniature chest.

Top and bottom of the chest are identical, but the shape on the edges can be different. The front edges of the sides are also molded. Note that the base riser is the same shape as the top and bottom, but ½ inch smaller.

All edges of the four drawer fronts are shaped also. These fronts are added to the boxes that are the drawers, so the drawers are made first, to fit the openings created in the case by the dividers. Do not attach the hardware until all surfaces have been sanded smooth and the stain and finish have been applied. A glossy finish is recommended.

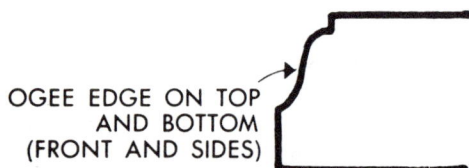

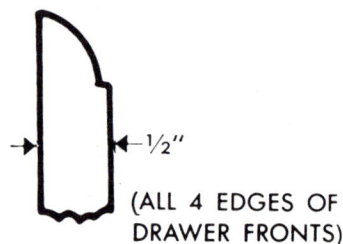

OGEE EDGE ON TOP AND BOTTOM (FRONT AND SIDES)

½"

(ALL 4 EDGES OF DRAWER FRONTS)

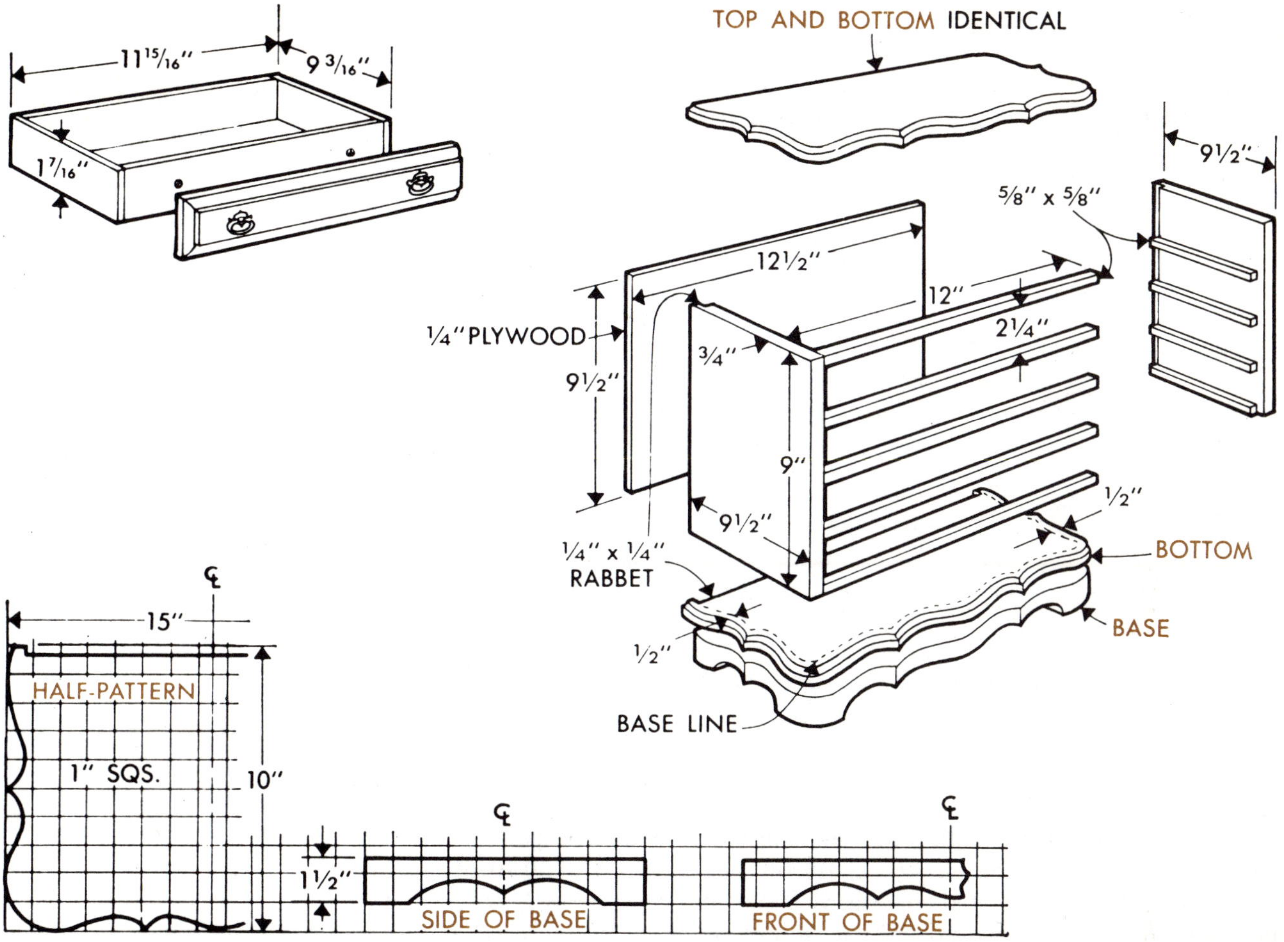

11$^{15}/_{16}$"   9$^3/_{16}$"

1$^7/_{16}$"

TOP AND BOTTOM IDENTICAL

9½"

$^5/_8$" x $^5/_8$"

12½"

12"

¼"PLYWOOD

¾"   2¼"

9½"

9"

¼" x ¼"
RABBET   9½"   ½"   BOTTOM

½"   BASE

BASE LINE

₵

15"

HALF-PATTERN

1" SQS.   10"

1½"

₵   ₵

SIDE OF BASE   FRONT OF BASE

MAHOGANY-VENEERED CHEST OF DRAWERS

This furniture-reproduction project is in the style of George Hepplewhite, circa 1780. The elegant chest of drawers with drop-front desk top is made of selected mahogany and mahogany veneer, with inlays of satinwood and ebony.

The great variety of construction details will present a challenge to even the most discerning craftsman. Also incorporated in the chest are several "hides" or secret hiding places and locks which will place additional demands upon the builder.

Begin construction of the chest by building the case. The top and bottom pieces fit into rabbets in the sides. Fasten the back in place using glue and screws. Make the drawer supports of plywood as shown and fasten in place. If you are going to use the drawer lock-hide, as shown in the drawing, you will have to drill holes in each divider for the sliding pin. Cut and fit the dividers between the top drawer and the pull-out supports. The pull-out supports actually are "pencilbox" hides and are locked in the case by the spring steel and block mechanism shown.

Build the pencil boxes using the locked rabbets and fit the locking mechanism in place.

Enlarge the squared drawing for the legs and aprons, "post-block" the legs up to the thickness needed and cut the legs and aprons on a band saw. Glue and dowel the legs and aprons together. Fasten the leg and apron assembly to the case using plenty of glue, glue blocks and screws.

Cut the drop leaf and fasten it in place mortising the hinges for a neat fit. Cut the ¾-inch plywood filler to match the remaining portion

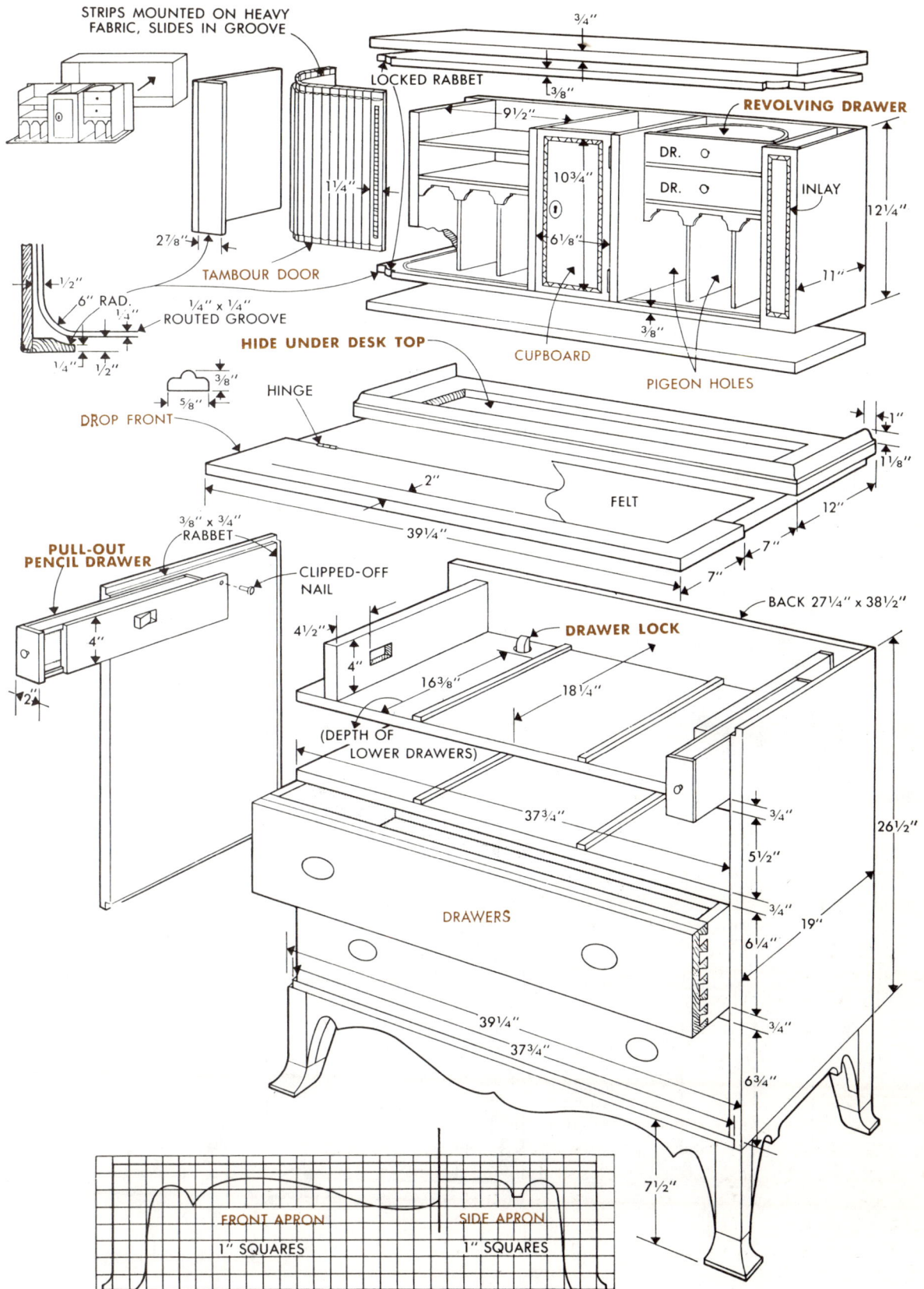

STRIPS MOUNTED ON HEAVY FABRIC, SLIDES IN GROOVE

LOCKED RABBET

3/4"

3/8"

9 1/2"

REVOLVING DRAWER

10 3/4"

DR.

DR.

INLAY

12 1/4"

6 1/8"

11"

1 1/4"

2 7/8"

TAMBOUR DOOR

1/2"

6" RAD.

1/4"

1/4" x 1/4" ROUTED GROOVE

1/4"   1/2"

3/8"

CUPBOARD

PIGEON HOLES

HIDE UNDER DESK TOP

3/8"

5/8"

HINGE

DROP FRONT

2"

FELT

1"

1 1/8"

39 1/4"

12"

3/8" x 3/4" RABBET

PULL-OUT PENCIL DRAWER

CLIPPED-OFF NAIL

7"

7"

BACK 27 1/4" x 38 1/2"

4"

4 1/2"

DRAWER LOCK

2"

4"

16 3/8"

18 1/4"

(DEPTH OF LOWER DRAWERS)

3/4"

37 3/4"

5 1/2"

26 1/2"

DRAWERS

3/4"

19"

6 1/4"

39 1/4"

37 3/4"

3/4"

6 3/4"

FRONT APRON

1" SQUARES

SIDE APRON

1" SQUARES

7 1/2"

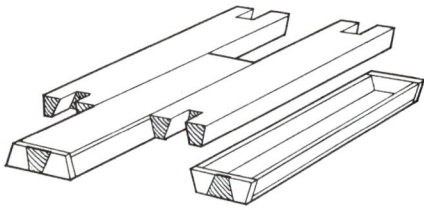

DRAWER-FRONT HIDE

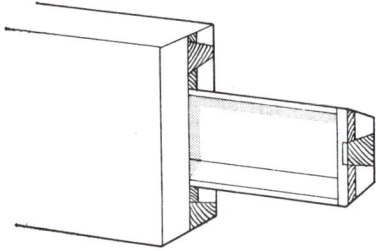

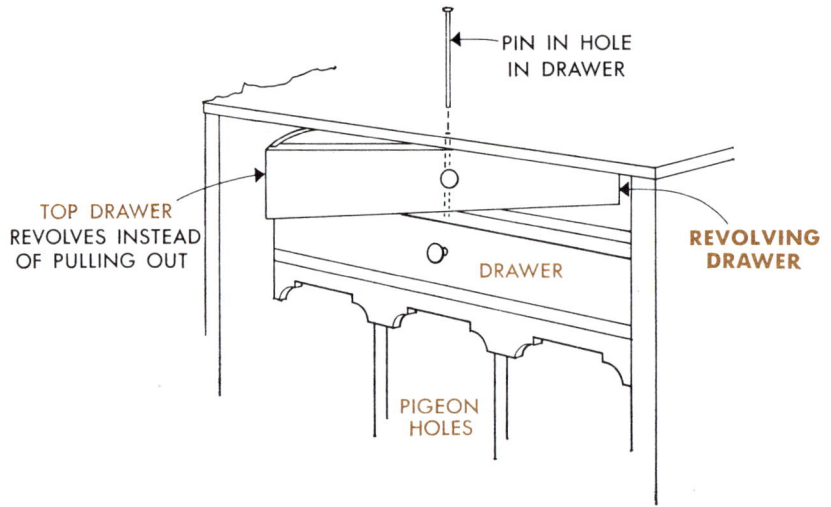

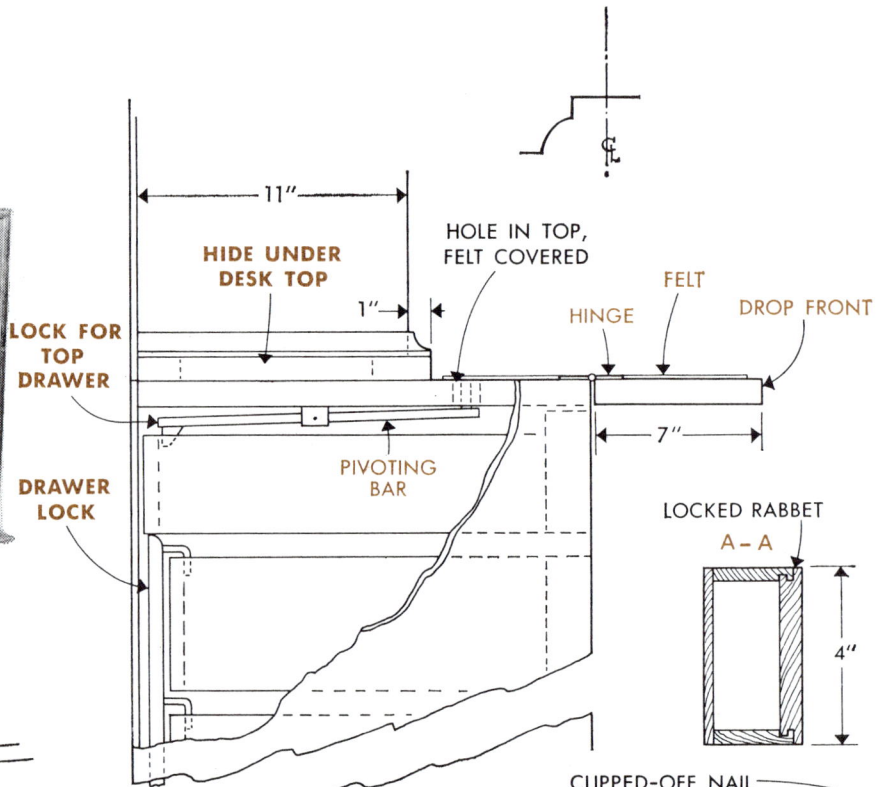

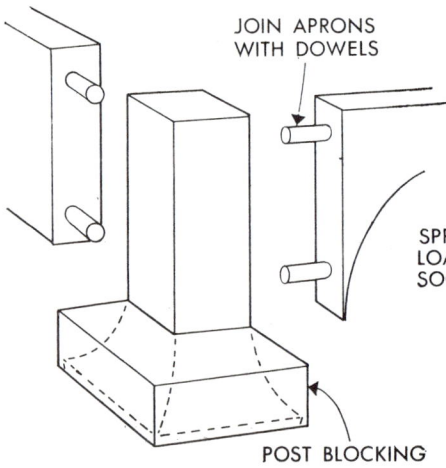

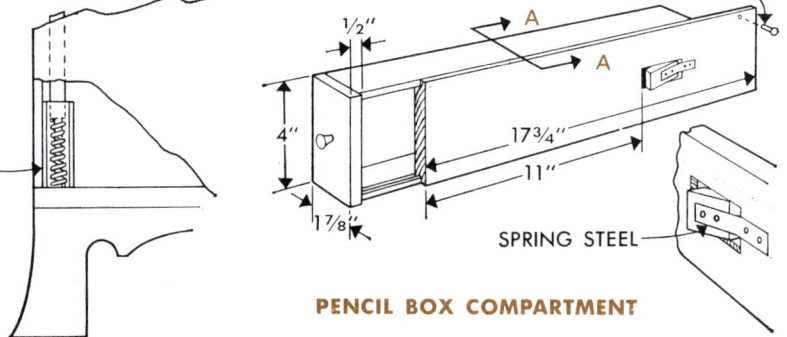

TOP DRAWER
REVOLVES INSTEAD
OF PULLING OUT

PIN IN HOLE
IN DRAWER

DRAWER

**REVOLVING
DRAWER**

PIGEON
HOLES

11"

**HIDE UNDER
DESK TOP**

HOLE IN TOP,
FELT COVERED

1"

HINGE

FELT

DROP FRONT

**LOCK FOR
TOP
DRAWER**

PIVOTING
BAR

7"

**DRAWER
LOCK**

LOCKED RABBET

A – A

4"

JOIN APRONS
WITH DOWELS

SPRING-
LOADED
SOCKET

POST BLOCKING

CLIPPED-OFF NAIL

A

A

1/2"

4"

17¾"

11"

1⅞"

SPRING STEEL

PENCIL BOX COMPARTMENT

of the chest top and glue and screw in place. If you wish, make a hide by cutting the center out of this board, making it a frame.

Construct the drawers to the sizes shown. The top drawer extends to the back of the case, while the lower drawers have to clear the sliding-pin mechanism. Construct the secret drawer-front compartments as shown.

Make the sliding-drawer locking pin, drill a hole down through the top of the case and slide the pin in place down through the drawer dividers. Make a small block, fit it with a spring and glue in place in the bottom of the case to receive the pin.

Build the pin lock and the top-drawer-lock as shown.

Now to build the desk portion. This is not permanently fastened to the chest, but is made to fit down into a "rim" of molding fastened to the chest top.

Make the outer case of the desk top, the inner case, including the pigeon-hole assembly and the routed grooves for the tambour doors. Note that the top drawer of the pigeon-hole assembly pivots instead of pulling out. Make the tambour-door strips of cloverleaf screen molding. Cutting their ends down allows them to slide easily around the curved portion of the track. Glue the pieces to a dark piece of cloth. Slide the tambour doors in place, slide the inside case into the outer case and fit the side pieces in place as shown.

Veneer the chest and desk using contact cement. After the veneer is applied, sand, stain and finish to suit. Cut the felt writing surface to fit and glue it in place using contact cement.

The hardware shown is authentic reproduction hardware.

CHOPPING BLOCK

Inclusion of a chopping block in your kitchen counter not only adds a luxury look to a kitchen, but also provides a highly practical feature: an area where meat and other foods can be cut without damaging existing counter tops.

Ideally the block should be adjacent to the sink and food disposer, so foods can be washed and scraps and trimmings dropped into the sink. It should also be within comfortable distance of the refrigerator to save steps.

In the example shown the chopping block is located directly above the automatic dishwasher and it projects the same distance as the rest of the counters. In your own kitchen you can make the block any width you desire.

You may prefer the backboard to be of the same laminate as the rest of the counter; if you want this back to be the same as the block, make it long enough so you can cut off a section to create the backboard.

The material for the block is hard maple, purchased as 2 x 2-inch roughsawed turning squares. These are available in 24- and 30-inch lengths. Each square first is surfaced to be true, then the pieces are trimmed to 1-5/8 inches, which allows for final sanding. (You want the thickness the same as the counter-top front; two ¾-inch pieces of plywood, plus 1/16-inch laminate, which is 1-9/16 inch.)

Trim all pieces the same length, true and square. Lay the pieces on a flat surface, such as a saw table, and arrange them for the best look. Use a jig to drill holes in the center of each one, and 3 inches from each end. Cut ¼-inch steel rod to length and thread each end.

True up turning squares by running over jointer-planer, shaper or with radial-arm saw set up as a planing shaper.

Make up a simple jig to drill the three holes in each strip, then counterbore the holes in the end blocks for the nuts.

Use a rip fence on the table saw, plus a square to assure that you glue up the chopping block absolutely square.

Use a good waterproof glue and liberally smear two edges of each strip. Place the side that will be the top down.

Use progressively finer grits on a belt sander to do the final smoothing. If you use block for backboard, cut it off now.

Ordinary cooking oil is used as finish. Apply and let soak in, then rub in thoroughly. In future, clean with steel wool.

Now, glue and clamp the pieces to create the block, then slip in the rods and tighten up the nuts on each end. The end blocks are counterbored to permit the nuts to be recessed. Let the waterproof glue set for at least 24 hours, then remove the clamps and scrape off any excess glue. Use a sander with progressively finer grits to smooth the block.

Finish the block by applying liberal coats of any household vegetable oil, adding it until the wood will absorb no more. For future maintenance, scrub with fine steel wool and repeat the oil treatment.

GRAND-FATHER CLOCK

An old-fashioned grandfather clock seems to have a fascination for most people from childhood on. The stately height, the soothing ticking, the sonorous chimes all create a feeling of calm and peace that takes us back to a time when life was much less hectic.

But, when we start pricing these lovely clocks, whether they be a true antique or a good reproduction, we find they can cost as much as a thousand dollars and up. The solution to the dilemma is to build your own. It will take time, and painstaking attention to cabinetwork and fitting, but the task is not really difficult and the finished product is well worth the time and effort.

Clear pine, and single, wide boards, rather than glued-up stock are used for all parts, except for the back which is pine-veneered plywood. If you prefer, however, plywood, either pine or hardwood-faced, can be used for most of the panels. Solid hardwood also can be used.

A shaper was used for a number of operations on the original clock; if you don't have one of these tools in your shop you can substitute stock molding of appropriate shape, gluing and bradding it to the edges of the stock. Half-round and quarter-round molding are readily available for the edges of the top of the base, and the lower part of the hood, while glass-bead molding can be substituted for the shape of the upper edge of the pediment.

Begin the clock by carefully laying out the back (1) on ½-inch plywood. Cut it out, using a circular saw as much as possible, then finishing the cuts with a handsaw. Use the same procedure on the waist sides (2) (figure 1). Now cut the rabbets along the back edges of the

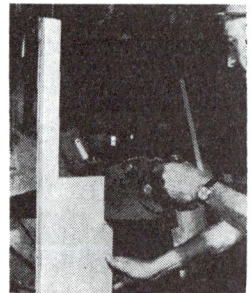

1. Power tools can be used for most cuts, but handsaw needed to finish corners.

2. Rabbets ½"x½" are cut along the back edges of the sides to accept the back.

3. Check the sides for fit against the back, then glue and nail back into the sides with 2d nails.

4. Waist-base spacer blocks are glued and clamped in place, excess glue is wiped away.

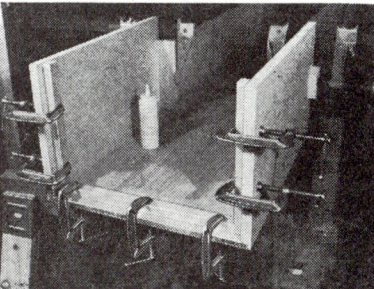

5. Side and rear support rails for floor are fitted, glued and clamped in place. Locate them accurately.

6. Fine-bladed saw is used to cut front base cover, then half-round molding is cut.

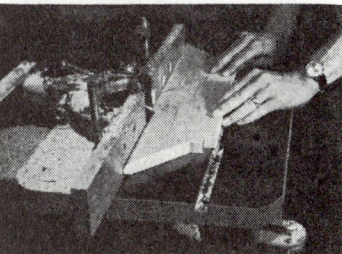

sides (figure 2) remembering the sides should be a pair. Cut away a section of the rabbets at top and bottom to accommodate the projections of the back that go over the base and hood sections. Check the sides for fit against the back, then apply glue liberally and nail the back into the rabbeted sides (figure 3) with 3d nails.

Cut the two waist-base spacer blocks (3) and glue and clamp them in place (figure 4). The base sides (5) come next. Cut the ½ x ½-inch rabbets along the back edges, then glue and clamp them in place, also using 2d finishing nails driven through the back.

The two side floor-support rails (9-A) and the rear rail (9-B) now are cut to size, then glued and clamped in place (figure 5). The front rail is fitted after the front panel is in place.

Use a fine-bladed saw to cut the miters and notches on the front base-cover plate (11) and shape the half-round and lip along the front edge (figure 6). Check for fit, then glue and clamp it in place. Cut, miter and edge the side cover plates (12) in the same way and glue and nail them in place with 4d finishing nails into the top of the base sides (figure 7).

The lower-waist door stop (14) can now be cut and fitted in place. Secure it with two 4d finishing nails through each side. Next comes the lower-waist crosspiece (13), again glued and secured with two nails at each end (figure 8).

To give the case more rigidity, momentarily move to the top of the case and fit the waist-top crosspiece (20), gluing and nailing it in place as you did the lower one. Then fit the door stop (21) beneath it (figure 9) and glue and clamp the two pieces together to assure there will be no gap between them.

Move back to the base and cut nine triangular-shape blocks from scrap, to support the lower-waist molding when it is fitted in place. Glue the blocks where indicated (figure 10) making sure the molding fits over them properly before fitting them permanently.

The base floor (9) now is cut and fitted to butt tightly against the three support rails, then is glued and nailed in position.

Raised-panel cutting is tricky, so take extra care on this step. The board for the panel (6) must be absolutely flat or you will have trouble. Slight bowing, however, can be handled by clamping the panel tightly between a couple of pieces of flat stock while you make the raising cuts. It may help to make a few trial cuts on scrap stock first. The saw blade should have a good set so it won't bind and overheat. There are a number of ways to make raised panels, but the one used for this clock was to make edge cuts on a table saw (figure 11). Marks from the saw teeth then are sanded off with a fine-grit belt (figure 12). Use a dado blade to cut the tongues on the panel edges.

The stiles and rails (7,8) for the panel are cut on the shaper, or made up from rabbeted stock and small quarter-round. Miter the corners carefully, then glue the frame around the panel. A framing clamp with corners was used to hold the assembly and for pulling the frame into square (figure 13).

While the glue is setting on the front-panel assembly, cut the lower-waist molding. Cut and assemble the front section (48) first, trimming until the ends align with the corners. Miters are cut on the sides (49), leaving them slightly long. When the miters fit perfectly, the ex-

MATERIALS LIST

1. Back: ½″x18½″x87″ pine plywood (1)

1″ Clear Pine or ¾″ Plywood (parts 2-35)

2. Waist Sides:	10″x64¾″ (2)
3. Waist—Base Spacers:	1¾″x10″ (2)
4. Waist—Base Spacer, Front:	2″x17¼″ (1)
5. Base Sides:	12½″x23″ (2)
6. Raised Panel:	16¾″x17¼″ (1)
7. Panel Stiles:	1-3/8″x19″ (2)
8. Panel Rails:	1-3/8″x19½″ (2)
9. Base Floor:	12″x17½″ (1)
9A. Side Support Rails, Floor:	1″x12″ (2)
9B. Front, Rear Support Rails, Floor:	1″x16″ (2)
10. Front Backing Strip, Base Bottom:	3½″x19″ (1)
11. Front Cover Plate, Base:	4¾″x20″ (1)
12. Side Cover Plate, Base:	3¼″x14″ (2)
13. Lower—Waist Crosspiece:	3″x14″ (1)
14. Lower—Waist Door Stop:	3½″x12½″ (1)
15. Front Foot:	4″x20½″ (1)
16. Right, Left Foot:	4″x14″ (1 each)
17. Waist—Door Stiles:	2″x38″ (2)
18. Waist—Door Top Rail:	5″x10¾″ (1)
19. Waist—Door Bottom Rail:	3″x10¾″ (1)
20. Waist—Top Crosspiece:	2¼″x14″ (1)
21. Top Door Stop:	2¼″x12½″ (1)
22. Hood Base Plate, Front:	5″x19″ (1)
23. Hood Base Plate, Side:	2½″x13½″ (2)
24. Hood Sides:	11¼″x19″ (2)
25. Hood Top:	12″x17″ (1)
26. Dial—Frame Sides:	3¼″x19″ (1 right, 1 left)
27. Dial—Frame Top:	7″x11¼″ (1)
28. Dial—Frame Bottom:	1½″x11¼″ (1)
29. Arch Spacer Plate, Front:	1¼″x5¼″x17″ (1)
30. Glass Retainer, Top:	5¾″x12″ (1)
31. Glass Retainer, Side:	5/8″x11″ (1 right, 1 left)
32. Glass Retainer, Bottom:	5/8″x12″ (1)
33. Hood Side Door, Sides:	¾″x8½″ (2)
34. Hood Side Door, Top and Bottom:	¾″x7″ (2)
35. Pediment:	11-7/8″x18″ (1)
36. Finial Base Block:	½″x1½″x2¾″ (1)
37. Finial Base, Block Molding:	½″-cove molding x 2¼″
38. Pediment Top Casing:	½″x2″x9¾″ clear pine (2)
39. Pediment Casing Front Trim:	½″-cove molding x 8¼″
39A. Casing Trim, End Pieces:	½″-cove molding x 1¼″
40. Pediment Sides:	¾″x6″x14″ (1 right, 1 left)
41. Pilasters:	split from 6″x6″x15″ single turning, clear pine (2)
42. Works Mounting Plate:	¾″x3½″x13½″ (1)
43. Works Adjusting Shim:	¼″x¾″x2¾″ (2)
44. Chime—Mounting Block:	3-3/8″x6″x6½″ hardwood (1)
45. Finial:	4″x4″x5″ clear pine (1)

7. Side base covers are mitered, carefully fitted in place, glued and nailed into the top of the base sides with 4d nails.

8. Lower-waist cross-piece is glued and secured with two 4d finishing nails in each end. Countersink nails, cover with putty.

9. Door stop is fitted underneath waist-top crosspiece; pieces are clamped together.

10. Nine triangular-shape blocks are cut from scrap stock, glued under the lower-waist molding to provide strength.

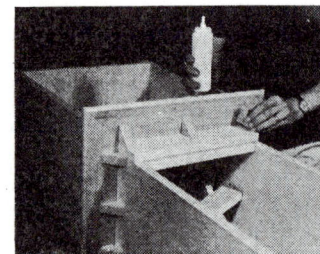

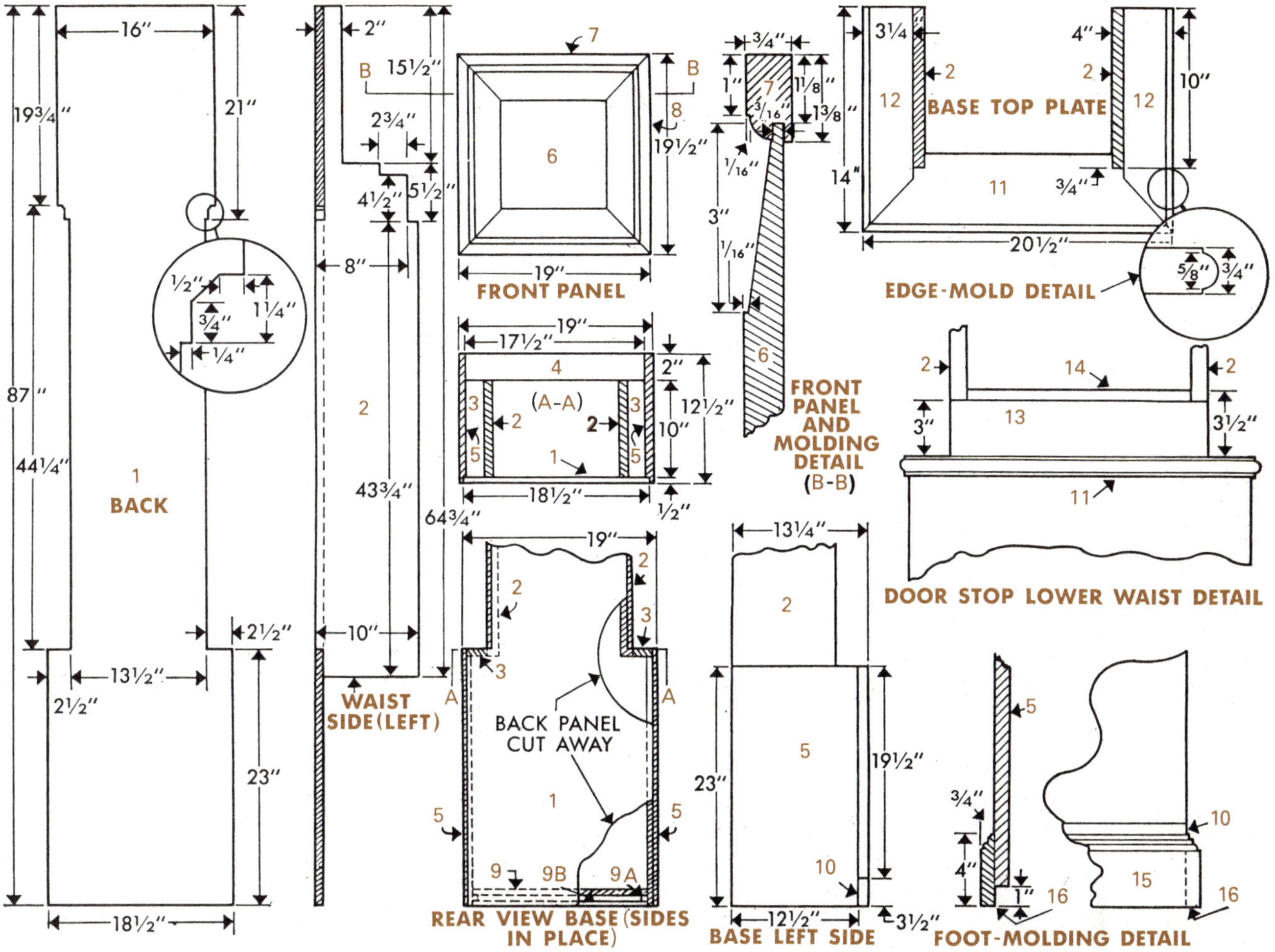

BACK
WAIST SIDE (LEFT)
FRONT PANEL
(A-A)
FRONT PANEL AND MOLDING DETAIL (B-B)
BASE TOP PLATE
EDGE-MOLD DETAIL
DOOR STOP LOWER WAIST DETAIL
BACK PANEL CUT AWAY
REAR VIEW BASE (SIDES IN PLACE)
BASE LEFT SIDE
FOOT-MOLDING DETAIL

Moldings, Waist

46. Upper Front:	¾"x1¾" bed molding (WP74)x16"
47. Upper Sides:	(WP74) 11¾" (2)
48. Lower Front:	¾" x 3¼" crown molding (WP51) x 19"
49. Lower Sides:	(WP51) 13" (2)

Glass, Single Strength

Dial:	11¼"x16" (1)
Waist Door:	10¾"x34-1/8" (1)
Hood Side Door:	5½"x7" (1)

Miscellaneous Hardware

Waist Door Hinges:	1½" brass butt (3)
Waist Door Knob:	1"-diameter brass (1)
Waist Door Latch:	2" brass (1)
Hood Door Hinge:	1" brass butt (2)
Hood Door Knob:	½"-diameter brass (1)
Clockworks (model shown):	U-1 grandfather 8-day movement supplied with black serpentine hands, 43"-pendulum, 6½"-diameter spun-brass bob, brass shells and weight.
Dial (model shown):	D-9 moving moon phase.

11. There are several ways to cut a raised panel; edge-cutting on a table saw is one.

cess on the ends of the sides is cut off. The molding is glued to the backing blocks and a few 2d finishing nails driven along the edges.

The front-panel assembly now is glued and clamped in place (figure 14) and the front backing strip for the base bottom (10) fitted. Cut and miter the front-foot molding (15), edging it on the shaper or by fitting appropriate-size glass-bead molding to its edge. Fit it the same way as the waist molding, then glue and clamp it in place. Remember, the foot projects 1 inch below the bottoms of the sides and the front backing strip. Complete the foot by cutting and fitting the sides (16).

Back to the top of the case. Use a square to mark a guide line on each side for the upper-waist moldings (47). Double-check the alignment by laying the square across the front of the case to see if the two guide lines match up. Now, place a section of the molding along the guide line and, using the back edge of the molding for a guide, mark the outline of the molding on the square corner where the back projects through the waist sides. Carefully cut along the guide line (figure 15). The molding now should be supported by the back of the case. Cut and fit the moldings, again gluing and countersinking the small nails (figure 16).

Since this molding will be subject to shock from time to time as the hood is raised and lowered, cut some support blocks and glue them into the slot formed by the molding and the case (figure 17). The case body now is finished.

Cut the stiles and rails for the waist door to size and shape the glass rabbets before sawing the arch in the top rail (18). Dowel the frame together and glue and clamp it (figure 18). When the glue has set, cut the decorative molding on the inside edge of the frame (figure 19). If you are using softwood, tack some scrap wood in the rabbeted section to give the router-bit pilot more support so it will not burn the relatively thin section.

Check the door for fit, mortise the hinges and install the knob.

The 3-piece hood base plate is made the same as the top plate for the base. Cut the sides (23), edge and miter them. Cut the front section (22) and miter and notch it. Check the assembly for fit against the sides and upper molding. Glue and reinforce the assembly with a pair of long finishing nails through each of the side members.

Cut and edge the sides of the dial frame (26) and the top and bottom (27 and 28). The molded edges now must be cut away for joining the various pieces (figure 20) which will take time and care. Cut the glass rabbets in the back surfaces of the various pieces as indicated, then glue and clamp the assembly. When the glue has set, cut notches in the upper corners to accept the pediment sides (figure 21).

Cut the hood sides (24) and on one of them lay out the opening for the access door. Bore an entry hole and very carefully, with a jig or saber saw and using a fine blade, make the cutout for the door (figure 22). Complete the sides by cutting the wide rabbets ¼ inch deep into which the pediment sides will fit (figure 23). Remember, the access door is in the right side (facing the clock).

Before you begin to assemble the hood, cut the four pieces for the dial-glass retainer (30, 31, 32) and miter and rabbet them to fit, then lay them aside.

12. Marks of saw blade are removed by using fine-grit paper on belt sander. Use fine-grit to assure that no sanding scratches will show on finish.

13. Handy tool for forcing stiles and rails around raised panel, also squaring up assembly, is framing clamp with corners.

14. Front-panel assembly is fitted, glued and clamped in place on the front of the clock-case base.

15. Outline of molding is marked on projections of back on each side; it is cut with jig saw.

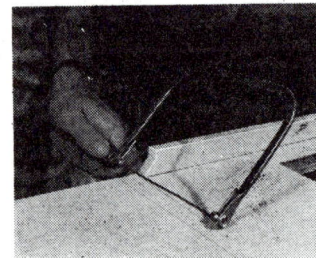

16. Molding then is fitted and mitered, glued and attached with small nails countersunk.

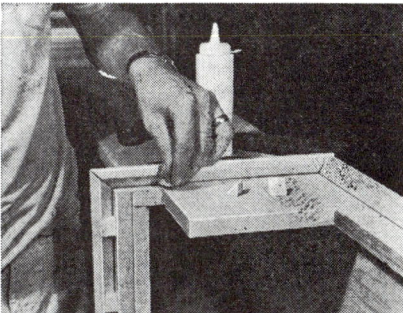

17. Because projecting molding may be subject to shock from removal and replacement of hood, use support blocks.

18. Stiles, rails of waist door are rabbeted for glass before cutting curve, doweling together.

19. Router is used to form molding on inner edge of assembled frame of waist door; use care.

It is critical that the clock hood be square at all points, so it's a good idea to assemble it on a surface you are sure is flat; a saw table is excellent. Glue and clamp the dial-frame assembly to the sides, checking to keep them square. When the glue has set, turn the hood assembly upside down and glue and nail on the base-plate assembly (figure 24). Turn it over again and fit the hood top (25).

Assemble the frame for the glass access door (33, 34), making it slightly oversize. Trim it to fit, then mortise the hinges and drill the hole for the knob. Hinges are on the rear edge of the door. Thin stock can be glued inside the cutout for the door to provide a stop.

The front pediment (35) comes next, and the Materials List calls for a board larger than necessary, to permit laying out the design. Trim the part to size, miter the ends and use a fine blade in a jig saw for the curved cuts. Be especially careful when cutting the arch for the dial. If it is a little crooked it will be almost impossible to true it up by sanding.

Cut the front arch-spacer (29) to size, then use the pediment as a pattern to mark the arch (figure 25). Use a shaper (figure 26) or a router to cut the molding along the arch and bottom edges. The dial arch and the two cutouts at the top of the pediment now are sanded smooth with a small drum sander set absolutely vertical to the work.

Cut and edge the pediment sides (40) next, again cutting them a bit long. Get the miters to fit exactly, then trim off the back edges of the pieces to fit. Glue and clamp the three pieces of the pediment to the hood (figure 27). The pediment top casings (38) have both ends and the front edge shaped. As an alternative, use door stop or casing, and rip to the required width. Shape the molding ends with a jig saw and file. Position the casings and nail and glue them in place (figure 28).

Colonial door stop is available in 1-7/8-inch widths and can be used by cutting the casing-trim end pieces (39-A) 1/8 inch shorter.

The two pieces of pediment-casing front trim (39) now may be cut, the ends mitered and the pieces carefully glued in place. Again, precision counts. The quality of these miter joints can make or break the appearance of the clock. Finish off the pediment casings by cutting and fitting the four trim end pieces (39-A).

Cut the finial base block (36), drill the 3/8-inch hole for the finial and mount the block on the center flat of the pediment with the back of the block flush with the back of the flat.

Cut the short length of cove molding for the base block (37) and use a jig saw to cut the ends to match the profile of the molding. Glue it in place under the base block.

The easiest way to make the two pilasters (41) is to make your turning square from two pieces of 3 x 6-inch stock glued together. Thoroughly paint the two surfaces with glue, then sandwich a piece of glossy paper (like a slick magazine cover) between them when you clamp them to dry. Locate your turning center at the joint, and when you are finished with the turning (figure 29) it can easily be split with a chisel or sharp knife. If you don't have access to a lathe, a little scrounging around the local junk shop or lumberyard should produce a stock turning, such as a chair leg or stair rung, that can be sawed lengthwise and substituted. The same holds true for the finial. If you don't have the equipment to make your own, you should be able to

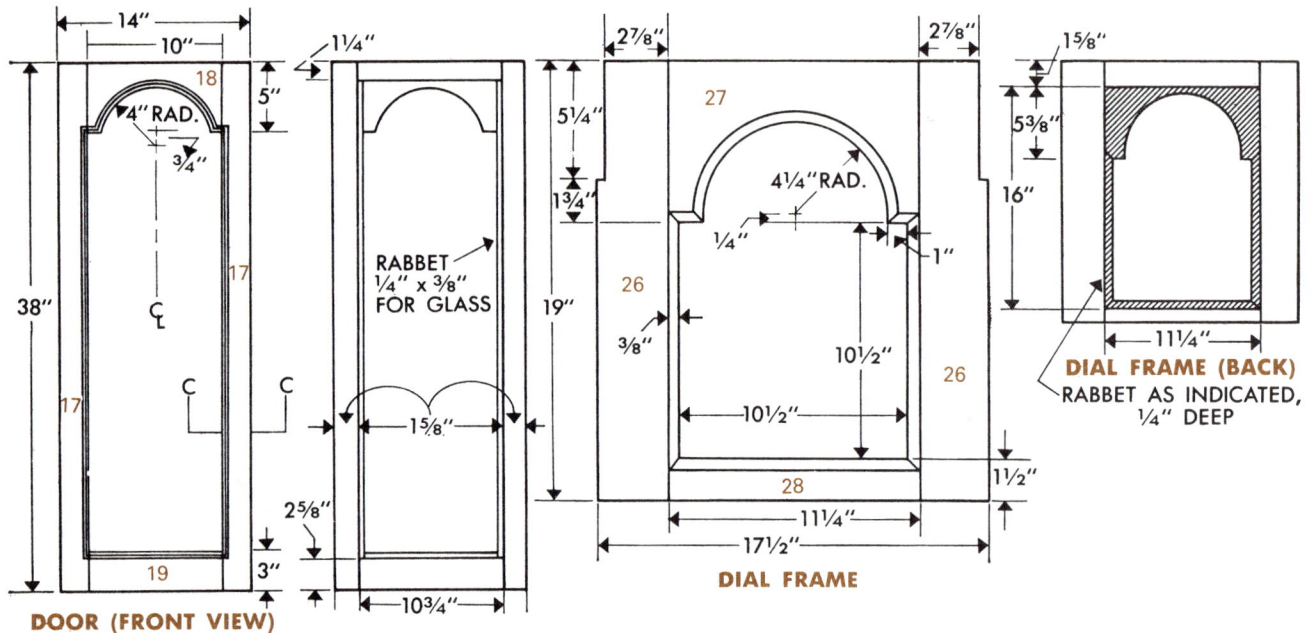

DOOR (FRONT VIEW)

DOOR (REAR VIEW)

RABBET ¼" x ⅜" FOR GLASS

DIAL FRAME

DIAL FRAME (BACK)
RABBET AS INDICATED, ¼" DEEP

4¼" RAD.

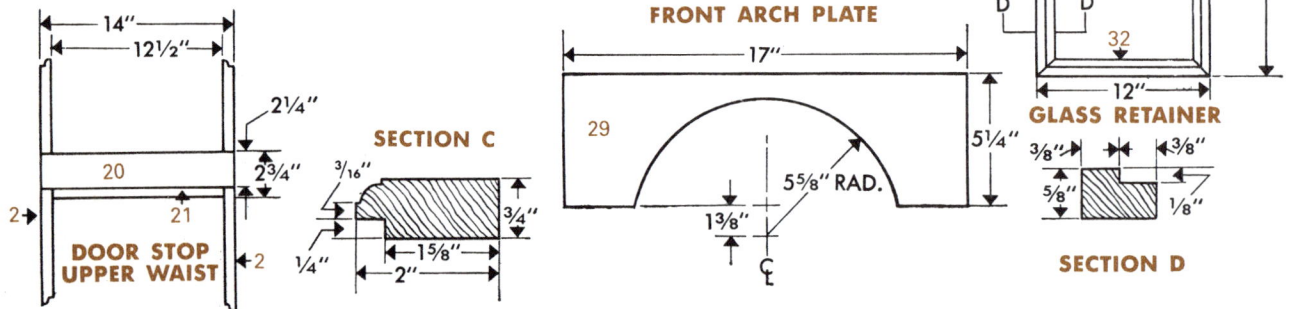

DOOR STOP UPPER WAIST

SECTION C

FRONT ARCH PLATE

5⅝" RAD.

GLASS RETAINER

SECTION D

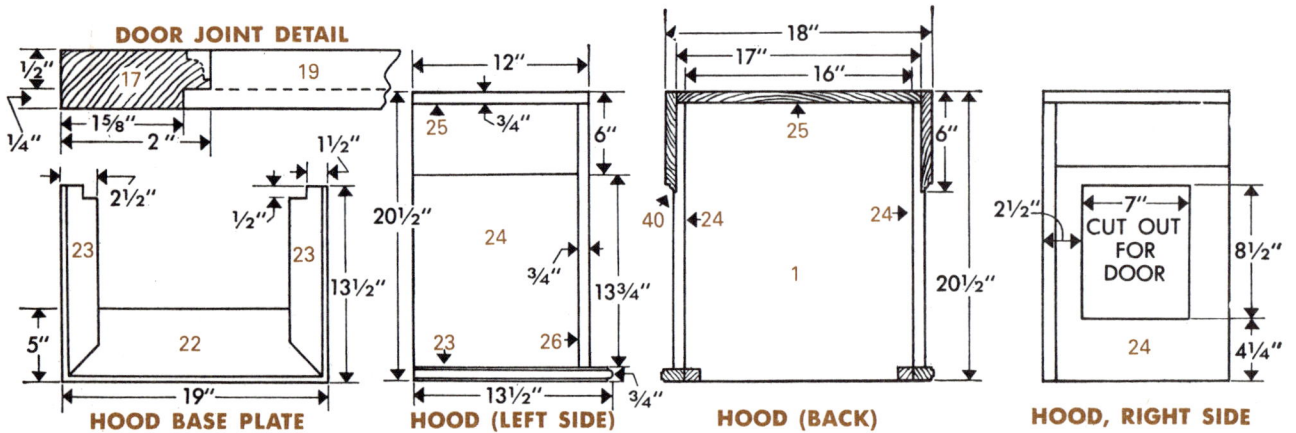

DOOR JOINT DETAIL

HOOD BASE PLATE

HOOD (LEFT SIDE)

HOOD (BACK)

HOOD, RIGHT SIDE

CUT OUT FOR DOOR

FINIAL BASE BLOCK, TOP VIEW

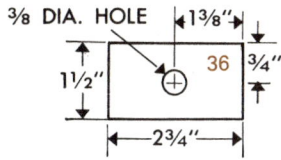

3/8 DIA. HOLE 1 3/8"
1 1/2"
36 3/4"
2 3/4"

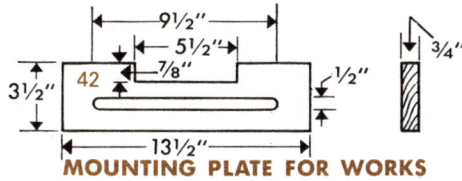

9 1/2"
5 1/2"
7/8"
3 1/2" 42 1/2"
13 1/2" 3/4"

MOUNTING PLATE FOR WORKS

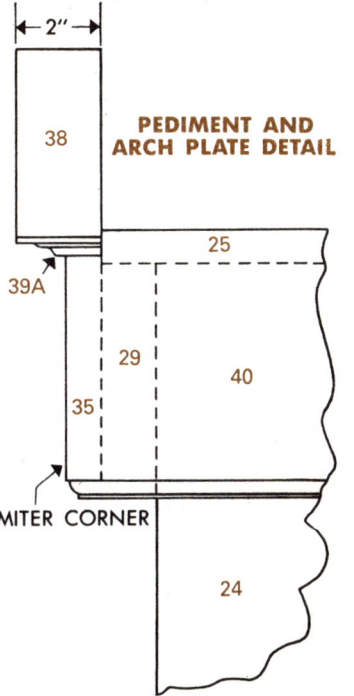

PEDIMENT AND ARCH PLATE DETAIL

2"
38
25
39A
29 40
35
MITER CORNER
24

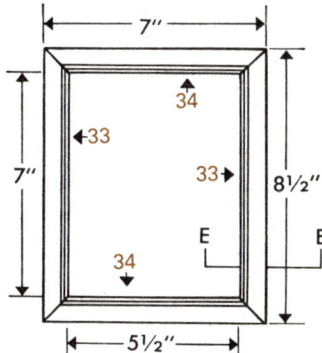

7"
34
33
7" 33 8 1/2"
E E
34
5 1/2"

HOOD SIDE DOOR

MOUNTING BLOCK AND SHIM INSTALLATION DETAIL

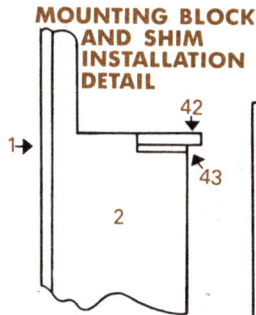

42
1
43
2

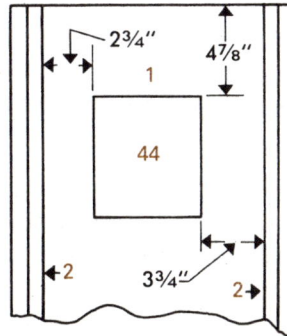

2 3/4"
1 4 7/8"
44
2 3 3/4" 2

CHIME BLOCK LOCATION

SECTION E

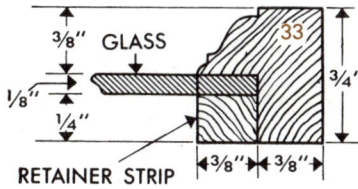

3/8" GLASS
33
1/8" 3/4"
1/4"
RETAINER STRIP
3/8" 3/8"

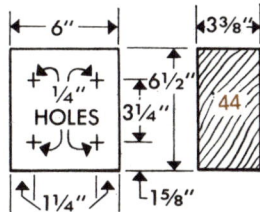

6"
3 3/8"
1/4"
6 1/2"
HOLES 3 1/4" 44
1 1/4" 1 5/8"

CHIME MOUNTING BLOCK

FINIAL

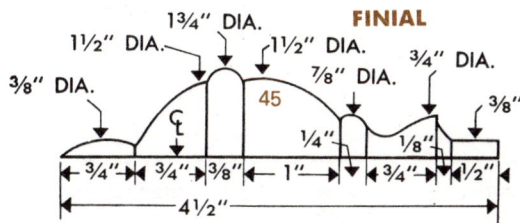

1 3/4" DIA.
1 1/2" DIA. 1 1/2" DIA.
7/8" DIA. 3/4" DIA.
3/8" DIA.
45 3/8"
1/4" 1/8"
3/4" 3/4" 3/8" 1" 3/4" 1/2"
4 1/2"

PEDIMENT AND TRIM DETAIL

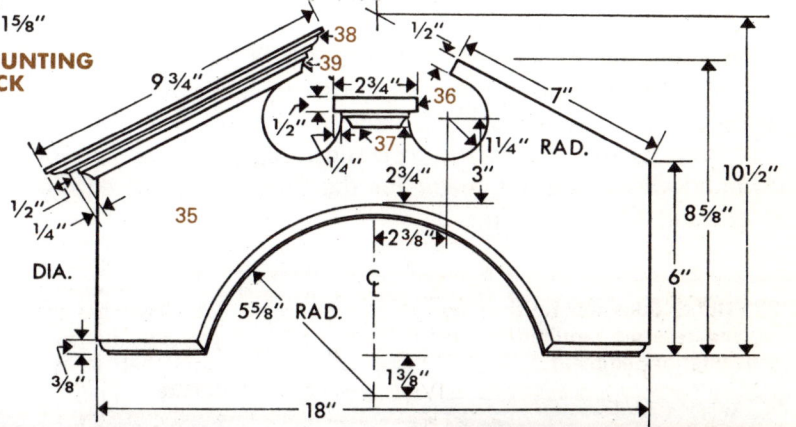

38
39 1/2"
9 3/4" 2 3/4" 36
1/2" 7"
1/2" 37
1/4" 1 1/4" RAD.
1/2" 2 3/4" 3
1/4" 2 3/4" 10 1/2"
DIA. 35 2 3/8" 8 5/8"
5 5/8" RAD. 6"
3/8" 1 3/8"
18"

PILASTER

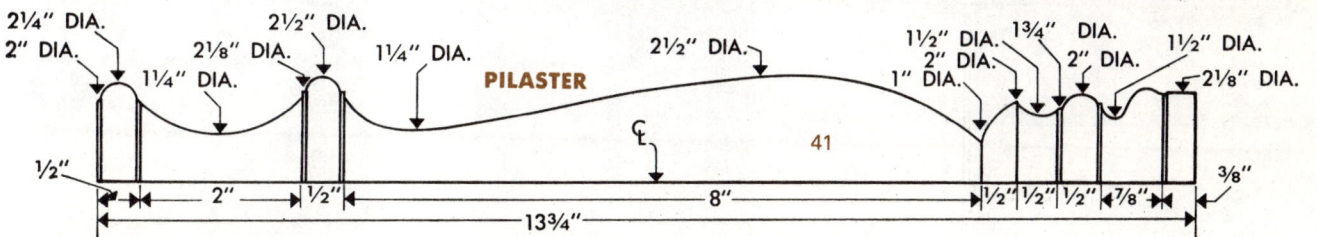

2 1/4" DIA.
2" DIA. 2 1/2" DIA.
2 1/8" DIA. 1 1/4" DIA. 2 1/2" DIA. 1 1/2" DIA. 1 3/4" DIA.
1 1/4" DIA. 2" DIA. 2" DIA. 1 1/2" DIA.
1" DIA. 2 1/8" DIA.
41
1/2" 3/8"
2" 1/2" 8" 1/2" 1/2" 1/2" 7/8"
13 3/4"

find one at the local lumberyard or they may be obtained from the same sources that sell clock works.

If you do your own turnings, especially in pine, don't be miserly with the sandpaper. Really give the work a good going over, particularly with the very fine finishing grits. It's surprising how sanding marks suddenly appear with the first coat of stain.

Now it's time to go over the entire clock case and do your finish sanding. Work on all surfaces with progressively finer grits of sandpaper until they are glass smooth. Give special attention to the large moldings at the top and bottom of the waist. They may look smooth, but often a little sanding will reveal small ripples left from the shaper or router bits. Sand the molding until these ripples are gone. Now also is the time to make sure all nail heads are recessed and the holes filled with wood putty. The best method of applying the putty is with a small palette knife of the type used by artists in oil painting. They are available from shops that carry oil-painting supplies.

Now is the time to fit the hood to the body of your clock. If you have done everything right, it will slip into place easily, and the hood sides will fit snugly against the sides of the back. The hood top should butt tightly against the top of the back and the hood plate should fit up against the upper waist molding with no gapping. Line up everything, then join the two parts with a brass piano hinge, locating the hinge between the hood and the case back. Put in just a few screws, then swing the hood up to make sure it clears all parts and does not bind.

If the hood is all right, then remove it again for a moment. Cut the mounting plate for the clock works (42) and the two adjusting shims (43). Drill the holes through the ends of the plate and the shims, then mount the plate in its notches, with the shims underneath, with the 3-inch brass screws and finishing washers.

Depending on the works you choose for your clock, the mounting plate may be a different size, and require a different location. Chimes will require a block, and instructions for the chimes and works will explain the required dimensions of blocks and the spacing between works and chimes.

Because of these factors, it is suggested you have the clock works on hand when you get ready for the final fitting of required plates, blocks and adjusting shims.

20. Parts for the dial frame are cut to size, inner edges molded, then notched for assembly.

21. Assembled dial frame next has upper corners notched as indicated to accept pediment.

22. Be careful in making cutout for access door in one hood side. Use very fine saw blade.

23. Hood sides are finished by cutting recesses required to accept sides of pediment.

24. Assemble the hood on perfectly flat surface to assure that it is true and square.

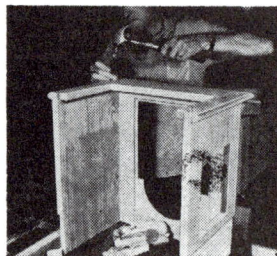

25. Spacer plate for front arch is cut to size, then cutout is marked, using pediment as pattern.

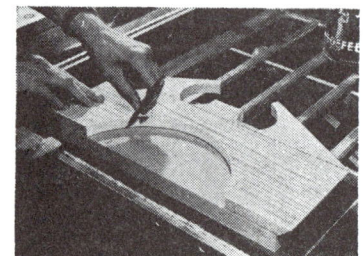

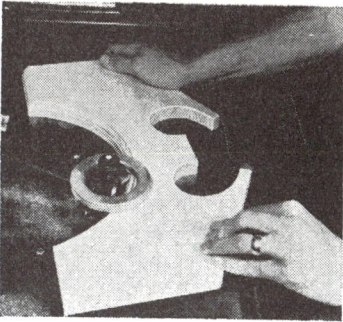

Finishing the clock is up to the builder. Some makers want a modern, light finish, while others will stick with the traditional darker "colonial" colors. In all cases, be sure your sanding is complete, and polish the wood between coats of varnish or clear lacquer so the final product is a lustrous, but soft, "hand-rubbed" finish.

26. Arch and lower edge of pediment are shaped on shaper or with portable router.

27. Miters between front and sides of pediment are fitted tight, then three pieces are glued on.

28. Casings for top edge of pediment are glued and nailed in place. Back surfaces are flush.

29. Two pilasters are turned from glued-up, split stock that is separated after turning is made.

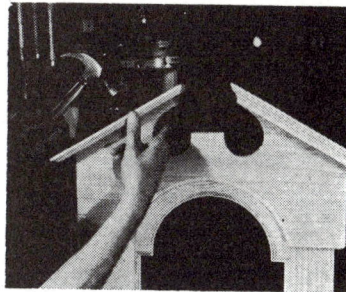

TURNED COMPOTE

While the dictionary defines "compote" as a dish with a stem for holding fruit, you can also include cookies, candies, nuts and snacks. For the lathe craftsman it's a fine project.

Cut five rings and a disk from ½-inch hardwood, alternating the colors as shown. Glue up this assembly, clamping it well. Turn a disk for your faceplate, then hold the assembly to the disk with a No. 14 x 1½-inch screw. Run the lathe at slow speed when roughing to shape.

The base of the stem is turned on the faceplate also, while the stem is a between-centers job. Enlarge the hole in the bowl to accept the tenon on the end of the stem and glue it in place. When turning the stem, size it for a snug fit in the base. You can stain and finish the various pieces while they still are in the lathe.

This compote also can be used to hold potted plants, and in some areas there is a demand for this type turning in florists, garden supply and novelty shops. It could be a source for a few extra dollars. You could make it in several sizes, both larger and smaller.

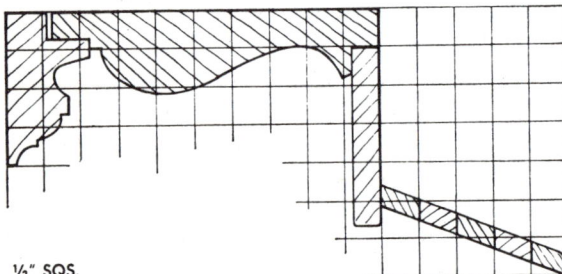

Bowl is turned from glued-up assembly of five rings and a disk of ½" hardwood stock. It is held on disk.

Base of stem also is faceplate turning, but it can be held with screws through faceplate, as it is thick enough.

SIDE VIEW

½" SQS.

SWINGING CRADLE

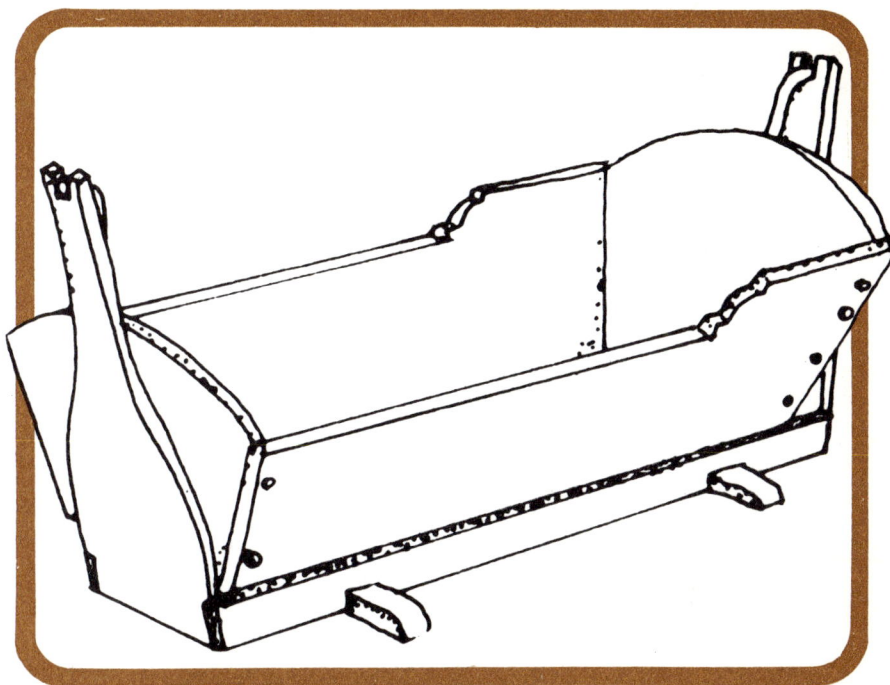

Copied from an antique on which the head, foot and bottom of the cradle were of 1-1/8-inch stock and the stand of 7/8-inch material, this reproduction uses 1-inch stock throughout (¾ inch net). If you wish to use the heavier lumber, have a lumberyard plane 1¼-inch stock to the proper thickness (which will cost more).

The design of this cradle is such that the bed portion is easily removed from the stand, should it be carried to another room, or if it is to be used in an automobile.

Start construction by making patterns from the squared drawings for the uprights of the stand, and the raised portion of the sides. These can be changed slightly in profile to suit your particular taste, but those shown are copied from the original antique.

The metal hangers are 3/8-inch steel rod, one end bent at right angles, while the other end is hammered flat and three holes are drilled to accommodate No. 12 wood screws.

The cradle headboard is glued-up from two pieces, but all other parts of the cradle can be cut from 1 x 12 stock. Duplicating the original, pine or fir is the stock used. Note that the measurements for the head, foot and sides of the cradle are for the outside surfaces AFTER the 15-degree bevel has been cut along the bottom edges. A ¼ x ¾-inch rabbet is cut along the ends of the sides to accept the head and foot in the cradle. Use glue and no. 6 x 1-inch screws to attach the sides and ends. Counterbore for all screws and fill the recesses with wooden plugs. This will make the cradle appear assembled with pegs.

The stand for the cradle consists of the uprights, two stretchers and two "feet." The stretchers are notched to accept the feet. A bevel of 8 degrees is cut along the lower edge of each of the uprights. Note that a ½ x 4-inch notch is cut on the lower end of each edge of the uprights to accept the ½-inch thickness of the stretchers, resulting from cutting a ¼ x ¾-inch rabbet in the ends of the stretchers.

Measure down 1 inch from the top of each standard on the center line and drill a 3/8-inch hole. Saw down from the top to make the slot in which the metal brackets hang.

Set the cradle portion on the floor and attach the brackets so their tops are 19 inches above the floor; this will assure the cradle will hang level (assuming the notches are equal in length). To assure that the notches are identical, cut both uprights at the same time, clamping or tacknailing the pieces of stock together. Also make the angles at the tops of the brackets equal.

The cradle shown was stained and given an oil finish. You may finish your cradle to suit your own taste, but keep in mind that any finish must be nontoxic to a child.

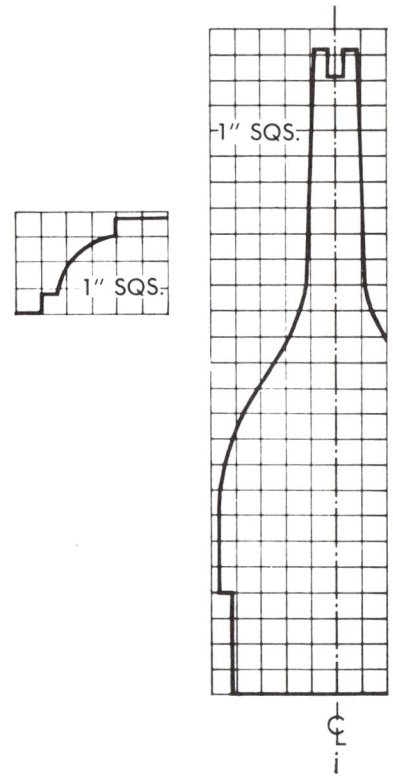

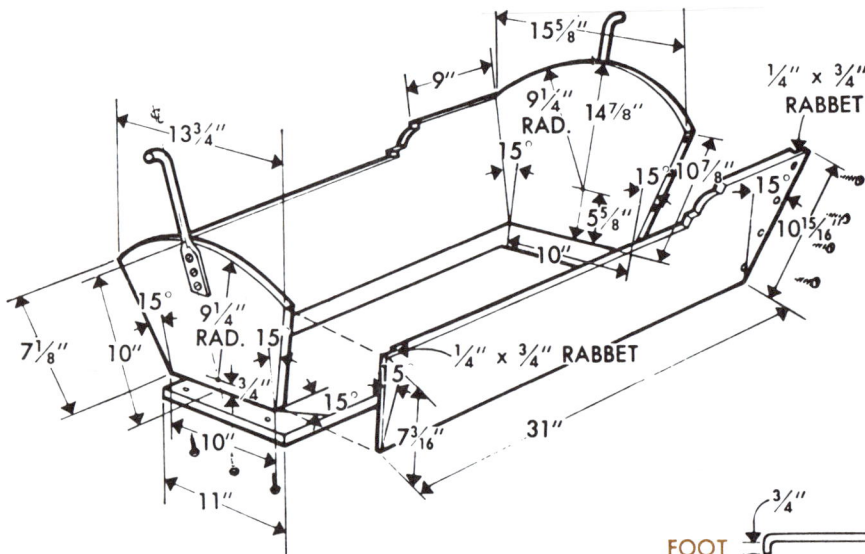

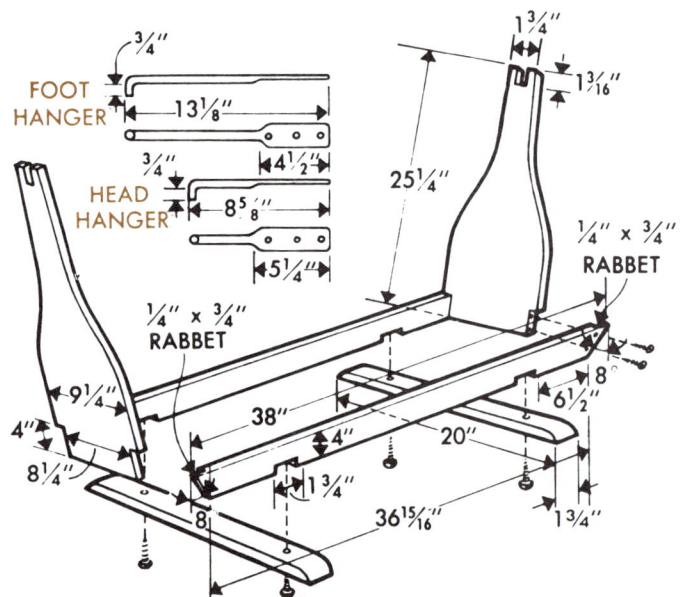

CROQUET SET

All you need is a flat patch of lawn, a lathe and a few spare evenings and you, too, can have happy neighbors whacking croquet balls all over your yard. The game has been played for centuries, was once a favorite of royalty and can be played by anyone.

Make the balls first; make a template from heavy cardboard to make sure you turn true spheres. (It is considered bad form to handicap an opponent with an egg-shape ball.) The six balls are cut from hard-maple turning squares. If you wish, cut slight grooves to set off, and make it easier to paint, the identity stripes on the balls. Turn the spheres as far down as possible, break off the scrap and stubs, then sand the ends smooth.

The mallet heads come next. Turn them from 3 x 3 inch turning squares 10 inches long. Taper the ends, and again, if you wish, cut slight grooves for the painted rings. Mallet handles can be made from 1-inch dowels, or you can turn them from scratch, adding the paint rings. Fit handles to mallets, holding them with waterproof glue.

The wickets (nine are required) are made from heavy-gauge wire, and can be formed uniformly and easily by bending them around a simple wooden jig.

Remember, each ball and mailing mallet should be coded with color stripes (green, red, blue, yellow, black and orange). These colors are easy to obtain in outdoor enamel in the small quantities required.

Last items to be made are the end stakes, and they too can be made from 1-inch dowels or turned from squares. Grooves can be cut in them to separate the paint stripes. These end stakes have a stripe of each of the colors used on the mallets and balls.

MATERIALS LIST

Balls:	4"x4"x6" maple turning squares (6)
Mallet Heads:	3"x3"x10" maple turning squares (6)
Handles:	1"x24½" dowels (6)
End Stakes:	1"x16" dowels (2)

Stand

Base:	¾"x5"x20" softwood (1)
Feet:	¾"x1"x7" softwood (2)
Uprights:	1"x22¼" dowels (4)
Top:	¾"x5"x18½" softwood (1)

Miscellaneous

Nylon Rope
Wire for Wickets
Paint

Now for the stand, the all-important keeper of the equipment when it's not in use. The 5 x 20½-inch base is cut from 1-inch pine or other softwood. Bore the four 1-inch holes for the uprights (dowels), then cut the slots for the mallet handles. If you have a bit large enough, the job will be easier and neater if you bore the 1¼-inch-diameter ends of the slots first, then cut out the centers with a saber saw. Cut the two feet for the base, sand them smooth and glue and nail them in place.

Cut the 5 x 18½-inch top from 1-inch softwood and round the corners to a 1-inch radius. Locate and bore the 1-inch holes for the uprights, making them only ½-inch deep. Cut the 3¾-inch holes for the balls, then make the slots for the mallet handles in the same way as in the base.

Bore the four holes for the ropes, then assemble the base, uprights and top. Use waterproof glue and pin the uprights in the top and base with small finishing nails through the sides.

Sand all surfaces of the stand, then give it a couple of coats of paint. The green used for the balls now can be finished with two coats of varnish and the stripes painted on them. Finish the end stakes.

When all the finish has dried, thread a short length of nylon rope or cord (clothesline will do) through each of the rope holes on one side. Secure them with a small knot on the underside of the top. Place the mallets in their slots, then lay the end stakes diagonally across them. Loop the two pieces of rope over the stakes and thread the ends through the two remaining holes. Pull the ropes snug, but not so tight the stakes cannot slide in and out, then secure the ropes with two more knots and cut off the excess rope. The end stakes thus positioned hold the mallets and balls securely in the rack, and also create a carrying handle. Wickets are stored over the top, between the two groups of mallets.

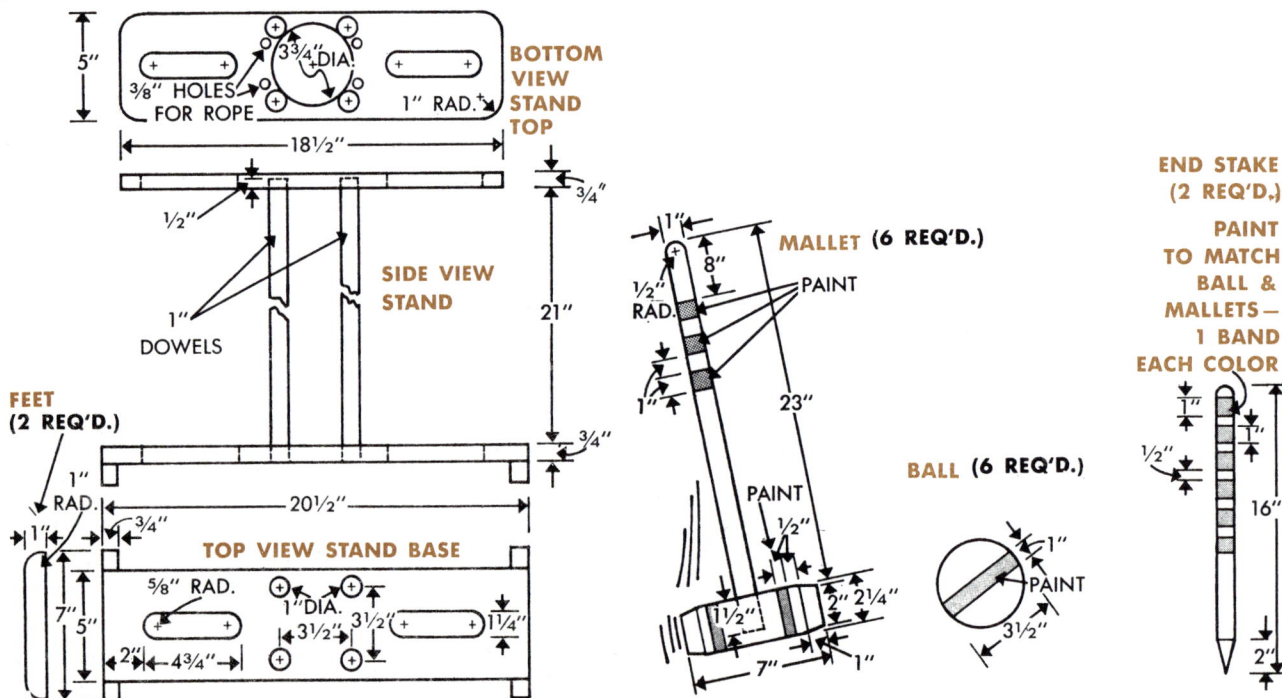

DISH CUPBOARD

Patterned after the old-time cupboards that, in some cases, reached from floor to ceiling, this piece of furniture provides both storage and display for anything from fine china to knickknacks. Simply changing the hardware, and adding grilles to the glass doors will change the styling to Mediterranean.

Edge-joined pine planks were used for the original, dowels inserted to reinforce the joints, but veneered plywood would simplify construction and make it stronger.

Start construction by cutting the L-shaped sides, remembering to make a pair, one righthand and one lefthand, if your plywood is good one-side. If you are using planks you need not be so careful, but do watch for the best grain to be on the outside.

Cut the dadoes for the shelves and the center horizontal divider that extends to the front to form a small ledge.

Check your own requirements at this point to determine if you need to cut more or fewer dadoes to accommodate the number of shelves to fit your own needs. Note that the dado for the "ledge" is positioned so the shelf sets on the projections of the sides. Also make the rabbets on the inner edges of the backs of the sides in which the ¼-inch hardboard of plywood panel will fit.

Three pieces of 1-inch stock (¾ inch net) are laminated to create the top and the base for the cupboard. A router or shaper is used to cut the decorative beading on these members and on the strip of stock fitted to the lower edge of the drawer front. A single bead is shaped along the front edge of the stock used for the upper-door frames. If plywood is used for the lower doors, cut grooves to simu-

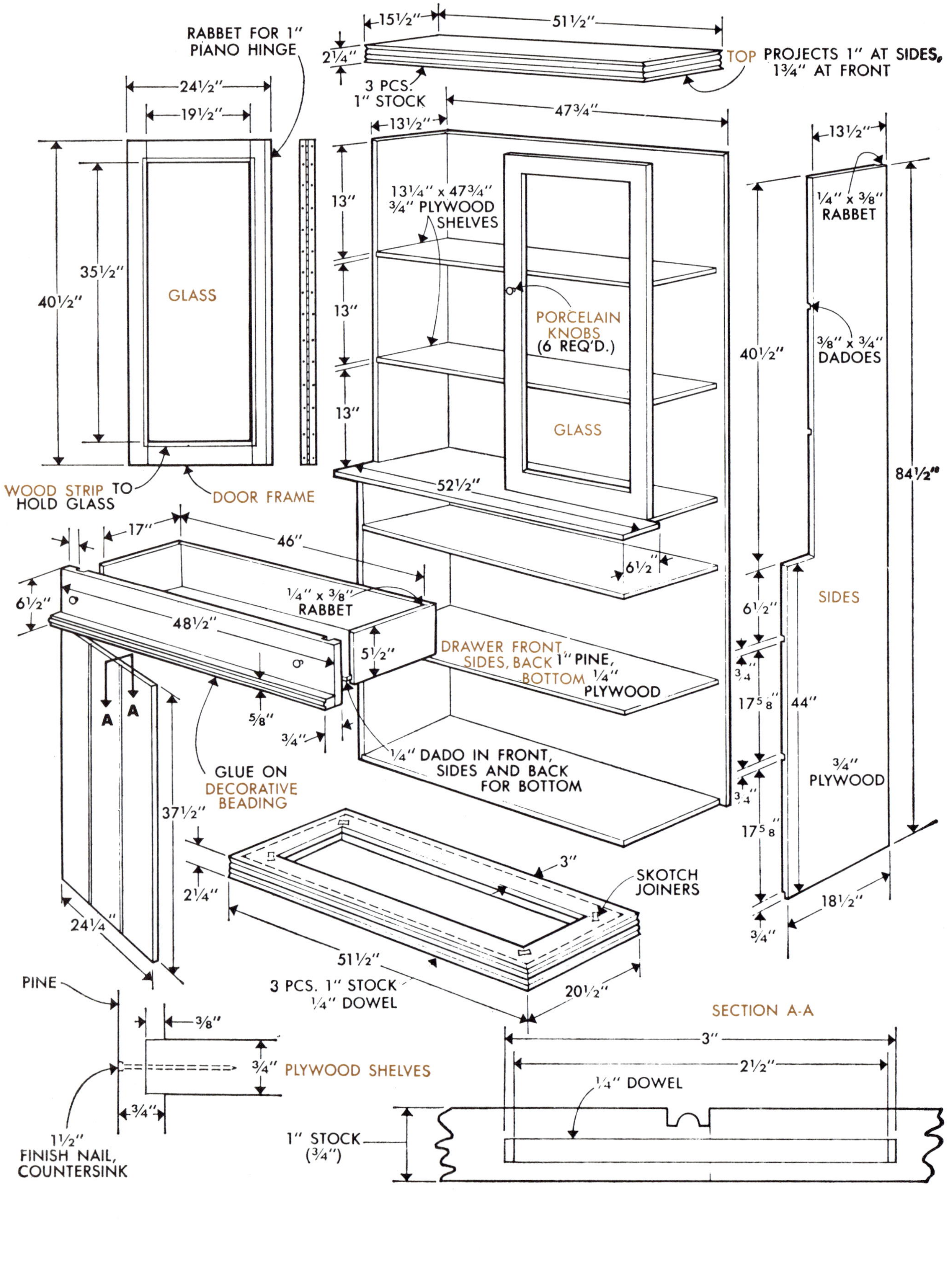
RABBET FOR 1" PIANO HINGE
24½"
19½"
40½"
35½"
GLASS
WOOD STRIP TO HOLD GLASS
DOOR FRAME
15½"
51½"
2¼"
3 PCS. 1" STOCK
TOP PROJECTS 1" AT SIDES, 1¾" AT FRONT
47¾"
13½"
13"
13"
13"
13¼" x 47¾" ¾" PLYWOOD SHELVES
PORCELAIN KNOBS (6 REQ'D.)
GLASS
52½"
6½"
40½"
13½"
¼" x ⅜" RABBET
⅜" x ¾" DADOES
84½"
SIDES
6½"
¾
17⅝"
44"
¾
17⅝"
¾" PLYWOOD
18½"
¾"
17"
46"
6½"
¼" x ⅜" RABBET
48½"
5½"
DRAWER FRONT, SIDES, BACK 1" PINE, BOTTOM ¼" PLYWOOD
A A
⅝"
¾"
¼" DADO IN FRONT, SIDES AND BACK FOR BOTTOM
GLUE ON DECORATIVE BEADING
37½"
2¼"
3"
SKOTCH JOINERS
24¼"
51½"
20½"
3 PCS. 1" STOCK ¼" DOWEL
PINE
⅜"
¾" PLYWOOD SHELVES
¾"
1½" FINISH NAIL, COUNTERSINK
SECTION A-A
3"
2½"
¼" DOWEL
1" STOCK (¾")

Molding head in table saw was used to cut decorative edge on base and top of original cabinet.

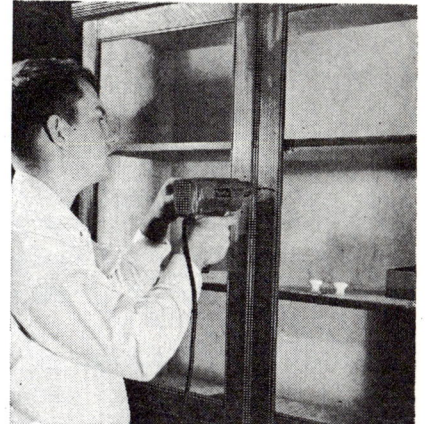

Holes for porcelain "early American" knobs are drilled to suit size of screws, just above center of cupboard doors.

late planking.

Check your dimensions after the cupboard is assembled, then make the drawer to fit the opening in your particular cabinet. If you have built many projects you will know that variations can occur, and drawers should be fitted individually. For the finish choose your favorite stains; or match the decor of the room in which the cupboard will be used.

CHILD'S DESK

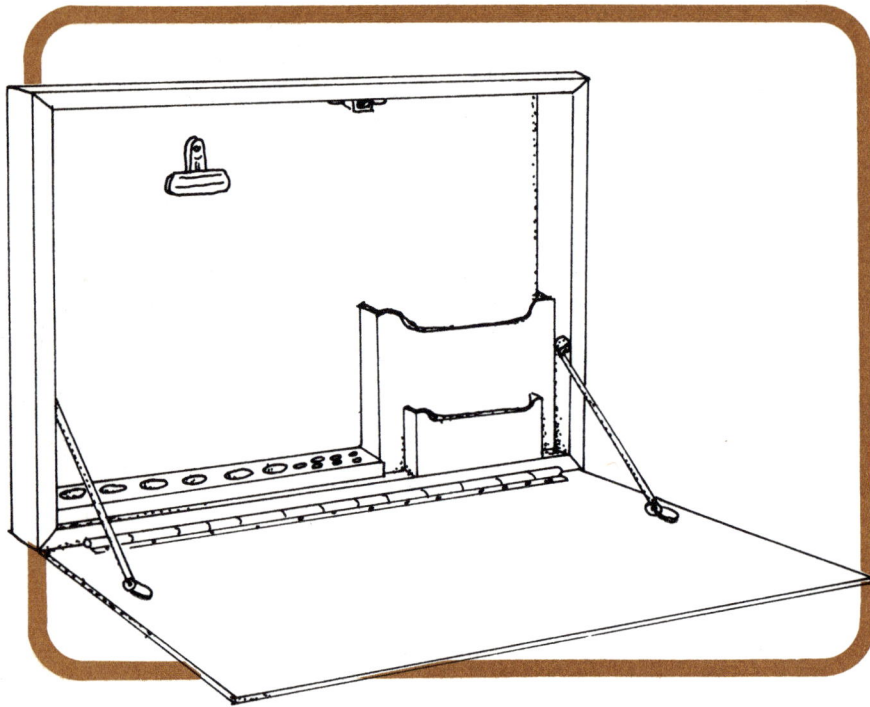

This attractive wall-hung desk doubles as a blackboard when the writing surface is held up by the magnet catch, the outside surface being coated with blackboard paint.

Construction is simple, the corners of the case being joined by rabbet joints, with rabbets on the inside back edges of the sides, top and bottom to accept the hardboard back. Glue and screws are used at the joints. The crayon rack and book holder are glued and bradded together of ¼-inch hardboard and 1-inch stock (¾-inch net) as indicated. The piano (continuous) hinge is attached with "Pop" rivets, as screws will not hold in the hardboard. The shelf supports also are attached with rivets, being left slightly loose so the supports will pivot. The paint holder is simply a block of wood drilled for paint jars and brushes.

The face of the writing surface (when the desk is closed) can be framed or sections of alphabet blocks can be glued around the edge to create a frame, which also hides the projecting rivets.

The spring-type paper clip is riveted to the back, a washer used under the rivet head.

MATERIALS LIST

Cabinet
Back:	¼"-hardboard x 17¼" x 26½" (1)
Sides:	¾"x3-3/8"x17¾" (2)
Top, Bottom:	¾"x3-3/8"x27½" (1)
Front:	¼"-hardboard x 18¼" x 27½" (1)

Crayon Rack
Front:	¼-hardboard x 3" x 7¼" (1)
Sides:	½"x¾"x3" (2)
Bottom:	½"x¾"x7¼" (1)

Book Rack
Front:	¼"-hardboard x 7" x 9¾" (1)
Sides:	¾"x1½"x7" (2)
Paint Holder:	¾"x2¼"x16" (1)

Miscellaneous
Lid Supports:	6" (2)
Piano Hinge:	1½"x24" (1)
Magnetic Latch:	(1)
Clamp-Type Paper Clip:	(1)
"Pop" Rivets:	for ¼"-material (15)
Glue	
Chalkboard Paint	

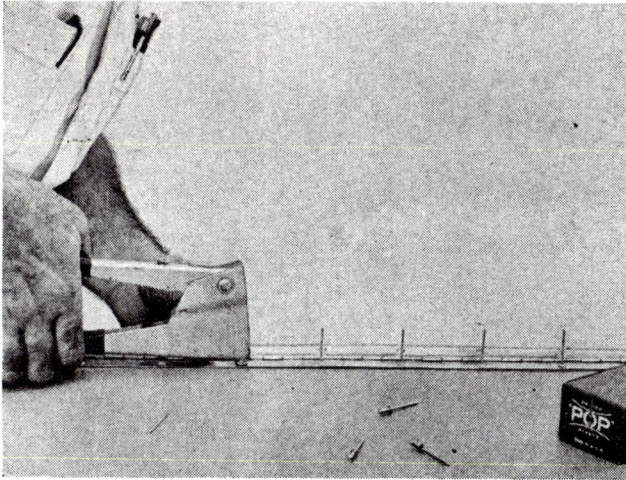

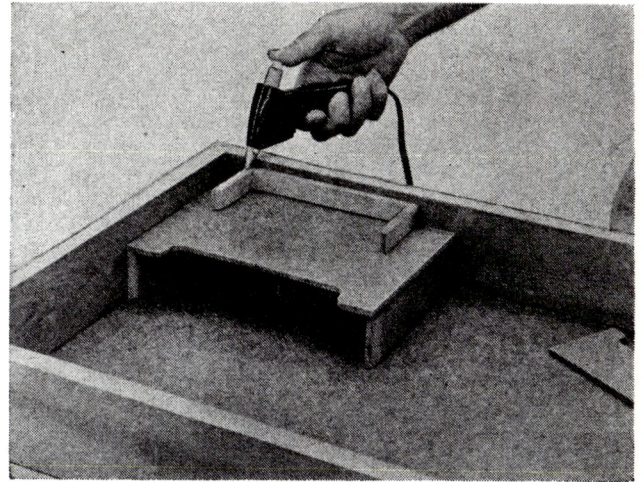

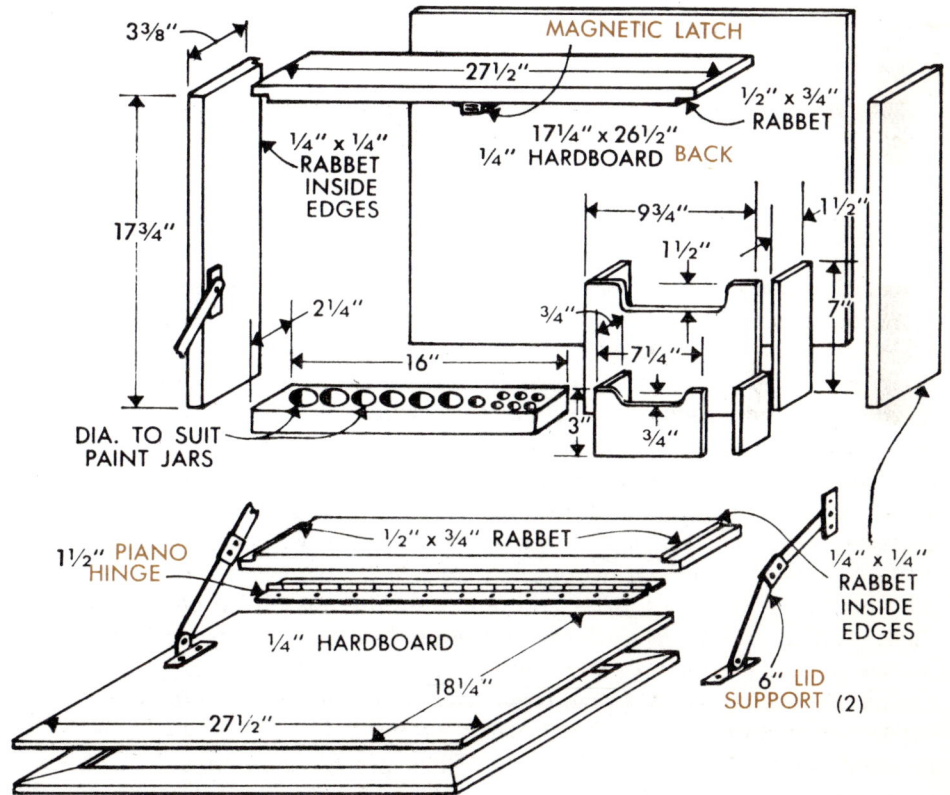

3⅜"

27½"   MAGNETIC LATCH

½" x ¾" RABBET

¼" x ¼" RABBET INSIDE EDGES

17¼" x 26½" ¼" HARDBOARD BACK

17¾"

9¾"

1½"

1½"

2¼"   ¾"

7¼"   7"

16"

3¾"   DIA. TO SUIT PAINT JARS

¾"   3"

½" x ¾" RABBET

1½" PIANO HINGE

¼" HARDBOARD

¼" x ¼" RABBET INSIDE EDGES

18¼"

27½"

6" LID SUPPORT (2)

GOVERNOR WINTHROP DESK

This handsome, all-mahogany desk is a real challenge for the home craftsman who likes to build classic furniture. Legend has it that the 13 panes of glass in each of the doors represent Governor Winthrop's original 13 colonies. In modern practice, as glass now can be obtained in almost any size, a single sheet is used, with a thin wooden grille in front to simulate the original dividers.

Carefully check the drawing for overall dimensions of the upper and lower parts of the desk. Except where noted, all stock is 1-inch material (¾-inch net), which means that hardwood plywood can be used. The drawer fronts must be cut from 2-inch or thicker stock (you may have to stack the lumber and glue up a "sandwich" to be band-sawed to shape). If it is necessary to laminate the drawer fronts from several pieces, then veneer them with mahogany. That's what the old-timers did, even when they had large pieces of solid stock; veneer has a much more beautiful grain pattern than solid wood. Rabbets are cut in the ends of the drawer fronts while they are still "in the square" before band-sawing.

Two of the drawers are identical in size, while the top one is 5 inches high, and fits inside the pull-out slides. The bottoms of each of the drawers is tempered hardboard. Unless you will store heavy items in the drawers, 1/8-inch hardboard should be strong enough. Drawer sides are attached to the fronts with screws or dowels through the sides into the ends of the fronts in the rabbets.

In the upper, book case section, note that the shelves rest on pegs fitted in holes bored in the sides. This arrangement permits adjusting the spacing to accommodate whatever size items are to be placed in

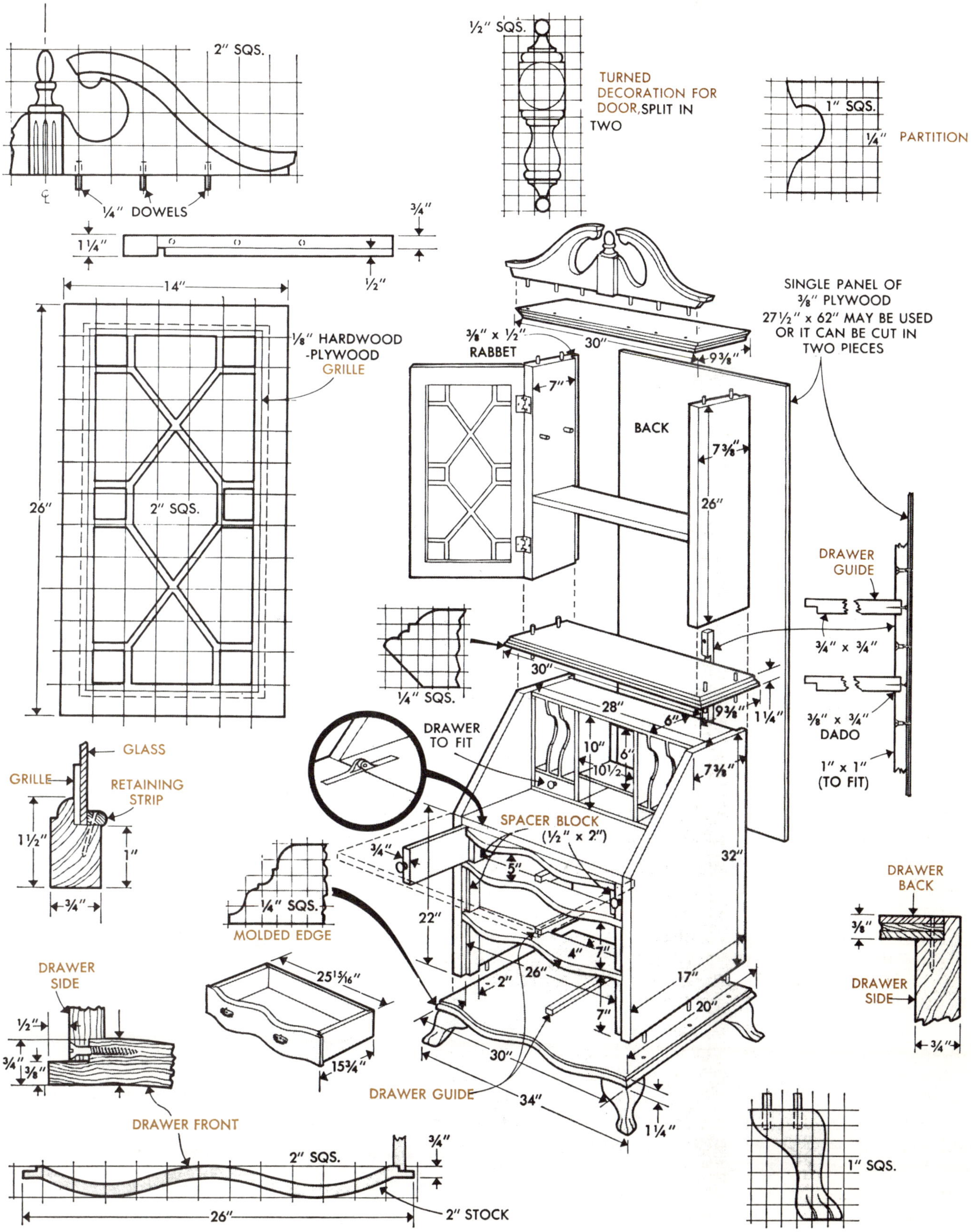

2" SQS.
¼" DOWELS
¾"
1¼"
½"
½" SQS.
TURNED DECORATION FOR DOOR, SPLIT IN TWO
1" SQS.
¼" PARTITION
14"
⅛" HARDWOOD -PLYWOOD GRILLE
26"
2" SQS.
⅜" x ½" RABBET
30"
9⅜"
SINGLE PANEL OF ⅜" PLYWOOD 27½" x 62" MAY BE USED OR IT CAN BE CUT IN TWO PIECES
7"
BACK
7⅜"
26"
DRAWER GUIDE
¾" x ¾"
⅜" x ¾" DADO
1" x 1" (TO FIT)
¼" SQS.
30"
28"
6"
9⅜"
1¼"
DRAWER TO FIT
10"
6"
10½
7⅜"
GLASS
GRILLE
RETAINING STRIP
1½"
1"
¾"
SPACER BLOCK (½" x 2")
¾"
5"
32"
¼" SQS.
MOLDED EDGE
22"
7"
4"
26"
2"
17"
20"
7"
DRAWER BACK
⅜"
DRAWER SIDE
¾"
DRAWER SIDE
½"
¾"
⅜"
25 15/16"
15¾"
30"
34"
1¼"
DRAWER GUIDE
DRAWER FRONT
2" SQS.
¾"
26"
2" STOCK
1" SQS.

the book case.

The hinged desk swings down and is supported on the curved front of the desk, plus the two pull-outs at the sides of the top drawer. For the back of the desk you can use a single piece of 3/8-inch plywood, or it can be in two pieces, which will permit the desk being taken apart for easier moving.

A guide rail is provided for each of the drawers to assure that they run true and free. A support for the guides is glued to the inside of the back of the desk.

Inside the desk, pigeonholes are installed, plus a small door 6 inches high. The door is embellished with a split turning.

Probably the most difficult parts of the desk to make are the feet. If you think of them simply as short cabriole legs you should have no problem. Cut one side of the leg from a block, then tape the cut-off pieces back on the block and cut the same profile on the adjacent face of the block. After this operation, filing, rasping and sanding will create the roundness necessary.

LACQUERED DESK (ca. 1715)

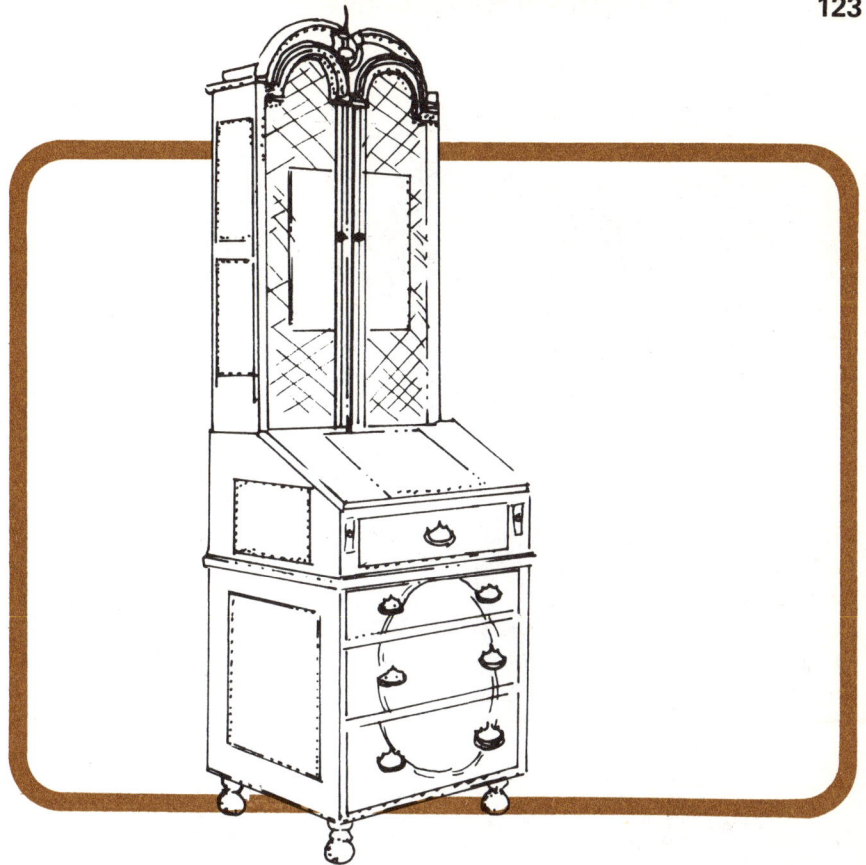

Styled after a lacquered desk (cabinet) made in the 1700's, this piece of furniture has been redesigned to be practical in modern homes, to be made with modern materials, and yet maintain the grace and beauty of the original.

Birch plywood can be used for the cases of the three pieces—chest of drawers, desk and cabinet—that make up the desk, plus hardwood and softwood for the various molding and trim. As did the early craftsmen, use gesso to conceal the fact that a variety of woods was used, and to fill in joints that were not quite accurate. Although gesso can be used to fill in imprecise work, try to keep joinery as accurate as possible in the interest of sturdy construction. The gesso you use will probably be a modern acrylic-base material; also the enamel you use to simulate the "lacquer" finish. Ironically, the lacquer finish on the original was developed as an imitation of the lacquer used on furniture imported from the orient to Europe over 200 years ago.

Suggested colors include red, blue or other "oriental" or "Chinese" colors to fit with the decor of the room in which the cabinet will be located. To simulate age, apply liquid gel medium in which is mixed a small amount of acrylic burnt umber. This is simply brushed on and allowed to dry; do not wipe it off as is the usual practice with antique glaze. Apply more in some spots and less in other (wiping with a cloth dampened in water will remove it, as it is water-soluble, but is waterproof when dry) to give it the look of age. Apply more in recesses in the molding and less on flat surfaces that would receive wear.

Construction of the three pieces is quite basic, with plywood sides dadoed and rabbeted to accept the shelves, tops, bottoms and

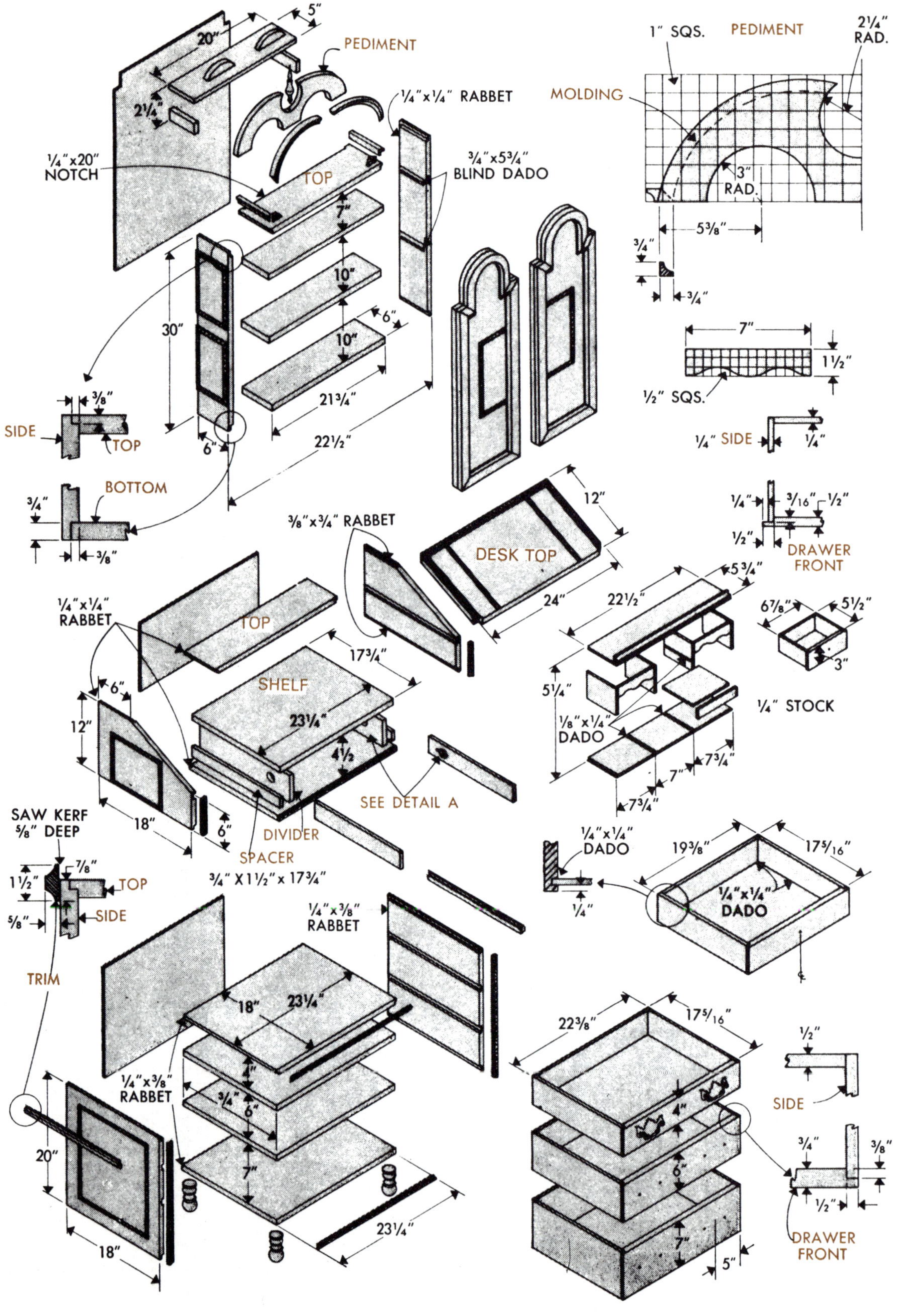

5"
20"
PEDIMENT
2¼"
¼"x¼" RABBET
¼"x20"
NOTCH
TOP
7"
¾"x5¾"
BLIND DADO
10"
10"
6"
30"
21¾"
22½"
6"
SIDE
⅜"
TOP
BOTTOM
¾"
⅜"
1" SQS.
PEDIMENT
2¼"
RAD.
MOLDING
3"
RAD.
5⅜"
¾"
¾"
7"
1½"
½" SQS.
¼" SIDE
¼"
12"
DESK TOP
24"
¼"
3/16"
½"
½"
DRAWER
FRONT
⅜"x¾" RABBET
¼"x¼"
RABBET
TOP
17¾"
SHELF
23¼"
4½"
6"
12"
18"
6"
SEE DETAIL A
DIVIDER
SPACER
¾" X 1½" x 17¾"
22½"
5¾"
6⅞"
5½"
3"
5¼"
¼" STOCK
⅛"x¼"
DADO
7¾"
7"
7¾"
SAW KERF
⅝" DEEP
1½"
⅞"
TOP
⅝"
SIDE
TRIM
¼"x¼"
DADO
¼"
19⅜"
17 5/16"
¼"x¼"
DADO
¼"x⅜"
RABBET
18"
23¼"
4"
¼"x⅜"
RABBET
¾"
6"
7"
20"
18"
23¼"
22⅜"
17 5/16"
4"
6"
7"
5"
½"
SIDE
¾"
⅜"
½"
DRAWER
FRONT

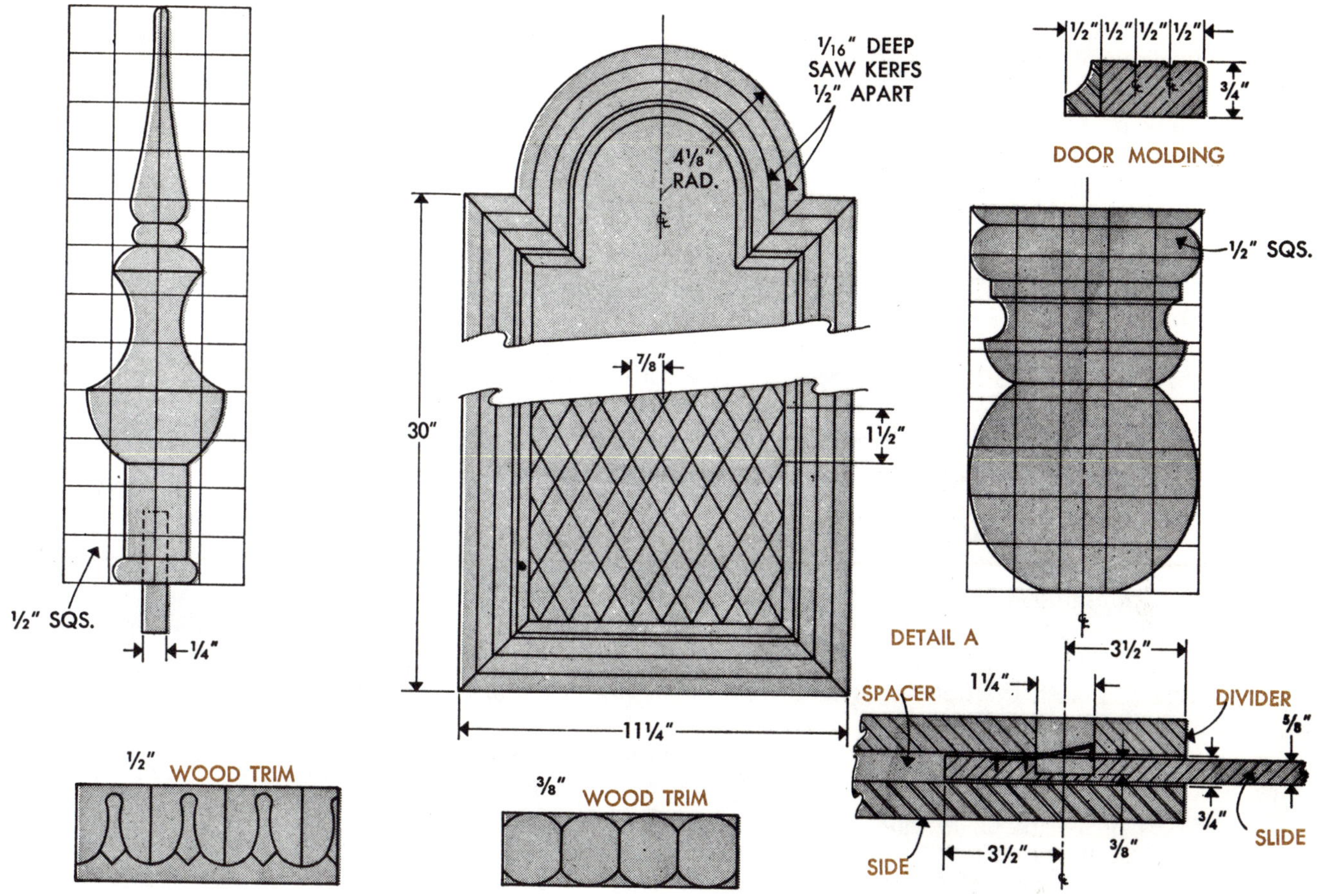

½" SQS.
¼"
1/16" DEEP SAW KERFS ½" APART
4⅛" RAD.
30"
⅞"
1½"
11¼"
½"|½"|½"|½"
¾"
DOOR MOLDING
½" SQS.
DETAIL A
3½"
1¼"
SPACER
DIVIDER
⅝"
¾"
SLIDE
⅜"
SIDE
3½"
½" WOOD TRIM
⅜" WOOD TRIM

MATERIALS LIST

Chest of Drawers

Case:	¾"-plywood (except as noted)
Side:	18"x20" (2)
Top:	18"x23¼" (1)
Shelf:	17¾"x23¼" (2)
Bottom:	18"x23¼" (1)
Back:	¼"x19¼"x23¼" (1)
Drawers:	¼"x½" ¾"-plywood
Front:	¾"x4"x22-3/8" (1)
Side:	½"x4"x17-5/16" (2)
Back:	½"x3½"x21-3/8" (1)
Front:	¾"x6"x22-3/8" (1)
Side:	½"x6"x17-15/16" (2)
Back:	½"x5½"x21-3/8" (1)
Front:	¾"x7"x22-3/8" (1)
Side:	½"x7"x17-5/16" (2)
Back:	½"x6½"x21-3/8" (1)
Bottom:	¼"x17-15/16"x 21-7/8" (3)
Trim:	5/8"x1½"x18" (2)
Leg:	2½"x2½"x4" (or ready-made units)

Desk

Case:	Plywood
Side:	¾"x12"x18" (2)
Bottom:	¾"x18"x23¼" (1)
Shelf:	¾"x17¾"x23¼" (1)
Top:	¾"x6"x23¼" (1)
Desk Top:	¾"x12"x24" (1)
Divider:	¾"x4½"x17¾" (2)
Spacer:	¾"x1½"x17¾" (2)
Pull-out:	5/8"x2-7/8"x17¾" (2)
Drawer Front:	¾"x4½"x19-3/8" (1)
Drawer Side:	½"x4½"x17-5/16" (2)
Drawer Back:	½"x4"x18-3/8" (1)
Drawer Bottom:	¼"x17-5/16"x 18-7/8" (1)
Pigeonholes:	¼"-plywood or hardboard
Top, Bottom:	5¾"x22½" (1 each)
Partitions:	5"x5" (4)
Shelf:	5"x7" (1)
Drawer Front:	3"x6-7/8" (1)
Drawer Side:	3"x5½" (2)
Drawer Back:	2½"x6-3/8" (1)
Drawer Bottom:	5½"x6-5/8" (1)
Molding:	¾"x¾"x22½" (1)
Cabinet:	¾"-plywood or solid stock (except as noted)
Side:	6"x30" (2)
Top:	6"x21¾" (1)
Bottom:	6"x21¾" (1)
Shelf:	5¾"x21¾" (2)
Pediment Top:	5"x20" (1)
End, Top Compartment:	2¼"x5" (2)
Pediment:	7"x24" (1)
Finial:	2"x2"x6" (1)
Door:	11¼"x34-1/8" (2)
Door Trim, Straight:	2"x25' (approx.)
Door Trim, Curved:	8½"x8½" (2)

backs. The chest of drawers is a simple box with shelves in which standard drawers are fitted. The short legs can be turned, or you can buy them ready-made.

The desk part is a little more difficult: make it to slip inside two trim strips on the chest, then use a couple of wood screws through the bottom to hold it on the chest, yet permit easy removal. The desk top is shortened to clear the doors. The open space above the upper edge of the top is filled by a molding attached to the pigeonhole assembly. The molding keeps the pigeonhole unit from sliding all the way back in the desk, so a "secret" compartment is created behind it. Its depth will be determined by how deep you make the pigeonholes. The seeming undersize of the pullout slides is necessary, as a couple of coats of gesso and enamel increase the size to a snug fit in the opening. Machine-carved molding is glued and bradded to the front of the chest and along three edges of the dropdown top. Note that the lower corners of the top are notched, so the molding on the chest front does not prevent the top pivoting down to be level. A sample molding pattern is shown, but you might wish to select a different style to make your cabinet more individual.

While dimensions are given for the parts of the pigeonhole assembly in the Materials List, it is strongly recommended that you cut and fit the parts to match the opening in your particular desk, in case it varies slightly from the sizes given.

Be sure to make the holes in the dividers (next to the slides) before you assemble the desk. The side of the opening toward the front of the desk is flat, so the "spring," bent from a piece of sheet metal, will jam against it and prevent the slide from being pulled out inadvertently. To remove the slides (another place for a secret compartment), you must remove the desk drawer, then reach in and depress the springs.

With the chest and desk finished you have a complete piece of furniture and you might want to stop here, as the relatively low profile suits a room where you want to maintain free wall space. In this case, make the drop-down top the full length of the slanting sides.

However, the cabinet with its curving pediment, doors with molding and gold "grille" create the real beauty of this piece of furniture. Molding for the doors can be two pieces: ¾ x 1½ inch with a ½ x ¾-inch molding attached, or it can be one piece shaped as indicated. The saw cuts are easy to do. The curved part of the molding on the doors requires first cutting a curve in a rectangle of ¾-inch stock, shaping a molding on this inner curve, then using a veining bit in a router to produce grooves to meet the saw cuts in the straight molding. The outside curve of the molding then is cut with a band, jig or saber saw.

Don't try to shape a narrow strip of molding with either a router or shaper; it will too easily be thrown from the cutter and your hands will be dangerously close to the spinning knives. Cut the inside curve on a larger piece of wood, shape the inner edge, then saw the strip free of the block. Use this same method for the curved molding that goes on the pediment. The pattern in the drawing for the pediment molding is the same width the full length; the photo shows the molding tapering down at each end. You do this by using a larger radius for the inner curve than the outer, but you move the center of the arc away

Complete assembly is shown here, all covered with gesso. Not coated at this stage are frames of molding.

Stacked together are the plywood "carcasses" of the chest-of-drawers, desk and cabinet. Edge trim was removed.

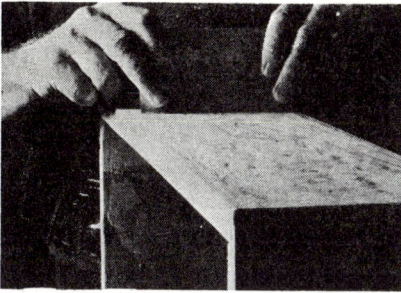

Coats of gesso were sanded smooth, leveled even more accurately with aid of cabinet scraper, more coats applied.

Art prints were trimmed to appropriate size, taped to various surfaces, then molding was positioned to frame them.

Before any molding was applied, art prints were placed in various locations, studied for appearance.

When molding frames had been applied, and coated with gesso, inside and outside of unit was painted with acrylic.

from the center used for the outer arc. Practice this on paper before transferring it to the wood.

Also note that the half-round pieces cut out of the pediment later are glued and bradded behind the same openings, on top of the small part of the cabinet.

Some antique cabinets display actual oil paintings on the cabinet doors and sides, while others are decorated with decoupage. The example desk was decorated with the latter method. Museum-quality art prints that are run through a press for eight or ten colors, rather than the usual four, were used. These prints are much more attractive, although they can be somewhat expensive.

For your furniture you might prefer French provincial or pastoral scenes. Just remember that the style of the piece is European and dates from the late 1600's through the 1700's. Tape your prints to various surfaces after trimming the borders, then stand back and "eye-ball" the cabinet until you feel you have achieved a pleasing arrangement. Mark around the prints and glue and brad a narrow beaded molding to create "frames" for the prints. However, the large oval print on the drawer fronts does not have a frame. It is glued in place, then sections are cut from it with a razor knife. This allows for clearance between drawers and shelves.

With the frames in place and the cabinet complete, three coats of gesso are applied, each being sanded thoroughly. On flat surfaces a cabinet scraper does a good job but leaves marks that require light sanding. Acrylic enamel is brushed on next; two coats should do the job, but more might be required.

When the enamel dries apply glue on the prints, then gold leaf to the molding, using gel medium thinned with water as an adhesive. (Gel medium comes as a cream in tubes, and as a liquid; use the liquid for all work.) The three screws used to hold the cabinet to the desk top, and the two holding the desk to the chest should be removed and the three pieces worked on separately. About four books of 22-carat gold leaf are required, but the imitation leaf can also be used, being somewhat less expensive. The cost difference is really not large enough to justify the difference for use on this really fabulous piece of furniture. A single application of the leaf will probably break and "craze," but do not try to make a solid application. Gold leaf on antiques has the same crazed and worn look.

Antiquing comes next. Brush on the gel medium colored with burnt umber on all surfaces, including the gold leaf and the prints.

The cabinet is placed on its back and a pattern of diamond shapes made to fit around the prints inside the molding on the doors. Carbon paper is used to transfer the pattern. Heavy gold thread is adhered to the lines, using gel medium (which dries clear) as an adhesive. Each thread should be cut slightly long. Stretch it along the line over the glue, then cut off the ends with a razor knife. This job is tedious and time-consuming but it enhances the appearance of the piece appreciably.

With the rest of the finishing done the varnish is applied. Work on each piece separately, with the cabinet on its back, and apply coat after coat of varnish until the prints melt into the surfaces of the cabinet, and the gold threads on the doors are below the surface of the finish. Quite a few days are required for varnishing, as each coat has to dry for 24 hours. Do not rush the job; allow the proper drying time and you will have a deep, rich finish that will have the look of age and the quality that only a true craftsman can create. You may use a urethane varnish.

Hardware is fitted on the cabinet before any finish is applied, then it is removed and not reinstalled until all finishing is complete. For the pull-out slides you may only find matching small knobs with machine screws which are threaded the full length. Cut off the heads, bore "force-fit" holes in the slides, then use epoxy glue and turn the screws into the holes, turning the knobs and screws together.

Now stand back and admire your work and wait for compliments from friends.

In answer to some questions you might have in mind: Yes, you can build it all of hardwood and stain and varnish or lacquer it. However, it would lose some of the character with an ordinary finish. Yes, you can use paints other than acrylic; just be sure all finishing materials are compatible. Yes, you can use one of the wax-type rub-on gilding materials in place of the gold leaf.

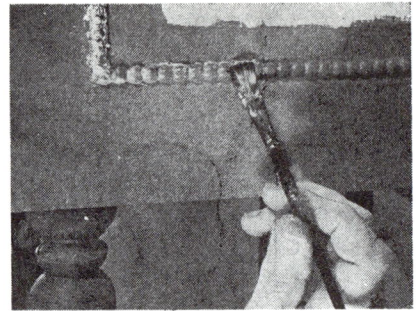

Gold leaf was applied by using thinned gel medium as an adhesive. Leaf was allowed to set, then gently brushed.

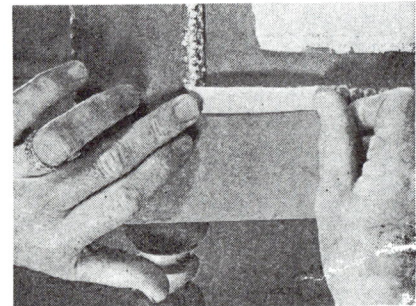

Leaves of paper and gold were cut into strips, applied to narrow molding as shown. This method minimized waste.

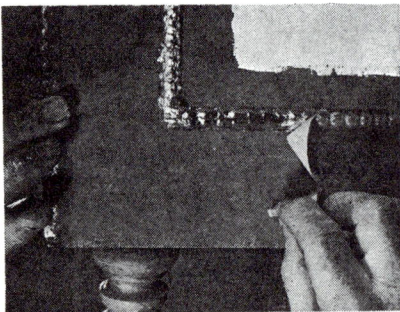

Gold leaf adhered only partly to "carved" molding, as shown here where paper is removed. This job takes time.

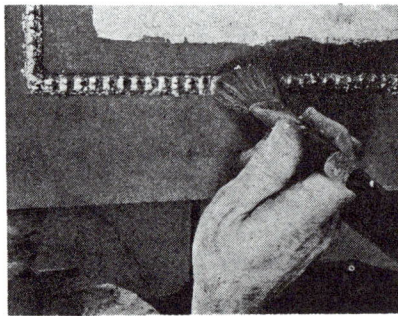

Soft-bristle brush is used to "pounce" leaf to make it fit contours of the molding. There is some waste.

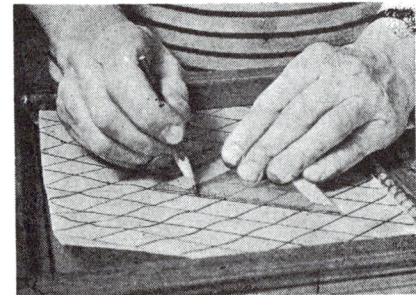

Triangular pattern was drawn on sheet of paper fitted over door, inside molding and frame; carbon transferred design.

Gold cord was glued to door, on lines from pattern, using gel medium as a "glue." Each was fitted in place.

For front of chest of drawers (extending over desk drawer) a large oval print was trimmed about two inches.

Burnt umber was mixed with gel medium to create "antiquing." This was simply brushed on, and was not wiped.

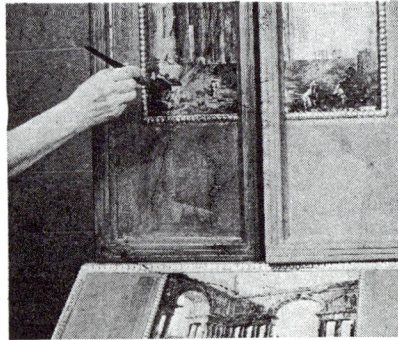

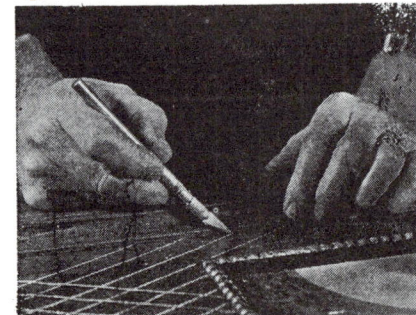

ROLL-TOP DESK

1. Sides of rolltop part of desk are cut with band or jig saw. Cut both together to assure they are identical.

2. Smooth edges of sides with sander to accept trim. Clamp them together to keep them same size and shape.

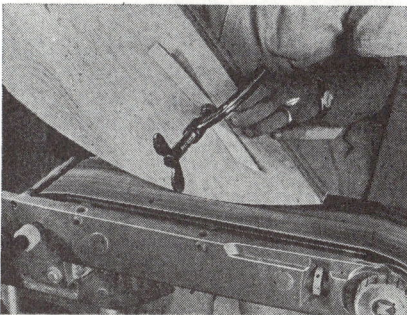

A full-size rolltop desk is a real collector's item and is in great demand. However, it is too large to fit in the average home. Both a student-size and full-size rolltop desk are shown and described in the following paragraphs. The full-size desk has been scaled-down to ensure that it will readily fit in rooms of average size.

Ordinary fir plywood can be used for the student's desk, but hardwood-plywood would make a more attractive item if it is to be used in a living room. Fir plywood also can be veneered to create almost any wood finish. The advantage of plywood is that you can cut large panels in one piece; using solid hardwood will make it necessary to edge-glue stock, and the finished product will be fairly expensive. Solid stock can be used on the drawer fronts, as shown in the photos. This does provide a better appearance if you are looking for an early American look.

Start construction by cutting the curved sides of the upper part of the desk (figure 1). Tack-nail them together to make sure they are identical. The edges must be sanded to accept thin strips of trim, so leave them nailed together, or clamp them and sand the edges, keeping them square.

The grooves for the rolltop are cut next, using a portable router. A router bit in a drill press or radial-arm saw also could be used. Quite likely it will take several passes to make the grooves.

Sides, bottoms and backs of the drawers are cut next, being ripped from ½-inch plywood (figure 4). Ripping the stock will assure that all matching pieces are the same width. Pick up the dimensions of the drawers from the drawings and from the materials list. One caution: be sure that you use the correct drawing with the proper materials list. There is a student-size and a full-size desk, and dimensions vary considerably. The only similarity is in the rolltop slats; for both desks the cross-sections are the same; the lengths are different.

Next, cut the desk top from ¾-inch plywood to the dimensions given. The edges of the top are trimmed with lengths of 1 x 2 with mitered joints. Glue and nail the trim pieces with 4d finish nails (figure 5) then countersink the nails and fill the depressions with wood putty.

On the prototype desk the legs were made from rough 2 x 2s that were planed down to 1¾ inch square (figure 6). You can use finished 2 x 2s, but be sure they are 1¾ inch. Some are as small as 1-5/8 inches square, which is somewhat undersize for the desk, especially the full-size model. With the legs sanded smooth (it's much easier to do this before assembly) rout or saw the ¼-inch grooves in them 17 inches down from the tops (figure 7). Shown are panels of ¼-inch plywood being fitted between the legs; you can use heavier material and still fit the grooves if the edges are rabbeted to create a ¼-inch edge.

When the student desk was first assembled, the drawers were made so the sides projected below the bottoms, and these projections then fitted in guides nailed and clamped at the bottoms of the drawer sections (figure 8). The redesign is shown in the drawing; trial and error proved that a flat shelf offers better support and easier action. The drawers were redesigned accordingly, and a single guide on the support shelves keeps the drawers aligned.

The lower part of the desk; legs, top, panels and drawer supports now are assembled. Keep the assembly square and use glue and nails as required. Clamp all assemblies firmly, and allow plenty of time for the glue to set.

Assemble the drawers (figure 9) after checking the drawer openings, and making any changes in dimensions necessary to permit the drawers to fit easily. There should be at least 1/16 inch clearance for the drawers, and even 1/8 inch will not be excessive if all edges are true and square.

The top can be attached by gluing, and driving finishing nails down through the top into the upper ends of the legs. This should be sufficient to hold it in place, as the "apron" of 1 x 2s fits snugly against the legs. For additional strength you can drive a few nails through the apron into the legs. Countersink and cover the nail heads with wood putty.

Put the finished lower portion of the desk, fitted with its drawers, aside and go back to the rolltop section. Cut the top, false back: (there is no other back to permit easy access to the rolltop, should it need repair or maintenance) and the pigeonhole dividers. Do not assemble any of these at this point.

Now comes the only really difficult operation in the construction of the desk, the rolltop itself. Cut to the length required enough strips of 1-inch stock to provide the slats. It would be a good idea to make a couple extra slats in case of damage or error.

Cut rabbets on the ends of the pieces of stock, then rip them to width (figure 10). If the stock is smooth and clear, it will require only sanding. Slats can be run over the jointer to assure a true, smooth

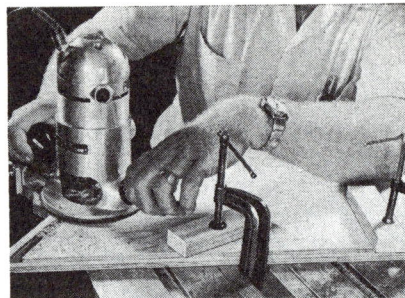

3. Most accurate, easiest way of cutting slots for rolltop is with portable router, using glue.

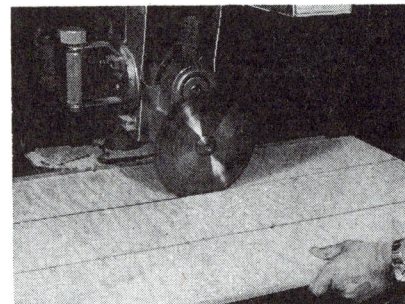

4. Drawer backs, bottoms and sides are ripped from ½" plywood. By ripping, identical sizes are assured.

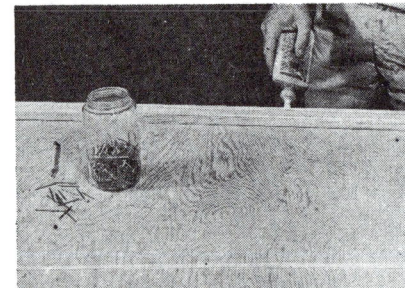

5. Edges of desk top are covered with 1x2 strips to give bulk. Fasten with 4d finish nails, set and fill with putty.

6. On original, rough 2 x 2s were planed down to 1¾" square for legs. Regular 2 x 2s (1¾" sq.) can be used.

7. Router or circular saw is used to cut dadoes in legs for side panels.

8. Redesign eliminates double guides, substitutes supports, single guides.

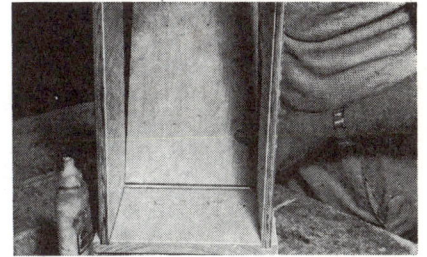

9. Solid stock was used on drawer fronts with plywood for rest.

10. Rabbeted stock is ripped to create slats for rolltop; wood is clear stock.

11. Planing was extra step; in most cases sanding of slats is enough.

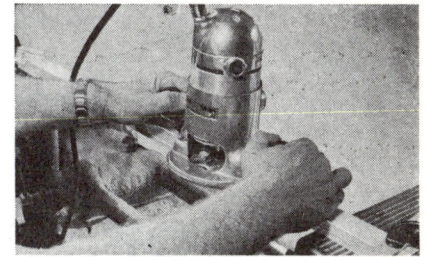

12. Bottom slat of rolltop is wider, has handholds cut in it with router.

13. Contact adhesive on slats and canvas; slats are tapped into place.

14. Before applying finish, go over all surfaces and sand them carefully.

15. Finished student's desk "in the white" before finish is applied.

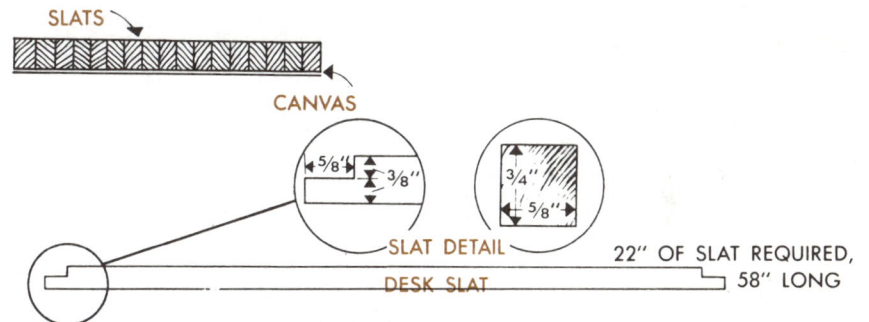

SLATS

CANVAS

5/8"   3/8"

3/4"   5/8"

SLAT DETAIL

22" OF SLAT REQUIRED, 58" LONG

DESK SLAT

surface (figure 11). Handholds are cut in the lower slat of the rolltop (figure 12) but knobs or handles also could be installed.

The final step in the top assembly is to apply contact adhesive to a piece of medium-weight canvas, and to the slats and tap the slats into firm contact with the canvas (figure 13). Cut the canvas slightly larger than needed, and definitely longer. You can always cut it and remove a slat if it is too long.

Fit the finished top between the grooved sides, attach the top and false back to which the partitions are fastened. This assembly is positioned on the top and fastened with a finishing nail toenailed at the front and back of each side. Set the nails and cover the back one with wood putty. The front nail will be concealed with the trim strip applied to the curved upper edges of the sides.

With the desk completely assembled, go over every surface and sand it carefully (figure 14). Your finished desk, "in the white," will appear as in figure 15. Double-check for any blemishes in the wood, then apply stain, varnish or lacquer and wax to create the finish of your choice.

FULL-SIZE DESK

12″ — 62″ — 11″

6″ RAD. — 14″ — 28″ RAD. — 19″ — 11″ — **SIDE FOR FULL-SIZE DESK**

14″ — 59-1/8″ — 6″ RAD.

FALSE BACK

FACE WITH 1/16″ PINE

3/4″ **PLYWOOD SIDES**

12″ — 3″

30″ — **HAND PULLS** — **BOTTOM SLAT** — 3/8″ DEEP x 1/2″ WIDE GROOVE ROUTED

PIGEONHOLE DIVIDERS — 8″ — 12″ — 30″

1/4″ **PLYWOOD BACK PANEL** — 1 x 2 **EDGE TRIM** — 12″ — 8″ — 60″ — 3/4″ **PLYWOOD TOP**

"MODESTY" PANEL — 1/4″ x 1/4″ **DADO** — **DRAWER SIDE 1/2″**

27½″ — 14″ — 4¾″

17″ — 7⅞″ — **DRAWER SLIDES** — 11″

1/4″ **PLYWOOD SIDE PANEL** — 30″ — 26″ — 3″ — 7⅞″ — 14″

DRAWER — 14″ — **FILE DRAWER**

2 x 2 **LEGS** — 14″ — 24″ — 1/4″ x 1/2″ **RABBET** — **NOTE: ALL DRAWER PULLS SAME AS ON STUDENT DESK**

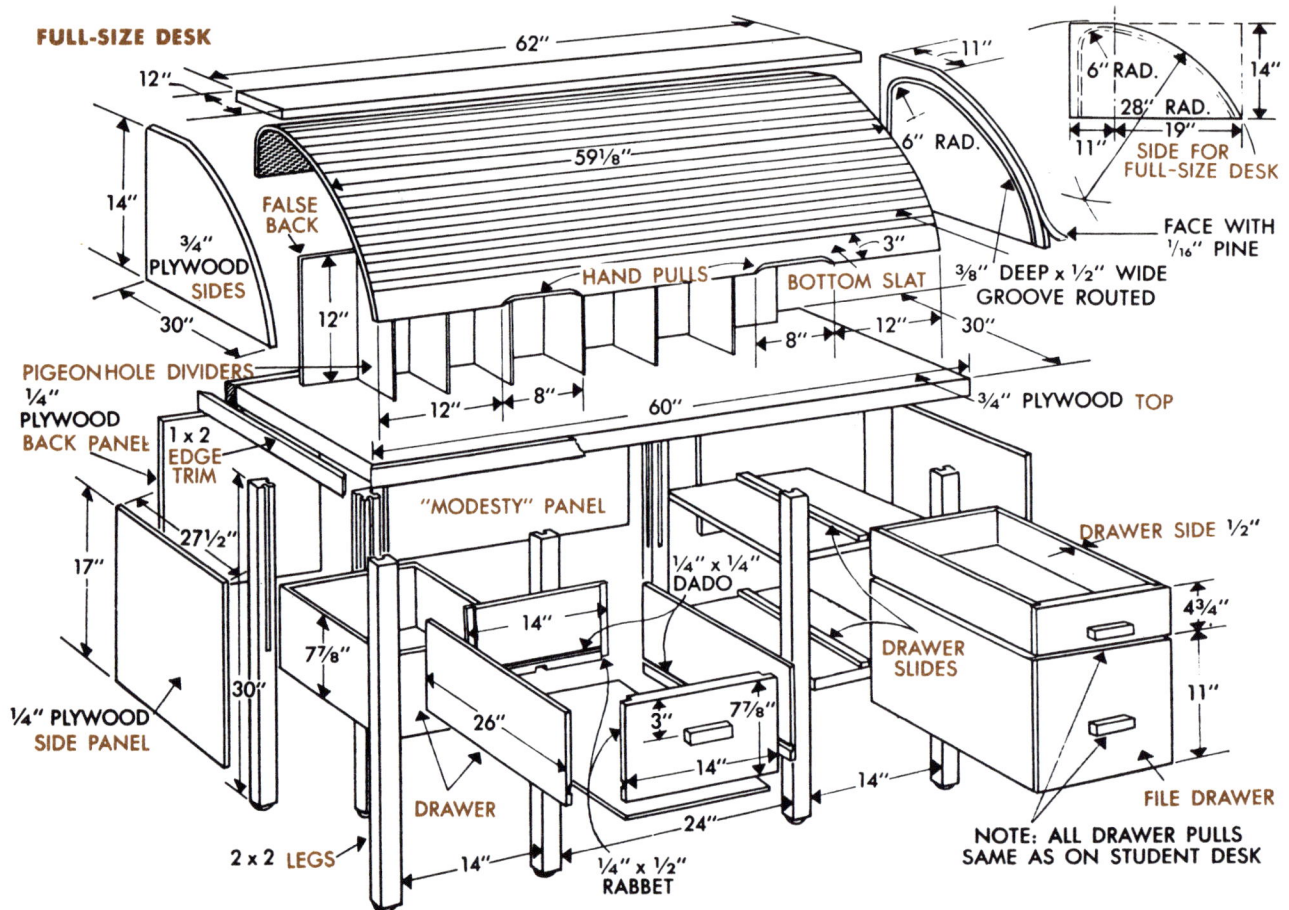

FULL-SIZE DESK MATERIALS LIST

Rolltop Section
Top:	¾″x12″x62″ (1)
Side:	14″x30″ ¾″-plywood (2)
False Back:	12″x57-7/8″ ½″-plywood (1)
Pigeon Dividers:	8″x12″ ¼″-plywood (6)
Slats:	5/8″x¾″x59-1/8″ (approximately 35)
Bottom Slat:	¾″x3″x59-1/8″ (1)

Case
Top:	30″x60″ ¾″-plywood (1)
Edge Trim:	1x2x31½″ (2)
Edge Trim:	1x2x61½″ (2)
Legs:	2x2 (1¾″x1¾″)x30″ (8)
Side Panels:	17″x27½″ (2)
Inside Panels:	17″x27½″ (2) (not in drawing)
Back Panels:	14½″x17″ (2)
"Modesty" Panel:	17″x24½″ (1)

Drawer Supports:	15½″x28″ (4)
Drawer Guides:	½″x¾″x28″ (4)

Drawers
All Bottoms:	13″x26-7/8″ ¼″-plywood (4)
Lefthand Sides:	¾″x7″x26¾″ (2)
Lefthand Front:	¾″x7-7/8″x14″ (2)
Lefthand Back:	½″x7″x14″ (2)

Righthand Top Drawer
Side:	½″x4″x26-7/8″ (2)
Front:	¾″x4¾″x14″ (1)
Back:	½″x4″x14″ (1)

Righthand Lower Drawer
Side:	½″x10-1/8″x27-7/8″ (2)
Back:	½″x10-1/8″x14″ (1)
Front:	¾″x11″x14″ (1)

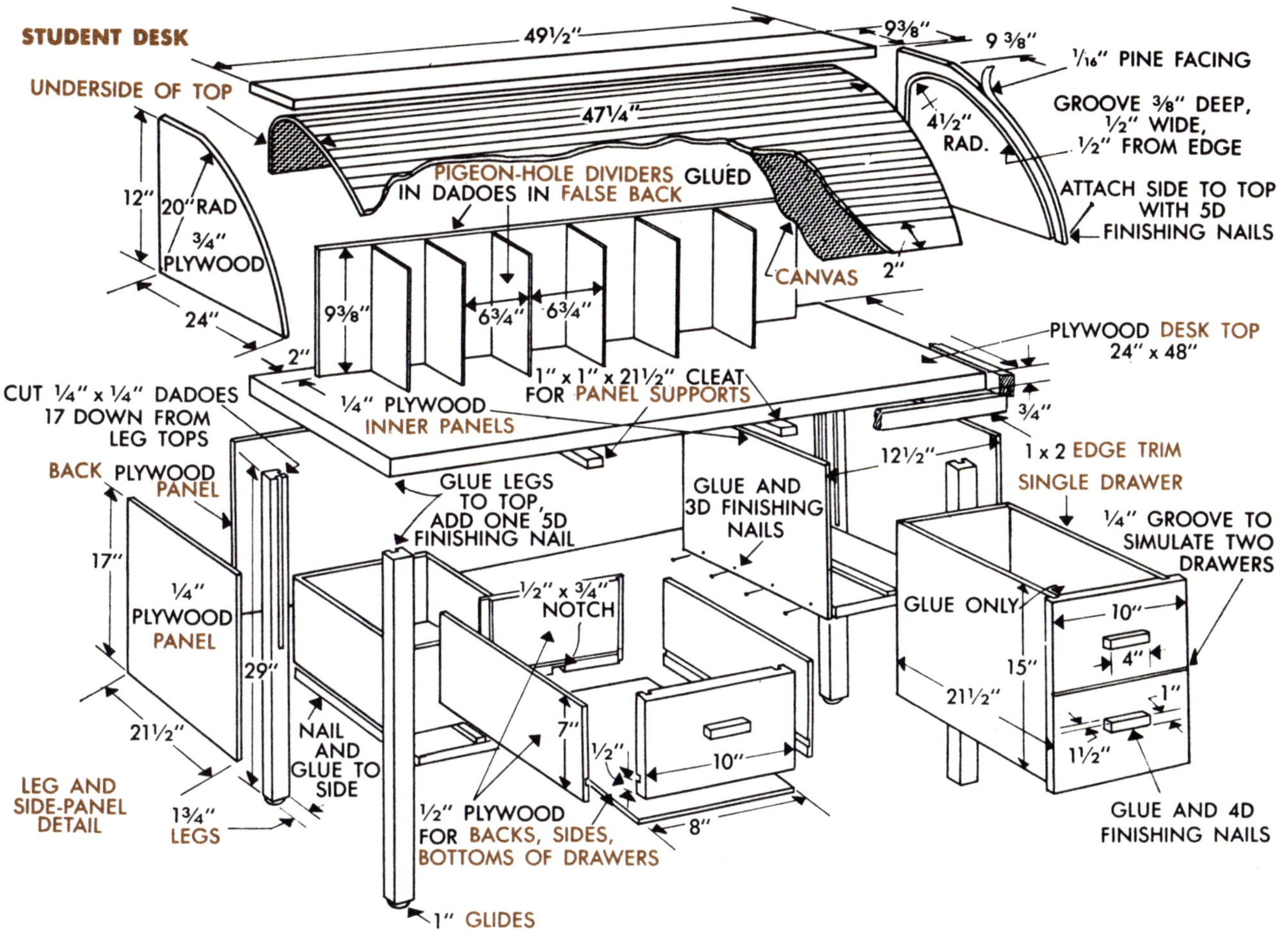

STUDENT DESK
UNDERSIDE OF TOP
49½"
9⅜"
9 ⅜"
1/16" PINE FACING
GROOVE ⅜" DEEP, ½" WIDE, ½" FROM EDGE
47¼"
4½" RAD.
12"
20" RAD
¾" PLYWOOD
24"
PIGEON-HOLE DIVIDERS GLUED IN DADOES IN FALSE BACK
ATTACH SIDE TO TOP WITH 5D FINISHING NAILS
CANVAS
2"
9⅜"
6¾"
6¾"
2"
PLYWOOD DESK TOP 24" x 48"
CUT ¼" x ¼" DADOES 17 DOWN FROM LEG TOPS
¼" PLYWOOD INNER PANELS
1" x 1" x 21½" CLEAT FOR PANEL SUPPORTS
¾"
BACK PLYWOOD PANEL
GLUE LEGS TO TOP, ADD ONE 5D FINISHING NAIL
12½"
1 x 2 EDGE TRIM
GLUE AND 3D FINISHING NAILS
SINGLE DRAWER
¼" GROOVE TO SIMULATE TWO DRAWERS
17"
¼" PLYWOOD PANEL
½" x ¾" NOTCH
GLUE ONLY
10"
4"
15"
21½"
1"
29"
7"
½"
10"
1½"
21½"
NAIL AND GLUE TO SIDE
LEG AND SIDE-PANEL DETAIL
1¾" LEGS
½" PLYWOOD FOR BACKS, SIDES, BOTTOMS OF DRAWERS
8"
GLUE AND 4D FINISHING NAILS
1" GLIDES

STUDENT-SIZE DESK MATERIALS LIST

Rolltop Section

Side:	12"x24" ¾"-plywood (2)
False Back:	9-3/8"x46½" ½"-plywood (1)
Pigeonhole Dividers:	8"x9-3/8" (6)
Top:	9-3/8"x49½" ¾"-plywood (1)
Slats:	5/8"x¾"x47½" (approximately 32)
Bottom Slat:	¾"x2"x47¼" (1)
Canvas, Medium Weight:	22"x45¾" (1)

Case

Top:	24"x48" ¾"-plywood (1)
Edge Trim:	1x2x25½" (2)
Edge Trim:	1x2x49½" (2)
Legs:	2x2s (1¾"x1¾")x29" (4)
Side Panels:	17"x21½" ¼"-plywood (2)
Inner Panels:	17"x21½" ¼"-plywood (2)
Back:	17"x45½" ¼"-plywood (1)
Drawer Supports (notched for legs):	11½"x21½" (3)
Drawer Guides:	½"x¾"x21½" (3)
Cleats, Panel Support:	1"x1"x21½" (2)

Drawers

Front:	10"x16" (1)
Front:	8"x10" (2)
Side:	15"x20-7/8" ½"-plywood (2)
Side:	7"x20-7/8" ½-plywood (4)
Back:	7"x9" (2)
Back:	9"x15" (2)

SCHOOL-MASTER'S DESK AND SWIVEL CHAIR

SCHOOLMASTER'S DESK

Patterned after the desks colonial schoolmasters once used at the front of classrooms, this compact unit would be ideal for a small home office, kitchen headquarters or a study center for a student. The chair has the early American look, but combines a touch of the modern with a lazy-susan bearing that permits the chair to rotate 360 degrees.

The desk is made of four separate sections: the base, the book case, the top and the pigeon-hole compartments. Start by making the base, cutting the pieces from 1-3/8-inch stock.

Rabbets are cut in the ends of the side pieces to accept the back member. The ½ x ¾-inch dado cut in the back runs its full length, being stopped by the rabbets on the side members. The dadoes in the side pieces are cut 7-15/16 inches long, starting from the back ends. It will be necessary to finish the blind ends of the dadoes with a chisel, to square them off to accept the scrolled side pieces. The stretcher, positioned 6-9/16 inches from the back, is ¾-inch stock and is attached with dowels or finish nails and glue, as are the side and back members. Strips of ¾-inch stock are glued and nailed inside the base to accept the shelf that is glued and nailed to the strips.

The next step is to make patterns by enlarging the squared drawings, for both the scrolled pieces of the book case, and the back of the pigeon holes.

Cut out the scrolled sides for the book case, then dowel and glue lengths of stock to make the sides. The scrolled pieces are glued and doweled to these sides.

You can use plywood for the sides and back (not for the scrolled

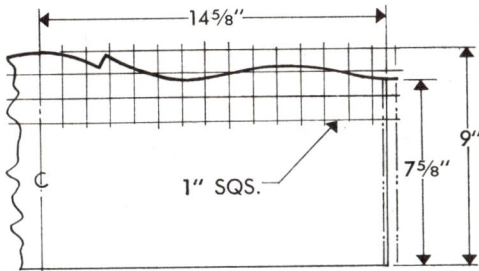

TOP-COMPARTMENT BACK DETAIL

1" SQS.

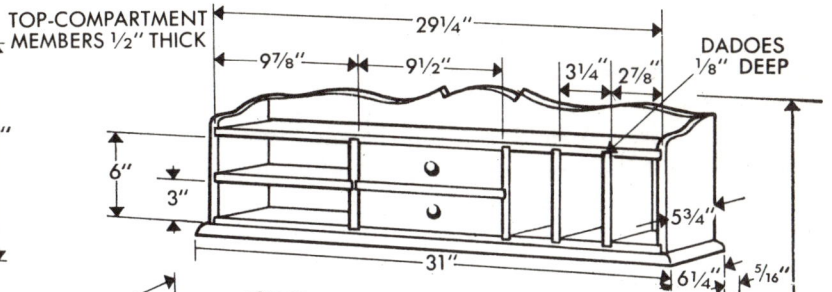

TOP-COMPARTMENT MEMBERS ½" THICK

DADOES ⅛" DEEP

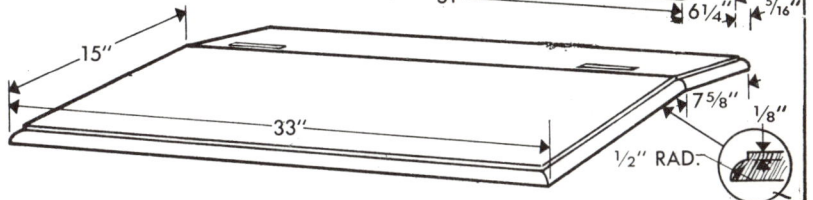

SECTION A—A

SCROLL DETAIL

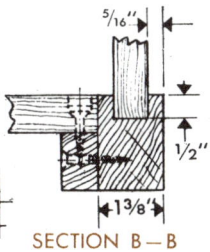

SECTION B—B

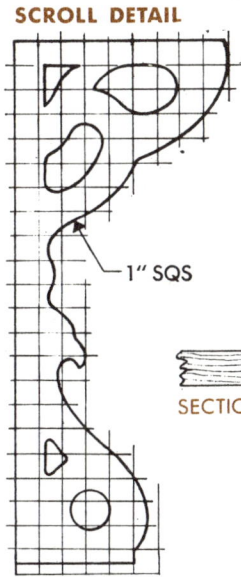

1" SQS

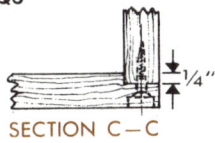

SECTION C—C

NOTE:
ALL STOCK ¾"
UNLESS OTHERWISE SPECIFIED.
ALL WOOD SCREWS #10 x 1¼" FH.
COUNTERBORE AND PLUG ALL
EXPOSED SCREWS

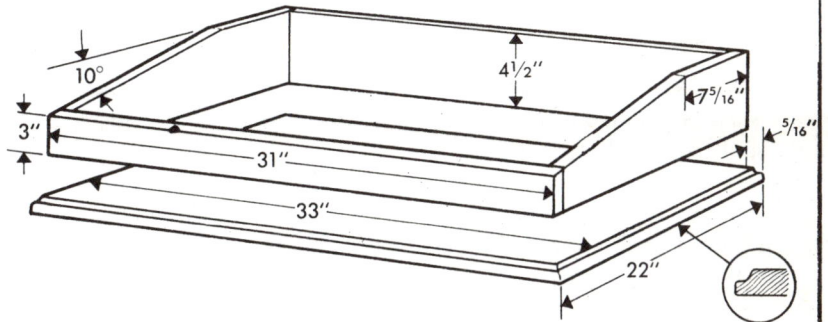

½" RAD.

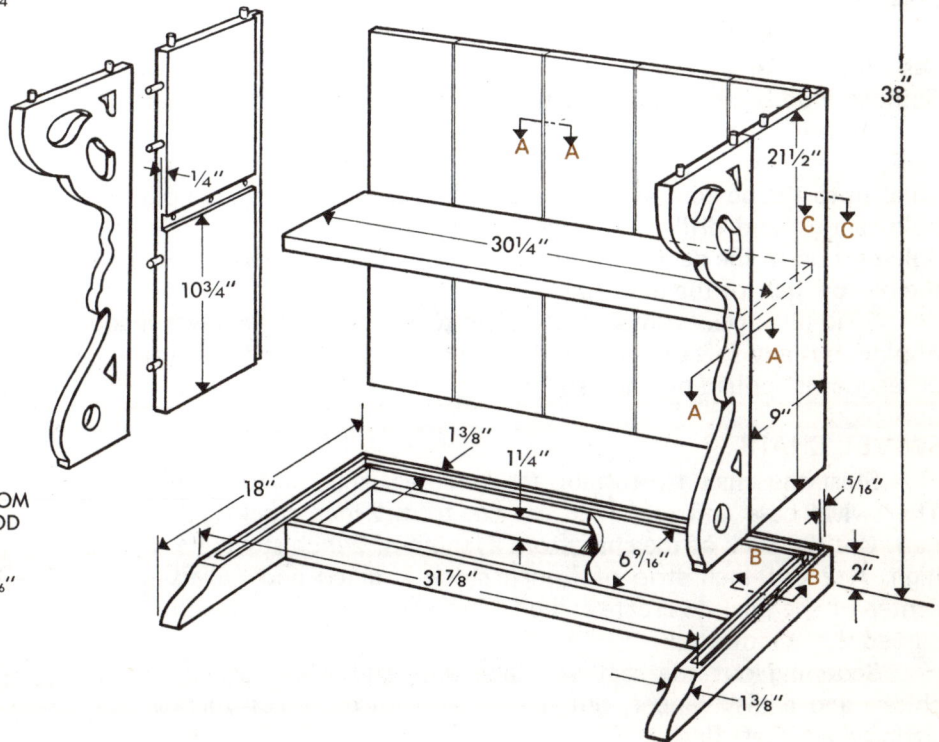

DRAWER BOTTOM
¼" PLYWOOD

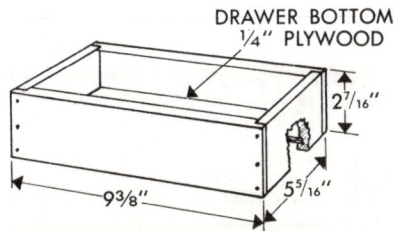

DRAWER DETAIL

section, as the edge-grain would show) but if you do, cut shallow V-grooves to simulate the chamfered edges of strips of solid stock as indicated in Section A-A.

The shelf dadoes in the sides are cut, of course, before attaching the scrolled parts. Assemble the back and sides, the sides being rabbeted to accept the back, installing the shelf at the same time. Clamp and square-up the assembly and put it aside to let the glue set. All screws are countersunk to later be covered with wood putty.

The desk top is next: Glue and screw together the sides, front and back, and just screw on the narrow top piece. Also hinge the lift-up top to the strip. Note that the edges of the top and bottom of the desk are shaped with a router or shaper. If you do not have these tools, glue and brad strips of stock molding to the edges, cutting the pieces smaller to accommodate the widths of the molding. If you use plywood, the molding is ideal to hide the edge-grain.

Cut out the bottom of the desk, but do not install it. Instead, position it on the book case section (be sure the glue has set in the book case) and drill through the bottom of the desk into the upper edges of the sides for 3/8-inch dowels. Four are used in each side. Remove the desk bottom and glue and screw it to the desk members. Dowels now are glued into the holes in the sides, being allowed to project slightly less than ¾ inch.

Glue the book case assembly into the base, then fit the desk onto the book case, using plenty of glue on the dowels, but not so much that you have a problem cleaning away the excess.

Use the pattern you have previously made and cut out the back for the pigeon-hole section. Now cut out the various pieces and partitions from ½-inch stock and glue and brad the pigeon-hole section together.

Next, drill four holes down through the narrow section of the desk top, making them a size to be shank-clearance holes for No. 10 flathead wood screws. Position the pigeon-hole section on this narrow strip, locating it so there is 1 inch on each side, and 5/16 inch at the back. Reach inside the desk with a pencil and mark up through the holes onto the bottom of the pigeon-hole section. Remove the pigeon-hole section and drill pilot holes for the screws. Return the pigeon-hole section to the desk top and fasten it by driving screws up through the narrow part of the desk top.

Sand all surfaces smooth and stain to suit. The original was made of pine, but any soft or hardwood could be used. A satin-finish varnish or lacquer is applied over the stain.

SWIVEL CHAIR

Start the chair by turning the four legs and the three spindles. The swivel base and seat then are cut from 2-inch stock (1¾ inches net). Cut the back of the chair from a length of 2-inch stock 4¼ inches high. A 2 x 10-inch strip of ¾-inch stock is glued and nailed at the center of the back to create a "lip" when the assembly is sawed to the curved shape indicated.

Scooping out the seat will take time and work, using gouges, chisels and a disk sander, but it will be a lot more comfortable for sitting than if left flat.

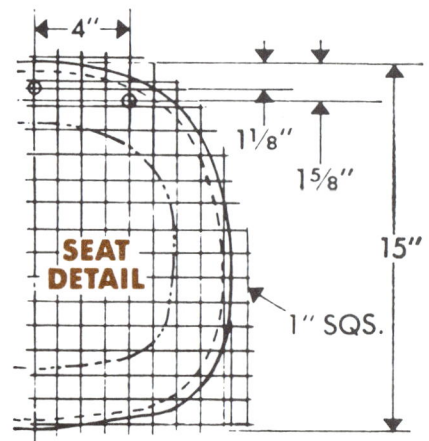

SEAT DETAIL

4"

1⅛"

1⅝"

15"

1" SQS.

LEG DETAIL

1¼" DIA.   2⁵⁄₁₆"   15⅞"   2"

½" SQS.

BACK-SUPPORT DETAIL

1⅛"   11⅛"   ¾" DIA.   1⅜"   1½"

9⁄₁₆" DIA.

BACK DETAIL   1" SQS

C   C   2"   ¾"   3½"

9⁄₁₆" DIA.

SECTION C-C

1¾"

9⁄₁₆" DIA.   7⁄₈"

14°

16½"   1¾"   14°

1¾"

1¼" DIA.
11½" DIA.
¼" RAD.

B   B
GRAIN

1" DIA.
SWIVEL

1" DIA. (FOR SWIVEL SCREW ACCESS)

15½° TRUE

SECTION B — B

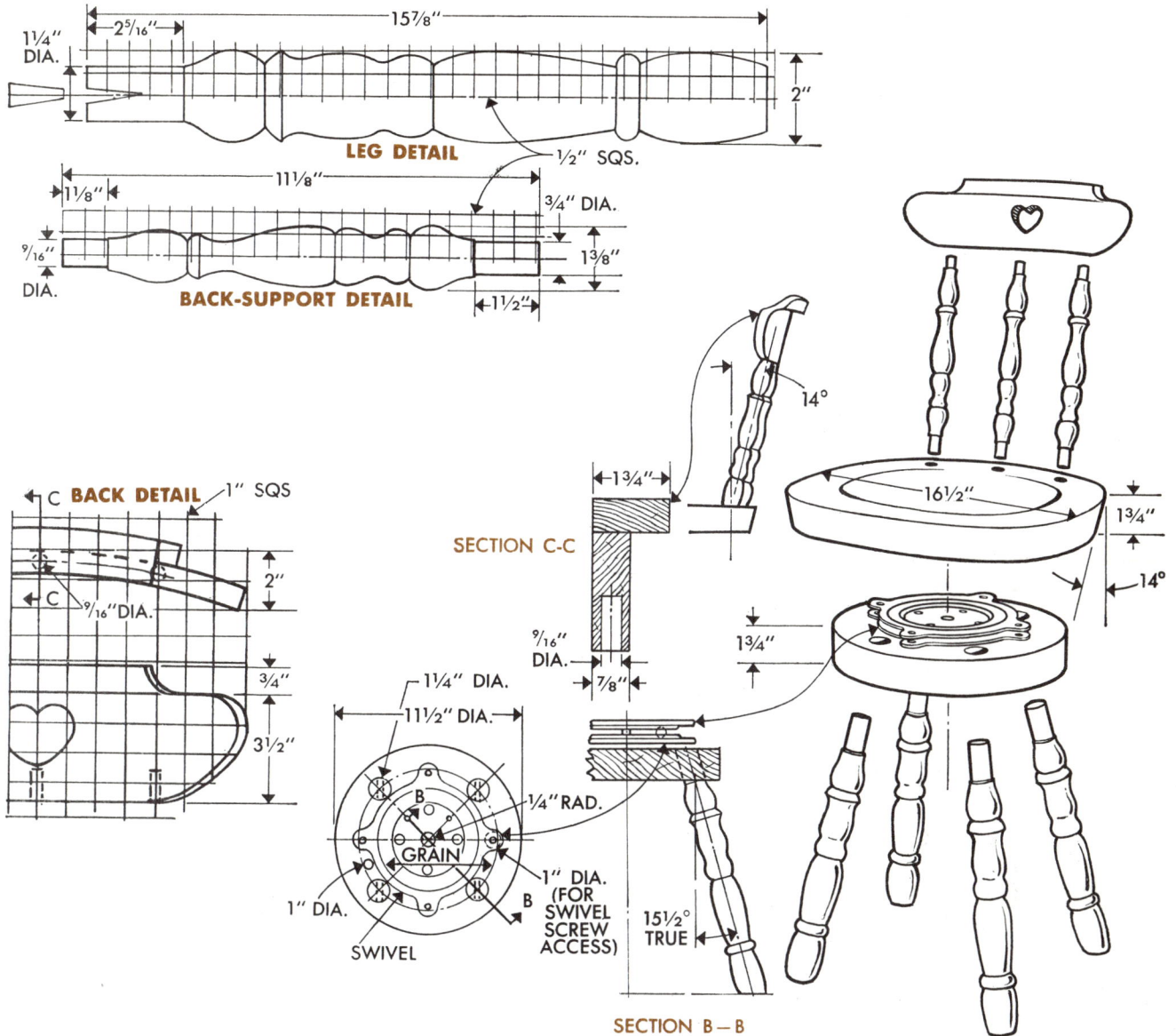

Cut notches in the upper ends of the legs and insert them in the holes drilled in the base. (Note there is also a 1-inch hole; it will be used for attaching the lazy Susan.) Position the slots at right angles to the grain, apply glue to the wedges and drive them in. Be sure the slots are positioned as indicated, because if they are in line with the grain, the wedges quite likely will sooner or later split the base. When the glue has set, sand down any projecting portion of the wedges.

Assemble the seat, spindles and back. When the glue has set, locate the lazy-Susan bearing in the center of the underside of the seat, mark the screw-hole locations and drill pilot holes. Drive the screws snug, but not quite home, then remove them, and the bearing.

Now, locate the bearing on the center of the leg base, mark the hole locations and drill the pilot holes. Drive these screws solidly to hold the bearing.

Turn the seat upside down, then position the base, with bearing attached, over the seat. By looking through the 1-inch hole you can position the bearing over one hole, then drive the screw almost home, but loose enough to permit moving the bearing to locate one other hole. Once you have driven screws in two of the holes in the bearing, the other holes will be in alignment, and you can turn the base to align the 1-inch holes over the screw-hole locations.

At this time, set the finished chair on a flat surface. If any of the legs is longer than the others, or the chair rocks, shim up the shorter legs to get the chair to set level. Now, using a block of wood about ¼ inch thick, and a sharp pencil, slide the block and pencil around each leg to mark it for cutting. Carefully cut on the lines you have made, then round the cut edges and tap on glides to the bottoms of the legs that now will fit parallel to the floor.

Stain and finish the chair the same as the desk.

If lazy-Susan bearings are not available, get a heavy-duty bearing, of the type designed for about 200-pound loads. This is the type of bearing used for swivel tables that support television sets. The lighter types of bearing, as used for lazy-Susan trays and the like, will not be strong enough to support the weight of a person sitting in the chair.

TRESTLE DESK

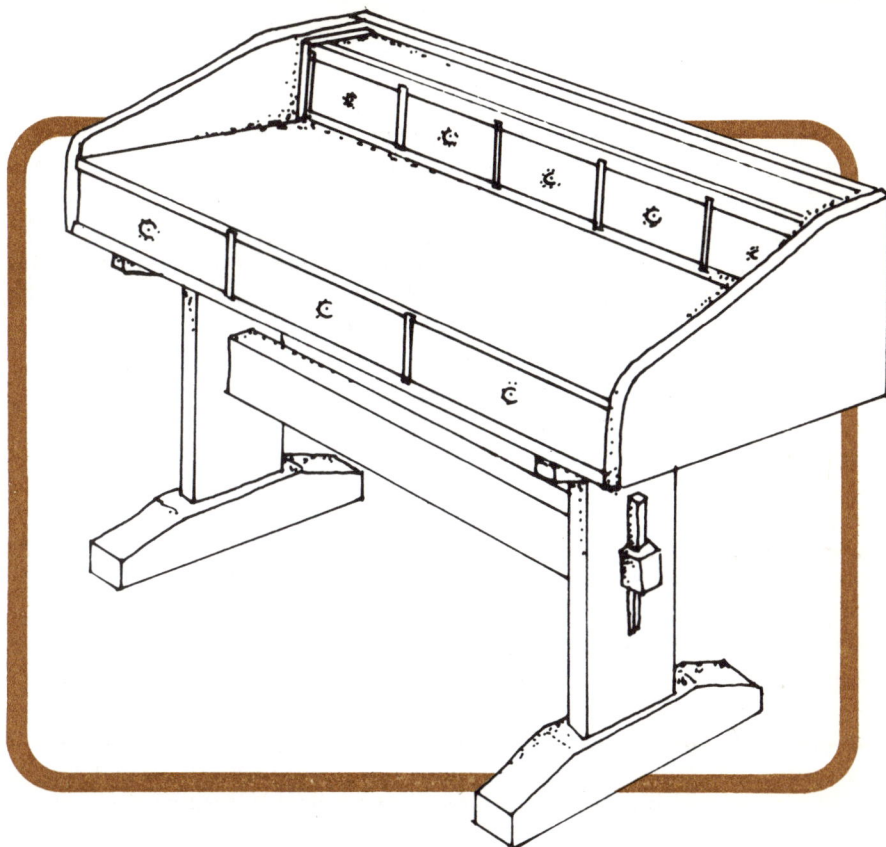

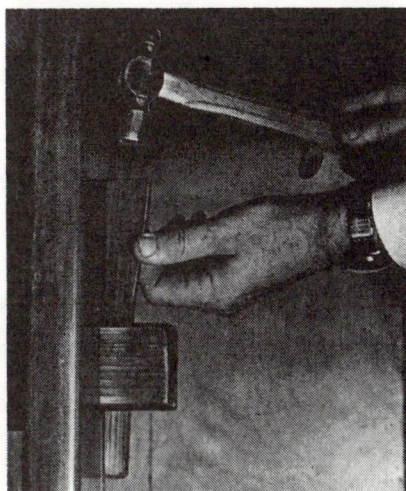

Made of low-cost pine shelving and common structural lumber, this attractive desk rivals any commercial reproduction in appearance and workmanship, and the price of the materials for the assembly is only a fraction of the cost of a factory-made item.

When you select the wood at the lumberyard, find out which is the lowest-cost lumber that has been stored indoors, or at least under cover, for three to six months. The desk top and bottom, as well as the drawer fronts, are cut from 1-inch (¾-inch net) pine shelving. The end pieces of the desk are made of 1¼-inch material, pine or hemlock. Legs and feet of the desk are 2 x 8 structural pine and 4 x 4 cedar post, respectively, as per the drawing. The trestle between the ends is a length of 2 x 4.

Choose wood that is generously endowed with tight knots, as they will add beauty to the finished product. Knots that come loose during construction can be glued back in place. Cracks and checks in the lumber also add to the character, but be sure they are not extensive enough to create weakness.

Start from the bottom and work up. Cut all structural members to the dimensions shown. Make the 1½ x 6-inch mortises in the feet to receive the legs, whose bottom ends are shaped to tenons to fit. A mortising attachment for a drill press does a fast job of cutting the mortises, but this tool is not essential to the craftsman who keeps his wood chisels sharp. Use a quality casein or white glue on all joints. Case-hardened or 6d cut nails (flooring nails with square heads) add realism to the antique look of the completed desk.

The ends of the trestle are mortised ½ x 1 inch to receive the wedges. These joints need not be glued as they permit quick disassembly should the desk later be transported to another location. Carriage bolts near the tops of the legs also aid in easy disassembly.

Three 1 x 8s are edge-glued to create panels for the writing surface and the bottom of the desk. Separators between the drawers, and the 1¼-inch ends produce a rigid structure. Cut nails are used on the glued joints and set just flush with the surface.

The top shelf is built and fitted last. Note that the separators for the small drawers are dadoed in place, like those for the larger drawers below. Dimensional stability and a good finished appearance result from this method of assembly. After nailing and gluing in place, the top shelf is finished by installing ¼-inch quarter round at each end against the sides.

The five smaller upper drawers are made in the same manner as the lower drawers. Sides and backs of the drawers are ½-inch pine. Although not quite authentic, 1/8-inch hardboard or plywood is used for the bottoms of the drawers. All the drawer pieces are cut at one time to assure uniformity of size and make assembly easier. Brads and glue make all joints secure.

Before assembling the drawers, the fronts are decorated as shown. The groove around the edges of each front is made with a 1/8-inch router bit. If you do not have a portable router, a bit can be checked in a drill press, with the press turning at maximum speed. Concentric circles at the centers of the drawer fronts are made with a fly-cutter, or with various-size hole saws. White porcelain knobs are centered in the decorations to add an authentic antique look.

After all joints have been assembled long enough for the glue to set completely, the finishing operations can be done. First, all exposed corners and edges are drastically rounded to simulate wear. A radius of about ¼ inch is made with a plane or coarse file or rasp. The radius should not be uniform, but rather of random configuration to simulate the wear of many years. Final sanding should be with fine-grit paper to reproduce the sheen and patina created by both age and countless contacts with people.

Distress marks may be added before sanding, if a real "antique" finish is desired. Striking with a tire chain, rolling nails under a rolling pin, beating with a hammer, are some of the techniques frequently used for distressing.

Either a light or dark stain may be employed with equal success, depending on one's preference. A "fruitwood" provides a warm, light-brown color. The stain is applied with a brush and promptly wiped off with a cloth. Shading around corners and edges can be blended in by hand, or by the use of a spray gun, if desired.

After the stain has dried at least one full day, an oil finish can be applied. Refined tung oil is excellent for a one-coat satin finish. Boiled linseed oil also is used by many craftsmen. The oil is applied with a brush, and preferably is heated before application so it penetrates the wood more readily. If the wood is particularly absorbent, a second coat may be indicated.

After the oil has been applied for 15 or 20 minutes, it is rubbed briskly with a clean, dry cloth to remove excess oil and dry the wood. A uniform satin sheen will indicate that the wood has been dried and

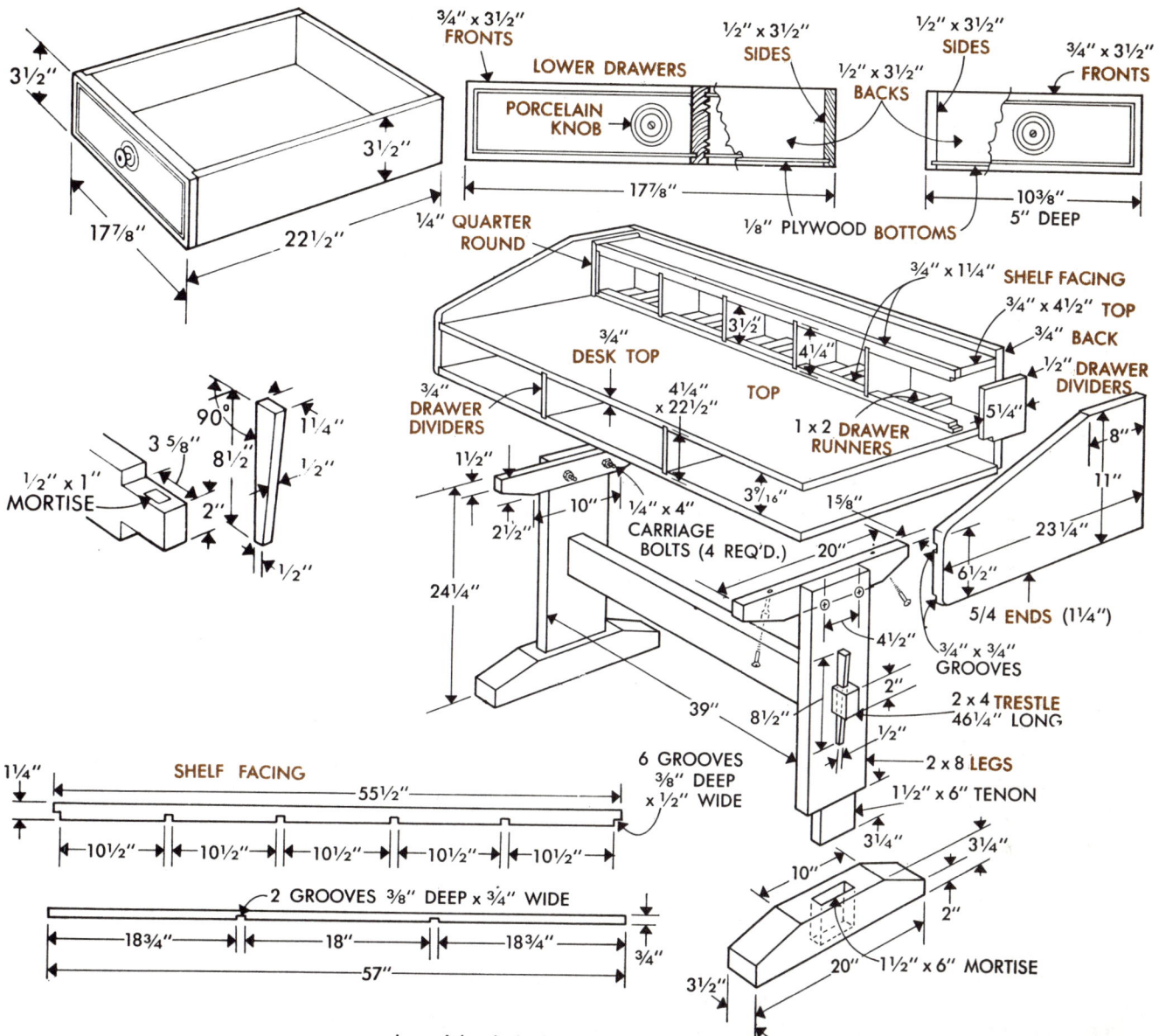

3½"

17⅞"   22½"

3½"

3½"

¾" × 3½"
FRONTS

LOWER DRAWERS

PORCELAIN KNOB

½" × 3½" SIDES

½" × 3½" BACKS

½" × 3½" SIDES

¾" × 3½" FRONTS

17⅞"

1/8" PLYWOOD BOTTOMS

10⅜"
5" DEEP

¼" QUARTER ROUND

¾" × 1¼" SHELF FACING

¾" × 4½" TOP

¾" BACK

½" DRAWER DIVIDERS

DESK TOP

3½"

4¼"

¾"

¾"
DRAWER DIVIDERS

4¼" × 22½"

TOP

5¼"

8"

11"

90°

1¼"

8½"   ½"

2"

½"

3⅝"

½" × 1" MORTISE

1½"

2½"

10"

¼" × 4" CARRIAGE BOLTS (4 REQ'D.)

1 × 2 DRAWER RUNNERS

3⁹⁄₁₆"

1⅝"

20"

23¼"

6½"

5/4 ENDS (1¼")

24¼"

39"

8½"

4½"

¾" × ¾" GROOVES

2"

½"

2 × 4 TRESTLE 46¼" LONG

2 × 8 LEGS

1½" × 6" TENON

3¼"

SHELF FACING

1¼"

55½"

10½"   10½"   10½"   10½"   10½"

2 GROOVES ⅜" DEEP × ¾" WIDE

18¾"   18"   18¾"

57"

¾"

6 GROOVES ⅜" DEEP × ½" WIDE

10"

3¼"

2"

20"   1½" × 6" MORTISE

3½"

burnished. It is a good idea to follow this treatment in a month or so with another coat of oil and a brisk rubbing and burnishing. Polishes and waxes should not be used.

If the oil finish is used, remember that varnish or lacquer cannot later be applied, as the oil will prevent the finish from setting hard. For a more permanent finish, but one that gives a "hand-rubbed" look, a penetrating sealer is good. Even the type used for hardwood floors can be employed. The sealer can be obtained in both light and dark shades, and since it actually penetrates the wood, there is no surface finish to chip or crack, and any minor damage can be repaired by applying more of the sealer with fine steel wool.

The drawers should be finished outside the desk, which also permits brushing stain and finish inside the openings into which the drawers fit. The two wedges also should be finished before they are inserted in the slots in the trestle.

VICTORIAN DOLL HOUSE

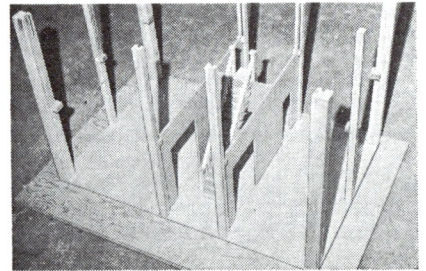

First floor is fitted on base, partitions parallel to stairway and short wall under stair are installed.

Second floor fits on cleats attached to columns. Bannister fits around stairwell. Note notches in corners of roof.

There's a touch of nostalgia in this unusual doll house that is patterned after the architecture of the 19th century when the vogue was restrained elegance. They did not have air conditioning in those days, but the high ceilings assured a cool house in the summer—unfortunately, also cool in the winter.

Actual construction of the doll house is quite simple. You can build it in one of two ways, either with ready-made shutters sold by unfinished-furniture shops and mailorder houses, or with shutters you make yourself. These instructions include plans for making shutters. The builder can save a considerable amount of money by spending time. Ready-made shutters can cost from 30 to 50 dollars, just for these components.

Before you start building, determine where in the house you will locate the doll house. The narrow width of the base is 29¾ inches, and this will be a close squeeze through some interior 30-inch doors when the door stops are considered. If a door is less than 30 inches, you will have "built a boat in the basement." In such a situation, make the base, porch and porch columns easily removable. This will make the house 6 inches narrower for easy moving.

Start construction by gluing and nailing the posts to the floor that is a 24 x 36-inch piece of ½-inch plywood. Note that the corner posts are grooved on two sides 1½ inches down from the top to accept the ends of the shutter stops. The two posts at the front and back of the house are grooved the full length inside to hold the partitions upstairs and downstairs that parallel the stairway. The center posts at the ends of the house are grooved 13 inches down from the top to

Here partitions for second floor are in place and shutter stops are attached to columns. Partition corners are notched.

Two shutters that form end of houses are hinged to open fully, provide access to the house. Shutters fit against stop.

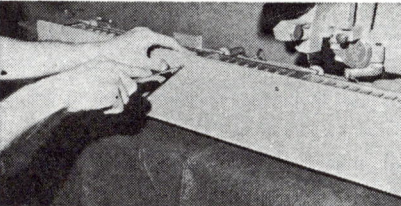

Gallery posts are attached to balcony by driving screws up through the floor. A spot of glue under each post helps.

Screws are driven down through the floor of the gallery (balcony) to secure the columns that support it at each end.

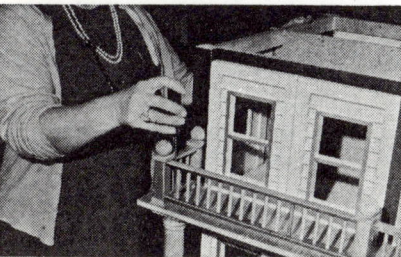

accommodate the ends of second-floor partitions.

Small blocks are glued to the columns at the corners and ends of the house to support the second floor. The partitions by the stairway support the floor at the center of the house. The floor and partitions are cut from ¼-inch plywood, hardboard or particleboard.

After this basic framework is up, cut and fit the shutters, altering some to accept doors or windows (or make your shutters to fit around these) and attach or hinge them to the posts. Both shutters on each end of the house are hinged, as is the center one at the back of the house. All others are nailed and glued to the shutter stops and the floor. Screws or nails are driven up through the floor to hold shutters.

After the shutters are fitted, set them aside and paint them before installing. Make the stairway, either from a solid block as indicated, or from stringers, risers and treads to be more realistic. Glue the upper end of the stair to the partition, and glue and screw the lower end to the floor. Glue and brads are used to install the second floor, then the stairwell railing (a real exercise in patience) is made and installed.

Attach the painted shutters, then make the porch and its railing. If you don't have a lathe, the porch columns can be assembled from dowels, or made square. The gallery posts can be assembled from square blocks and wooden beads if you lack a lathe.

Construction of the roof is the trickiest part of this project, but even it is not difficult if you keep in mind that all the rafters are cut at 45 degrees, except for the jack rafters at the corners and these require 45 x 45-degree compound miters.

Begin by cutting the end and side plates to size, with 45-degree miters on both ends. These are joined together with glue and finishing nails. Care should be taken to ensure that this basic frame is square.

Cut six side and end rafters (A) making sure all cuts are carefully measured and precisely cut.

These rafters are first nailed in place on the bottom plate, then the top brace is inserted and all the rafters glued and nailed to it. This job requires four hands to position properly.

Now comes the hard part; cutting the compound-miters on the jack rafters (B). The photographs and drawing show how to accomplish this. A radial arm saw is used to make the compound miters, but a good miter box and a jig will work just as well. Just be sure all your measurements are correct before you make the cuts, and be extra sure

Construction of roof is hardest part; make all cuts carefully and accurately, but remember, they will be concealed.

Cutting compound miters on jack rafters requires accurate measurements, careful cuts. Check direction of angles.

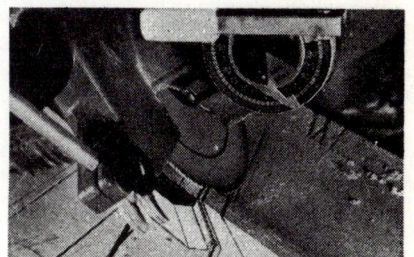

3/16" × 7/16" RAIL
(LENGTH TO FIT)

1/2" SQS.

1/2"

14"

1 1/4"

PORCH COLUMN

1/2"

2 1/2"

2 1/2"

FIRST TREAD

3/4"

3 1/2"

1/4"

1/4"

1/16" 1/8"

1/8"

1/8"

50°

3/4"

2 1/2"

STAIR BALLUSTER
(28 REQ'D.) 3/16" × 1/2"

STAIRWELL RAILING

3/16" SQ.
LOWER END
SHOULDERED
TO 1/8" DIA.

1/4" × 1/4" × 3"
BALLUSTERS

4 1/2"

10 1/2"

3 3/8"

11/16"

3/4"

11/16"

12" RISE

5/16"

3/4"

9 3/8" RUN

5 3/4"

SECOND-FLOOR NEWELL POST

4 3/8"

7/16" SQ.

15/16"

15/16"

FIRST-FLOOR NEWELL POST

1/8"

7"

7"

7"

10"

TYPICAL 10"
SHUTTER (6 REQ'D.)

2"

4" × 7"
WINDOWS
(16 REQ'D.)

2 3/4"

3/4"

1/4"

1/4"

1/4"

4"

1"

7"

7/8" DIA.

1/4"

1/4"

3 1/2"

1/4"

1 1/8"

GALLERY POST
7/8" × 7/8" SQ.
(4 FULL-SIZE AND
2 HALF-SIZE REQ'D.)

(4 REQ'D.)
7" SHUTTER

5"

HOLES THROUGH
BOTTOM RAIL

RAIL

1/4" × 3/4"

1/4" DOWELS

6"

4 7/16"

15 1/4"

8"

11 1/4"

1"

38"

HOLES 1/8" DEEP
IN TOP RAIL

1 3/4"

8 3/8"

4 1/2"

5 SAW CUTS
1/32" DEEP

FRONT AND
BACK DOOR 1/2"
PLYWOOD

FRONT AND BACK-DOOR SHUTTER
(FRONT DOOR OPENS, REAR DOOR
FIXED, ENTIRE SHUTTER IS HINGED)

23 7/8"
(TYPICAL)

8"

7"

3"

8"

STAIR TREADS ¼" STOCK
(15 REQ'D., INCLUDING
SHORT ONE)

ROOF SHEATHING
⅛" PLYWOOD

SHINGLE DETAIL

¼"

1¼"

3"

¼"

1/16"

GRAIN

DORMER SASH

12"

1 3/8"

45 x 45
COMPOUND ANGLE
ON JACK RAFTER

45°

ROOF SHEATHING

RAFTERS
¾" x 1"

SECTION
SHUTTER

2"

3/8"

¾"

4"

5"

36"

24"

¾" x 1¾"

45°

2"

¾"

12"

PLATE

21½"

33½"

¾" x 1¼"
STOP

45°

45°

45°

CORNER POSTS
1½" x 1½"

¾"

23"

23"

PARTITION

15½"

12¾"

11¼"

¾" x 1"
POST

¾" x 1"

⅛"

1"

SECOND-FLOOR
PARTITIONS

SECTION
LOUVER

½"

7"

3"

3"

3"

3"

3"

11½"

SHUTTER
STOP

¾"

¾"

¼" x ¼"
TENON

¾"

7⅛"

5¾"

6½"

1¼"

½"

¾"

¼"

¼"

STILE AND
RAIL
SECTION

SHUTTER
STOP

¾"

SHUTTER

STAIRWELL

¾" x ¾"
NOTCH CORNERS

¼" PLYWOOD OR
PARTICLEBOARD

22½"

5½"

3½"

1½" x 1½"

34½"

10"

15¼"

CORNER POST

2 7/16"

1½"

2½"

2 7/16"

SECOND
FLOOR

SECOND FLOOR
PLAN

3"

7⅛"

12"

3"

7"

FIRST-
FLOOR
HALL
PARTITION

HALF-LAP
JOINT

13"

25"

23"

2½"

2½"

7¾"

12"

2½"

7" x 8"

WINDOWS
(6 REQ'D.)

8¾"

8¾"

3"

1" x 1"

BRASS BUTT
HINGES TYPICAL

6"

36"

24"

½" PLYWOOD
FLOOR

4¾"

29¾"

42"

6½"

FIRST-FLOOR
PLAN

BASE ¾" PLYWOOD

¼"

1"

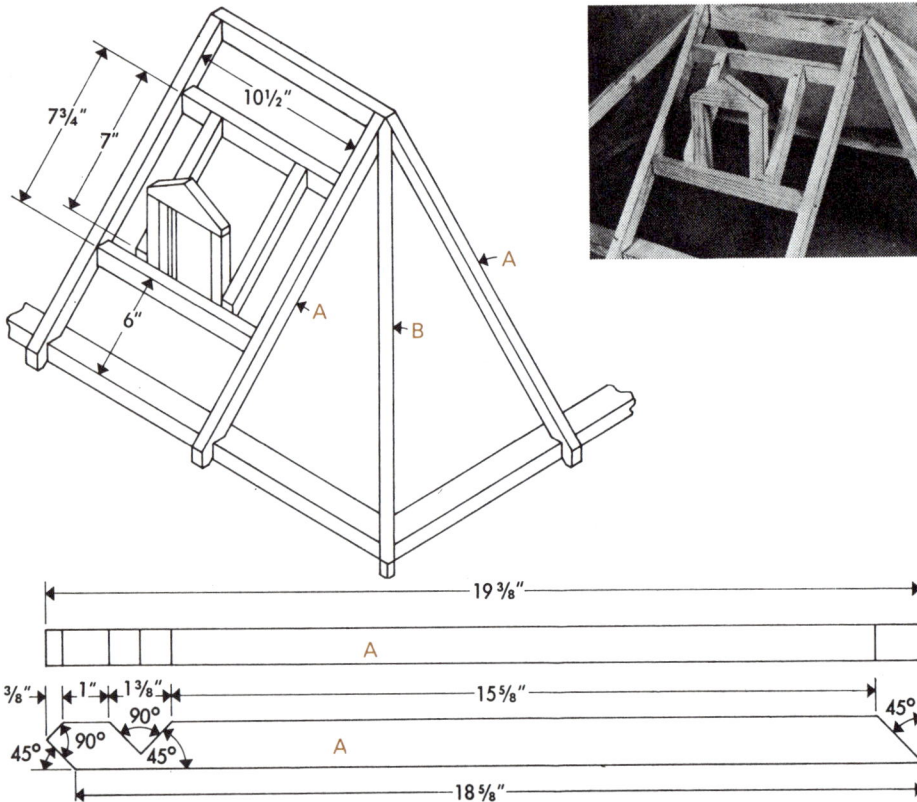

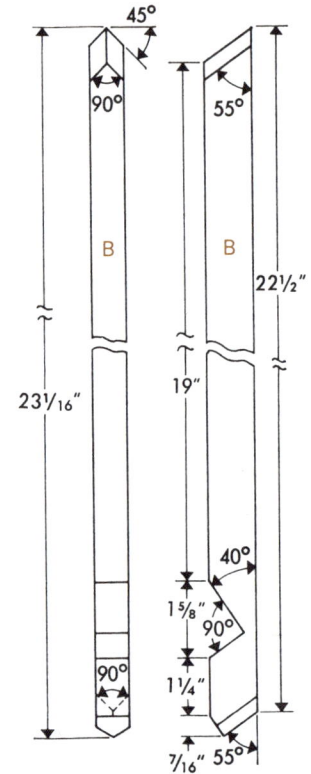

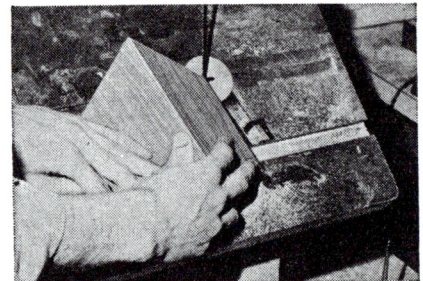

Roof framing is the most difficult part. Here it is shown fitted to the body of the house.

Dormer is installed, then roof "decking" behind it is glued in place. Cutout in decking makes it more realistic.

Plywood roof for dormer has edges cut at angle to fit snugly against slope of the roof; shingles cover joint.

the angle of the cut is facing the proper direction. After cutting the rafters, they are glued and nailed in position.

The dormer construction comes next and is then placed between the side rafters. Construction can be a little tricky, but remember, all the edges and joints will be covered by the plywood roofing and shingles, so a perfect fit is not necessary.

For realism the individual shingles can be made from cedar. However, you will spend many tedious hours completing this task. To save time and patience cut strips of stock with the shingle profile, then score the strips at random to simulate shingles. It will save a lot of time and work. Position the shingles to have a 2-inch exposure.

To complete the project attach four swivel-type 2-inch casters under the base for easier moving. The house does weigh enough to make it difficult to move easily.

DRESSER CADDY

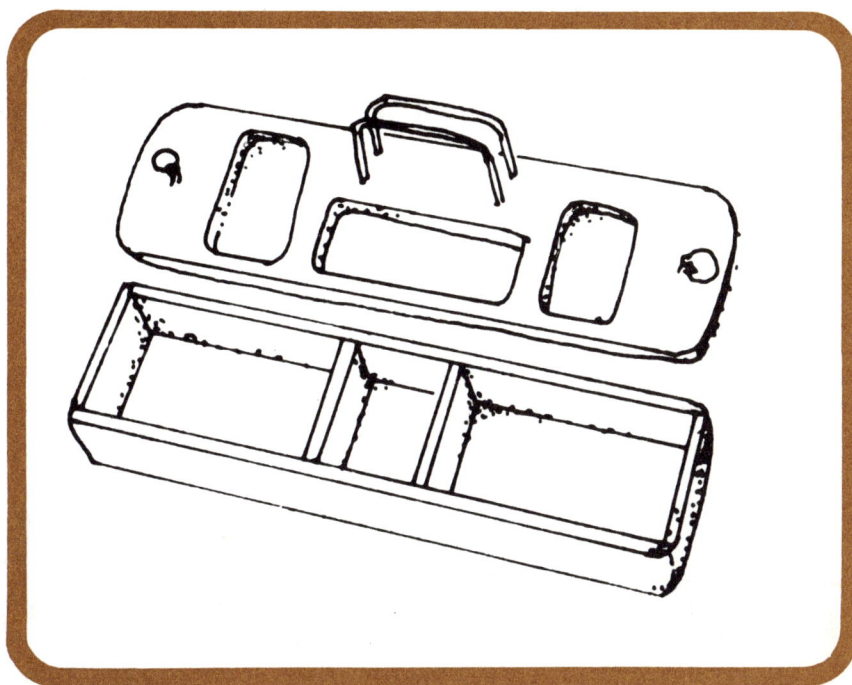

Solve the problem of clutter in the bedroom with this dresser caddy, designed to hold a variety of items that usually end up on finished surfaces. The caddy features recesses on top, a billfold holder and a divided tray underneath. Built with basic hand and power tools, this simple, yet attractive piece is a good project for the youngster in the family. This is a gift for Dad that will please Mom.

Start construction with the top tray, made from a solid piece of 1½-inch hardwood stock. Mark the outline of the recesses and the holes for the brass rod to be used for the billfold holder. Cut the recesses with a router or, outline and remove waste with a chisel. The offsets in the tray can be made with a router or dado blade. First, set up for a ½-inch wide rabbet and, with several passes, cut to ¾ inch deep around the bottom of the piece. Start the second cut at the inside of the first one, but go only 3/8 inch deep. Make the contour on the upper edge with a shaper or hand plane and sand to shape.

The bottom tray is a simple box with two partitions. Make a 1/8 x ¼-inch rabbet in the bottom edge of all sides. The ends are simply glued and bradded between the front and back, as are the partitions. Make the bottom from either 1/8-inch hardwood plywood or hardboard and glue and brad in place. Round the corners with a rasp and sandpaper.

If you haven't drilled the holes for the brass rod, drill these. Cut the brass rod into 10½-inch lengths and bend to shape using a piece of dowel to round the corners.

Brass ring-type drawer pulls may be added to compliment the brass billfold holder. These may be left off entirely or some other trim of your choice added. A good idea would be to change the hardware and finish to match your bedroom furniture.

If you wish to make one for a woman the bottom tray can be partitioned into smaller compartments to hold jewelry. In this case, the billfold holder could be changed to a "tree" for necklaces or earrings. This is a very versatile design that can be adapted to many imaginative uses.

You will probably want to sand and finish the piece before you insert the rod into the top. Just glue it into the drilled holes. A final touch could be to add a felt or flannel pad on the bottom. When finished, you have an attractive and functional piece that keeps things organized and protects the finish of your furniture.

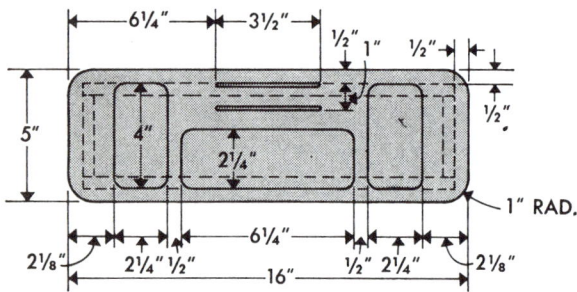

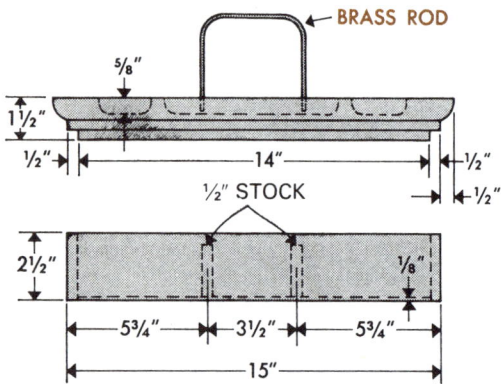

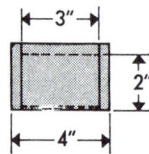

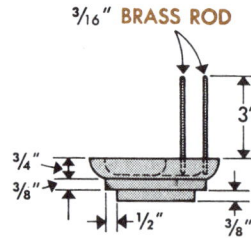

TOY EARTH MOVER

Junior engineers who are planning extensive excavating in the sandbox will welcome the addition of this giant-size off-road earth mover to their line of equipment.

Sturdy construction from ¾-inch hardwood assures long life. Easy movement is the result of the "oversize" wheels that are 4 x 6-inch rubber-tined replacement mower wheels. They can be purchased at lawnmower dealers and hardware stores.

Work on the project can be started with either the tractor or trailer. The floor of the trailer on which the hopper sets is cut from ¾-inch stock, then the hopper sides, back, front and bottom are cut as indicated. "Dry-assemble" the hopper, then mark along the sides to indicate the position of the bottom. Next, cut the curved shapes that are fitted to the inner surfaces of the sides and glue these "overlays" in place. Assemble the trailer with its hopper and fit the kerfed block at the front to accept the forward edge of the light sheet metal that forms the hopper. If you don't have a piece of sheet metal handy in the shop, cut a couple of large food tins apart, make one or two lap joints and solder them. The easiest metal to use, of course, is the lightweight do-it-yourself aluminum available in most hardware stores. Brads are easily driven through it along the edge into the overlays. It may be necessary to first punch holes in the metal.

Make the hitch for the trailer, as dimensioned. Although ¼-inch aluminum is indicated, you can use 1/8-inch stock, which might be more readily available at your local hardware store. Cut and assemble the axle housing for the trailer.

Start the tractor next, first making the floor. The sides require

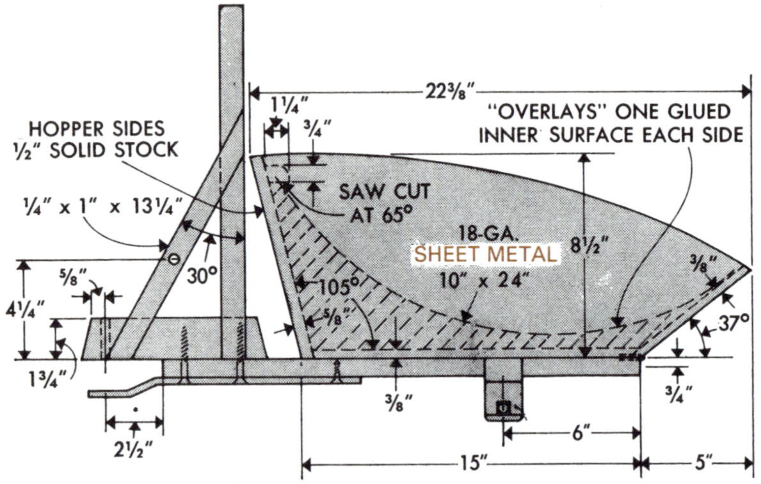
HOPPER SIDES
½" SOLID STOCK
¼" x 1" x 13¼"
22⅜"
1¼"
¾"
"OVERLAYS" ONE GLUED
INNER SURFACE EACH SIDE
SAW CUT
AT 65°
18-GA.
SHEET METAL
10" x 24"
8½"
⅜"
37°
30°
105°
⅝"
4¼"
1¾"
⅜"
¾"
2½"
6"
15"
5"

HARDWOOD
HOIST ASSEMBLY

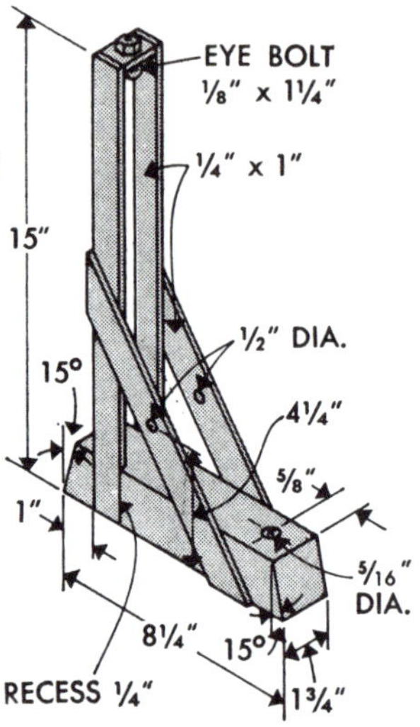
EYE BOLT
⅛" x 1¼"
¼" x 1"
15"
½" DIA.
15°
4¼"
⅝"
1"
5/16"
DIA.
8¼"
15°
RECESS ¼"
1¾"

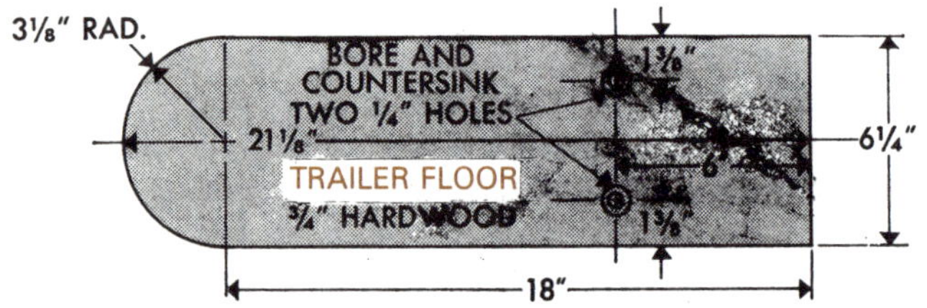
3⅛" RAD.
BORE AND
COUNTERSINK
TWO ¼" HOLES
1⅜"
21⅛"
6"
6¼"
TRAILER FLOOR
¾" HARDWOOD
1⅜"
18"

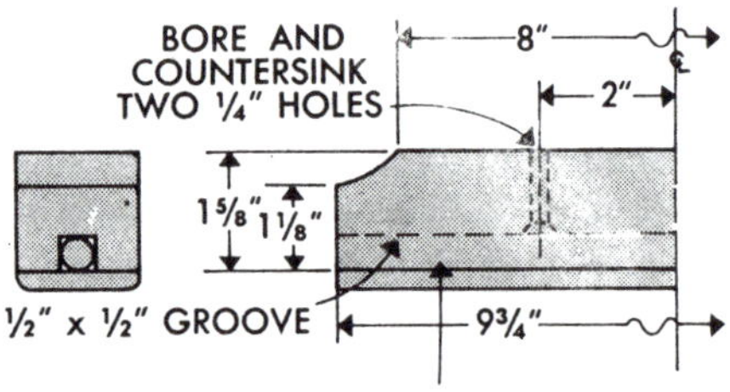
BORE AND
COUNTERSINK
TWO ¼" HOLES
8"
2"
1⅝"
1⅛"
½" x ½" GROOVE
9¾"

CAB AXLE HOUSING

TRAILER AXLE HOUSING

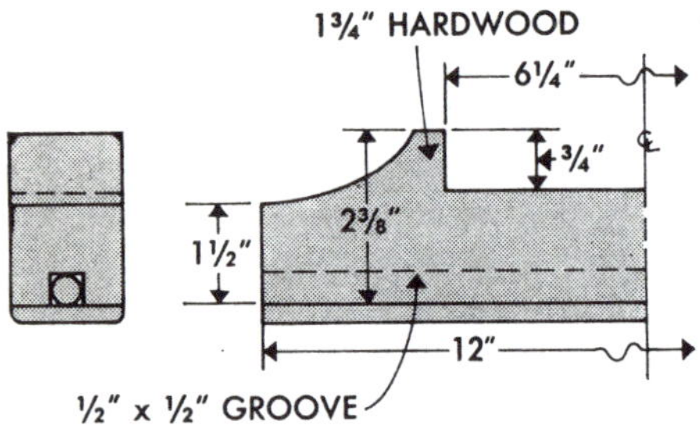
1¾" HARDWOOD
6¼"
¾"
2⅜"
1½"
12"
½" x ½" GROOVE

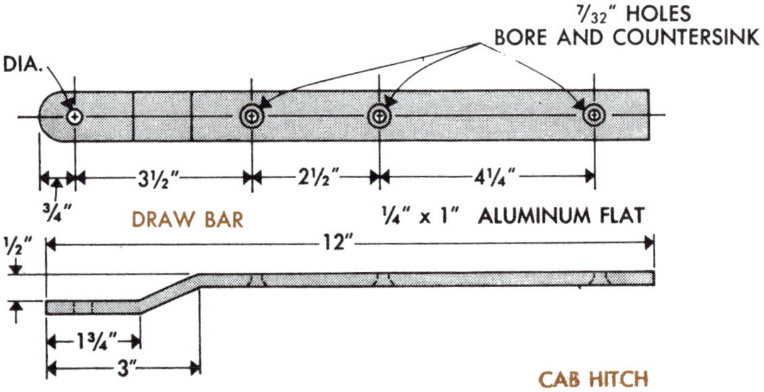
7/32" HOLES
BORE AND COUNTERSINK
5/16" DIA.
3½"
2½"
4¼"
¾"
DRAW BAR
¼" x 1" ALUMINUM FLAT
½"
12"
1¾"
3"

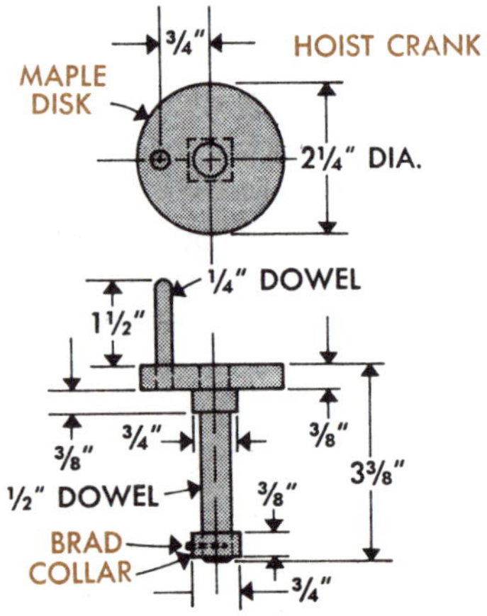
¾"
HOIST CRANK
MAPLE
DISK
2¼" DIA.
¼" DOWEL
1½"
¾"
⅜"
⅜"
3⅜"
½" DOWEL
⅜"
BRAD
COLLAR
¾"

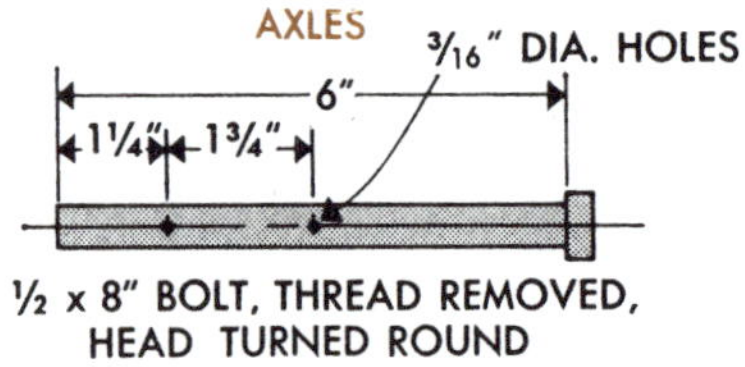
AXLES
3/16" DIA. HOLES
6"
1¼"
1¾"
½ x 8" BOLT, THREAD REMOVED,
HEAD TURNED ROUND

CAB HITCH

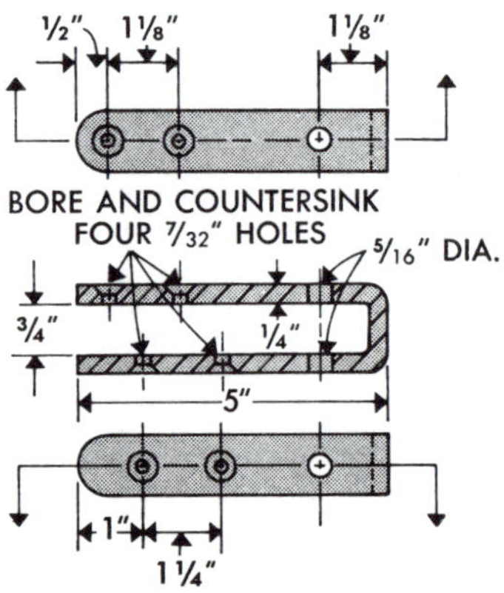
½"
1⅛"
1⅛"
BORE AND COUNTERSINK
FOUR 7/32" HOLES
5/16" DIA.
¾"
¼"
5"
1"
1¼"

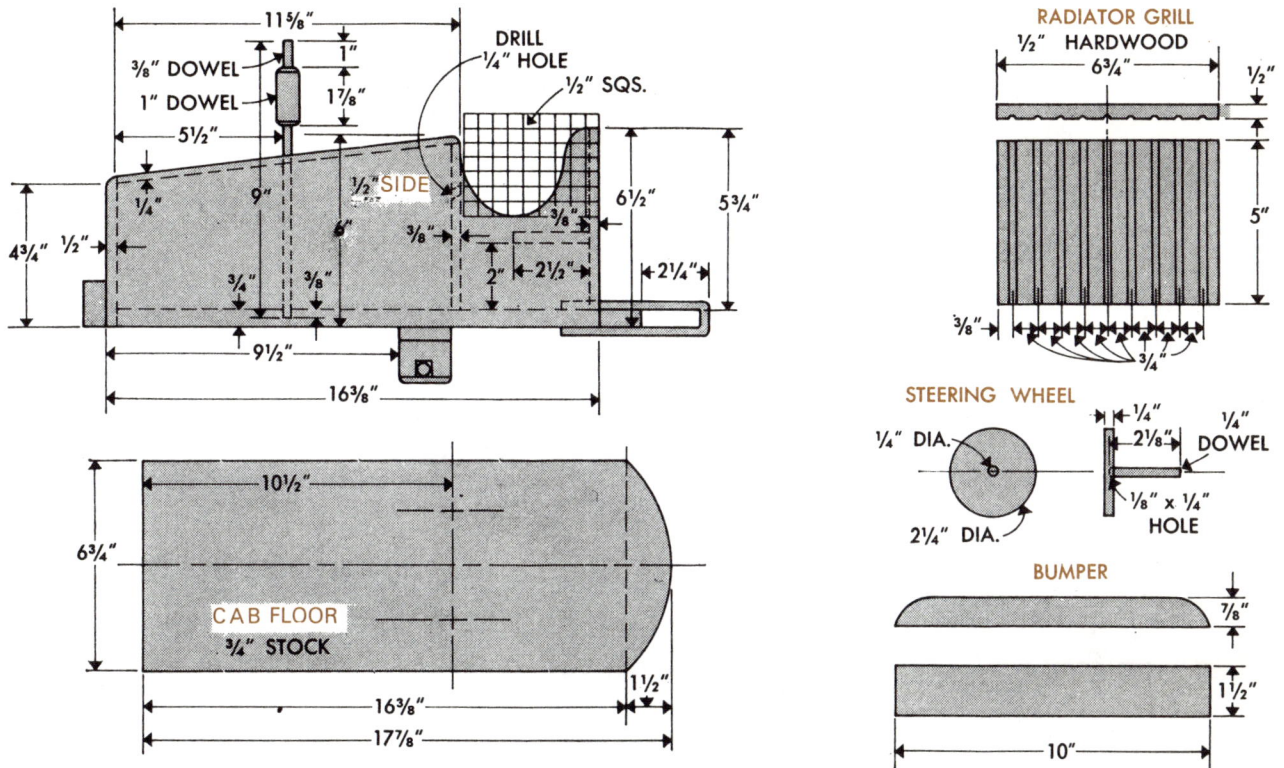

Diagram labels (side view, top left):
- 11 5/8"
- 3/8" DOWEL
- 1" DOWEL
- 5 1/2"
- 1"
- 1 7/8"
- DRILL 1/4" HOLE
- 1/2" SQS.
- 1/2" SIDE
- 9"
- 6"
- 4 3/4" 1/2"
- 1/4"
- 3/4" 3/8"
- 3/8"
- 6 1/2"
- 5 3/4"
- 3/8"
- 2"
- 2 1/2"
- 2 1/4"
- 9 1/2"
- 16 3/8"

Cab floor:
- 10 1/2"
- 6 3/4"
- CAB FLOOR 3/4" STOCK
- 16 3/8"
- 17 7/8"
- 1 1/2"

RADIATOR GRILL
- 1/2" HARDWOOD
- 6 3/4"
- 1/2"
- 5"
- 3/8"
- 3/4"

STEERING WHEEL
- 1/4" DIA.
- 2 1/4" DIA.
- 1/4"
- 2 1/8"
- 1/4" DOWEL
- 1/8" x 1/4" HOLE

BUMPER
- 7/8"
- 1 1/2"
- 10"

making a pattern by enlarging the squared drawing that provides the shape of the "cockpit." Cut the other parts to the sizes shown. Note that the seat also could be a solid block, rather than the 3/8-inch piece indicated. The block, if one is used, as well as the back of the trailer, must be notched to fit over the hitch. If you use 1/8-inch stock rather than the 1/4-inch shown, make the notch to fit. Be sure to make the hitch and install it on the base before assembling the tractor.

The axle housing is assembled on the underside of the base. When making the "radiator" use a block of hardwood about three times the required length. Saw the kerfs as indicated, then cut off the radiator to the proper width. This will keep your hands away from the saw.

The hoist assembly is made of hardwood strips to the dimensions shown. Note that the vertical members are recessed their thickness into the base block so the angled braces are parallel. When you attach the hoist to the trailer base, align it with the hitch, then drill through the hole in the hitch and through the base of the hoist, which assures that these holes will be in line and readily accept the hitch pin. The crank is fitted in the hoist in the holes in the braces, then is held in place by a collar that is bradded to it as indicated. Light chain or heavy cord is fastened to the "drum" of the hoist, run through a small pulley suspended from an eye bolt (or just through the eye bolt) and to the lower center edge of the front of the hopper that is pivoted to the base of the trailer with a couple of small strap hinges.

The axles for this rig are 1/2 x 8-inch cap screws with the threads removed and the heads turned or ground round. They are drilled as indicated to be attached with screws. Depending on the wheels used you may have to drill a hole near one end to accept a cotter key.

ETAGERE

Meaning a cabinet with open shelves for the display of knick-knacks, the word "etagere" is of French derivation.

For this version, start with the base, consisting of the four legs and shaped aprons joined with dowels. It will be necessary to glue up blocks for the legs, and the aprons also are glued up to be about 1¼ inches thick. It is not critical to make the aprons that thickness, but it does create a more rigid base. Glue blocks, cut 45 degrees at each end, are glued and screwed inside the base for further reinforcement.

The cabinet bottom is made next, and the edges are shaped, or a molding is glued and tacked on to provide a finished look. Bore four 1-inch holes, as indicated, to accept the corner posts of the cabinet. The back and sides of the cabinet are made up of rails, stiles (corner posts) and raised panels. You will need a shaper to create the curved tops of the panels, and to groove the curved rail. Turn a 1-inch-diameter tenon on each end of each corner post, and center-drill one end.

Fasten the assembled panels to the cabinet floor by driving screws up through the floor into the lower rails. The floor then is attached to the base by screws driven through the base in counterbored holes.

Attach the cabinet top, using glue in the holes for the corner-post tenons, plus a finishing nail that will be hidden by the square portion of the turned spacer. Eight of the spacers are the same, for the two lower shelves, but the upper spacers are slightly different. The ½-inch-diameter tenon on the lower end of each spacer fits in the hole bored in the upper tenon of the spacer below.

The upper trim pieces next are cut to shape and doweled to the

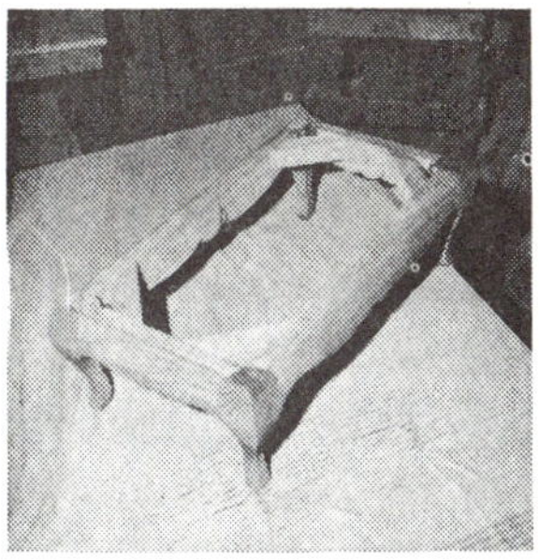

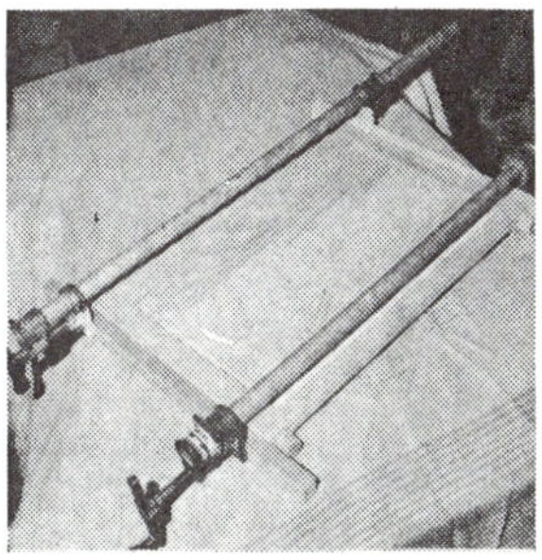

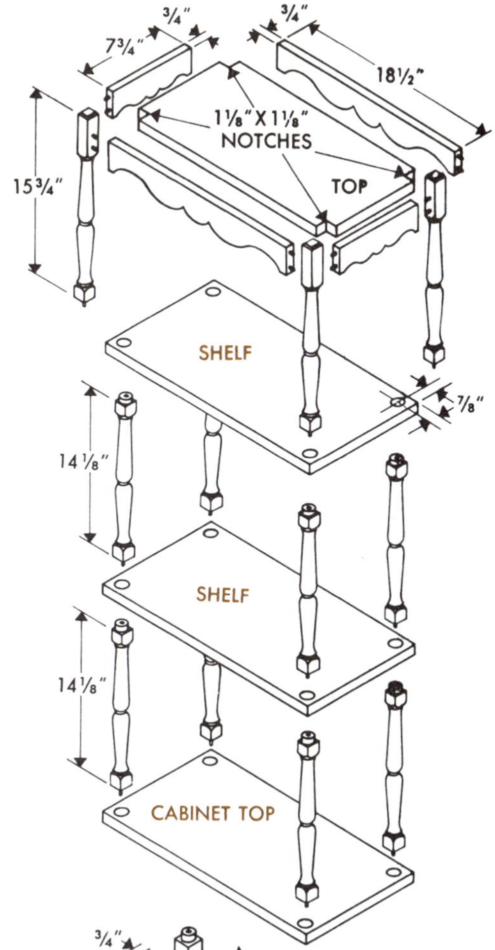
3/4"
7 3/4"
3/4"
18 1/2"
1 1/8" X 1 1/8"
NOTCHES
TOP
15 3/4"
SHELF
7/8"
14 1/8"
SHELF
14 1/8"
CABINET TOP

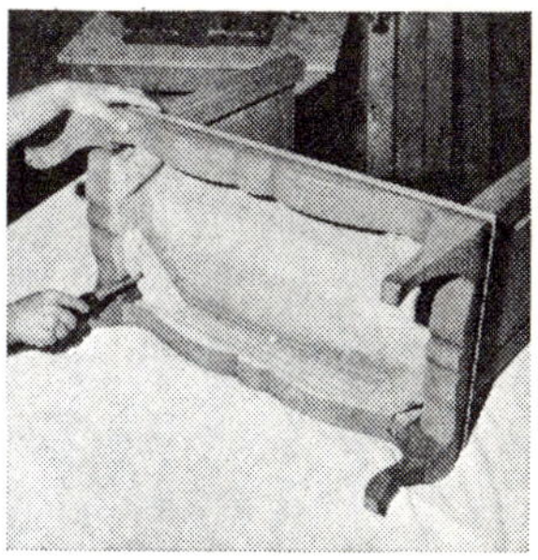

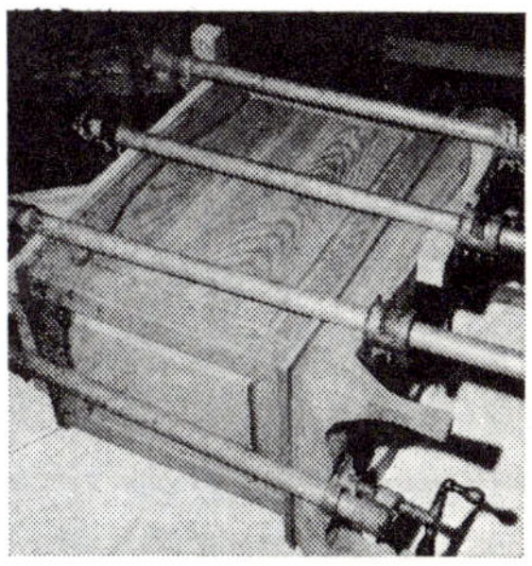

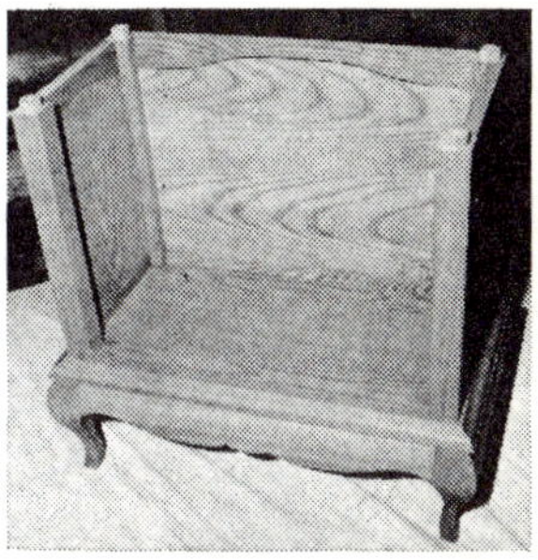

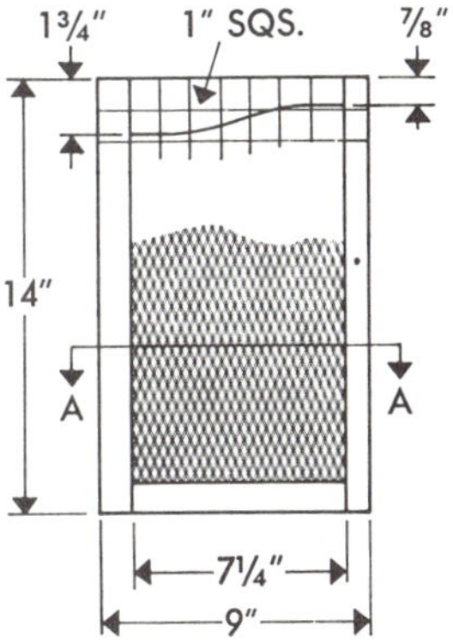
1 3/4"
1" SQS.
7/8"
14"
A
A
7 1/4"
9"

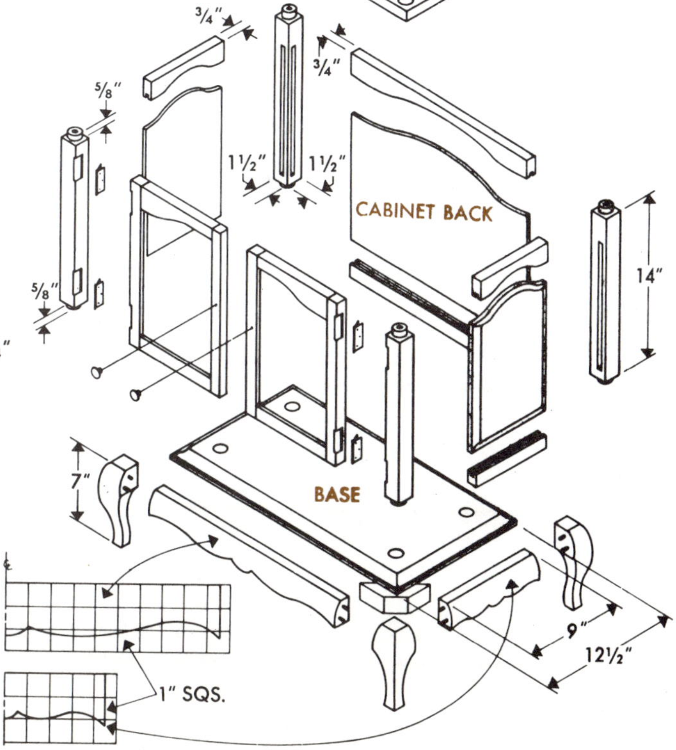
3/4"
3/4"
5/8"
5/8"
1 1/2"
1 1/2"
CABINET BACK
14"
7"
BASE
9"
12 1/2"
1" SQS.

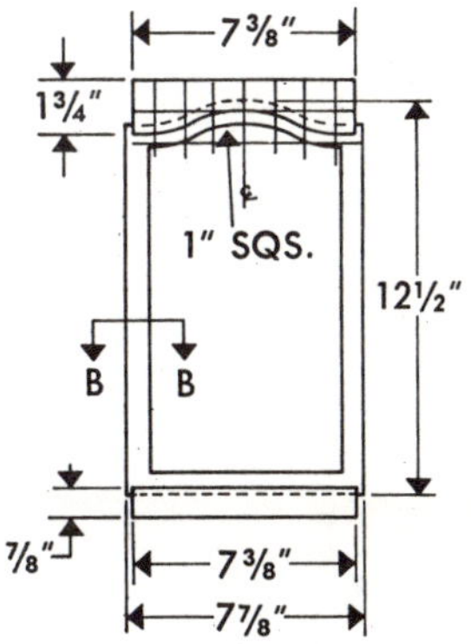
7 3/8"
1 3/4"
1" SQS.
12 1/2"
B
B
7/8"
7 3/8"
7 7/8"

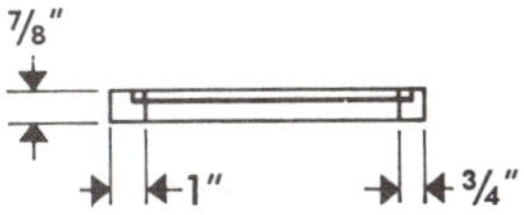
7/8"
1"
3/4"

SECTION A—A

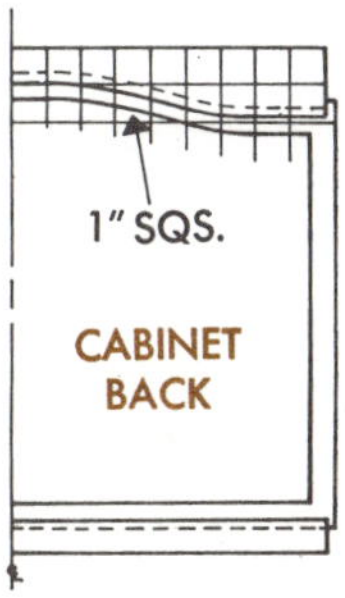
1" SQS.
CABINET BACK

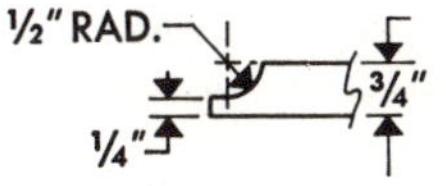
1/2" RAD.
3/4"
1/4"

SECTION B—B

square part of the upper spacers. The top then is notched and fitted on the upper edges of the trim pieces.

Doors for the cabinet are made now, as detailed, or you can leave the cabinet open. The arched doors, however, do add a final touch to the cabinet. Finish to suit.

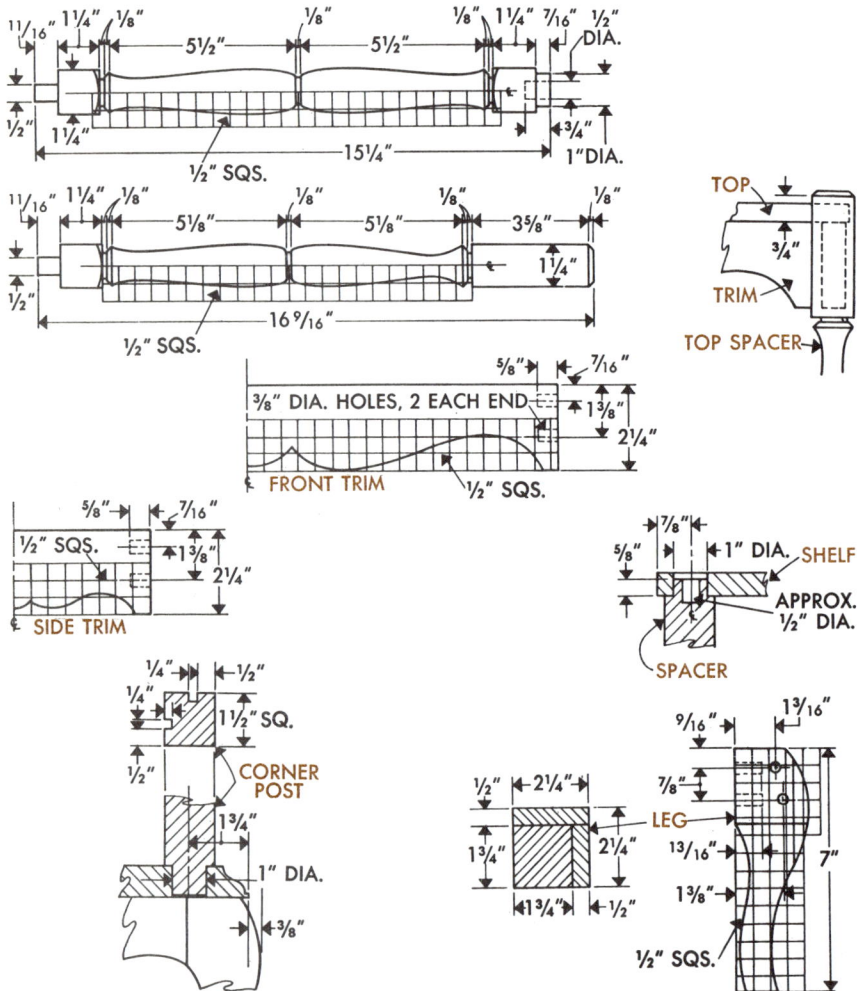

MATERIALS LIST

Top:	¾"x10"x20¾" (1)
Shelf:	¾"x10¾"x21½" (2)
Cabinet Top:	¾"x10¾"x21½" (2)
Cabinet Bottom:	¾"x12½"x23¼" (1)
Top Trim (front, back):	¾"x2¼"x18½" (2)
Top Trim (sides):	¾"x2¼"x7¾" (2)
Door (top rail):	¾"x1¾"x7¼" (pair)
Door (outer stile):	¾"x1"x8½" (2)
Door (inner stile):	¾"x¾"x8½" (2)
Door (bottom rail):	¾"x1"x7¼" (2)
Cabinet Corner Post:	1½"x1½"x15¼" (4)
Base Apron (front, back):	1¼"x1½"x19¼" (2)
Base Apron (side):	1¼"x1½"x9" (2)
Cabinet Side Panel:	¾"x7-7/8"x12½" (2)
Cabinet Side (upper rail):	¾"x1¾"x7-3/8" (2)
Cabinet Side (lower rail):	¾"x7/8"x7-3/8" (2)
Cabinet Back Panel:	¾"x12½"x18½" (1)
Cabinet Back (upper rail):	¾"x1¾"x18" (1)
Cabinet Back (lower rail):	¾"x7/8"x18" (1)
Leg:	2¼"x2¼"x7" (4)
Turned Shelf Spacers:	1¼"x1¼"x15¼" (8)
Turned Shelf Spacers:	1¼"x1¼"x16-9/16" (4)
Corner Glue Block:	1¼"x3"x6" (4)

TIFFANY LAMP

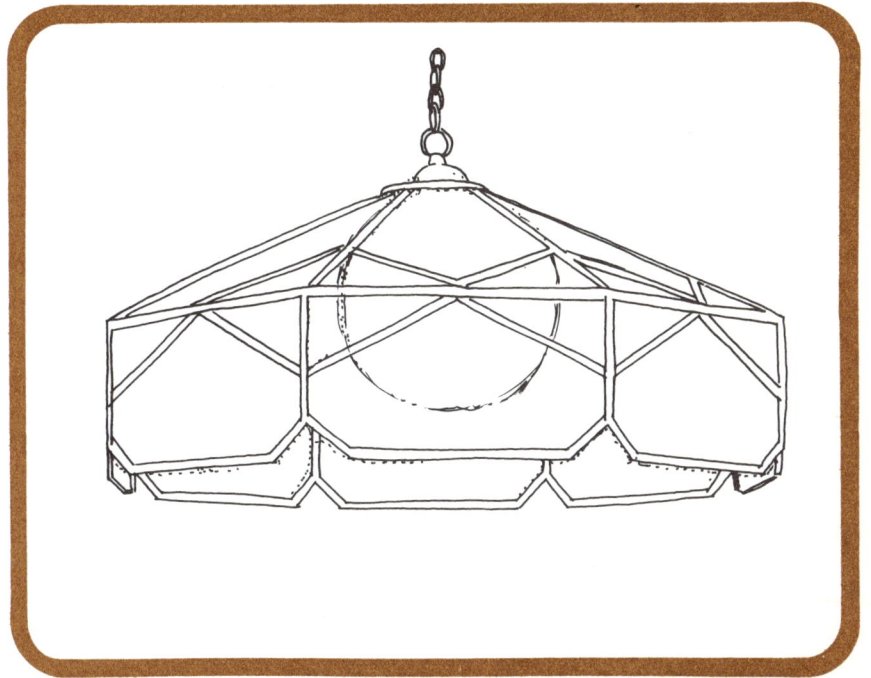

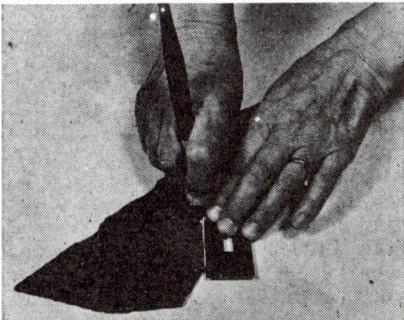

Diamond-tipped glass cutter makes the best cut on the heavy glass. It is held against a metal straightedge.

Cut-off line must be neatly scored with glass cutter, no breaks or skipped spaces. Pattern is held with tape.

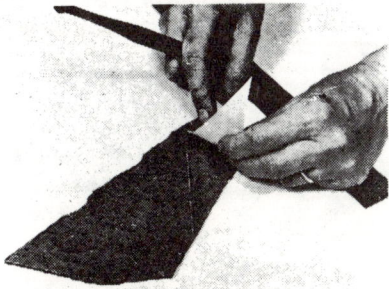

Light shining through the colorful sections of this stained-glass lamp creates a mood of Victorian elegance. The lamp can be made from supplies purchased in bulk or from a kit which contains precut glass. If you are a beginner in the art of working with glass, you may prefer to purchase a kit available from several sources. In either case your lamp creation can be built in just a few hours. Except for the cutting of the glass, assembling a lamp from kit or bulk materials is basically the same.

If you are using bulk materials the cutting of the glass is the first step. This is not a difficult operation, but it does take practice and you will have some waste. A diamond-tipped glass cutter is the best tool, but a heavy-duty standard cutter also can be used. As with any glass, first score a line with the cutter, then tap lightly along the score on the underside of the glass. You can watch the glass fracture along the line and fall into two pieces.

If you have purchased a kit you only need to assemble the pieces of stained-glass according to the pattern.

Soldering is the other skill required for stained-glass work. Even craftsmen who are skilled with iron or gun had best practice joining the lead cames before beginning to solder the actual lamp. Use a soldering "pencil" or low-voltage gun, as excess heat simply destroys the soft lead cames.

Apply oleic acid to the joint to be soldered, load the gun or pencil with solder and touch it to the joint. "Puddle" the solder smoothly, but don't overheat the lead.

Assemble the lamp lead and glass on a sheet of plywood. As

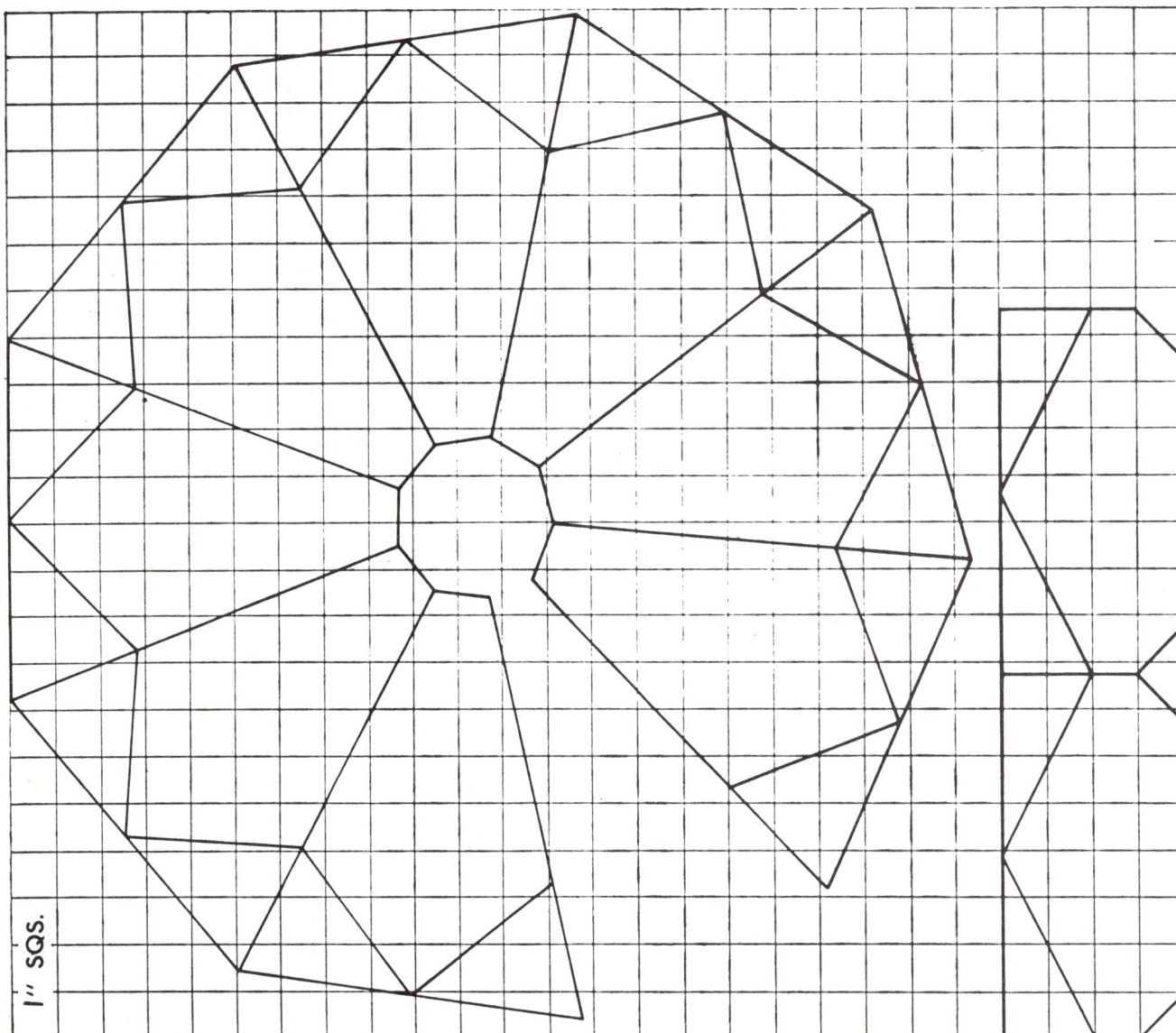

1" SQS.

shown in the photograph, tacking blocks to the plywood will hold the pieces in position while soldering. As sections of glass and cames are assembled, solder the joints. When the project is completely soldered on one side, turn it over and solder all joints on the other side.

Carefully bend the upper part of the lamp to shape and solder

To complete cutting the glass, hold with one hand and gently tap with the glass cutter along the scored line.

Enlarge the squared drawing and make a full-size pattern for both upper and lower portions of lamp.

Lead may be cut in several ways. One is a sharp pocketknife or X-acto knife. Tap on blade with hammer if necessary.

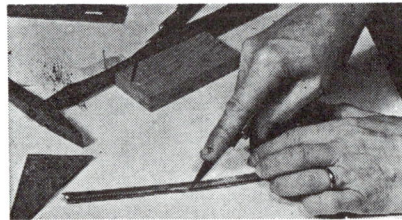

The cames come in a roll and will be somewhat twisted. Straighten by tapping a small block of wood on them.

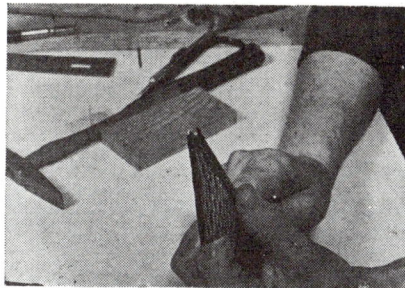

Glass pieces are carefully fitted into the U-shaped channels in the cames. Be careful of glass slivers that cut.

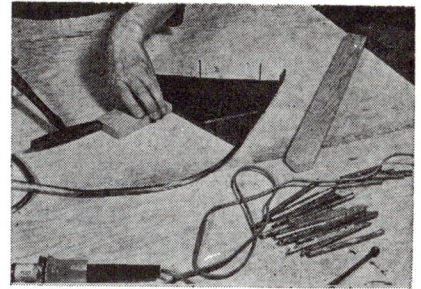

To start the lamp, fit the first pieces of glass into cames, drive a couple of nails in the work surface to hold cames.

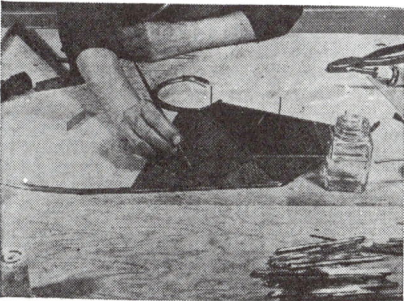

Oleic acid is used as a flux for soldering the cames together. It is brushed on all joints before soldering them.

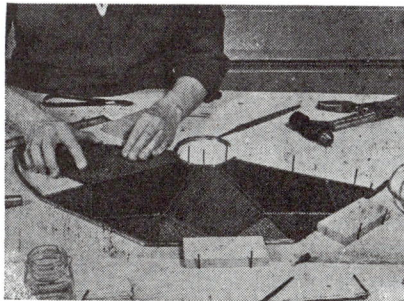

As pieces are fitted into place, they are held by nails and small blocks of wood. One long came encircles the outer edge.

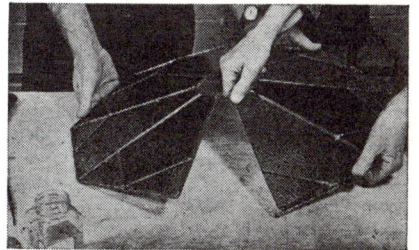

When all pieces are fitted together and soldered on both sides, the top portion of the lamp is carefully bent together.

Electrical fixtures, including a swag chain and a diffusing bulb of frosted glass, are fastened in place.

Lower portion is assembled on a long board, with a second board as a "backing." Sharpened stick "drives" points.

The lower portion is soldered on both sides and carefully bent to shape, then the joining pieces soldered together.

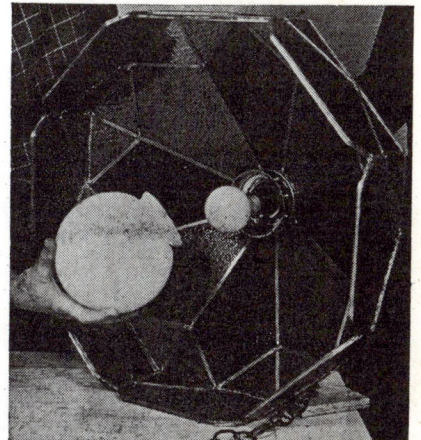

the seam. Follow the same process for the lower part of the lamp, then join it to the upper, shaping as necessary.

Now you are ready to insert the electrical fixtures and attach the swag chain.

Your new Tiffany lamp will enhance the appearance of almost any room. Hang the lamp over your dining room table, pool table, or near your favorite reading or easy chair.

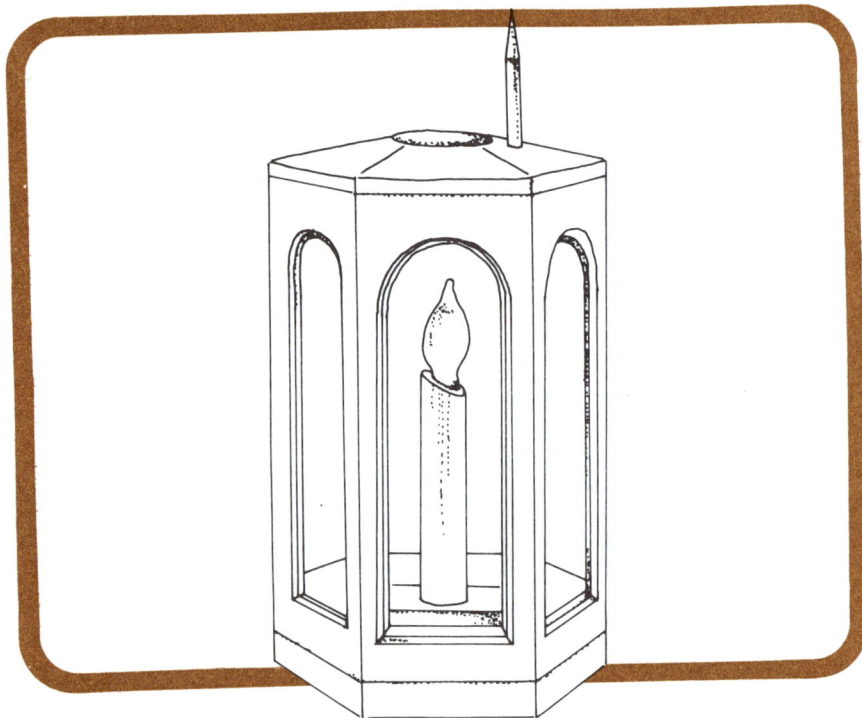

WOODEN LANTERN

Equally at home in a formal hallway or at a patio steak fry, this lovely wooden lantern is not complicated to make, but does require accurate cutting of miters and angles. Check your equipment for proper alignment before you start this project.

Lay out the top and base on 1½-inch pine, making sure each edge will be 5½ inches long (figure 1). After cutting them to shape, cut a ¼ x ¾-inch rabbet along each edge (figure 2). A fly cutter (figure 3) bores the access hole in the top. Note that the two ½ x ½-inch blind holes in the top and bottom are for the support rods, while the ¾-inch hole through the top is for clearance for the lifter rod.

Four vent holes are drilled in the base (figure 4) then bevels are shaped on the top (figure 5). The six sides are cut to shape, then a fly cutter is used for the arc at the top of the cutouts (figure 6). The opening is finished with saber or scroll saw (figure 7). A router or shaper is used to cut the glass rabbet (figure 8) and the molding edge on the opposite face of each side (figure 9). Both edges of each side are beveled (figure 10) and spline grooves are cut (figure 11). The rounded corners of the cutouts will have to be chiseled square (figure 12). When the assembly is glued (figure 13) a strap clamp or strong cord is used to assure tight joints. When the glue has set, cement a small block inside the lantern at the top of each cutout; this will hold the glass in place.

Assemble the lifter mechanism (figure 14) and check to see that it works freely. Glue the top in place and attach the base with screws only, to permit removing for cleaning. After applying finish to the lantern, install the glass with glazier's points. You can use either a real candle or an electric lamp shaped like a candle flame in a wooden holder, as indicated in the drawing.

MATERIALS LIST

Top and Base:	1½"x9½"x11" (1 each)
Sides:	¾"x5½"x15" (6)
Splines:	¼"x½"x15" (6)
Lifter Rod:	½"x20" dowel (1)
Support Rods:	½"x14¼" dowels (2)
Lifter:	¾"x2½"x8½" (1)
Feet:	1½"x1½"x2" (3)
Candleholder:	1¼"x3"x3" (1)
Optional Materials:	1½"x9¼" candle dowel
	candle-type bulb
	socket
	plug
	cord
	switch

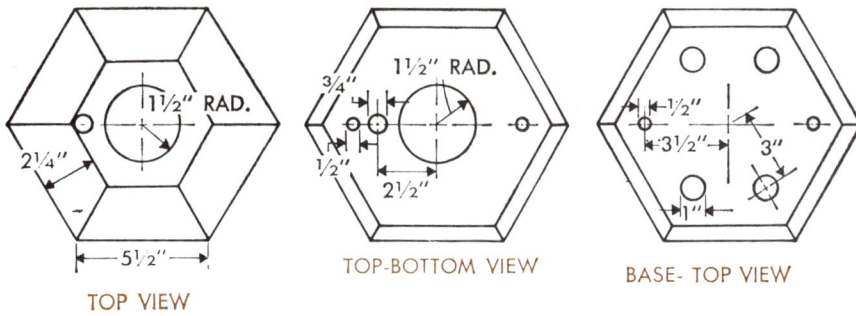

TOP VIEW

1½" RAD.

2¼"

5½"

TOP-BOTTOM VIEW

¾"
1½" RAD.
½"
2½"

BASE- TOP VIEW

½"
3½"
3"
1"

SPLINE-JOINT DETAIL

½"
¼"

LIFTER BASE

8½"
3½"
2½"
2¼"

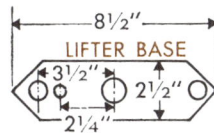

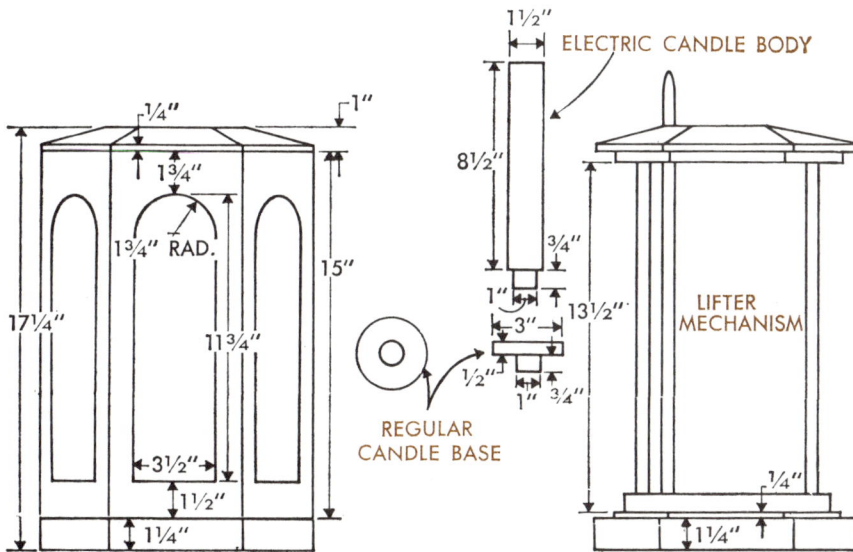

1. Hexagon-shape top and base are cut using 30-degree angle on saw to create corners of 60-degree. Lay out accurately.

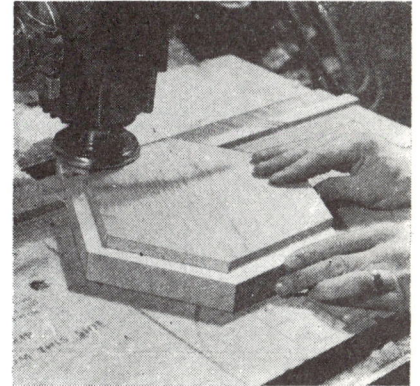

ELECTRIC CANDLE BODY

1½"
8½"
¾"
1"
3"
½"
1" ¾"

REGULAR CANDLE BASE

LIFTER MECHANISM

13½"

¼"
1¼"

¼"   1"
1¾"
1¾" RAD.
15"
17¼"
11¾"
3½"
1½"
1¼"

2. Rabbet ¼" deep by ¾" wide is cut on each edge, using planer, router or regular dado blade.

3. Fly cutter is used to bore 3" access opening in the top. Bore half way through from each side for clean cut.

4. Four vent holes 1" in diameter are next bored in the base, to provide ventilation for either candle or lamp.

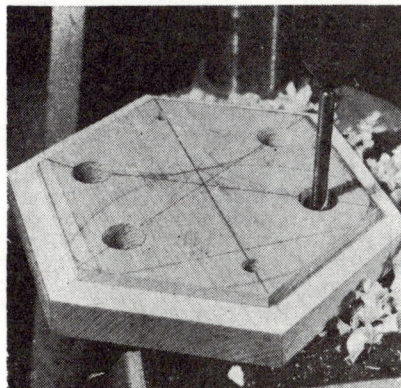

5. Bevels that give "character" to the top are either planed or cut with sharp planer blade that makes smooth cut.

6. Fly cutter again is used, this time to make the top arc in the cutout that is located in each of the six sides.

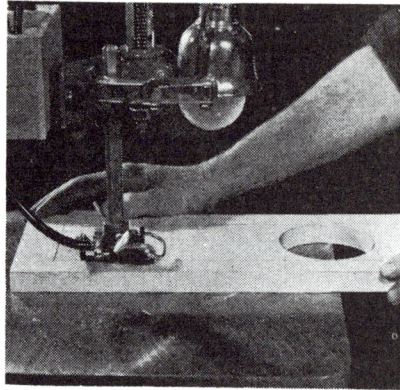

7. Scroll or saber saw is used to finish the cutouts. Make one side with opening, then use it as pattern.

8. Sand edges of cutouts carefully, then use router or shaper to cut 3/16" x ¼" rabbet to accept the glass.

9. Use the same method to make a decorative molding edge on the face side of the cutouts; use a pilot bit.

10. The next operation is to cut 30-degree bevels on the edges of sides. Be sure molded side of cutout is up.

13. Splines are inserted, with glue, and assembly is clamped by means of heavy cord, or with strap clamp.

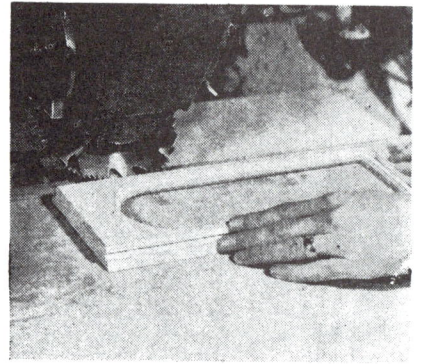

11. Dado blade makes quick work of cutting ¼" x ¼" spline grooves in edges of the sides square to surfaces.

14. Assemble lifter rod, support rods and lifter base and check to see that unit works freely for lifting light.

12. Both molding and rabbet for glass are cut with pilot bit, so sharp chisel is used to square up the corners.

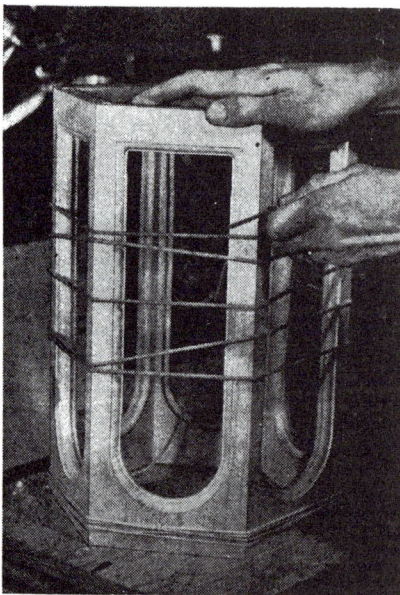

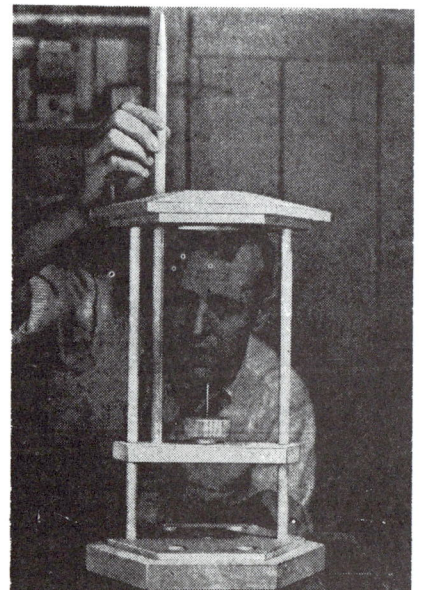

TOY ELECTRIC LOCOMOTIVE

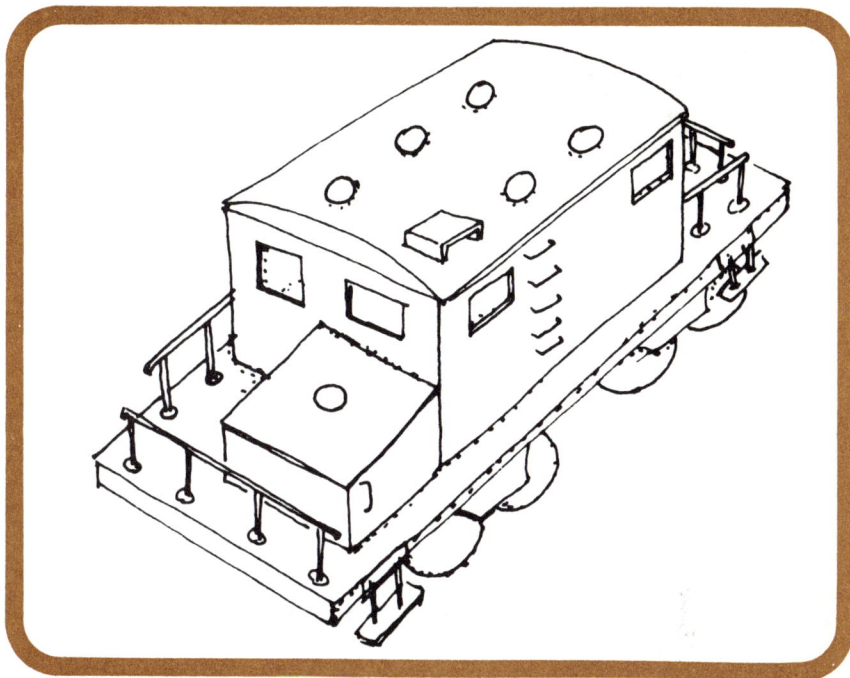

Locomotive cab without roof. Nail heads are countersunk and filled with wood putty. Note cleats inside ends and sides.

There's a touch of nostalgia about this electric locomotive that is patterned after a type that was used, and sometimes still is, as a "workhorse" to shunt cars from track to track in switching yards.

Construction is fairly simple, with all parts except for the railings, steps and grab irons being wood. Welding is called out for assembling the railings and steps, but you can solder these assemblies if you make sure the metal is shiny clean, and you use either acid-core wire solder, or bar solder with an acid flux.

The floor of the locomotive is a piece of 1-inch (¾ inch net) stock cut to the dimensions given. On the original the cab sides and ends were cut from ½-inch plywood. If you don't have stock this thin, use something heavier, but allow for the additional thickness in your dimensions. Cleats are fastened inside the upper edges of the ends and they are drilled to permit driving screws up through them into the roof. Cleats on the inside lower edges of the sides provide a means of attaching the assembled cab to the floor. Thus you can assemble the cab completely before screwing and gluing it to the floor.

The roof is shaped as shown, to a curved upper surface, then six holes are drilled and counterbored to accept the wooden drawer pulls that represent air vents. Two other drawer pulls, which should be slightly smaller in diameter, serve the same purpose on the motor enclosures at each end of the cab. They are attached by driving a screw from inside; no counterboring is required as on the roof.

As previously mentioned, the railings and steps are assembled and soldered or welded, depending on your facilities. A local welding shop also could do the job, but might be a bit expensive. The grab irons are

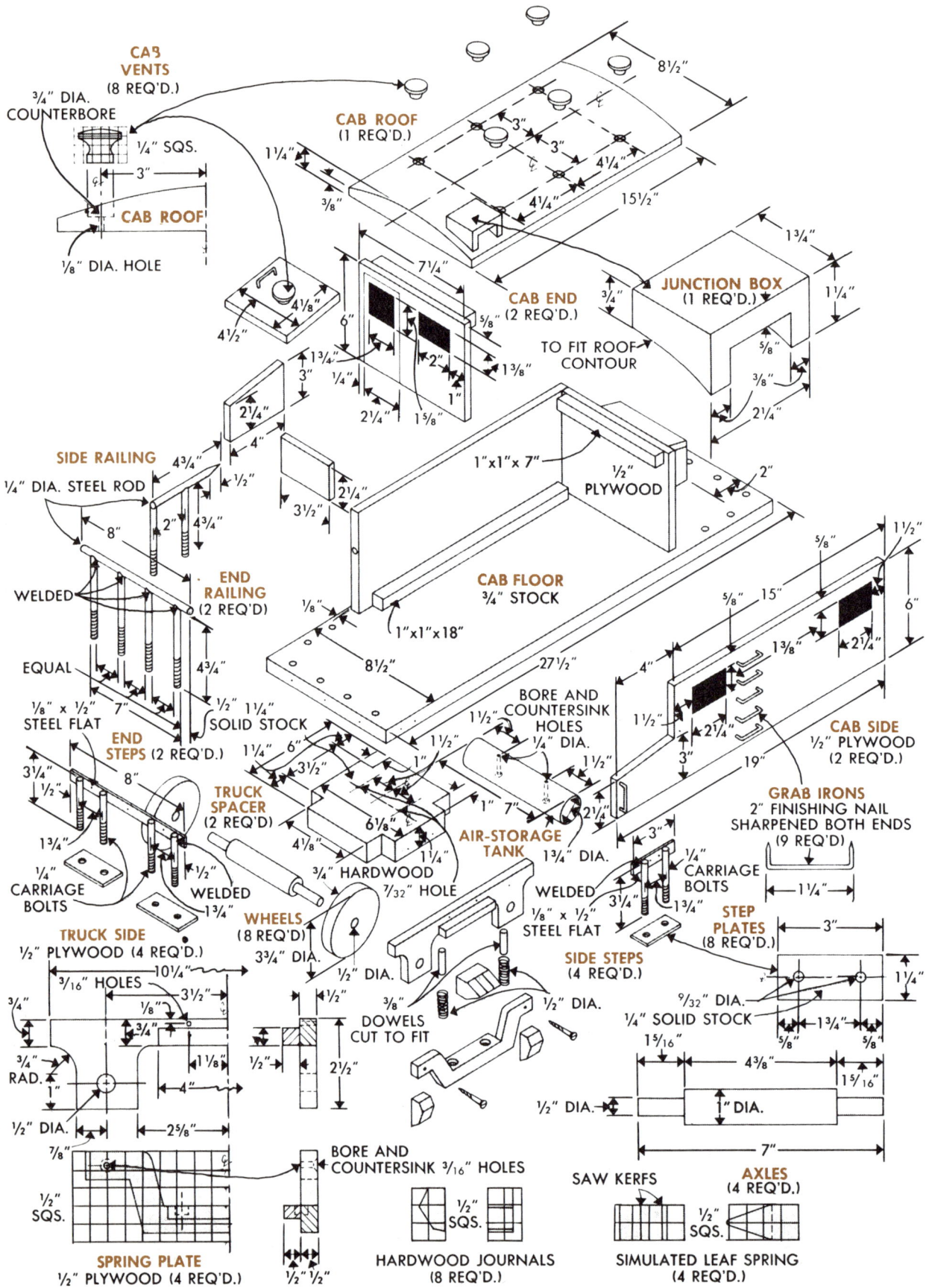

CAB VENTS
(8 REQ'D.)

3/4" DIA. COUNTERBORE

1/4" SQS.

3"

CAB ROOF

1/8" DIA. HOLE

CAB ROOF
(1 REQ'D.)

8 1/2"

3"

3"

4 1/4"

4 1/4"

15 1/2"

1 1/4"

3/8"

4 1/8"

4 1/2"

7 1/4"

6"

CAB END
(2 REQ'D.)

5/8"

2"

1"

1 3/8"

1 5/8"

2 1/4"

1 3/4"

1/4"

3"

1 3/4"

2 1/4"

4"

4 3/4"

1/2"

JUNCTION BOX
(1 REQ'D.)

1 3/4"

1 1/4"

5/8"

3/8"

2 1/4"

3/4"

TO FIT ROOF CONTOUR

SIDE RAILING

1/4" DIA. STEEL ROD

8"

2"

4 3/4"

2 1/4"

3 1/2"

1/8"

1" x 1" x 7"

1/2" PLYWOOD

2"

WELDED

END RAILING
(2 REQ'D)

EQUAL

1/8" x 1/2" STEEL FLAT

7"

4 3/4"

1/2"

1 1/4"

SOLID STOCK

CAB FLOOR
3/4" STOCK

1" x 1" x 18"

8 1/2"

27 1/2"

BORE AND COUNTERSINK HOLES 1/4" DIA.

1 1/2"

1 1/2"

1 1/2"

4"

15"

5/8"

5/8"

1 3/8"

2 1/4"

1 1/2"

1 1/2"

2"

6"

CAB SIDE
1/2" PLYWOOD (2 REQ'D.)

3"

19"

END STEPS (2 REQ'D.)

3 1/4"

8"

1/2"

1 3/4"

1/4" CARRIAGE BOLTS

TRUCK SPACER
(2 REQ'D)

1 1/4"

6"

3 1/2"

1"

6 1/8"

4 1/8"

1 1/4"

3/4" HARDWOOD

7/32" HOLE

WELDED

1 3/4"

1/2"

WHEELS
(8 REQ'D)

3 3/4" DIA.

1/2" DIA.

AIR-STORAGE TANK

1" 7"

2 1/4"

1 3/4" DIA.

WELDED

1/8" x 1/2" STEEL FLAT

3 1/4"

1 3/4"

3"

1/4" CARRIAGE BOLTS

GRAB IRONS
2" FINISHING NAIL SHARPENED BOTH ENDS (9 REQ'D)

1 1/4"

STEP PLATES
(8 REQ'D.)

3"

1 1/4"

9/32" DIA.

1/4" SOLID STOCK

1 3/4"

5/8"

5/8"

TRUCK SIDE
1/2" PLYWOOD (4 REQ'D.)

3/16" HOLES

10 1/4"

3 1/2"

1/8"

3/4"

3/4"

3/4" RAD.

1"

1/2" DIA.

4"

1 1/8"

2 5/8"

1/2"

4 1/2"

2 1/2"

DOWELS CUT TO FIT

3/8"

SIDE STEPS
(4 REQ'D.)

1/2" DIA.

1/2" DIA.

1 5/16"

4 3/8"

1 5/16"

1/2" DIA.

1" DIA.

7"

7/8"

1/2" SQS.

SPRING PLATE
1/2" PLYWOOD (4 REQ'D.)

1/2" 1/2"

BORE AND COUNTERSINK 3/16" HOLES

HARDWOOD JOURNALS
(8 REQ'D.)

1/2" SQS.

SAW KERFS

AXLES
(4 REQ'D.)

1/2" SQS.

SIMULATED LEAF SPRING
(4 REQ'D.)

simply 2-inch finishing nails sharpened at each end, then bent to the shape indicated and tapped into place on the sides of the cab after the painting is done.

The truck assemblies will take a little time, but are important in the realistic appearance of the locomotive. If you have a lathe, turn a cylinder to 3¾-inch diameter, then saw slices from it for the wheels. Alternatively, cut them on a band saw or jig saw.

Simulated windows are created by painting areas black, then masking with rectangles of paper. Cab is painted green.

Completed trucks look very realistic with both leaf and coil "springs," as on real locomotive.

Trucks are attached as indicated in the drawing. Square them up, so both are parallel and track in straight line.

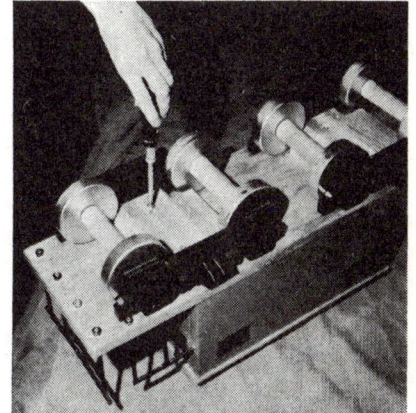

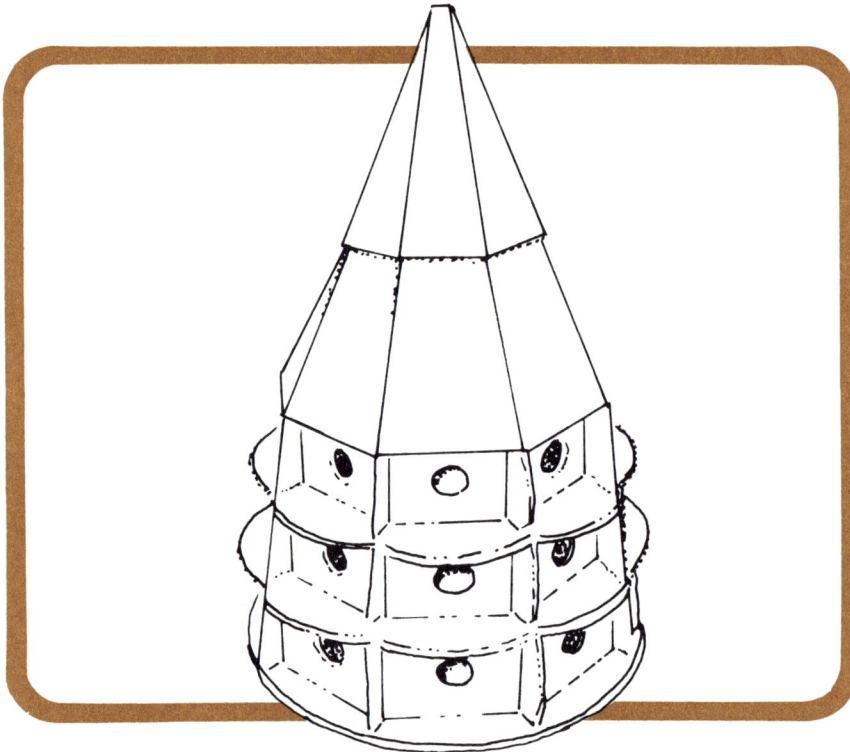

24-
APARTMENT
MARTIN
HOUSE

Largest and most beautiful of the swallow family, the purple martin feeds almost entirely on flying insects and can eat his weight (equal to about 2,000 mosquitoes) in insects daily. These birds are fastidious housekeepers, friendly and have a beautiful song. Over the years they have become sophisticated and no longer use hollow trees and other natural conditions for their homes, but have come to rely on man-made apartment houses.

In southern states the martin scouts arrive about the first of February, in the north in March and April. These scouts check for housing and insect supplies, then in about a week return south and guide the main flocks north. If your martin house is ready, you can almost be sure of full occupancy, and most birds will return to the same home every year.

The martin house described here is designed to be bolted to a 4 x 4 post, which should locate the house about 10 to 12 feet in the air. If the house is lower, it will attract starlings, who are a noisy nuisance. The house is designed so the floors can be separated for easy fall cleaning of the few wisps of straw that martins use for nesting.

Start construction by cutting a disk from ¾-inch plywood 27 inches in diameter. Using the same center, scribe a circle 24 inches in diameter. Now, using dividers or compass, mark off points along the inner circle 9-1/8-inches apart. These points locate the ends of the fronts of the first-floor apartments. Glue and screw the fronts to the base, and use glue between the ends of the fronts.

Cut the 2 x 4 joists to size, bevel the ends and half-lap them as indicated to form a 4 x 4-inch square around the post hole. Glue and

First floor is cut from disk of ¾"-plywood; apartment fronts are screwed to it. Note hole at center for post.

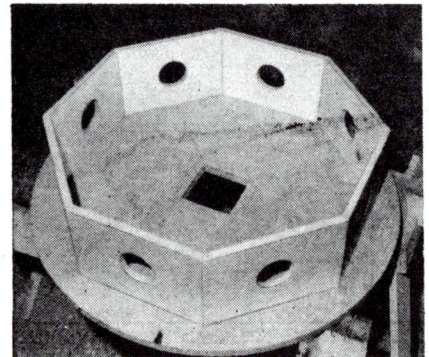

MATERIALS LIST

First Floor: ¾'' ext-grade plywood,
                27'' diameter (1)

Second Floor: ½'' ext-grade plywood,
              21'' x 21'' (1)

Third Floor: ½'' ext-grade plywood,
               19'' x 19'' (1)

"Ceiling:"   ½'' ext-grade plywood,
               19'' x 19'' (1)

All ½'' Solid Stock:

First Floor
Fronts: 6¼''x9-1/8'' (8)
Walls: 5¾''x8½'' (8)
Backs: 2½''x5¾'' (8)
Outside Dividers: 2''x4¾'' (8)

Second Floor
Fronts: 6''x8-3/8'' (8)
Walls: 5½''x7½'' (8)
Backs: 2¼''x5½'' (8)
Platforms: 4''x10'' (8)
Outside Dividers: 1¾''x4¼'' (8)

Third Floor
Fronts: 6''x7½'' (8)
Walls: 6''x7½'' (8)
Backs: 1½''x6'' (8)
Platforms: 4''x9½'' (8)
Outside Dividers: 1½''x3¾'' (8)

Roof
Lower-Roof Segments: 8¼''x13'' (8)
Upper-Roof Segments: 5''x13'' (8)
Joists: 2''x4''x38'' redwood (4)
Roof-Support Strips: ¾''x¾''
  length to suit (8)

Door Plugs: ½'' stock, 2¼'' diameter (8)

screw the joists to the base, driving the screws down through the base. Waterproof glue, of course, should be used for all joints.

Mark the outline of the second floor by tracing around the walls of the first and moving the line in the thickness of the fronts. Each of the floors fits inside the other. Repeat this operation for the third floor and the "ceiling" of the third floor, which is the same size as the floor.

The ends of the apartment walls now are beveled and they are installed with glue and screws on each floor. The backs are last, and are just glued; brads can be toenailed through the walls to hold the backs while the glue sets.

Fit one floor into another, and use a screw through every other front to hold them together. Do not use glue, to assure easy disassembly for cleaning. Fasten the "ceiling" on the third floor with screws, then cut the roof pieces to size and shape. Cut lengths of ¾ x ¾-inch stock beveled as shown, and glue and nail them to the inside faces of the lower-roof members with the lower edges 1 inch up from the lower edges of the roof pieces.

The outside platforms now are glued and screwed to the projecting edges of the second and third floors. Note they are not attached to the upper edges of the floor below. Again, this is to assure easy disassembly. The outside dividers are next; separate the floors and attach the dividers with screws driven from inside.

The 4 x 4-inch opening in the first floor will allow some space for air flow around a 4 x 4, and ventilation holes in the apartments allow an air flow into the center "air shaft" that runs to the "attic." To assure ventilation in the attic, bore a number of ¼-inch holes under the inner edge of the roof, parallel to it, through the upper edges of the fronts of the third floor, the ceiling and the support blocks.

The door plugs, assembled from two wooden disks and a pull, are to keep sparrows and other birds out until the martins return.

When the upper and lower roofs are assembled, it may be necessary to saw off the upper ends of the upper roof to make them even. Cut and fit an octagonal block in the resulting opening. Drill two 9/16-inch holes through one pair of joists to permit bolting the house to the 4 x 4 post, which is drilled to match.

"Walls" between apartments are glued and screwed to base. Bar clamp, or fixtures, hold walls while glue sets.

Back wall of each apartment is fitted next, being glued in place. Each back has a ½'' ventilation hole near top.

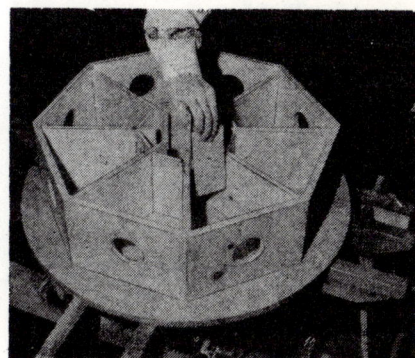

5/8"

3/4" x 3/4"
STRIPS BEVELED

BROKEN LINE INDICATES POSITION OF OVER-LAPPING TOP SEGMENT

13"

2"

4"

5"

13"

13"

8 1/4"

OVERHANGS ROOF 1"

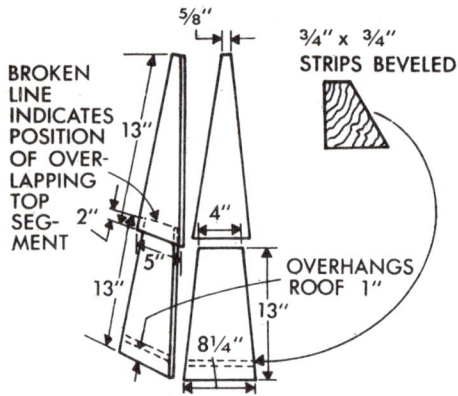

ROOF SEGMENTS
1/2" SOLID STOCK, 8 EACH

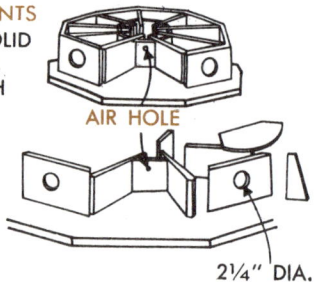

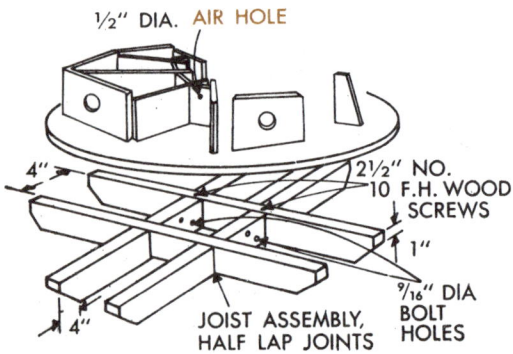

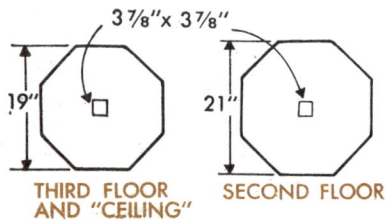

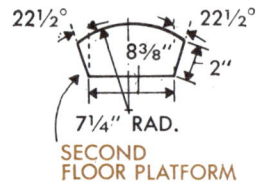

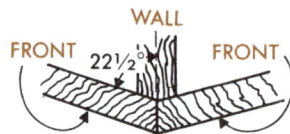

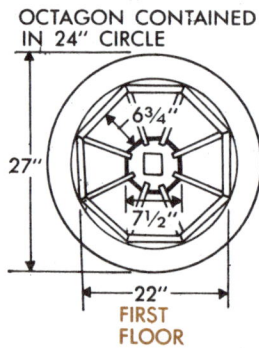

AIR HOLE

2 1/4" DIA.

1/2" DIA. **AIR HOLE**

4"

2 1/2" NO. 10 F.H. WOOD SCREWS

1"

4"

9/16" DIA BOLT HOLES

JOIST ASSEMBLY, HALF LAP JOINTS

3 7/8" x 3 7/8"

19"

21"

THIRD FLOOR AND "CEILING"

SECOND FLOOR

VENTILATION HOLES UNDER ROOF EDGE

THIRD FLOOR PLATFORM

22 1/2°

22 1/2°

6 3/4" RAD.

2"

7 1/2"

3"

22 1/2°

22 1/2°

8 3/8"

2"

7 1/4" RAD.

SECOND FLOOR PLATFORM

WALL

FRONT

22 1/2°

FRONT

OCTAGON CONTAINED IN 24" CIRCLE

6 3/4"

27"

7 1/2"

22"

FIRST FLOOR

Second and third floors are marked by tracing next lower floor, drawing line in the thickness of the stock on fronts.

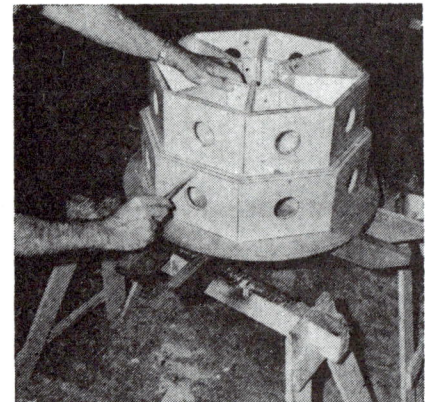

Each floor of apartments fits into one below resting on walls of apartments. Use screws, but not glue, in assembly.

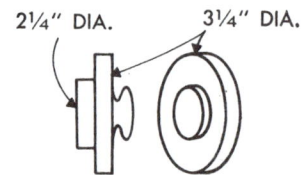

2 1/4" DIA.

3 1/4" DIA.

CHIPPENDALE MIRROR

Although seemingly complex, this mirror is quite simple and an excellent "first project" for anyone interested in making antique reproductions. Solid mahogany is used for the flat end pieces as well as for the molding. You will need 1 piece 7/8" x 12" x 24" for the frame, and one ½" x 18" x 24" for the scrolls.

If you cannot get ½ inch stock have a local cabinet shop or lumber dealer surface-plane the 18 inch piece to ½ inch, or use a safety planer in a radial-arm saw or drill press.

Enlarge the squared drawings of the scrolls and transfer the outline to the wood. With a hand coping saw or electric saber or bandsaw, cut the scrolls.

To make the frame, cut the 12-inch-wide piece of mahogany into 5 strips 1-5/16-inches wide (one for practice).

The shaper cutter used for the molding is made for use with a molding head for a radial-arm or table saw. Set the cutter at 38 degrees and adjust the height as shown. Use hold-downs directly before and after the cutter.

Cut the rabbets that hold the mirror and backboard and round the outside bead of the molding with medium-grade sandpaper.

After the molding is cut and sanded, the frame is mitered, glued and clamped. Once set, you can mortise the top and bottom to receive the scrolls. Cut the mortises on the ends then cut stopped-mortises on the sides. The extensions on the scrolls will cover any discrepancies of the stopped mortises.

Glue and clamp the scrolled endpieces in place.

Heavy plate-glass mirror should be ordered to the exact size

minus 1/16 inch and held in place by a backboard of ¼-inch plywood secured by glazier points.

The weight of the mirror makes using screw eyes a little risky, so "hang" the mirror using two picture hangers.

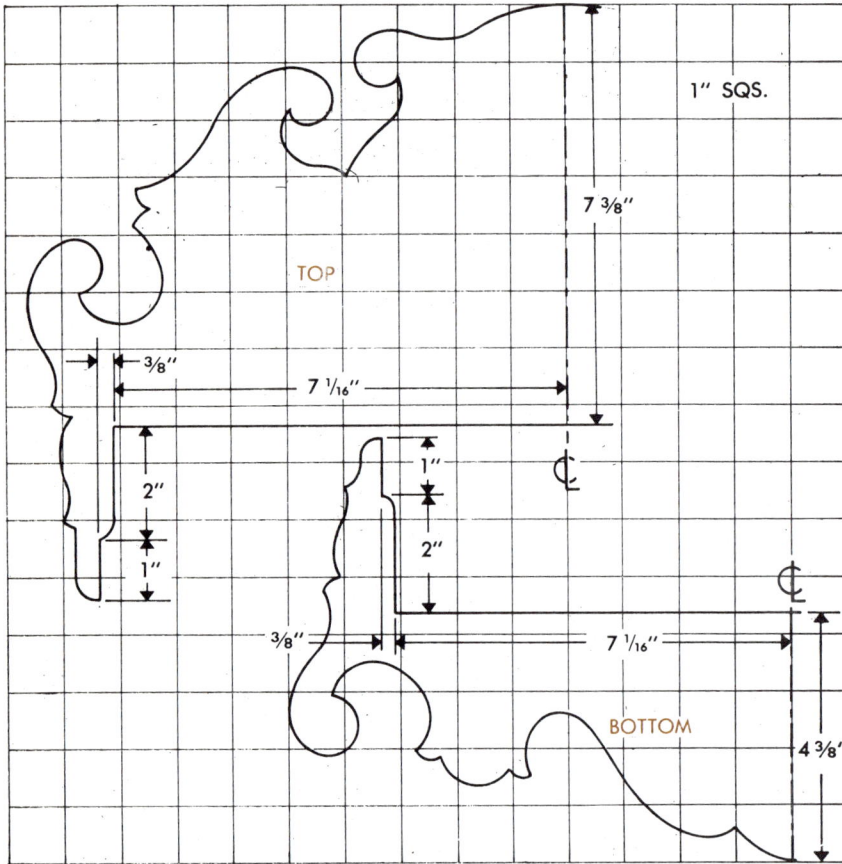

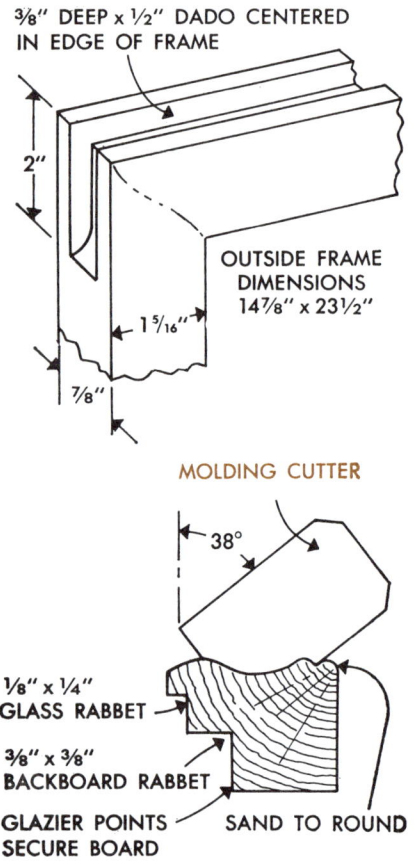

1" SQS.

7 3/8"

TOP

3/8"

7 1/16"

2"

1"

1"

2"

3/8"

7 1/16"

BOTTOM

4 3/8"

3/8" DEEP x ½" DADO CENTERED IN EDGE OF FRAME

2"

1 5/16"

7/8"

OUTSIDE FRAME DIMENSIONS 14⅞" x 23½"

MOLDING CUTTER

38°

⅛" x ¼" GLASS RABBET

⅜" x ⅜" BACKBOARD RABBET

GLAZIER POINTS SECURE BOARD

SAND TO ROUND

PATIO FURNITURE

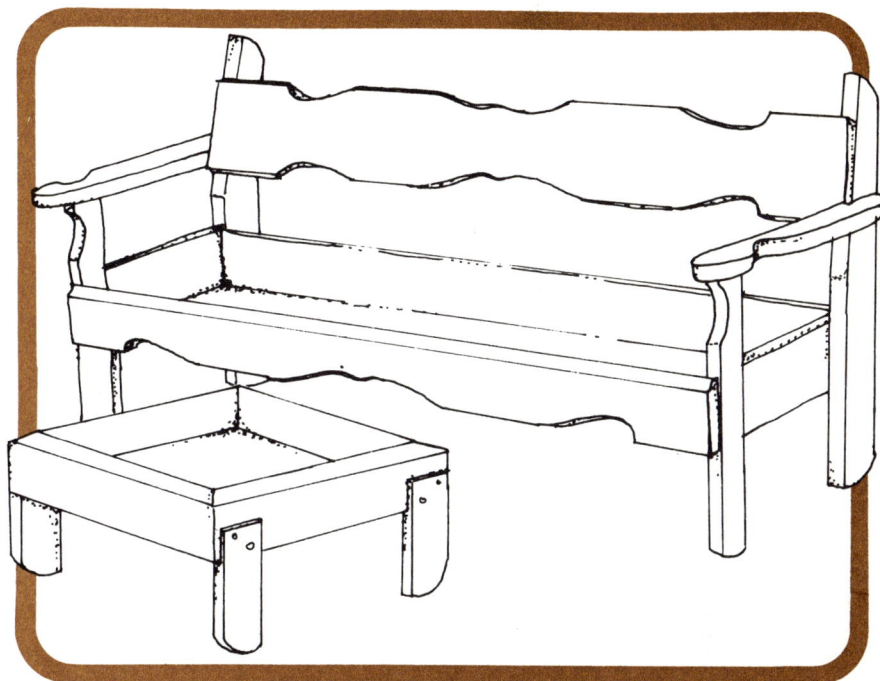

MATERIALS LIST

Sofa
Back Post:	1¾"x5"x36"	(2)
Leg:	1¾"x3½"x23"	(2)
Side Rail:	1¾"x6"x21¼"	(2)
Front Rail:	1¾"x6"x71½"	(1)
Back Rail:	1¾"x6"x69½"	(1)
Back:	¾"x9"x71½"	(1)
Stiffener:	2" x 2" x 69½" (1) Fir	
Arms:	1½"x3½"x28"	(2)
Cleats:	1"x1"x21¼"	(2)
Cleats:	1"x1"x65½"	(2)
Cushion Support:	Ext. grade plywood	
	¾"x21¼"x67½"	(1)

Ottoman
Frame:	1¾"x5"x25½"	(2)
Frame:	1¾"x5"x25¾"	(2)
Leg:	1¾"x4"x10½"	(4)
Cleat:	1"x1"x19¼"	(2)
Cleat:	1"x1"x22"	(2)
Cushion Support:	Ext. grade plywood	
	¾"x21¼"x22"	(1)

SOFA

Construction of the sofa is really rather simple. Start off by checking the details in the drawings, then shape the posts and legs. Next make the side rails and rabbet each end as shown in the drawing.

At this point you can assemble the side rail, the post and the leg, using glue and nails. The front rail and back rail are next. Note that the front rail is rabbeted at each end, but the back rail is not. The latter butts between the posts. When assembling, use plenty of glue and drive the nails so they cross-brace. For example, when you attach the back rail, drive nails through the rail into the ends of the side rail and, also from the outside of the post into the end of the back rail.

Next, make the back and the brace. The best bet is to make the back first and attach it. Then cut the brace to fit. Glue and clamps are used to attach the stiffener.

Shape up the arm as shown in the detail. Best bet is to attach it at the front first, using glue and a single gutter spike driven down into the leg. Then, at the rear, drill through for the ¼-inch carriage bolt.

Cut and attach the cleats with glue and nails. The cushion support does not have to be a single piece; you can make it up from odds and ends of plywood. If you do make the support from a single piece, drill a hole or two in it to drain away rain water that would accumulate.

OTTOMAN

The ottoman is a nice accessory because you can use it as a footrest when sitting on the sofa, or you can remove the cushion and use it as a serving table when you need more space for food and beverages at mealtime.

Details of the ottoman are shown. It is best to make and assemble the frame pieces first. The bevel on the top edge should be formed after the pieces are assembled. Next, make and attach the legs. It is not out of line to hold the legs in place with a couple of nails while you drill for and drive the screws. Finally, cut and attach the cleats and then the cushion support.

In all cases the parts should be sanded smooth before assembly. If you want a natural redwood finish, apply several coats of clear exterior sealer. For a darker finish, apply a penetrating walnut stain first. In all situations it is wise to use fine steel wool between coats to smooth previous applications before applying the next.

SOFA ASSEMBLY

OTTOMAN ASSEMBLY

Legs of ottoman are temporarily tacked in place and holes for screws are drilled and cleats are installed.

OUTDOOR WALL PLANTER

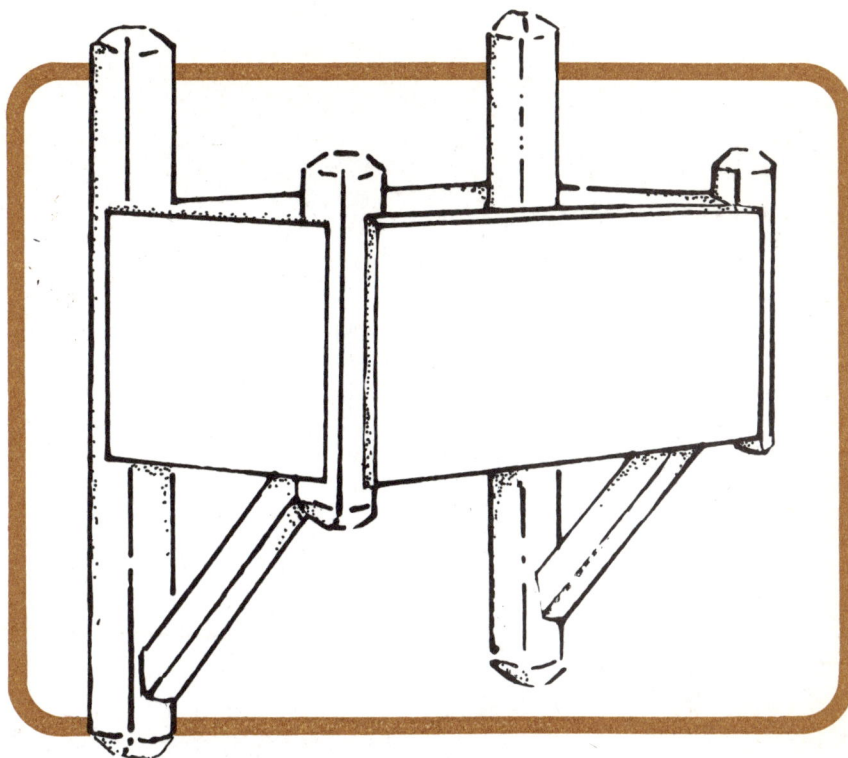

MATERIALS LIST

All redwood:

Back Post:	1¾''x1¾''x24''	(2)
Front Post:	1¾''x1¾''x12''	(2)
Front:	¾''x8''x20½''	(1)
Side:	¾''x8''x10½''	(2)
Back:	¾''x8''x21''	(1)
Bottom:	¾''x9''x21''	(1)
Brace:	1¼''x1¼''x12''	(2)

With the accent on outdoor living, a project to decorate a blank, exterior wall area is very much in order. There also is a practical reason for hanging these planters on a wall, since they provide visual relief without taking up patio or deck space.

Start by cutting front and back posts to length and chamfering both ends of each piece. Touch up the corners with fine sandpaper. Cut the front and the two sides to width and length, then cut the rabbets. Attach the front to the two front posts, using waterproof glue and 4d finishing nails. Since this is an outdoor project, you can substitute box nails for a "rustic" appearance.

Attach the sides to the front posts, then add the back posts. Cut the back to size and add it to the assembly. Best bet at this point is to measure the opening and cut the bottom to fit. The bottom must be notched at both forward corners to fit around the posts. It's a good idea to cut these notches slightly oversize to provide for water drainage. Use plenty of glue on the edges of the bottom and fasten with 6d nails.

Cut one brace to exact size by checking against the planter for good fit, then cut the second to match. Attach them with glue and nails; drill ¼-inch holes for the lag screws.

A natural, aged finish is complimentary to redwood, but you can stain, paint or seal the wood as you wish.

When you plant, put a 1-inch layer of gravel in the bottom of the planter before filling it with soil. What you plant depends on the exposure, and your local nursery can advise you on this.

(TYPICAL)

1″

1/2″

④

22″

⑤

6″

24″

③

②

⑦

①

45

1/2″

2″

12″

8″

1/2″

⑥

1″

12″

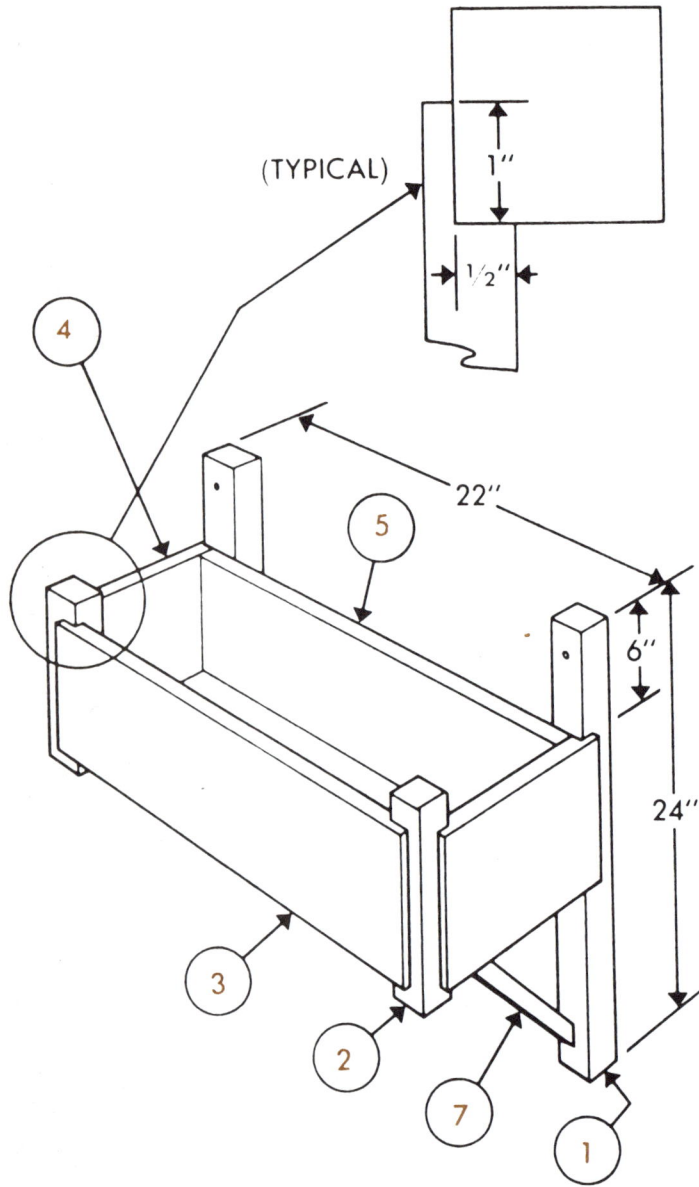
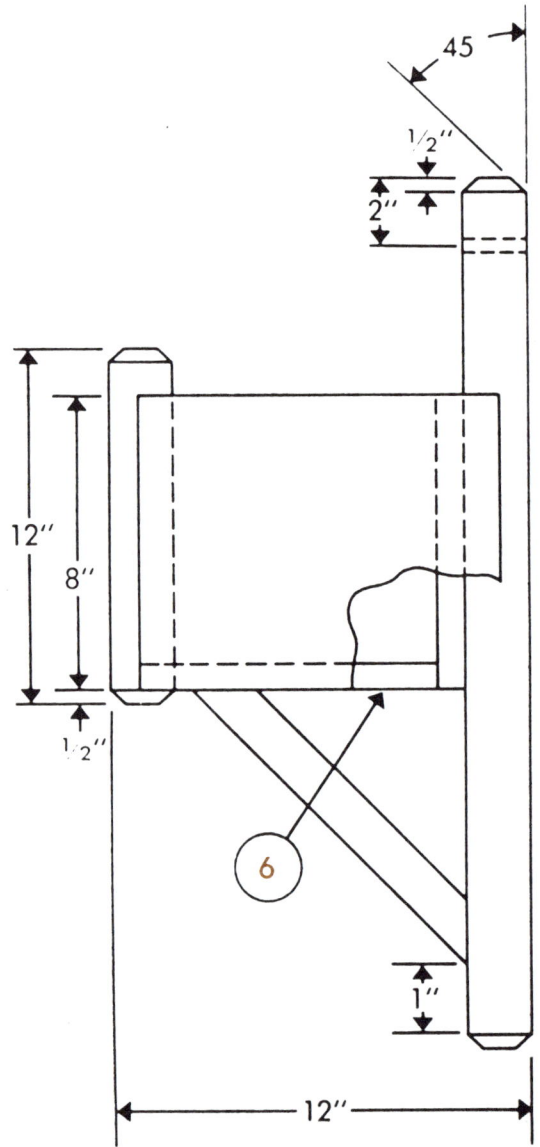

PATIO PLANTER AND TRAY

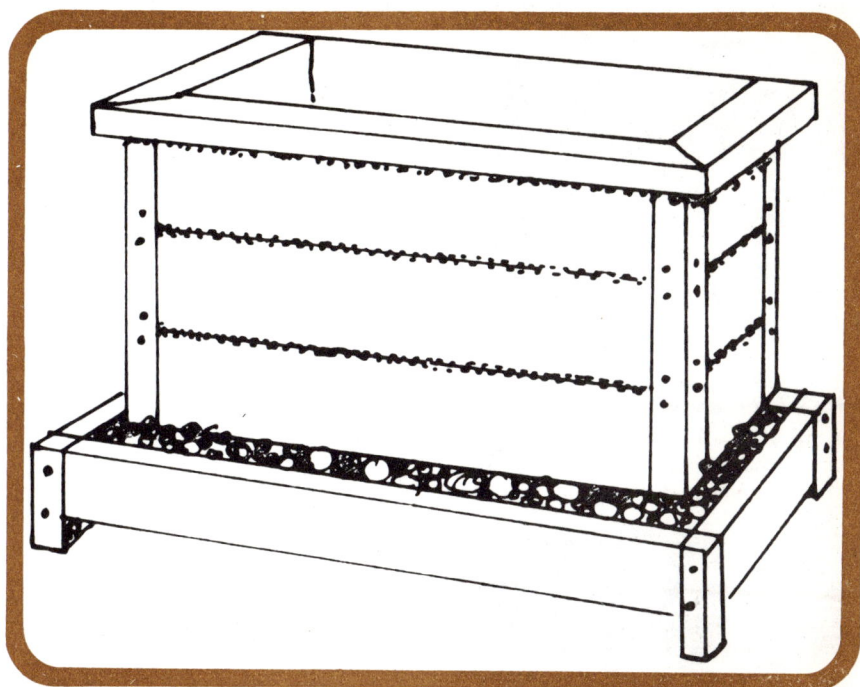

When dressed with colorful flowers or greenery, a concrete patio or wooden deck takes on a new and more attractive look. Short of leaving an open area for actual planting in soil, the best way to accomplish this is to make planter boxes for strategic spots. The planter shown is good looking and has great structural strength, despite the lack of complicated joints. It will fit almost anywhere—a pair of them, for example, are attractive flanking a door.

All material is 2-inch foundation-grade redwood. You can use better material, but this grade is less expensive than clear stock, and it looks rugged and like it belongs outdoors. Net dimensions of 2 x 6 stock are 1-5/8 x 5-5/8, generally.

Start construction by cutting the corner posts and boards required. As indicated in the drawing, all mating edges are chamfered to create a deep "V-joint." This makes the joints a point of interest, and is practical, as any later separation of joints will not be obvious.

Start assembly by nailing the posts and boards that form the front and back. All mating edges are coated with waterproof glue, and bar or pipe-fixture clamps are used to pull the boards together while you nail. Drill pilot holes if there is any tendency for splitting. Next, add the end boards, again using clamps while you nail. Lengths of 2-inch board are nailed on for the bottom. The top frame is cut as shown because the box was placed against a wall. If free-standing, add the fourth strip.

Cutting and assembly for the tray is the same as for the planter. You can use the planter without the tray, but it does add style.

Drill a few ½-inch drain holes in the bottom, then apply a coat of

Chamfering all mating edges creates deep V-shape shadow lines. Decorative stones are placed in tray.

USE 2" STOCK THROUGHOUT
(REDWOOD RECOMMENDED)

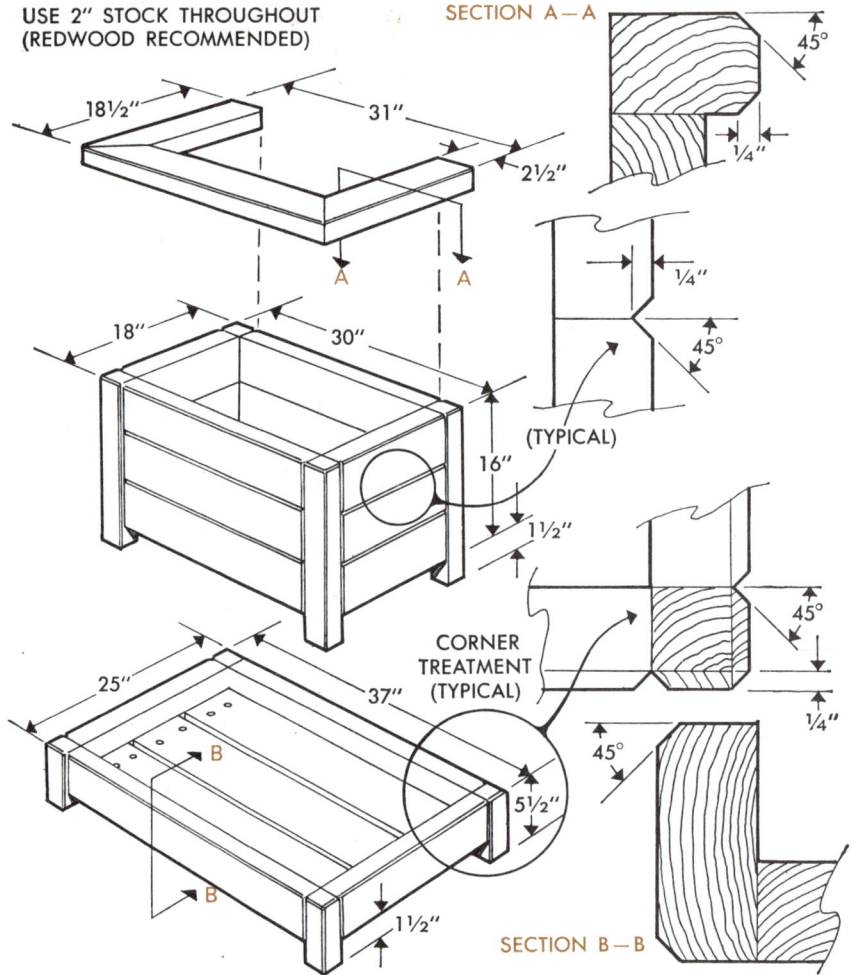

SECTION A—A

18½"   31"   2½"   45°   ¼"

A   A

18"   30"   16"   (TYPICAL)   ¼"   45°

1½"

CORNER TREATMENT (TYPICAL)

25"   37"   45°   45°   ¼"

B   5½"

B   1½"   45°

SECTION B—B

clear-resin sealer. Line both the planter and tray with plastic sheeting, stapling it in place (don't forget the drain holes) and put in a 1-inch layer of gravel for drainage before filling with earth. After the planter is in the tray, fill the tray with small stones.

PATIO SERVER

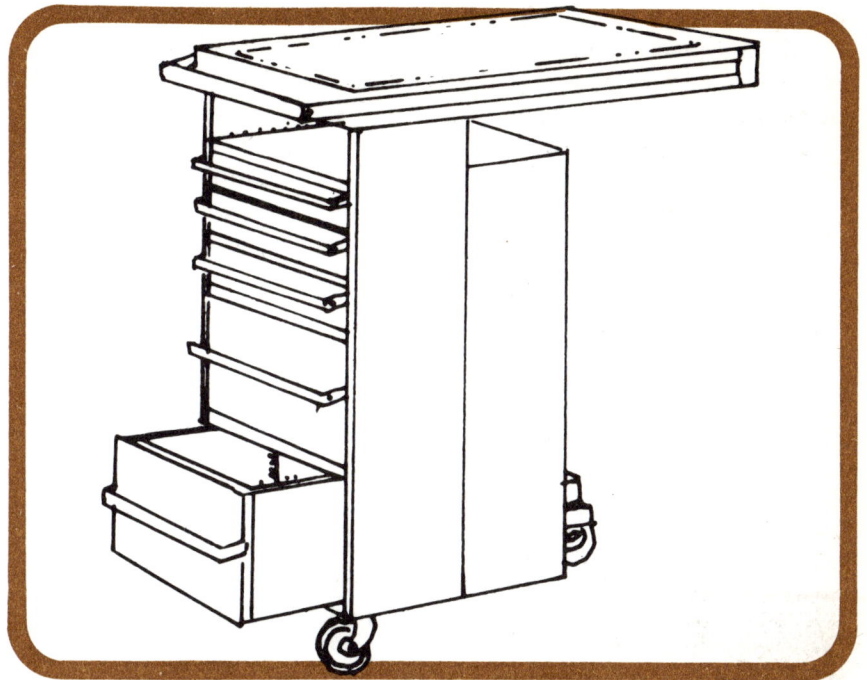

The design of this server is an adaptation of the traditional tea cart. Great for patio serving, it easily transports food and eating utensils to the patio table for dining. The cart holds silverware, cups, glasses and linens, while the top is large enough to hold the food for a meal. A chopping block, which is handily stored under the top, can be removed and placed on the cart or table for cutting and slicing. To make serving quick and efficient, the cart is designed to roll right over the table.

Although it is called a "patio" server, it also can be used in the house for moving a complete meal from the kitchen to the dining room. After the table has been set and the meal served, the cart rolls easily out of the way, and like a "silent butler" standing nearby, is ready and waiting to haul away the soiled dishes, silverware and the remains of the meal. The duplex receptacle on the end of the server top has an 8-foot cord (yours may require a longer cord) that is plugged into the house current to permit using toasters, electric frying pans, percolators, etc., right at the table.

The case of the server can be made of edge-glued solid stock, or from hardwood-faced plywood. If plywood is used, you may wish to make a shallow saw cut in the sides, as in the drawing, to simulate edge-glued boards. All stock listed in the Materials List is hardwood, unless otherwise noted (except for the sides, back and drawer fronts that can also be plywood), and all stock indicated as ¾-inch is what is normally called "1-inch stock." The aluminum used for the handles is the "do-it-yourself" type sold at most hardware stores. Be sure to get the ¼-inch material, as the more common 1/8-inch bars are a little too light to stand up to pulling on them if the drawers are heavily loaded.

Note that the casters are inserted in the lower edges of the sides, and in the caster support. If the server is to be used extensively on a rough patio, use plate-type casters and screw them to the bottom frame as well as the edges of the sides.

Stain and finish the project to suit; for outdoor use, consider an exterior-grade varnish that will stand occasional showers.

MATERIALS LIST

A.	Lower Top:	¾"x11-15/16"x14¾" (1)
B.	Back Panel:	¾"x16-3/8"x23-1/8" (1)
D.	Drawer-Glide Framing:	½"x1-5/8"x15½" (8)
F.	Drawer-Glide Framing:	½"x1-5/8"x11-15/16" (8)
G.	Bottom Framing:	¾"x2¾"x14¾" (2)
H.	Bottom Framing:	¾"x2¾"x6-7/16" (2)
J.	Caster Support:	¾"x2¾"x17¼" (1)
K.	Brace:	¾"x1¾"x8-1/16" (1)
L.	Sides:	¾"x12¾"x27-5/8" (2)
N.	Top:	1/16" plastic laminate x 16-3/8" x 27-11/16" (1)
O.	Top Support:	¾"x16-3/8"x27-11/16" (1)
P.	Top Frame:	¾"x2-9/16"x28½" (2)
Q.	Top Frame:	¾"x2-9/16"x18" (1)
R.	Inner Framing:	¾"x¾"x14-3/8" (1)
S.	Inner Framing:	¾"x¾"x21-5/16" (2)
U.	Top Handle:	¾"x1"x17½" (1)
V.	Handle Bars:	¼" x 1" aluminum bar x 31" (2)
W.	Cord Retainer:	¼" aluminum wire x 3-3/8" (2)
X.	Extension Cord (male plug):	8' (1)
Y.	Surface-Mounted Duplex Outlet:	1¼"x1¾"x5" (1)
Z.	Housing Back:	¼"x2-1/16"x17½" (1)
AA.	Housing Top and Bottom:	¼"x1½"x18" (2)
BB.	Housing Ends:	¼"x1½"x2-9/16" (2)
CC.	Carving-Board Facing:	9/16"x1½"x14-11/16" (1)
DD.	Carving-Board Strips:	13/16"x1½"x14-11/16" (14)
EE.	Handle Spacer:	1"x1"x1" (10)
FF.	Handle:	¼" x 1" aluminum bar x 14-11/16" (5)
GG.	Drawer Bottom:	½"x11-1/16"x13-11/16" (4)
HH.	Drawer Back:	½"x2½"x13-11/16" (2)
II.	Drawer Side:	½"x2½"x11-9/16" (8)
JJ.	Drawer Dividers:	½"x2-1/16"x11-11/32" (3)
KK.	Drawer Front:	¾"x2½"x14-11/16" (2)
LL.	Cup Hooks, Curtain Hooks:	3" (6)
MM.	Drawer Back:	½"x6-11/32"x13-11/16" (2)
NN.	Drawer Front:	¾"x6-11/32"x14-11/16" (2)
OO.	Glass Rack:	¼"x6¼"x14-9/16" (1)
PP.	Caster, Swivel:	3"-diameter (3)

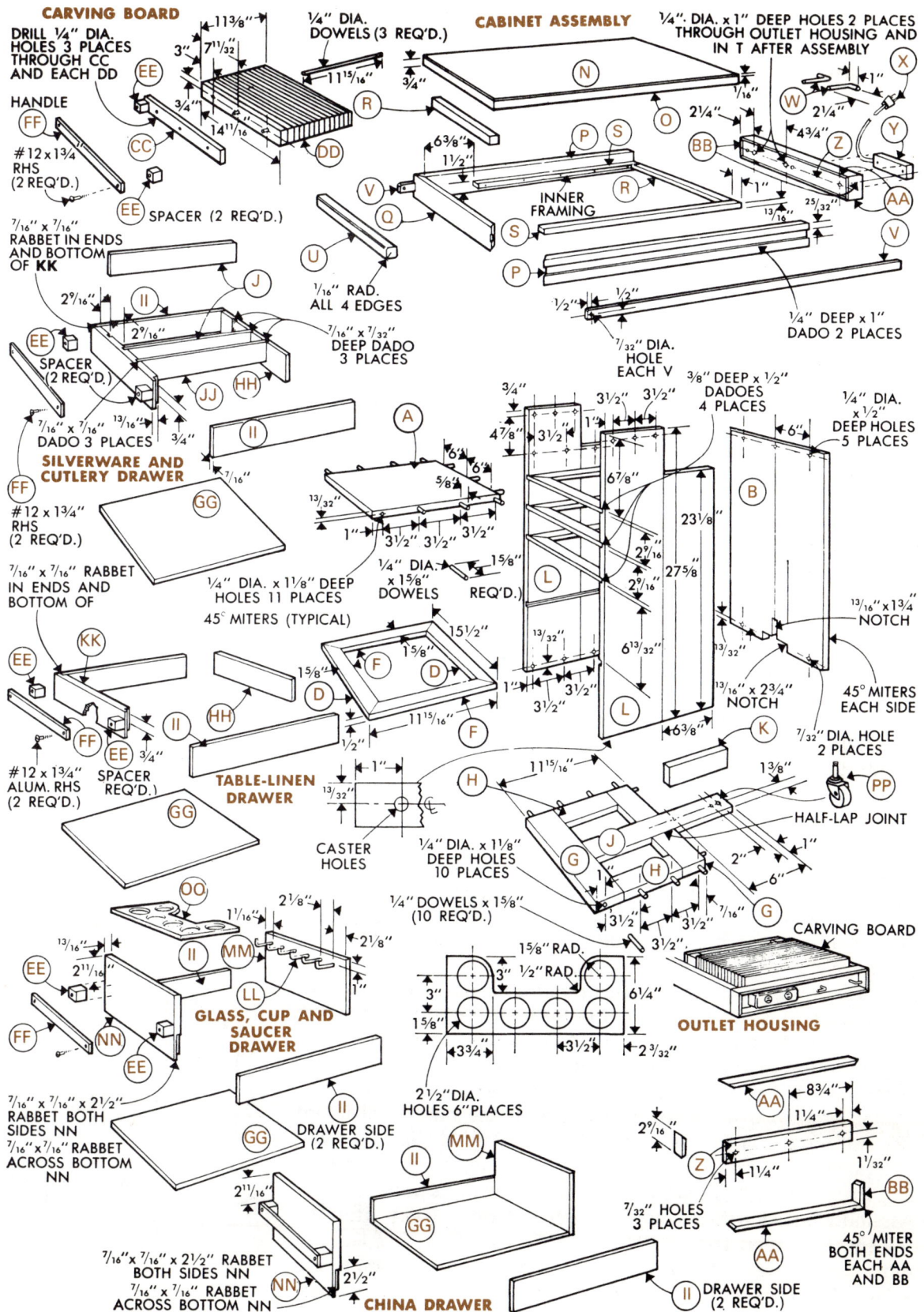

CARVING BOARD

DRILL ¼" DIA. HOLES 3 PLACES THROUGH CC AND EACH DD

HANDLE
FF

#12 x 1¾" RHS (2 REQ'D.)

EE SPACER (2 REQ'D.)

EE
CC
DD
R
EE

11⅜"
3" 7¹¹/₃₂"
¾"
11¹⁵/₁₆"
14¹¹/₁₆"
¾"

¼" DIA. DOWELS (3 REQ'D.)

CABINET ASSEMBLY

¼". DIA. x 1" DEEP HOLES 2 PLACES THROUGH OUTLET HOUSING AND IN T AFTER ASSEMBLY

N
O
P S
R
S
P
V
Q
U
BB
W
X
Y
Z
AA
V

¹/₁₆"
2¼"
4¾"
1"
2¼"
13/₁₆
25/₃₂
1"

6⅜"
1½"

INNER FRAMING

½" ½"

¼" DEEP x 1" DADO 2 PLACES

⁷/₃₂" DIA. HOLE EACH V

7/₁₆" x 7/₁₆" RABBET IN ENDS AND BOTTOM OF KK

EE SPACER (2 REQ'D.)

2⁹/₁₆"
2⁹/₁₆"
II
J
JJ HH

7/₁₆" x 7/₃₂" DEEP DADO 3 PLACES

1/₁₆" RAD. ALL 4 EDGES

7/₁₆" x 7/₁₆" DADO 3 PLACES

13/₁₆" ¾"

SILVERWARE AND CUTLERY DRAWER

FF

#12 x 1¾" RHS (2 REQ'D.)

7/₁₆" x 7/₁₆" RABBET IN ENDS AND BOTTOM OF

EE KK FF EE II HH

#12 x 1¾" ALUM. RHS (2 REQ'D.) SPACER REQ'D. ¾"

TABLE-LINEN DRAWER

II
GG
A
F D
D
F

7/₁₆"

¼" DIA. x 1⅛" DEEP HOLES 11 PLACES
45° MITERS (TYPICAL)

¼" DIA. x 1⅝" DOWELS REQ'D.

13/₃₂"
1" 3½" 3½" 3½"
6" 6"
5⅝"
1⅝"

¾"
4⅞" 3½"
3½" 3½" 1"
6⅞"
23⅛"
27⅝"
2⁹/₁₆"
2⁹/₁₆"
13/₃₂"
6¹³/₃₂"
1" 3½" 3½"
6⅜"
L L L

¼" DIA. x ½" DEEP HOLES 5 PLACES

3/₈" DEEP x ½" DADOES 4 PLACES

B

13/₁₆" x 1¾" NOTCH

13/₃₂"
13/₁₆" x 2¾" NOTCH

45° MITERS EACH SIDE

⁷/₃₂" DIA. HOLE 2 PLACES

15½"
1⅝"
1⅝"
11¹⁵/₁₆"
½"

K
H
G J H
G

11¹⁵/₁₆"
1⅜"
HALF-LAP JOINT
PP

2" 1"
6"

CASTER HOLES

1"
13/₃₂"

¼" DIA. x 1⅛" DEEP HOLES 10 PLACES

¼" DOWELS x 1⅝" (10 REQ'D.)

3½" 3½"
⁷/₁₆"

1⅝" RAD.
3" ½" RAD.
3"
3"
1⅝"
3¾" 3½" 2³/₃₂"
6¼"

2½" DIA. HOLES 6" PLACES

CARVING BOARD

OUTLET HOUSING

OO
II MM
LL
EE
2¹¹/₁₆"
13/₁₆"
FF NN
EE

1¹/₁₆"
2⅛"
2⅛"
1"

GLASS, CUP AND SAUCER DRAWER

7/₁₆" x 7/₁₆" x 2½" RABBET BOTH SIDES NN
7/₁₆" x 7/₁₆" RABBET ACROSS BOTTOM NN

GG

II
GG
MM
II
GG

DRAWER SIDE (2 REQ'D.)

2¹¹/₁₆"
7/₁₆" x 7/₁₆" x 2½" RABBET BOTH SIDES NN
7/₁₆" x 7/₁₆" RABBET ACROSS BOTTOM NN
NN
2½"

CHINA DRAWER

AA
Z
BB
AA
II

8¾"
1¼"
2⁹/₁₆"
1¼"
1¹/₃₂"

⁷/₃₂" HOLES 3 PLACES

45° MITER BOTH ENDS EACH AA AND BB

DRAWER SIDE (2 REQ'D.)

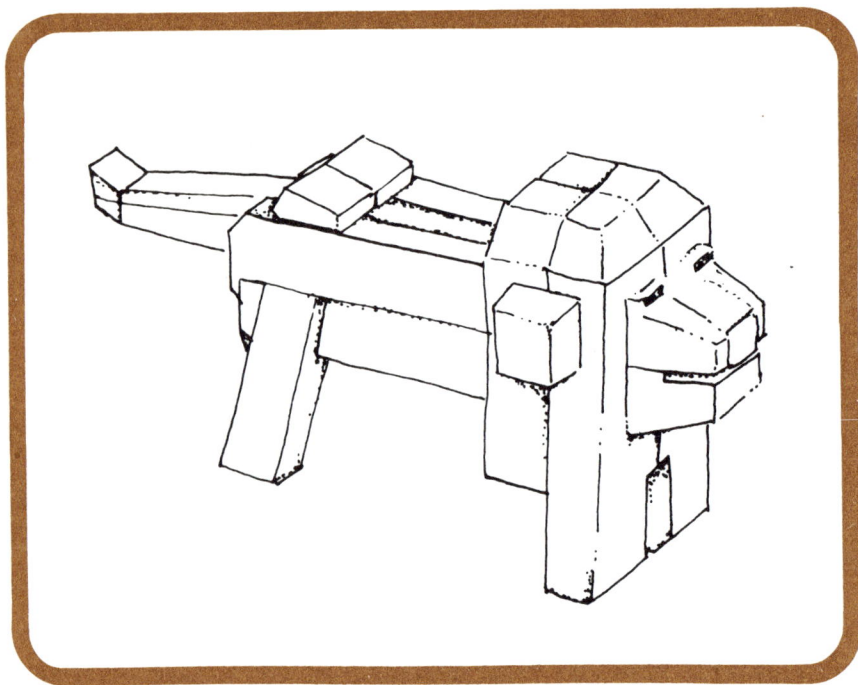

LION BLOCK PUZZLE

Putting together this little lion from the eleven pieces will be a challenge to anyone's ingenuity, and patience. It also will be a challenge to the craftsman who makes the puzzle, as the pieces must fit properly, and considerable filing and fitting will be required to make accurate joints.

A hardwood is required and scraps can be used because the pieces are all small. Make full-size patterns from the squared drawings, keeping in mind that there must be pairs of all pieces (right- and lefthand), except for parts A, B and F. If you have a mean streak in your personality, you might just make pairs of all pieces, and when the would-be puzzle worker got the handful of parts and looked at the photo of the lion, he might just have a problem assembling the puzzle with "parts left over."

A surface finish, such as lacquer or varnish is not recommended, as it would quickly be worn away by the constant friction of assembly and disassembly. A penetrating sealer would protect the wood, eliminate surface finish, and help prevent the parts from becoming soiled.

If the puzzle is to be made for a youngster, you might consider a bright-color, nontoxic paint. Painting each of the parts a different color would make it a fun assembly. When fitting the pieces as you make the puzzle, be sure to allow that slight extra tolerance to prevent the paint from causing too-tight fits between the various parts.

Assembly begins with horizontal member A on B. Next, fit in the legs C-1 and C-2, then D-1 and D-2; and E-1 and E-2. This leaves a recess to receive dowel F. G-1 and G-2 are next. Finally, turning F, the square "ears," 90 degrees counterclockwise locks all pieces in place.

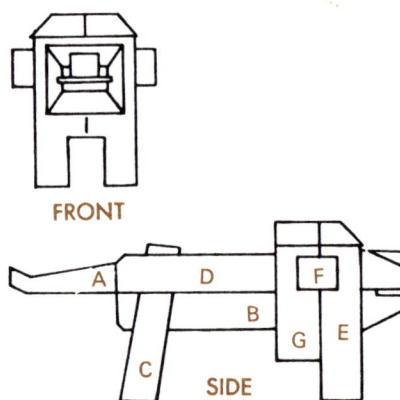

FRONT

SIDE

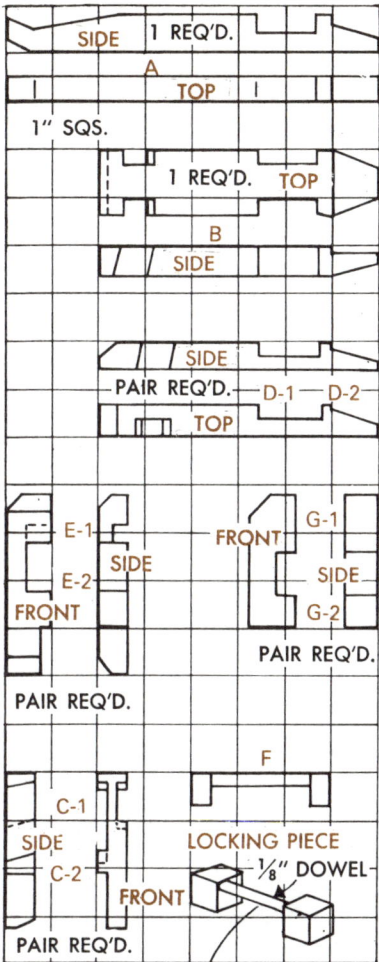

SIDE   1 REQ'D.
A
TOP

1" SQS.

1 REQ'D.   TOP
B
SIDE

SIDE
PAIR REQ'D.   D-1   D-2
TOP

E-1   FRONT   G-1
SIDE   SIDE
E-2   G-2
FRONT
PAIR REQ'D.
PAIR REQ'D.

F
C-1
LOCKING PIECE
SIDE   1/8" DOWEL
C-2   FRONT
PAIR REQ'D.

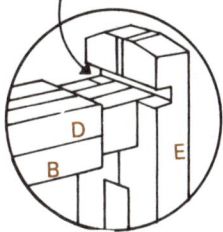

D   E
B

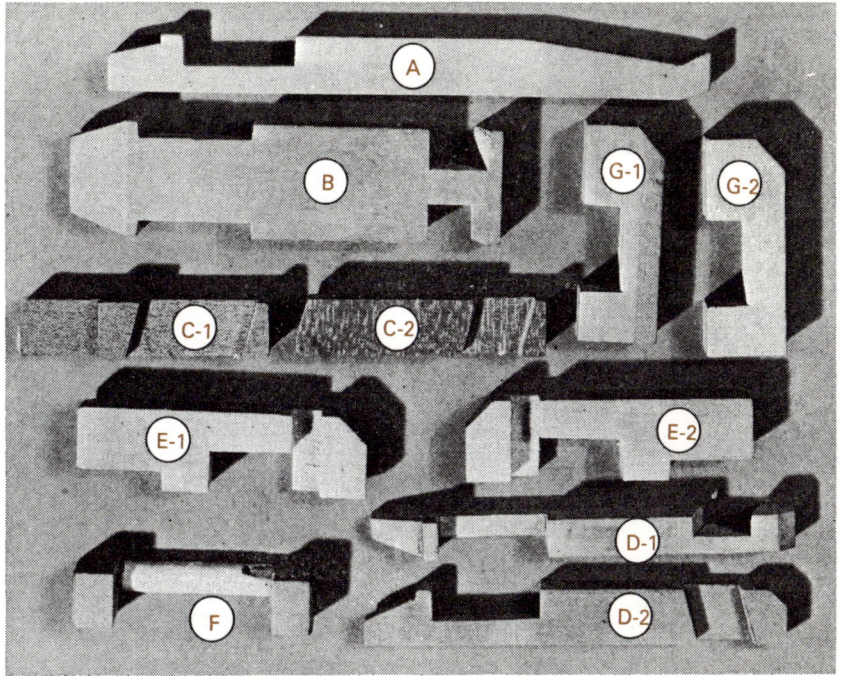

JUNIOR GRAND PRIX RACE CAR

Inspired by the Formula cars that run the Grand Prix circuit around the world, this car has been reduced to the basics so there are no compound curves in the bodywork. Power is supplied by the driver through a "pedal-power engine" and steering is quick and precise through a "butterfly" wheel.

Start construction by making a pattern for the sides by enlarging the squared drawing. Cut the two sides from ½-inch plywood. If you use a veneer plywood, be sure to make a pair with the good side out.

Cleats cut from 1-inch softwood are glued and screwed to the inner surfaces of the sides, flush with upper edges. Hardwood cleats for supporting the pillow-block bearings for the rear axle are glued and screwed in position, as indicated.

The front of the body is joined by the front-axle cleat, which first is grooved as indicated. Crosspieces at the top of the body are about 15½ inches long—which should be the distance between the ½-inch grooves in the axle cleat, less twice the thickness of the upper cleats inside the body. Cleats at the rear part of the body should be the same length.

The crank support is installed now, being glued and screwed to the center groove in the front-axle cleat at the forward end, while the back end is supported on two cleats glued and screwed under the seat.

To make the pedal drive you first weld (or have welded) a short length of ½-inch black-iron pipe to a piece of steel angle. Slot the angle as indicated, to permit tightening or loosening the belt. Drill a hole near the center of the pipe and tap for a grease fitting.

The crank can be made in two ways: First, bend a Z-shape which

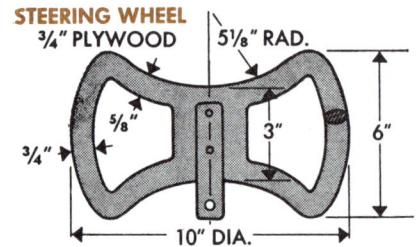

STEERING WHEEL
¾" PLYWOOD
5⅛" RAD.
⅝"
¾"
3"
6"
10" DIA.

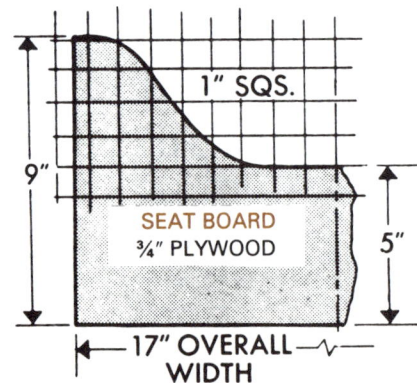

1" SQS.
9"
SEAT BOARD
¾" PLYWOOD
5"
17" OVERALL WIDTH

will be one arm with the pedal extension and the portion that goes through the pipe. Install the two shaft collars and pulley loosely, then weld on to this bent crank the other portion of the crank. Center the crank, tighten the collars and lubricate it with a grease gun.

The second method is to insert the rod in the crank support, heat the rod at the bending points and bend the crank to shape.

Install the rear bearings and axle with pulley. Align front and rear pulleys, install the belt and tighten.

The steering assembly is next. After it is installed and tested, cover the back and front of the body with do-it-yourself sheet aluminum.

The lights and airfoil are optional items. Finish the car in bright colors and patterns to suit.

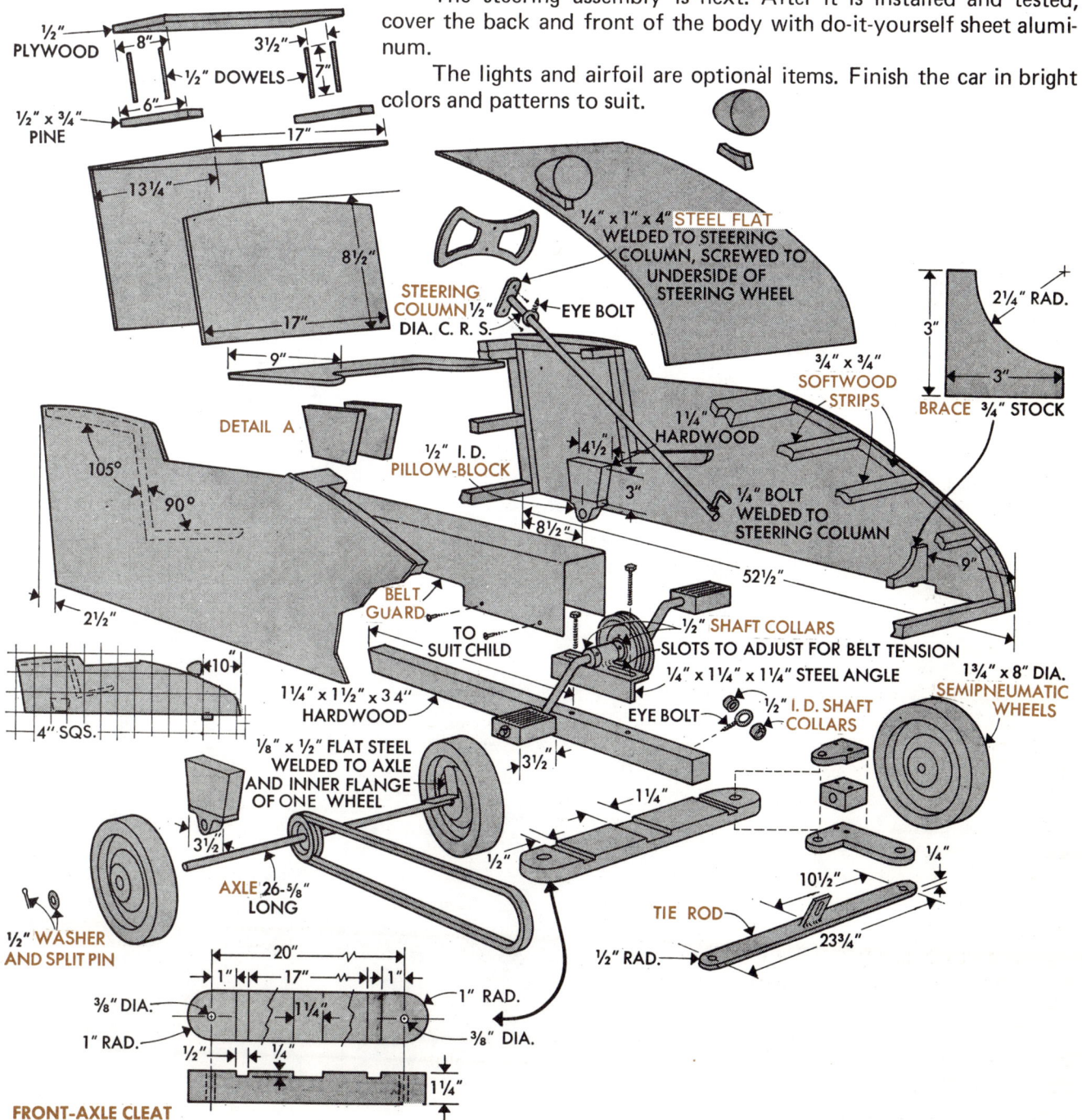

½" PLYWOOD
8"
3½"
½" DOWELS
7"
½" x ¾" PINE
6"
17"
13¼"
8½"
17"
9"

DETAIL A
105°
90°
2½"
10"
4" SQS.

STEERING COLUMN ½" DIA. C. R. S.
EYE BOLT

¼" x 1" x 4" STEEL FLAT WELDED TO STEERING COLUMN, SCREWED TO UNDERSIDE OF STEERING WHEEL

2¼" RAD.
3"
3"
BRACE ¾" STOCK

¾" x ¾" SOFTWOOD STRIPS

1¼" HARDWOOD
4½"
3"

¼" BOLT WELDED TO STEERING COLUMN

½" I. D. PILLOW-BLOCK

8½"

52½"

9"

BELT GUARD

TO SUIT CHILD

½" SHAFT COLLARS
SLOTS TO ADJUST FOR BELT TENSION

¼" x 1¼" x 1¼" STEEL ANGLE

EYE BOLT

½" I. D. SHAFT COLLARS

1¾" x 8" DIA. SEMIPNEUMATIC WHEELS

1¼" x 1½" x 34" HARDWOOD

3½"

1¼"

½"

¼"

10½"

¼"

⅛" x ½" FLAT STEEL WELDED TO AXLE AND INNER FLANGE OF ONE WHEEL

3½"

3½"

AXLE 26-⅝" LONG

TIE ROD
½" RAD.
23¾"

½" WASHER AND SPLIT PIN

FRONT-AXLE CLEAT

20"
1"
17"
1"
1" RAD.
⅜" DIA.
1¼"
1" RAD.
⅜" DIA.
½"
¼"
1¼"

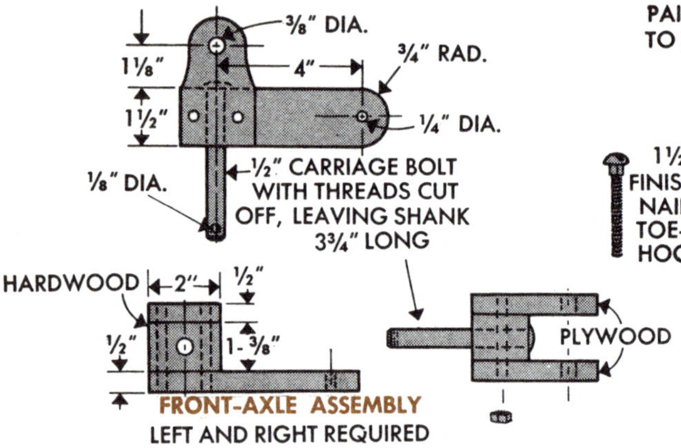

3/8" DIA.

1 1/8"

4"

3/4" RAD.

1 1/2"

1/4" DIA.

1/8" DIA.

1/2" CARRIAGE BOLT WITH THREADS CUT OFF, LEAVING SHANK 3 3/4" LONG

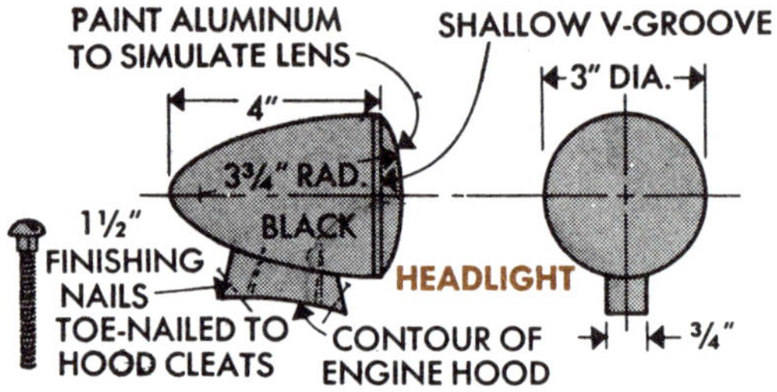

PAINT ALUMINUM TO SIMULATE LENS

SHALLOW V-GROOVE

4"

3 3/4" RAD.

BLACK

3" DIA.

1 1/2" FINISHING NAILS TOE-NAILED TO HOOD CLEATS

HEADLIGHT

CONTOUR OF ENGINE HOOD

3/4"

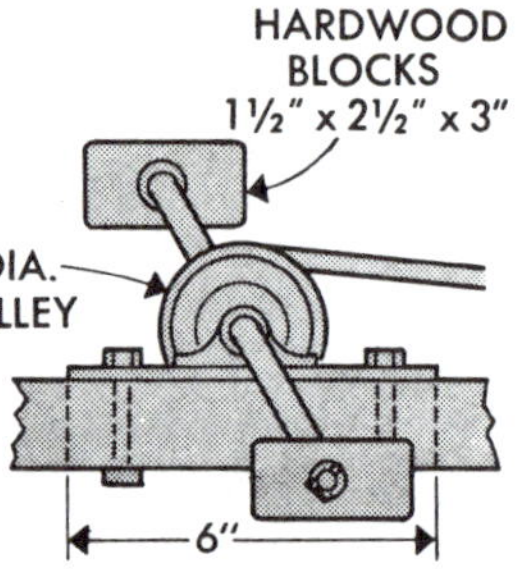

HARDWOOD BLOCKS 1 1/2" x 2 1/2" x 3"

HARDWOOD   2"   1/2"

1/2"

1 - 3/8"

PLYWOOD

FRONT-AXLE ASSEMBLY
LEFT AND RIGHT REQUIRED

3" DIA. V-PULLEY

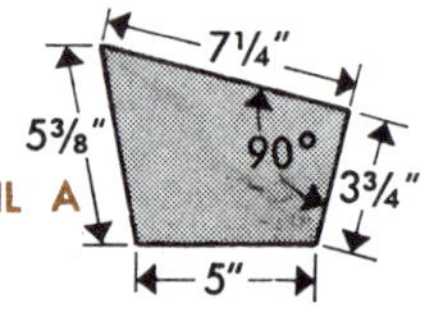

DETAIL A

7 1/4"

5 3/8"

90°

3 3/4"

5"

6"

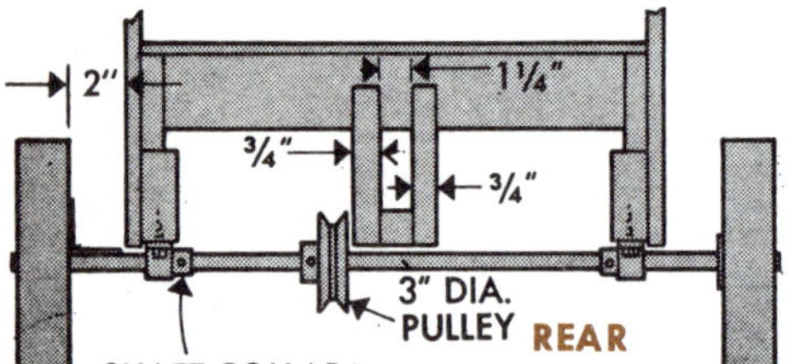

2"

1 1/4"

3/4"

3/4"

3" DIA. PULLEY

SHAFT COLLARS

REAR AXLE ASSEMBLY

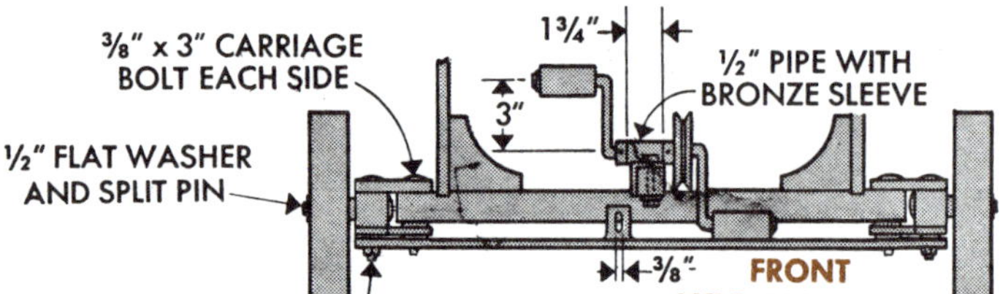

3/8" x 3" CARRIAGE BOLT EACH SIDE

1/2" FLAT WASHER AND SPLIT PIN

1/4" x 3" CARRIAGE BOLT EACH SIDE

1 3/4"

3"

1/2" PIPE WITH BRONZE SLEEVE

3/8"

FRONT AXLE ASSEMBLY

1/4"

1/2" RAD.

7/8"

1/4" DIA. BOTH ENDS

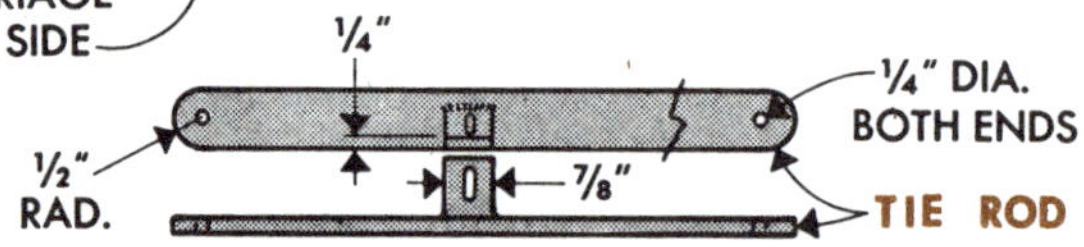

TIE ROD

BOOK RACK

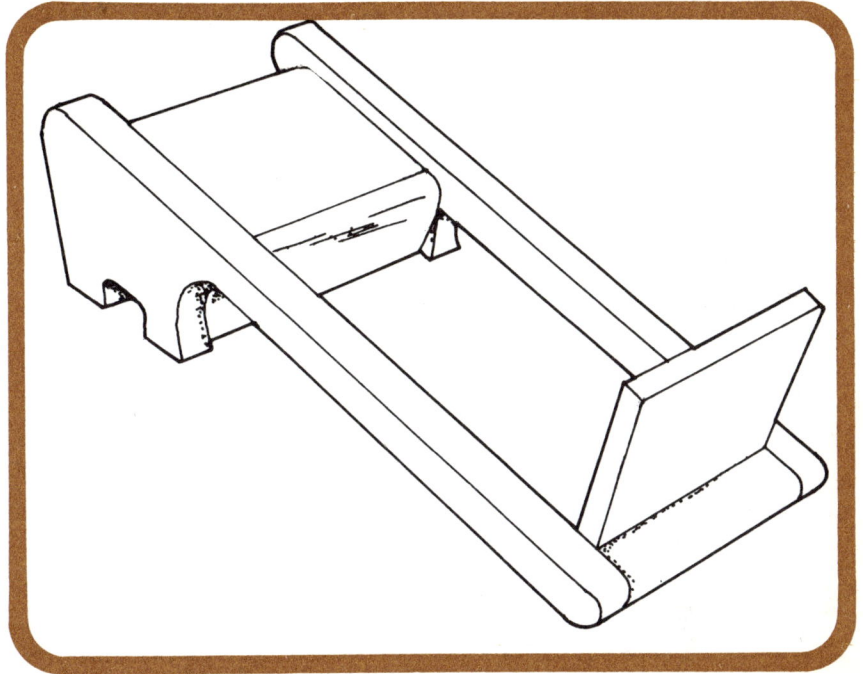

If you're looking for a project to use up some of those leftover wood scraps, give this one a try. None of the pieces are very large and the project takes but a few hours to build. The small globe is available at most stationery stores, or you may wish to substitute a small statuette or other item.

Projects of simple design such as this book rack are most attractive made of one of the hardwoods such as walnut, teak or even zebrawood.

Begin the project by cutting to length and width the two pieces to be used for the sides. Make the pattern for the sides, and transfer to one of the boards. Tack the boards together, nailing in the waste areas, and saw around the outline using either a band saw, jig or coping saw. Sand the pieces to match.

Make the platform that holds the globe in one unit then attach it to the sides. Round off the top edge of the platform as shown. Nail it in place keeping the lower edges of the sides and the platform flush; cut the book support and spacer to size. Round off the two edges of the spacer as shown and sand all exposed surfaces. Attach the book support to the spacer with countersunk wood screws. Fasten the book support-spacer assembly to the two sides using 2-inch brads for the spacer and No. 8 x 1¼-inch flathead screws for the support. Set all nails and fill the holes with wood filler. If you are using a dark hardwood, such as teak or walnut, finish with a penetrating sealer. This is flowed onto the surface until the wood will not absorb more. The surplus is wiped off and the project left to dry. After a day or two, rub down with fine steel wool and wax.

BOOK RACK ASSEMBLY

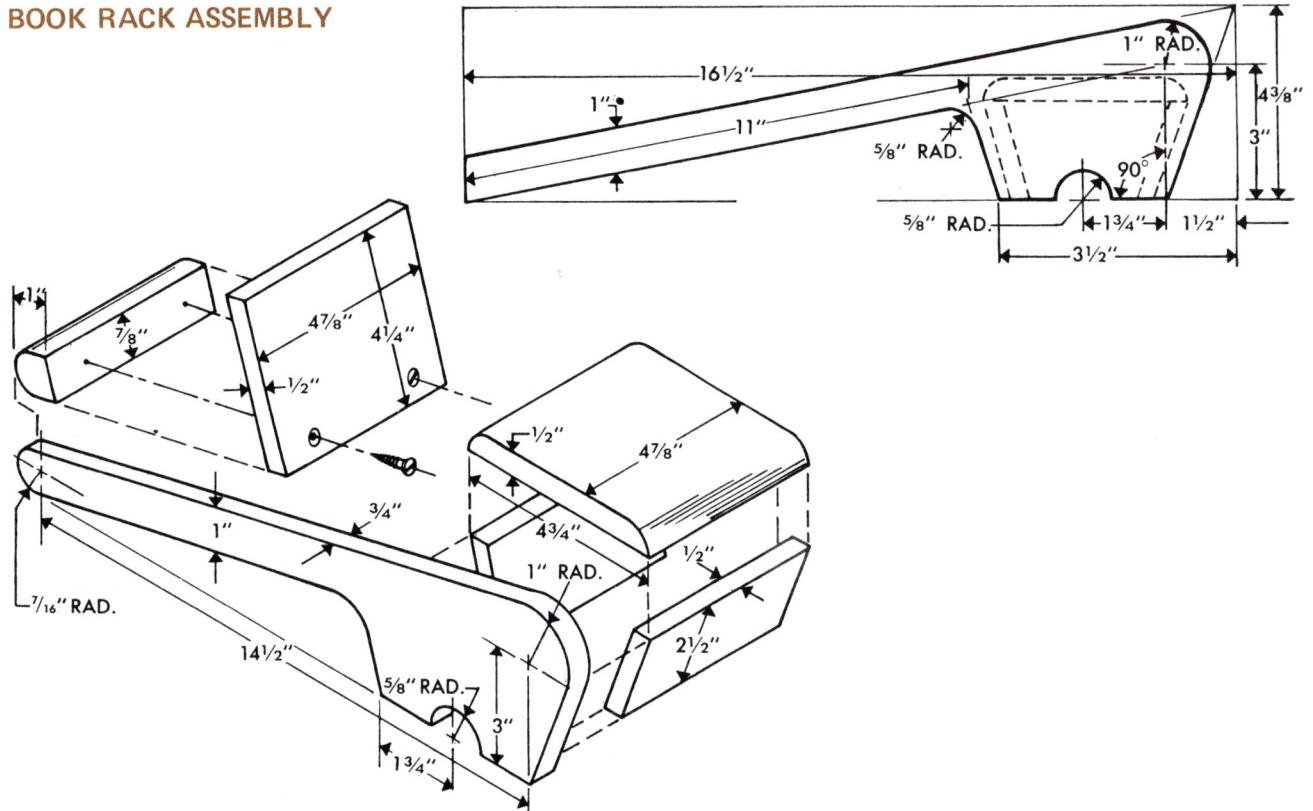

SPICE RACK WITH CLOCK

This unusual item is basically a spice rack, but it is combined with a clock, a slanted shelf for holding open cookbooks and two archtopped shelves for displaying conversation pieces and collectibles. The cook can refer to recipes, time the cooking, and have the necessary spices close at hand.

Begin construction by cutting the sides from patterns made by enlarging the squared drawings. Cut and sand the sides together to assure they will be identical. Dadoes are cut in the inner faces of the sides for the four shelves. Cut the dadoes that hold the slanting shelf, and the rabbets that accept the two backs of the decorative shelves (these rabbets may be stopped just below the second shelf). Make the four shelves, dadoing for the vertical partitions, and the sides of the clock cabinet. Rabbets are cut the full length of the two upper shelves to accommodate the top and bottom edges of the shelf backs. Cut the clock-cabinet sides that are ¼ inch narrower than the rack sides to allow for the ¼-inch backs of the two side compartments. Clamp and assemble the rack sides, the shelves, and the clock-cabinet sides with glue and finishing nails. Cut the clock face from 3/8-inch plywood and install. It is positioned by wooden cleats set back 1-3/8 inch from the front edges of the opening. The face is held against the cleats by ¼-inch quarter round. Miter the corners of the molding.

Cut the slanting shelf to size and glue and brad the decorative apron to its lower edge. The apron has a tenon on each end created by cutting ¼ x ¼-inch rabbets as indicated, and a dado is cut in its upper edge. The book ledge is attached to the apron before fitting to the shelf. "Dry-fit" the assembly in the dadoes in the sides, and when it fits properly, install with glue and brads. The top crosspiece is cut to shape and attached with glue and brads. Fasten the arches over the shelves against cleats located 5/8 inch from the front edges of the shelves and partitions. Fit the drawer slides to the vertical partitions and install the partitions in their dadoes. Note the drawer slides position the front of the drawers about ¾ inch from the front. At this point attach the upper shelf backs with brads.

The unusual spice drawers consist of a top, bottom and two bracket-shape sides. Spice bottles on the original had their lids fastened to the drawer fronts. The bottles were unscrewed from their lids when used. An alternative would be to put backs on the drawers with the bottles loose. Full drawers also could be made to hold loose spices. The drawer pulls are shaped from plywood. The clock numbers are cut and installed before putting on the clock hands. Battery-operated clock movements and hands are available from a number of sources.

The clock-spice rack may be finished in several ways. Flat varnish may be used, or you may wish to enamel, to match or contrast with kitchen decor. An "antique" color glaze could be used, making the rack a "color" accent piece.

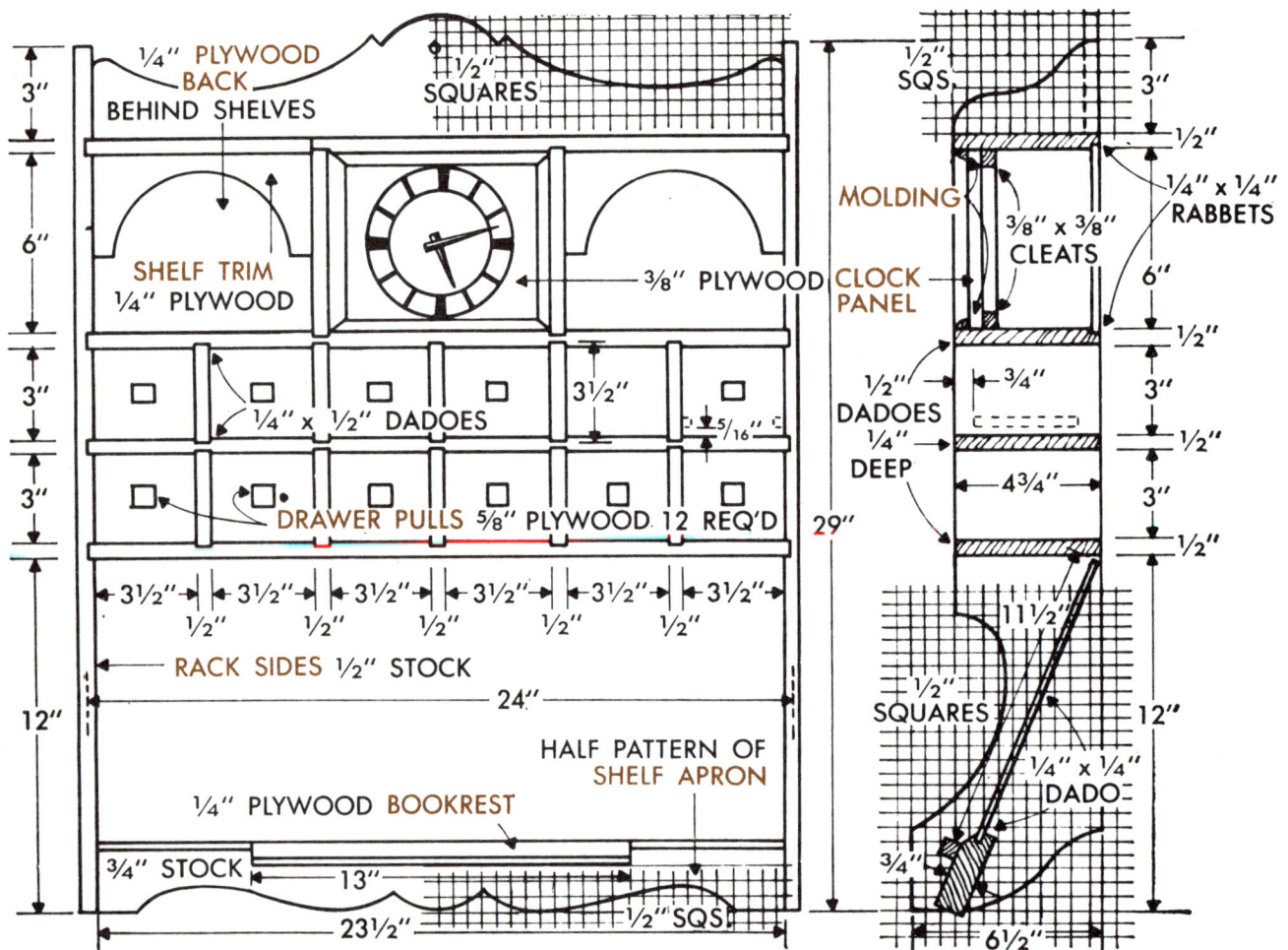

¼" PLYWOOD

7½"

3" RAD.

3½"

¾"   ¾"

DRAWER PULL

⅝"

¾"   ⅜"

DRAWER DETAIL

¾"

3⁷⁄₁₆"

LID

DRAWER SLIDE
¼" SQ.

¼"

2¹⁵⁄₁₆"

SPICE
JAR

⅜"

4¾"   3"

¼" PLYWOOD

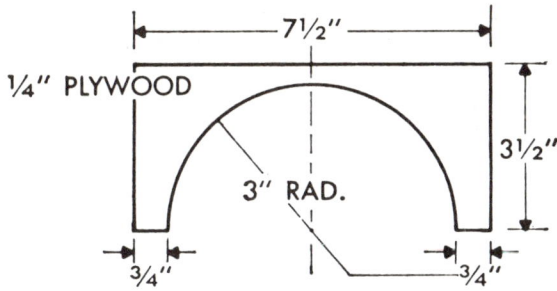

1.

2.

3.

1. Dadoes in the side accept the shelves and book shelf (saw guard removed for photo).
2. Rack is assembled using glue and brads.
3. Bookshelf is "dry-fit" before final assembly.
4. Spice bottles are fastened to the drawers.

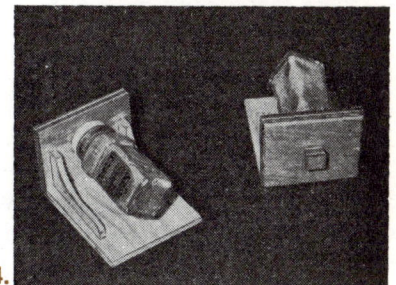

4.

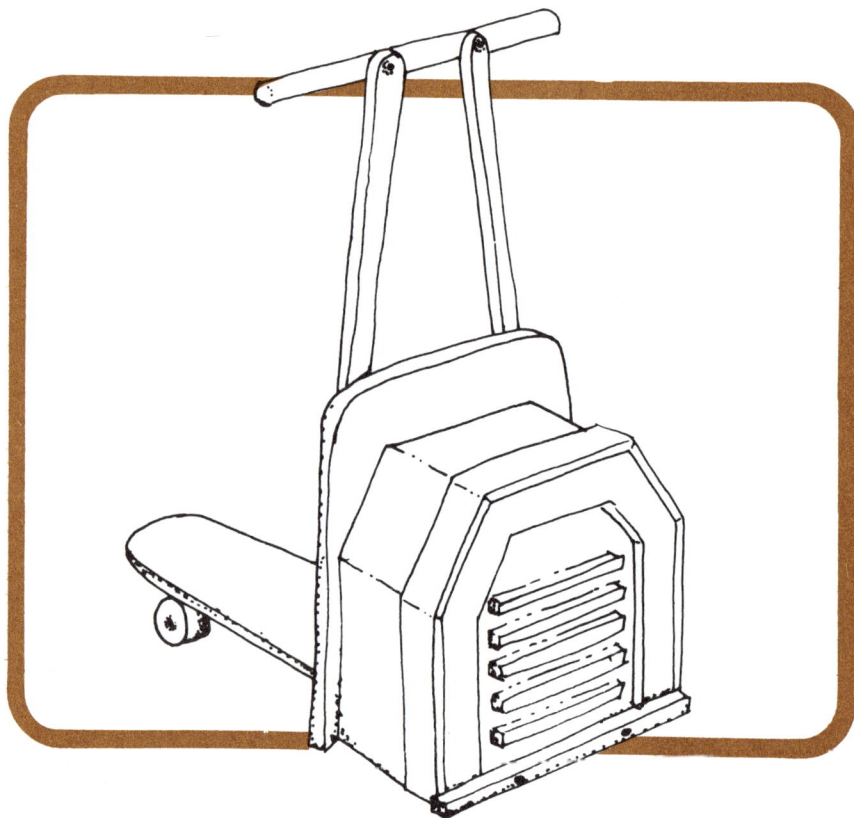

SKATE SCOOTER

If you remember the old-fashioned scooter made from a fruit box, length of 2 x 4 and the wheels from a single skate, then you might like to make an updated version. Combining the old with the new, the conventional 2 x 4 is replaced with a modern skate board. Safer than a skate board for small fry, and capable of providing plenty of fun, this scooter is designed to resemble an auto.

Skate boards may be purchased from mail-order houses and toy departments. Scooters with the metal wheels will make more noise, be rougher to ride, and will last longer than composition wheels, but the latter are recommended because they are less likely to skid and cause spills.

Begin construction by cutting the floor from ¾-inch exterior-grade plywood. Notches are cut in the back end of the floor to allow for attachment of the dashboard. The floor is fastened to the skate board with flathead wood screws.

Cut the handle uprights from 1-inch hardwood and attach to a 1-inch dowel with stove bolts. Be sure no rough edges of the bolts are left to cut small hands. Three holes are bored in each upright to permit screwing it to the dashboard assembly. Cut the dashboard from ¾-inch exterior-grade plywood to the size and shape shown. Round the corners to prevent injury.

Cut and fasten the engine-wall cleats to the dashboard with glue and screws. The engine walls are then cut to size and tack-nailed in place over the engine-wall cleats. It is easier to cut the parts to size and shape and dry-fit them, then disassemble and paint each piece.

When all joints match, glue and screw in place over the engine-

MATERIALS LIST

Skate Board:	Bought or made (1)
Dashboard:	¾"x13"x14" ext. grade plywood (1)
Wall Cleats:	7/8"x1"x30" solid stock (1)
Front Panel:	¼"x11¼"x11¼" plywood (1)
Engine Walls:	½"x5"x30" solid stock (1)
Panel Trim:	¼"x1¼"x10¾" plywood (1)
Wall Trim:	½"x1½"x36" solid stock (1)
Grill Bars:	¼"x½"x6½" solid stock (5)
Bumper:	5/8"x1"x13" solid stock (1)
Handle Uprights:	¾"x1"x23" hardwood (2)
Handle:	1" dowel x 14" (1)
Floor:	¾"x6¼"x10¼" ext. grade plywood (1)

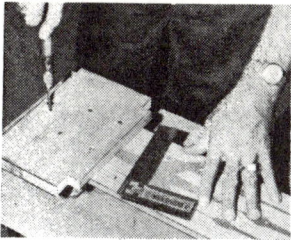

wall cleats and up against the dashboard. Cut the front panel to shape and fasten with finishing nails or screws to the front edges of the engine walls. A pattern can be made for the front panel by marking around the outside of the assembled engine walls. The front panel is outlined with trim and a trim-panel is fastened over it, making the grill. Grill bars and a bumper are cut from solid stock and added to the front panel for more realism. The dashboard assembly is fitted over the floor and attached with screws into the edges of the floor, then the handle uprights are attached with screws into the dashboard, making sure none of the screws protrude.

Paint the scooter with a nontoxic enamel, using strong contrasting colors. On the scooter shown the handles are finished natural, the bumper, grill and engine-wall trim painted gloss black, the front panel silver, and the dashboard and engine walls red.

All that remains is to stand back and watch the fun. It won't take youngsters long to learn how to balance the scooter, and make turns by leaning in the direction they wish to turn.

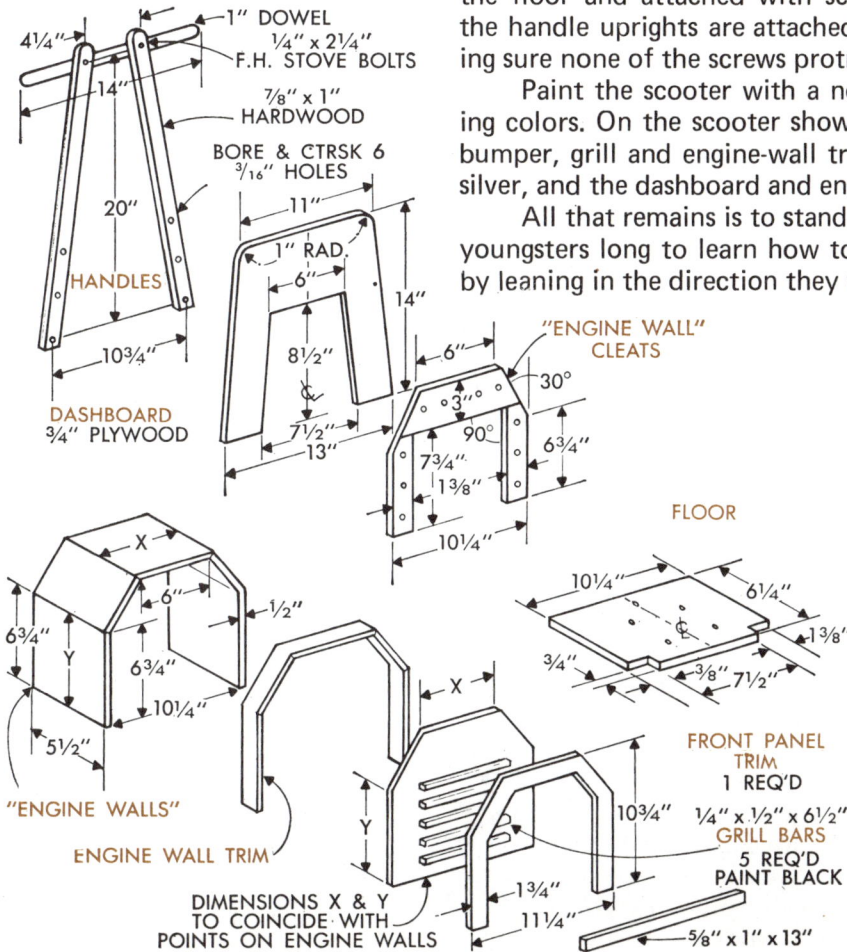

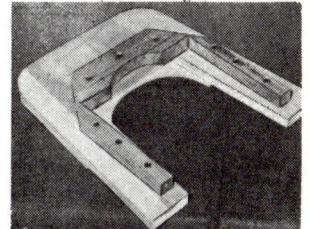

4¼"
1" DOWEL
¼" x 2¼"
F.H. STOVE BOLTS
14"
⅞" x 1"
HARDWOOD
BORE & CTRSK 6
³⁄₁₆" HOLES
20"
11"
1" RAD.
HANDLES
6"
14"
10¾"
8½"
"ENGINE WALL"
CLEATS
DASHBOARD
¾" PLYWOOD
30°
3"
7½"
13"
90°
6¾"
7¾"
1⅜"
10¼"
FLOOR
X
6"
½"
10¼"
6¼"
6¾"
1⅜"
6¾"
Y
10¼"
¾"
⅜" 7½"
5½"
FRONT PANEL
TRIM
1 REQ'D
"ENGINE WALLS"
X
10¾"
¼" x ½" x 6½"
GRILL BARS
5 REQ'D
PAINT BLACK
ENGINE WALL TRIM
Y
DIMENSIONS X & Y
TO COINCIDE WITH
POINTS ON ENGINE WALLS
1¾"
11¼"
⅝" x 1" x 13"

Fasten scooter floor securely to skate board with screws. Dashboard reinforced with cleats, engine walls fastened over cleats and up against dashboard with screws.

Each part is "dry-fitted" then painted and reassembled with screws. All corners and edges are sanded and rounded to prevent injury to small riders. Grill adds realism.

Assembly is fastened to the floor with screws into the edges of the floor. Attach handle uprights to the assembly with screws, making sure none of them project.

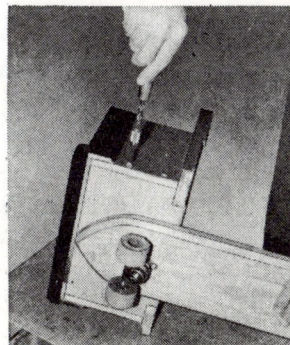

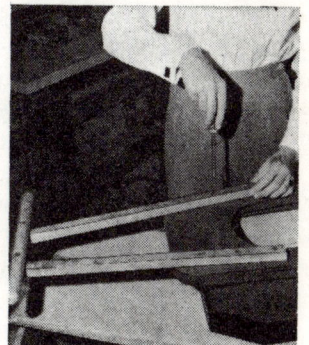

SALEM SECRETARY

This elegant secretary in the Hepplewhite style is attributed to a cabinetmaker by the name of Appleton, and is dated ca. 1809.

The secretary is a pretty straightforward example of plywood boxes fitted with drawers and doors. An attractive pediment that has urns at either end and a carved wooden eagle at the center rests on the 12½ x 40-inch top. The eagle is gilded to appear to be gold. The doors are fitted with small diamond-shaped pieces of glass in wooden frames. Glass was not readily available in large pieces in those days, so the smaller pieces were utilized. For modern construction you can use a single pane of glass and fit a grid over the front. If you make the grid readily removable it will make it much easier to clean the glass. For those who prefer realism in furniture reproductions, make the grid according to the cross section shown, then hold the small pieces of glass with thin strips of wood bradded to the inside of the openings.

The only part of the construction that may cause trouble is the dropdown writing surface which masquerades as a drawer front when it's closed. In the days when the secretary was built there were special quadrants made to permit easy lowering and raising of such writing surfaces. To solve the construction problem of trying to duplicate the action of the original quadrants use a friction lid support with a curved shape. To drop the surface, pull out at the top and push the bottom in slightly when it is horizontal. To raise it to the vertical position lift up, pull out slightly, then push it back to fit the "drawer" opening. Chains give added support.

Plywood may be used for most of the construction; mahogany plywood would be most authentic. You can use fir plywood and

GLASS GRILLE

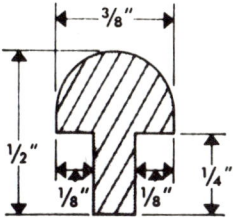

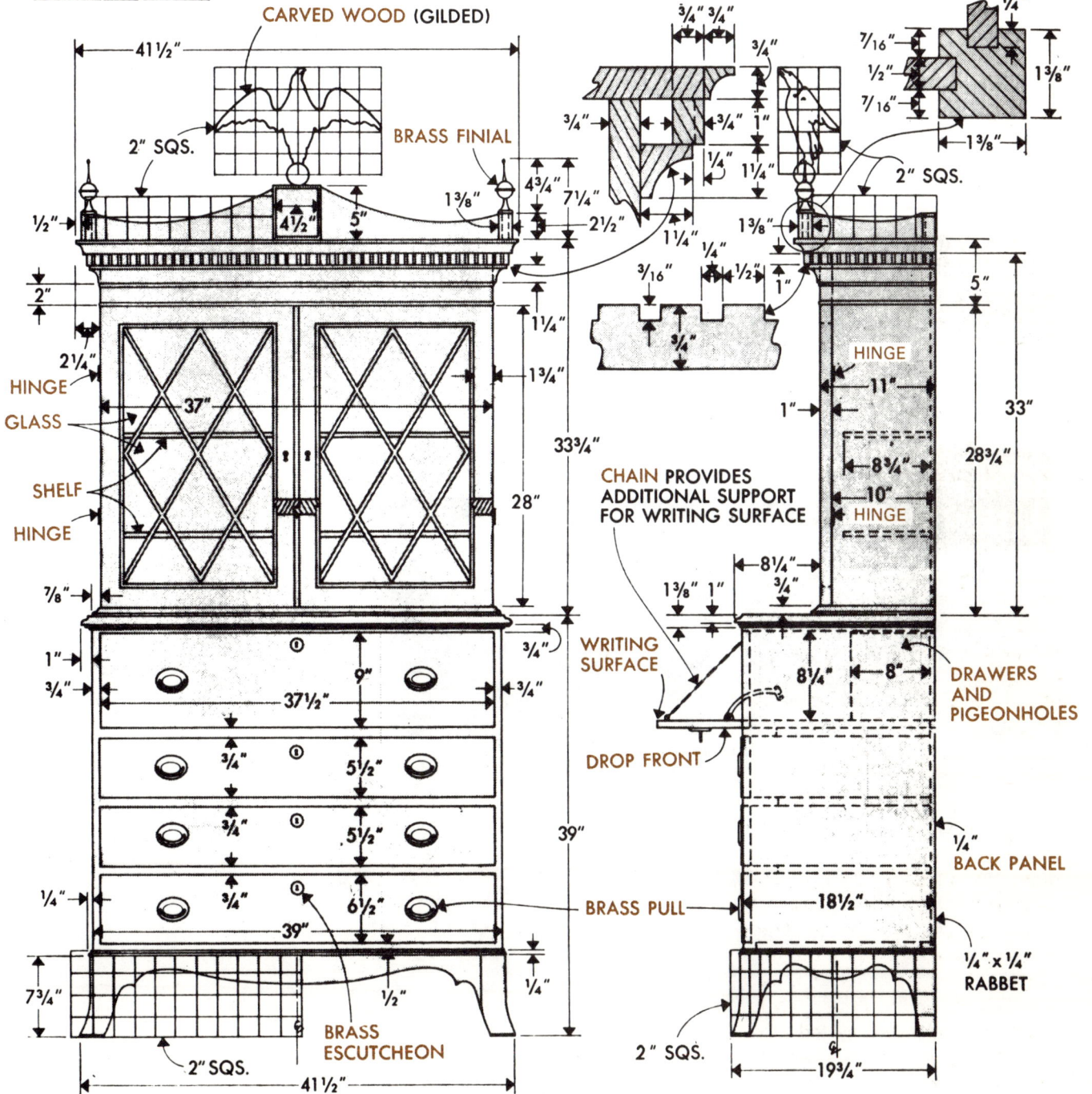

LOCATION OF LID SUPPORTS

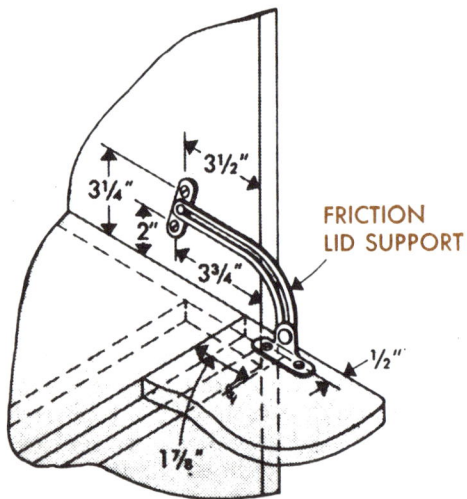

3½"

3¼"

2"

3¾"

FRICTION
LID SUPPORT

½"

1⅞"

Proper location of lid support is important, to assure action of drop-down surface.

When curved friction lid support is properly positioned, writing surface fits neatly when lifted up and pushed back.

veneer it with mahogany, which is better and less expensive. The legs must be built up of solid stock, and the four posts on top of the cabinet also are solid stock. Hardwood should be used for the door frames. Drawers are standard construction, with a single guide on the bottom of each, and a two-piece guide inside the chest in which the guide slides to keep the drawers square in the openings.

To lower writing surface you first pull top downward (on finished desk you pull on handles), let lower edge pivot.

When completely lowered, writing surface rests on crosspiece of cabinet, is supported by lid support.

EARLY AMERICAN SERVING SET

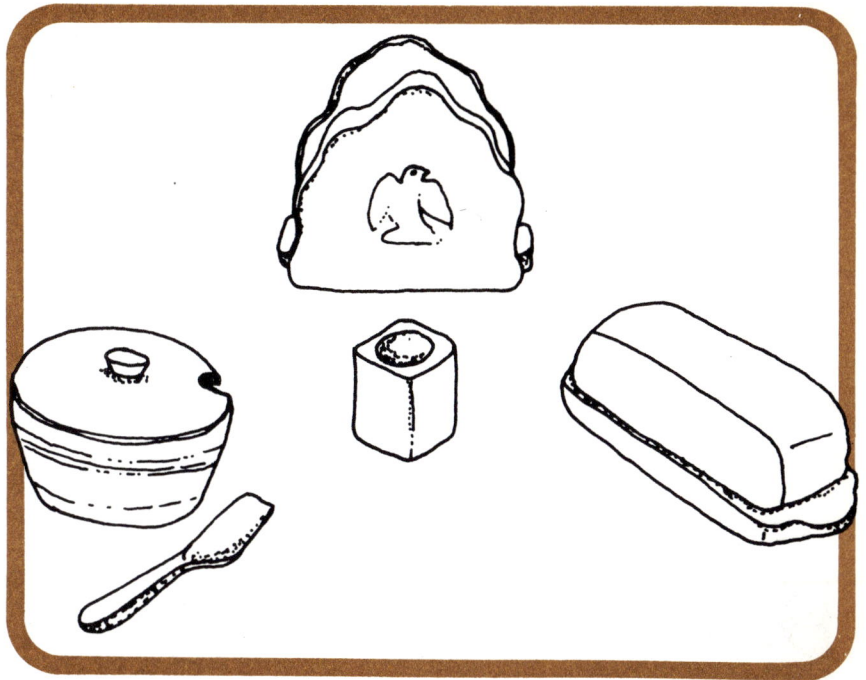

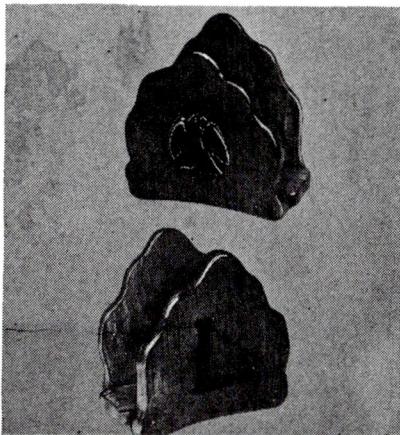

The rustic appearance of this set makes it attractive for either indoor or outdoor dining. It is also easy to build because any slight mistakes are lost in the rough-hewn design.

NAPKIN HOLDER

You can apply an eagle or other shape to the side of the napkin holder, rout an initial or even stencil a painted flower. Enlarge the squared drawing to make the sides, then rout or rasp the edges round. The bottom of the holder has angled edges to make the top of the holder flare out. The ends, but not the long edges, of the bottom are "distressed" to match the sides.

Apply an early American stain, then seal the wood with a satin varnish or clear lacquer.

Clear pine, or other straight-grained softwood is best for the project because it is easy to work.

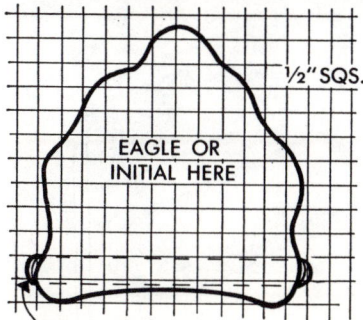

½" SQS.

EAGLE OR INITIAL HERE

THESE EDGES SANDED AFTER ASSEMBLY

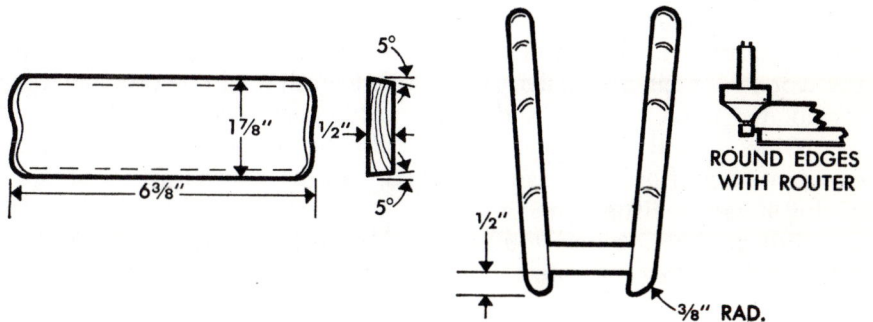

1⅞"

½"

6⅜"

5°

5°

½"

ROUND EDGES WITH ROUTER

⅜" RAD.

SUGAR BOWL AND SCOOP

You will need a lathe to turn the bowl for this part of the set, and a band or jig saw to make the scoop. Once the scoop is shaped it will have to be carved to create the hollow in the bowl.

Turn the sugar bowl and hollow the inside on a faceplate before making the lid. Because each craftsman will vary in his touch with the chisels, each bowl will vary slightly in diameter, so the lid then must be turned to fit its own bowl. The squared drawing gives the profile of the inside and outside of the bowl, but this shape can be varied somewhat to suit your own ideas of design.

After turning the lid for the sugar bowl, cut the opening for the handle of the sugar scoop. Keep the opening as small as possible, while still allowing easy fitting around the scoop handle.

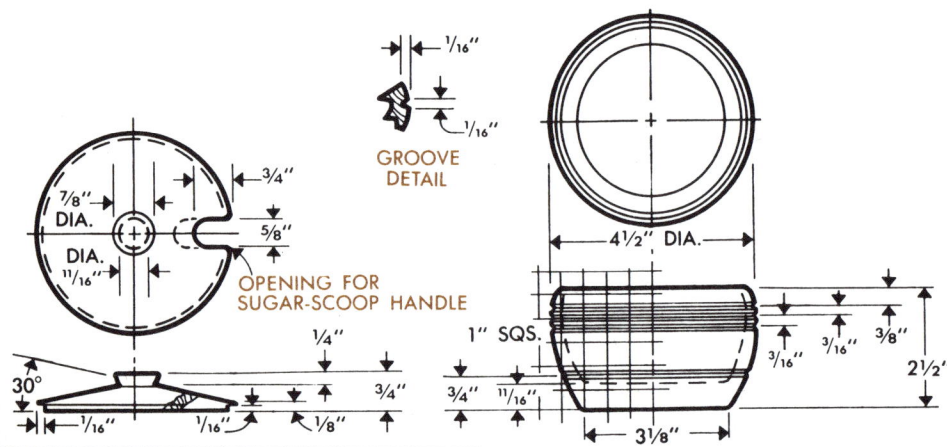

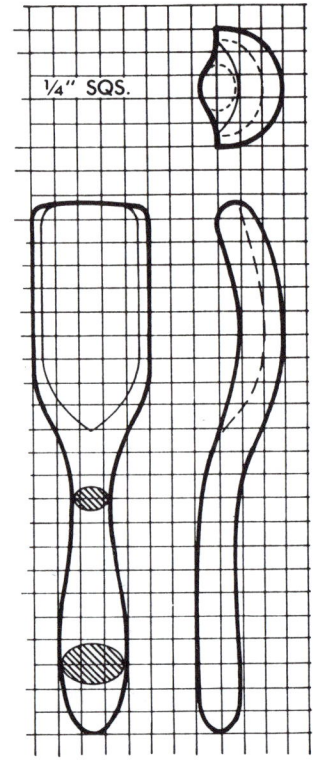

BUTTER DISH AND TOOTHPICK HOLDER

Both these items are carved from glued-up blocks to simplify construction and to assure there are no sections of weak cross grain.

For the butter dish cover you can cut a groove in a block of wood, then fit blocks at each end of the groove to create the recess that fits over a ¼-pound stick of butter or margarine. When the end blocks have been glued in place, use a rasp, file and sandpaper to shape the cover as indicated.

The dish on which the cover fits is cut from a solid piece of stock, being shaped with chisel and gouge to the profile indicated, then smoothed with consecutively finer grits of sandpaper, to prepare the wood for stain and sealer. A saladbowl finish could be used, as it is formulated to be nontoxic and it does not impart taste to food.

Glue is used to assemble the toothpick holder, but brass brads can be added after the finish is applied, to dress up the simple design of this attractive little item.

For an added touch you can carve the word "toothpicks" on the front of the holder, or rout it with a hand grinder and accessory router base.

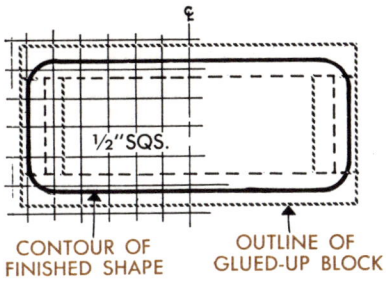

CONTOUR OF
FINISHED SHAPE

OUTLINE OF
GLUED-UP BLOCK

½" SQS.

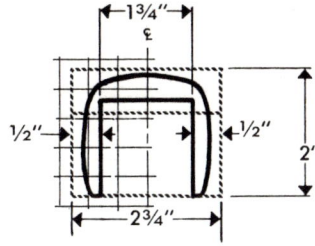

1¾"

½"   ½"

2"

2¾"

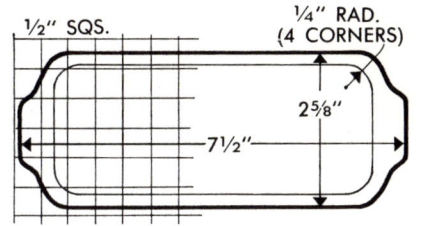

½" SQS.

¼" RAD.
(4 CORNERS)

2⅝"

7½"

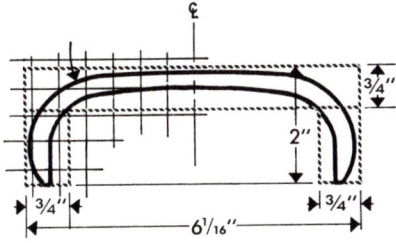

¾"

2"

¾"   ¾"

6 1/16"

OUTLINE OF COVER

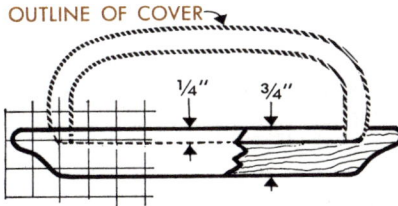

¼"   ¾"

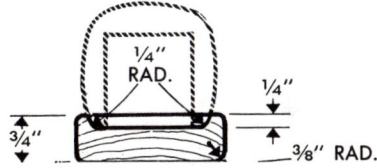

¼"
RAD.

¼"

¾"

⅜" RAD.

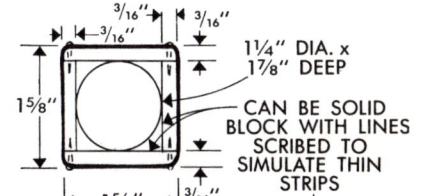

3/16"   3/16"
3/16"

1⅝"

1¼" DIA. x
1⅞" DEEP

CAN BE SOLID
BLOCK WITH LINES
SCRIBED TO
SIMULATE THIN
STRIPS

1⅝"   3/16"

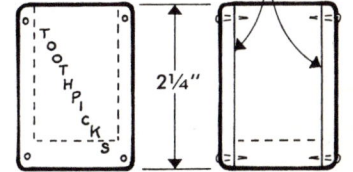

TOOTHPICKS

2¼"

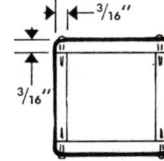

3/16"

3/16"

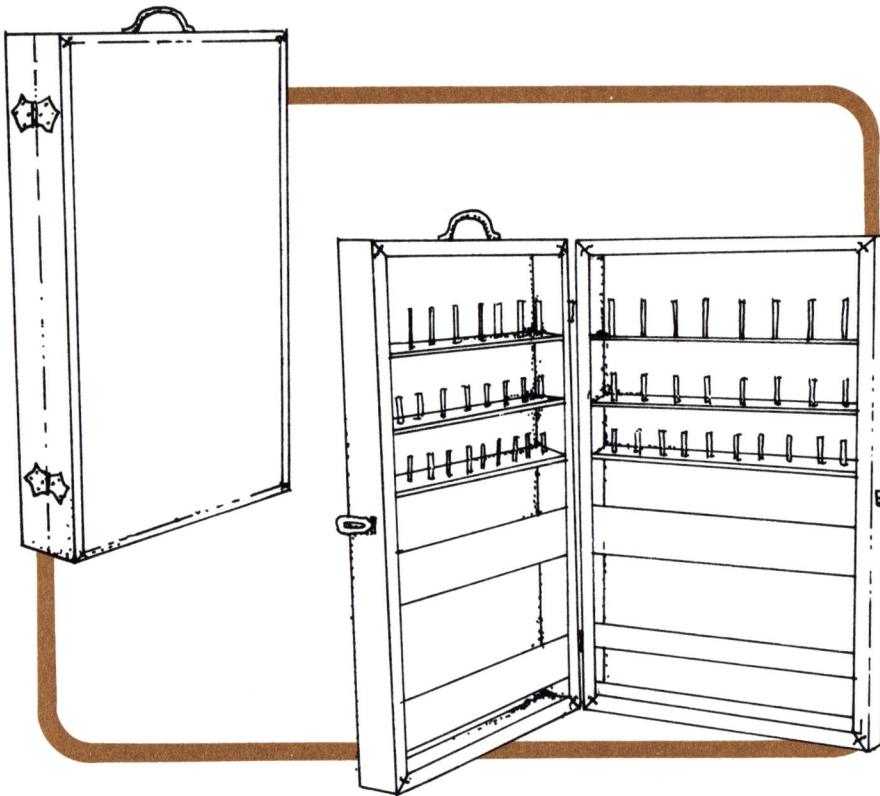

SEWING BOX

Although this sewing box looks a little complicated, it's really fairly simple and can be modified to suit the individual. To simplify construction the box is built as a single unit, then cut along the center line to produce two halves.

To begin construction, cut the ends and sides to size, carefully mitering the corners to 45 degrees. Then, without changing the saw angle, turn the boards over and groove the miters crosswise 1/8 x 5/16 inch on their center lines to accept 1/8-inch hardboard splines. Rabbet both inside edges of each end and side ¼ inch x 3/8 inch to accept the plywood sides. Cut ¼-inch dadoes in the two sides to accept the shelves. Assemble and glue the basic box, consisting of the two sides, the ends and the plywood front and back. Be sure the plywood sides are square. You may wish to use small brads along the plywood edges to hold the assembly until the glue sets. Wipe off any excess glue.

When the glue is dry, saw the box in half along the center line. Cut the ¼-inch plywood shelves, drill ¼-inch holes and glue the dowels for the thread spools in place. Mortise for the ends of the two 2¼-inch "bin faces" so the bottom edges are flush with the bottoms of the 1-3/8-inch shelves. This creates deep shelves ideal for odds and ends. Next mortise for the three "rails" in the bottom compartments. Glue and brad in place.

Stain the wood as you desire, finish with clear lacquer or varnish, and install hardware.

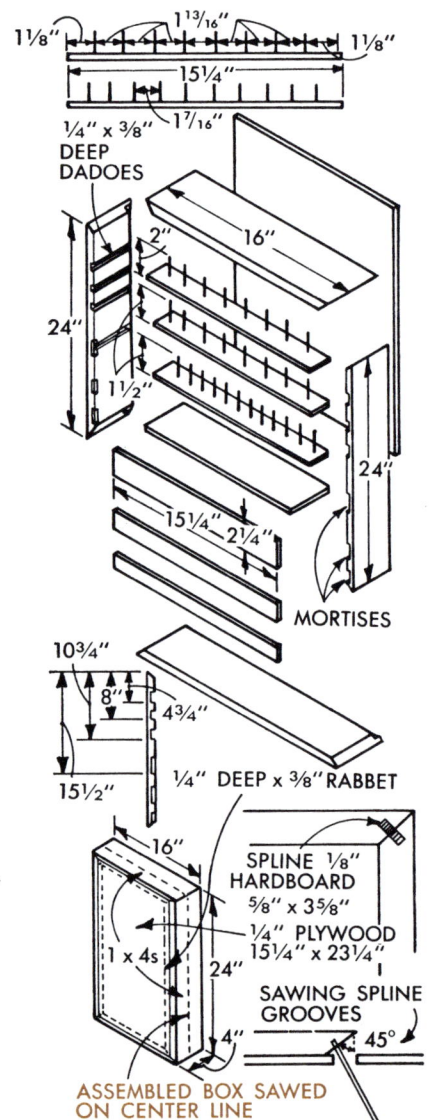

COOKBOOK SHELF

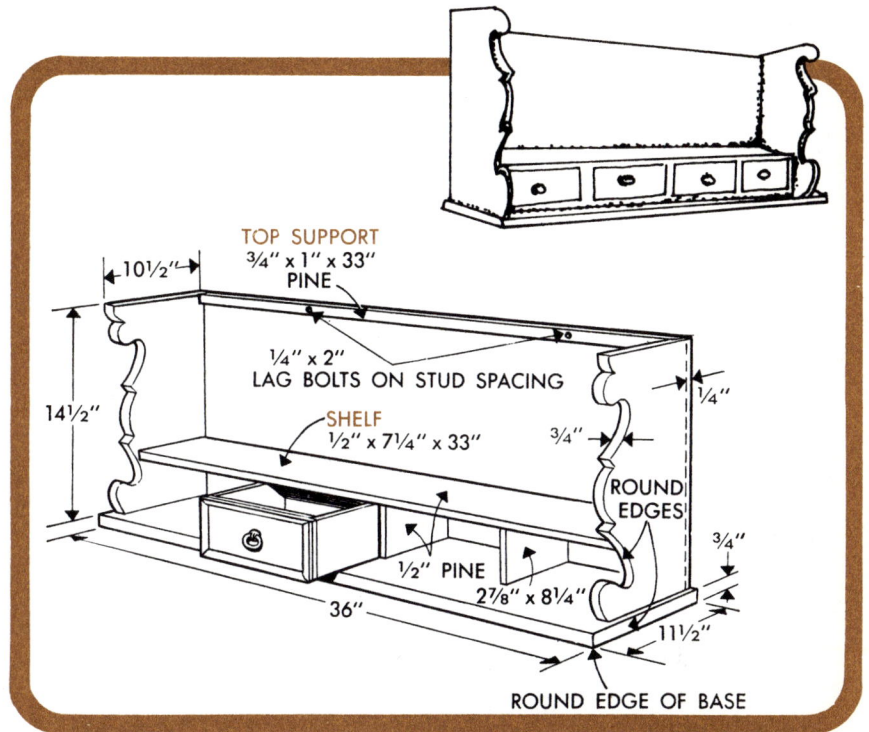

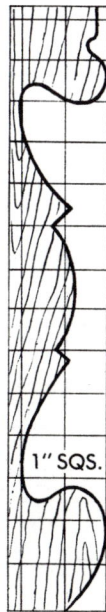

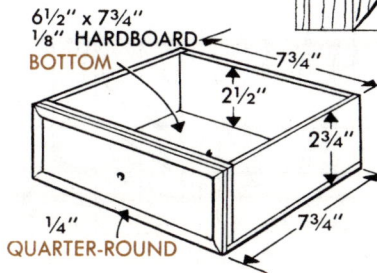

TOP SUPPORT
¾" x 1" x 33"
PINE

←10½"→

¼" x 2"
LAG BOLTS ON STUD SPACING

SHELF
½" x 7¼" x 33"

14½"

¼"

¾"

ROUND
EDGES

½" PINE

2⅞" x 8¼"

¾"

36"

11½"

ROUND EDGE OF BASE

1" SQS.

6½" x 7¾"
⅛" HARDBOARD
BOTTOM

7¾"

2½"

2¾"

¼"
QUARTER-ROUND

7¾"

One problem that every cook faces is where to keep the cookbooks. The volumes usually wind up in a drawer, shoved on top of the refrigerator, or stuck in some equally unhandy spot. For the gourmet cook, this shelf will keep the collection of French, German, Italian, Spanish and other specialty cuisine cookbooks within easy reach. The occasional, or less ambitious, cook can use it for the salad and 1,001-ways-to-serve-hamburger cookbooks.

The drawers are a handy addition which are great for trading stamps, coupons, car keys, credit cards and recipes clipped from magazines and newspapers.

The original design, as shown, is colonial, but a modification of the patterns of the ends will change the unit to suit any decor. Use a softwood for the ends, making a pattern from the squared drawing. The base and shelf are simple rectangles, as is the back. A strip under the base and one at the upper edge of the back are used to fasten the completed shelf to the wall, by using lag screws into the wall studs. A second method of attaching, possibly simpler, would be to install strips inside the upper edges of the sides, through which wood screws could be driven up into the underside of the wall cabinets. The two supporting strips then could be eliminated.

The shelf is finished to match the existing kitchen cabinets. Hardware should match that on the cabinets, or can be of your choice if the cabinets have no pulls.

FRETWORK SHELF

If you are a fretwork enthusiast here is a project that will take hours at the jigsaw, not only for the cutting, but for all the small holes that must be drilled to permit blade insertion.

The original was made from ¼-inch mahogany plywood and sprayed with three coats of clear Deft. After making a pattern by enlarging the squared drawing (and this pattern will take a lot of free-hand work) trace it onto the stock. Cut two at the same time by tacking the wood together; you can make several pairs at once if your saw will handle the cutting. After making each pair, cut ¼ inch from the straight edge of one. This cut edge then is butted against the surface of the other, to create a shelf with two equal-width sides.

The shelves all are identical in shape but vary in size. Glue and small screws are used to assemble the project.

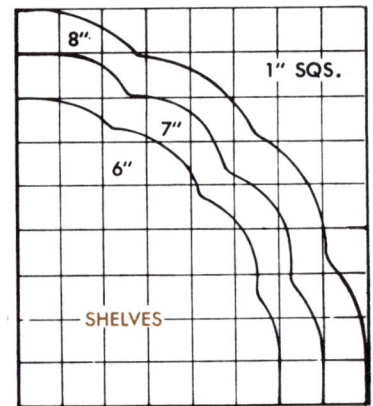

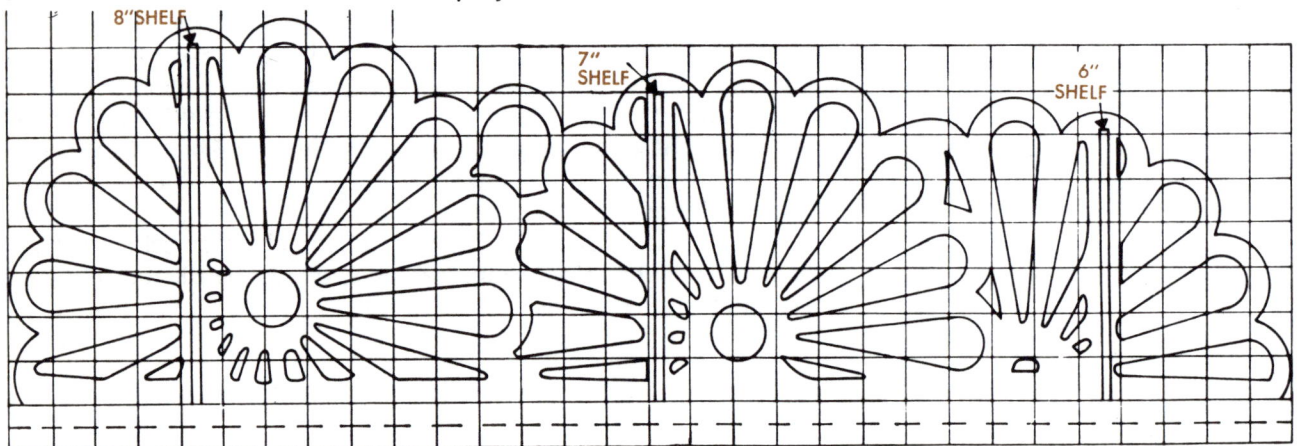

RUSTIC NOVELTY SHELF

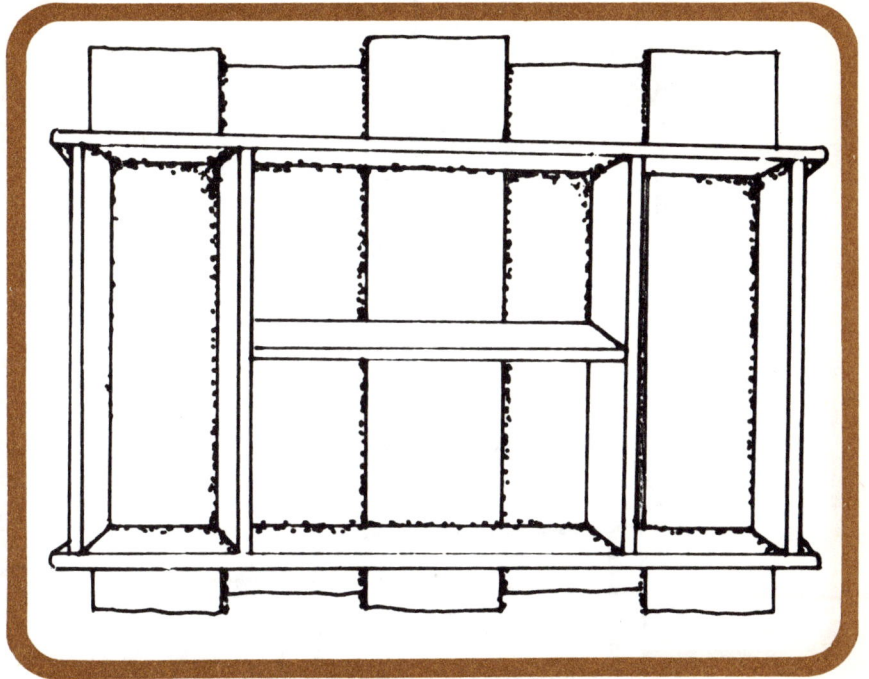

The back panel for this unique and attractive whatnot shelf can be cut from a single piece of hardwood plywood and the V-grooves cut with a saw, or separate strips can be cut. The latter method was used for the shelf pictured, the strips having the edges beveled and the five pieces then were glued to a sheet of plain plywood.

Using separate strips permits getting unusual grain effects, as illustrated. The shelves and uprights are cut from plywood and glued and nailed together with small finish nails. Countersink the nails and cover with wood putty. Screws are driven through the panel into the edges of the shelves to assemble the unit. Countersunk for the screws.

The original was finished by applying thinned black paint as a stain, then wiping it off. Thinned shellac was applied over the dried "stain." Gray, brown or cream color also can be used.

ONE-PIECE BACK PANEL
(OR SEPARATE STRIPS)

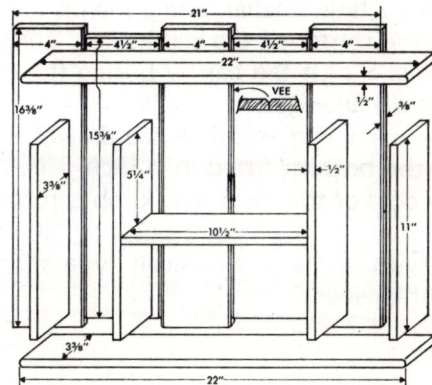

SCREW-TOP CANDLE STAND

As colonial as corn bread, this quaint little candle holder is simply a small cabinet with a screw mechanism that allows the candle-holder bar to be adjusted for height. The drawer in the cabinet, originally intended for flint and steel, provides handy storage for matches. With the exception of the drawer knob and the screw, all parts are pine.

Begin by cutting the top, bottom, sides and back of the cabinet. Glue and nail the box together. Cut the top block, round the upper edges, and cut the decorative dado on the sides. Locate the center and bore the hole, then thread with a 1-inch wood tap.

The completed block is glued in place on the top of the base. Cut a 8¼-inch length of 1-inch dowel and thread the entire length. Sand a slight chamfer on one end, then place a bit of glue on the threads of the other end, and turn it into the block. (Note that 1-inch internal threads require a hole smaller than 1 inch.)

Locate the center of the candle bar, bore and tap it 1 inch, then cut it to shape. Finish the bar by boring the candle holes in the ends and rounding off all edges.

Cut the parts and assemble the drawer. Construction is conventional, with the bottom fitted in ¼-inch deep dadoes cut ¼ inch from the bottom edges of the sides. The knob is turned from maple or other hardwood.

Finish with an early American type stain, followed by two or three coats of lacquer.

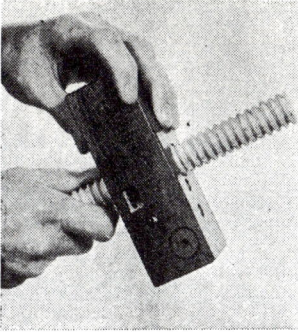
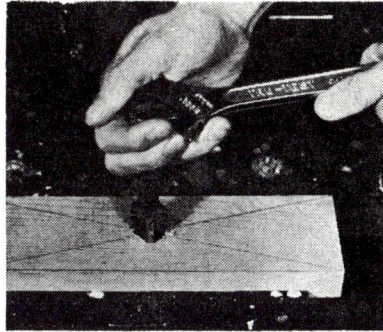

Special screw box is used to cut threads on the 1"-dowel used for the shaft. Candle bar is tapped before being cut to shape. Tap is similar to type used for metal pipe. End of screw is smeared with glue then turned into block. Small drawer knob can be turned on the lathe using a screw center.

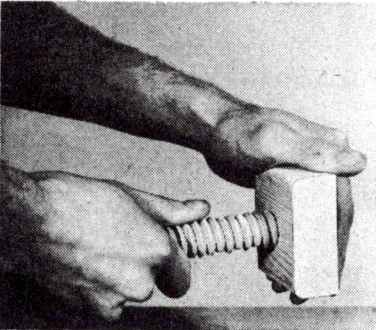
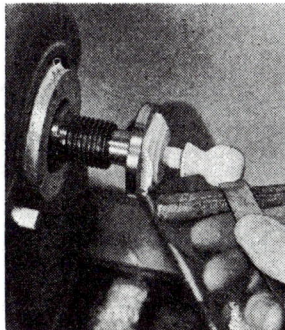

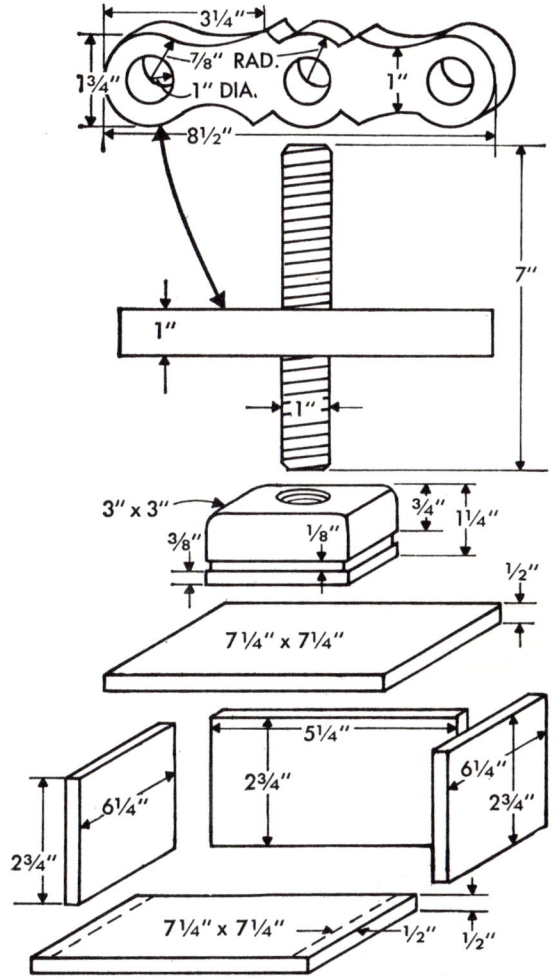
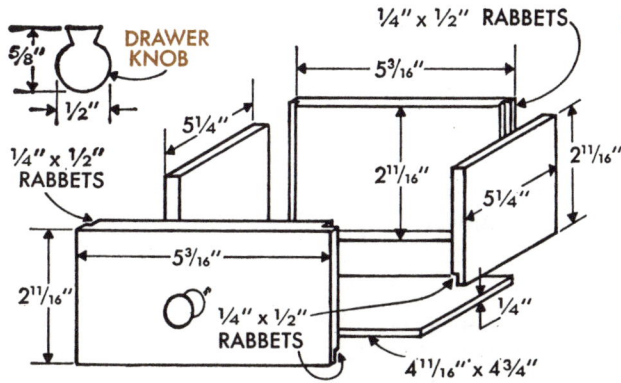

ROLL-AROUND STEP STOOL

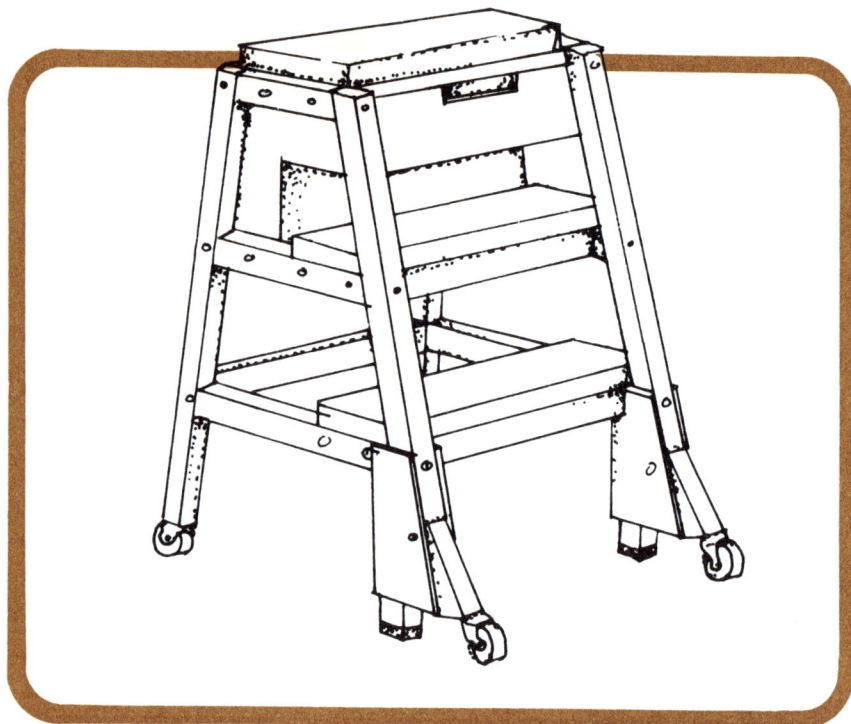

This versatile step stool rolls easily to any spot in the home or shop, then stops the moment you step or sit on it. It's of a height that is ideal as a seat for working in the kitchen, or at a workbench, and there is no problem reaching the highest cabinets or shelves when you stand on the steps. The handy storage compartment under the hinged top can be used for cleaning supplies or tools.

Hardwood is used for the legs, spreaders and other parts, except where other material is specified. Cut all parts to size, getting the dimensions from the Materials List and mark each part with the proper letter for easy assembly. The legs are splayed 10 degrees, so the ends of each spreader are cut at that angle. Other components can be fitted as you make the assembly, the proper angles marked and cut.

Note that the front stretcher on the bottom step is ½ inch shorter than the others, to accommodate the two gussets made of ¼-inch plywood, that fit inside the legs. Two other gussets, attached to the outside of these legs reinforce the short stationary legs when the spring-loaded legs pivot up as weight is applied to the stool.

Drill pilot or "profile" holes for all screws and use plenty of glue. Immediately after a joint is tightened with the screws, wipe off all excess glue.

For a kitchen the step stool can be stained and varnished; for the shop a good quality enamel would be more practical to clean.

CUSHION ASSEMBLY
STAPLE OR TACK

VINYL UPHOLSTERY

URETHANE CUSHION

45° MITER ALL CORNERS

$10\frac{1}{8}''$ $14\frac{3}{8}''$

$\frac{1}{4}'' \times 10\frac{1}{16}'' \times 14\frac{5}{16}''$
PLYWOOD SEAT PANEL

$\frac{1}{2}''$

$14\frac{3}{8}''$

NO. 8 x $\frac{7}{8}''$ F.H.S., 8 REQ'D.
DRILL $\frac{11}{16}''$ DIA. HOLE AND
C.S.K. (BOTTOM SIDE)

$9\frac{1}{8}''$

$9\frac{5}{8}''$

$\frac{3}{4}''$

$4''$ $5\frac{1}{4}''$

$4''$

$5\frac{1}{2}''$

$5\frac{1}{2}''$

$10°$

$5\frac{1}{2}''$ $5''$

$5\frac{3}{4}''$

$5\frac{1}{4}''$

$\frac{7}{8}''$

$\frac{7}{32}''$ DIA. HOLE
AND C.S.K. FOR
NO. 12 F.H.S.

$4\frac{1}{4}''$ $4\frac{1}{4}''$

$3''$

$\frac{3}{4}''$ $10°$ $\frac{5}{8}''$

$1''$

$20°$

$7\frac{1}{2}''$

$1\frac{5}{16}''$ $2\frac{5}{8}''$

DRILL $\frac{3}{8}''$
DIA. HOLE

$1\frac{1}{4}''$

$4\frac{3}{8}''$

$2\frac{1}{2}''$

DRILL $\frac{7}{32}''$ DIA. HOLE 3 PLACES

$6\frac{3}{4}''$

DRILL HOLE FOR
CASTER STEM
TO DIA.
AND DEPTH
DICTATED
BY CASTER

$\frac{5}{8}''$

DRILL $\frac{7}{32}''$
DIA. HOLE

$\frac{3}{4}''$

$4\frac{1}{2}''$

DRILL $\frac{23}{64}''$
DIA. HOLE
AND REAM
TO SLIGHTLY
UNDER $\frac{3}{8}''$
DIA. TO INSURE
TIGHT FIT WHEN
INSERTING
HINGE PINS

$3\frac{3}{32}''$

45° MITER
(TYPICAL TO ALL
EDGE MOLDINGS)

$14\frac{1}{2}''$

$5\frac{11}{16}''$ $10°$

$1''$

$\frac{3}{8}''$ $1\frac{1}{4}''$

$\frac{3}{4}''$

$2\frac{5}{8}''$

$10°$

45° x $\frac{1}{32}''$
CHAMFER ONE
END ONLY

$2\frac{13}{16}''$

DRILL $\frac{1}{16}''$ DIA. x $\frac{3}{4}''$
DEEP PILOT HOLE

$\frac{15}{16}''$ SCREW EYE

$1\frac{1}{4}''$ 5° ALL 4 SIDES

NOTE: TOP AND BOTTOM STEPS
ARE IDENTICAL EXCEPT
BOTTOM STEP FRONT
RISER IS $\frac{1}{2}''$ SHORTER
THAN ALL OTHER RISERS.

$15\frac{7}{8}''$ $4''$

$16''$

$15\frac{7}{8}''$

4" x $15\frac{7}{8}''$ STEP
TREAD, MAKE
FROM STANDARD
$\frac{1}{8}'' \times 9'' \times 24''$
STAIR TREAD

$4''$

$13\frac{}{16}''$

$4\frac{1}{8}''$

$11\frac{}{16}''$

TOP STEP
BOTTOM STEP

$\frac{11}{16}''$

$\frac{15}{16}''$

$\frac{13}{16}''$

$14\frac{1}{2}''$

$1\frac{1}{4}''$

$14''$

A B C D E F G H I J K L M N O P Q R S T U V W X Y Z AA BB CC DD EE

MATERIALS LIST

A.	Top Spreader:	¾"x1¼"x9-15/16" (2) hardwood
B.	Center Spreader:	¾"x1¼"x13-1/16" (2)
C.	Bottom Spreader:	¾"x1¼"x15-15/16" (2)
D.	Back Leg:	¾"x1¼"x22" (2)
E.	Front Leg:	¾"x1¼"x19-5/16" (2)
F.	Gusset:	¼"x4"x5-11/16" (4) plywood
G.	Hinge Pin:	3/8"—diameter x 1¼" aluminum rod (2)
H.	Tension Spring:	¼"—diameter x 1" (2)
I.	Caster:	1-5/8"—diameter swivel (4)
J.	Back Panel:	½"x9½"x14½" (1) plywood
K.	Side Panel:	½"x9-5/8"x11¾" (2) plywood
L.	Front Panel:	½"x4"x14½" (1) plywood
M.	Center Panel:	½"x5½"x13½" (1) plywood
N.	Upper Bottom Panel:	½"x5½"x13½" (1) plywood
O.	Bottom Panel:	½"x5¼"x13½" (1) plywood
P.	Seat Frame:	½"x1-5/8"x10-1/8" (2)
Q.	Seat Frame:	½"x1-5/8"x14-3/8" (2)
R.	Seat Panel:	¼"x10-1/16"x14-5/16" (1) plywood
S.	Cushion	1"x10-1/16"x14-5/16" (1) urethane foam
T.	Upholstery:	15-1/16"x19-5/16" (1) vinyl
U.	Molding:	1/16"x15/16"x16" (4) aluminum edge molding
V.	Molding	1/16"x15/16"x4-1/8" (4) aluminum edge molding
W.	Tread:	1/8" (2) rubber, standard
X.	Step:	1"x4"x15-7/8" (2)
Y.	Riser:	¾"x1¼"x14½" (4)
Z.	Leg:	¾"x1¼"x5¼" (2)
AA.	Leg Stop:	¾"x1"x1-5/16" (2)
BB.	Leg Pad:	½"x¾"x1¼" (2) rubber
CC.	Foot:	¾"x1¼"x3-3/8" (2)
DD.	Spreader:	1¼"x1¼"x14½" (1)
EE.	Hinge, Continuous:	1-1/16"—open x 24" (1)

BUTTERFLY TABLE

PLAIN-SAWED

QUARTER-SAWED

Fine cabinetwork from the 17th century is displayed in this butterfly table, the original of which is in the Metropolitan Museum of Art in New York. The term "butterfly," of course, refers to the shaped supports that pivot out to hold the leaves.

The solid lumber used for the top has warped with time. For this reason use a glued-up top, if solid lumber is used. Invert every other strip so you create a heartwood-to-heartwood and sapwood-to-sapwood combination on quarter-sawed lumber to minimize warping, while straight-sawed lumber alternates the direction of heartwood and sapwood to again reduce the chance of warpage.

To absolutely minimize warpage, use plywood. The rounded or molded edge can be filled and stained to match the surface.

Make patterns for the butterfly supports and the top by enlarging the squared drawings.

Short lengths of ½-inch dowel are inserted in holes bored in the upper and lower edges of the butterfly supports, to act as pivots. Matching holes, slightly larger than ½ inch, are bored in the underside of the top and the stretcher, to receive the dowels. Glue the dowels in the supports, let the glue set firmly, then assemble in the table. Be sure no glue enters the holes.

All four legs are turned to identical shape. The turning blocks are 1¼ inches square, which produces the square portions at the top and bottom. Any home-shop lathe with a capacity of 30 inches will handle the turnings. You can, of course, buy ready-made turnings of similar shape that can be used. Be certain that purchased legs have the square portions to fit apron and stretchers.

Note that the legs are splayed, looking at the narrow ends of the table as well as the long way. To get the angle for the splay on the sides, place the legs in pairs on a flat surface, with the upper ends 11½ inches apart, the lower ends 15¼ inches apart. Mark straight across the tops of the legs and cut on that line. Repeat this operation for the angles on the long sides of the table. The angles for the apron ends are determined at the same time.

The aprons are attached to the legs by doweling, or by making them ¾ inch longer at each end and using mortise-and-tenon joints. Use glue blocks inside three of the aprons, as indicated, to attach the top. Use screws only between the blocks and the top, and make the screw holes slightly oversize, to allow the top to expand and contract without loosening the screws or a glue joint. Stain and finish the table to suit your decor. Install glides on the ends of the legs.

1" SQS.

4¼"
8"
3⅜"
¼" ¼"
12"
3¾"
4"
SLANT SIDES AND FRONT TO FIT

DETAIL OF DRAWER

6⅞"
3/16"
1¼" ¾" 4¾" 1⅛"
24⅛" ¾"
4½" 1¼"
3/16"
13/16" 7/8"
3/16"
4½"
¾" 1⅛"
13/16" 1"
3/16" ¾"
1¼" 1¼" 23⅞" TO UNDERSIDE OF TOP VERTICALLY
4½"
¼"
1"
1¼"
1¼"
¾"

34½"
¾"
11½"
5"
1¼"
DRAWER SLIDE
24"
½"
15¼"

10¾"
12⅛"
13⅜"
8"
RULE JOINT
1" SQS.
5" ○3¾"
20"
VERTICAL
HALF-ROUND EDGE
1⅛" 1"
PIVOT
2¾"
10¾"

CAPE COD TABLE

Clean and simple in design, this table from the New England area is a fine exercise for the lathe enthusiast who likes early American furniture. While the design might immediately suggest hard maple as the wood to use, the original probably was made with a variety of woods, and several kinds of stock might be used, depending on the builders' preference, for the different parts of the table.

A clean-turning hardwood is recommended for the legs, while the top can be edge-glued from a softer material. Plywood is not recommended, because of the shaping of the edges of the top. Assemble the table legs to the aprons with mortise-and-tenon joints, as detailed, then make the drawer to fit the opening you create. The top is attached by driving screws up through the two front strips, plus glue blocks notched to fit around the legs and join the aprons.

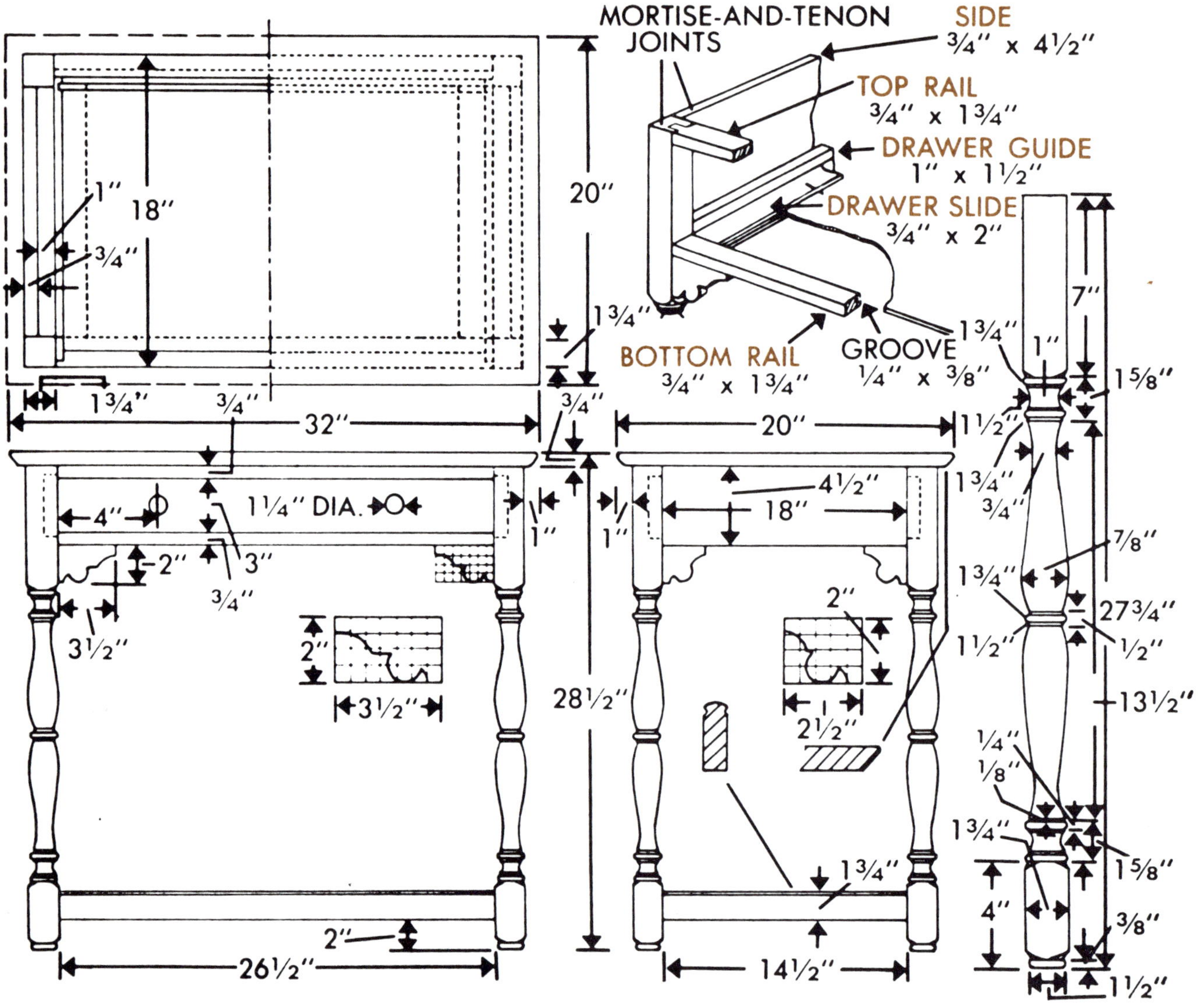

MORTISE-AND-TENON JOINTS

SIDE
3/4" x 4 1/2"

TOP RAIL
3/4" x 1 3/4"

DRAWER GUIDE
1" x 1 1/2"

DRAWER SLIDE
3/4" x 2"

BOTTOM RAIL
3/4" x 1 3/4"

GROOVE
1/4" x 3/8"

20"

1 3/4"

3/4"

1"

18"

1"

3/4"

1 3/4"   3/4"

32"

3/4"

20"

1 1/2"

1 3/4"
3/4"

4"

1 1/4" DIA.

4 1/2"

18"

1 3/4"

1 1/2"

7"

1 5/8"

7/8"

27 3/4"

1/2"

13 1/2"

2"

3"

3/4"

3 1/2"

2"

3 1/2"

28 1/2"

2"

2 1/2"

1 3/4"

1/4"
1/8"

1 3/4"

1 5/8"

4"

3/8"

2"

26 1/2"

14 1/2"

1 1/2"

1"

WAGON-SEAT COFFEE TABLE

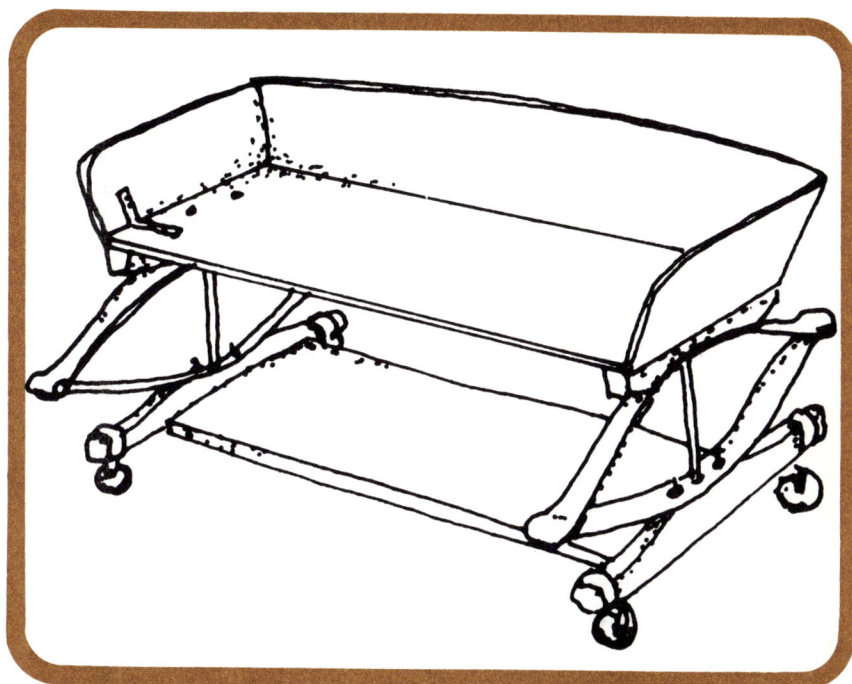

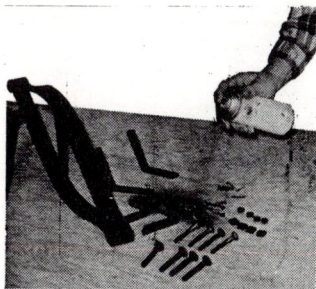

One antique in great demand—and short supply—is a wagon or buggy seat. They are used for everything from informal benches to flower stands to simple decorations for a porch on to a coffee table.

This reproduction is authentic in appearance. Best of all, it will cost only a few dollars, plus some time in the workshop.

If you can get some weathered lumber, it will add to the antique look of the project. If not, then distress the lumber by filing all edges to simulate wear, and do a little hammering and battering to create the look of age.

Edge-glue the pieces for the seat, then glue and nail them to the braces that are cut from 2 x 4s. Use square-head flooring nails, or shape the heads of regular nails to look like hand-forged fasteners. Cut the back and sides from 1 x 8 or 1 x 10 lumber. Glue and nail them to the edges of the seat, allowing the lower edges to project so they can be planed at an angle, flush to the underside of the seat.

Oak, hickory or other tough hardwood is used for the "feet." Attach the feet to the shelf with 2½-inch flathead wood screws.

The leaf "springs" are shaped from flat bar, joined at the ends with a 1¼-inch dowel, and reinforced at the center with a ½-inch steel rod welded at top and bottom. The springs and all metal parts are painted flat back; a spray can does the job in a hurry.

Finish to suit; the original has stain and a rubbed-on linseed oil. You may want an antique with glaze, or even a "Hitchcock" black with gold striping, such as used on new buggies. The casters may not be authentic, but they certainly make it a lot easier to move the seat, whether for cleaning or to relocate it in a room.

15″

2½″ RAD.
END
6″

13″

1″ SQUARES

2 HOLES ⅜″ DIA.

③ ⑯

BACK ②

⑪

⑨ SPRING "EYE"

TACK WELD

1¼″ ⑦

SPRING LEAVES

① SEAT

⑰

③

2½″ 1½″

3½″

3½″

⑱

⑫

BRACE ⑤ 7″

¾″

10″ RAD. ⑨

3½″

1¾″ 1⅜″ 1⅞″

9¼″

10¾″

⑩

⑭

⑦

⑧

④ **FOOT**

⑲

1¾″

⑮

1½″

④

⑥ **BRACKET**

3⅛″

¾″

CAP ⑮ ⑥

4 HOLES ⅜″ DIA. 3½″

4d FINISHING NAIL

⑬ 1⅝″ **CASTER**

2⅛″

⑬

MATERIALS LIST

1. Seat, edge glued: 1 x 3s or 1 x 4s x 35¼″ long
2. Back: 1x8x39¾″ (1)
3. End: 1x8x15″ (2)
4. Foot: 1-5/8″x1-7/8″ x21½″ (2)
5. Brace: 1-3/8″x1-5/8″ x12″ (2)
6. Bracket: ¼″x1½″x10″ steel flat (4)
7. Spring: 3/16″x1½″ x30″ steel flat (4)
8. Spring: 1/8″x1½″x 1′4″ steel flat (4)
9. Ferrule: 1¼″x2½″ dowel (4)
10. Shelf: 1x4x32½″ (3)
11. Strap, Sheet metal: 5/8″x7″ (2)
12. Strap: 1/8″x¾″x7″ steel flat (2)
13. Caster: 1-5/8″-diameter stem with socket (4)
14. Rod: ½″-diameter x 7½″ (2)
15. Cap, chair glide: ¾″-diameter (4)
16. Carriage bolt: 5/16″x2½″ (8)
17. Nut: 5/16″ hex (8)
18. Wood Screw: No. 10x¾″ FH steel (20)
19. Wood Screw: No. 10x2½″ FH steel (6)

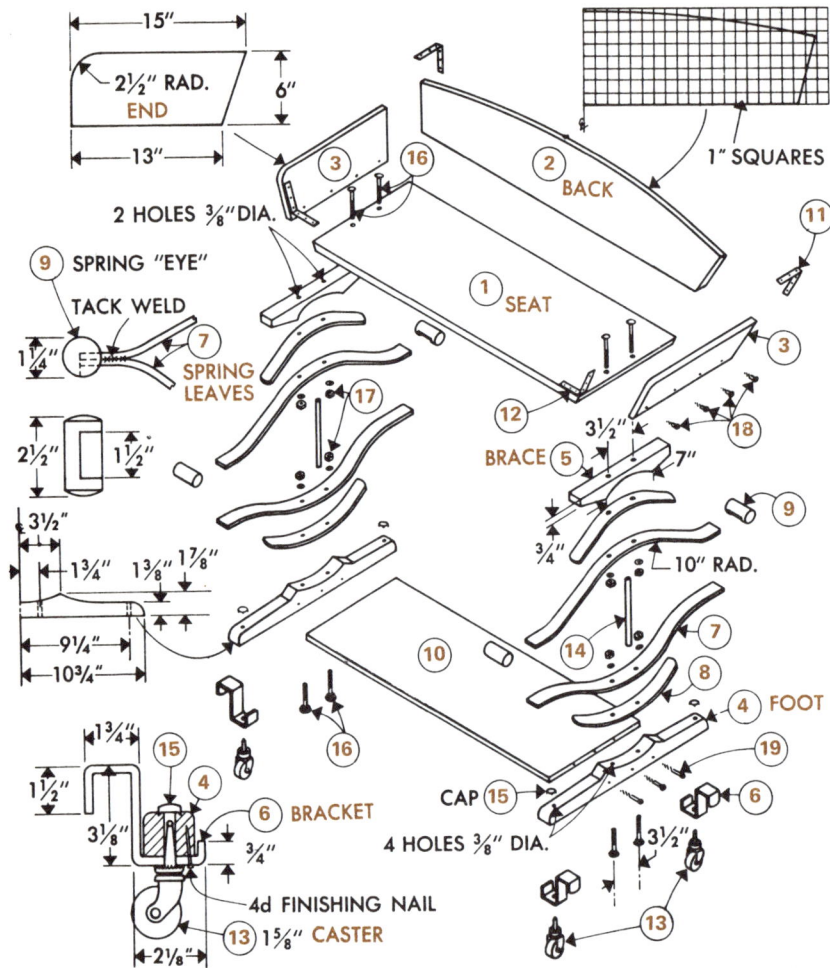

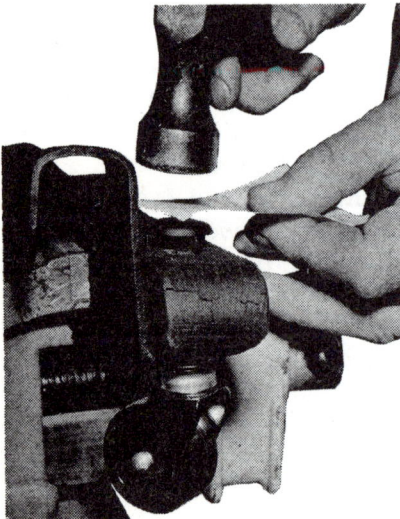

Metal chair glides of ¾″-diameter are fitted over holes for caster sleeves. These glides also are painted flat black.

Table feet here are being treated with boiled linseed oil. You also can stain, or use penetrating sealer.

WROUGHT-IRON COFFEE TABLE

Ornamental "wrought iron" combined with a glass top creates a truly distinctive coffee table for patio, porch or pool side. Best of all, no welding is required. All joints are assembled with blind rivets, which eliminates the need for a welder and the jigs and fixtures required to hold the sections while they are being welded.

The various shaped ornamental pieces are bent cold from mild steel. The jig is made by drilling two holes in a block of steel to accept two steel rods, spaced slightly more than the thickness of the steel flats that are bent into curved shapes.

In use, the jig is clamped in a vise and the work passed between the rods. The metal is bent slightly, moved a little, then bent again, to create a smooth, sweeping curve with no kinks. The 1/8-inch steel flats will not require heating but can be bent cold. The heavier material, such as the rods used for the legs, may require being heated to a cherry red with a propane torch to permit bending them into the required "hair-pin" shapes.

To assure uniformity and simplify construction, all pieces are cut to size before bending. Before cutting, however, make one test piece of each shape to determine the correct length. Bend the length to fit a pattern you have drawn full size. If your first section is too short, you can lengthen it; if too long, you can cut it and note the difference in length, so you can cut the other pieces to the right size.

You also can bend one section to shape and use it as a pattern for the other pieces. Because of the type of construction, slight variations in shape will not be noticeable, and will lend a "hand-shaped" look to the finished table.

MATERIALS LIST

Legs:	5/16"- or 3/8"-diameter steel rod x 37¼" (4)
Frame:	½"x½"x96" steel angle (2)
Brace:	1/8"x½"x2" (2)
Leg Scroll:	1/8"x½"x15" (4)
Side Scrolls:	1/8"x½"x15" (12)
End Scrolls:	1/8"x½"x13½" (8)
Rivets:	medium length (50 long (24)
Glass:	¼"x17-7/8"x30-7/8" (1)

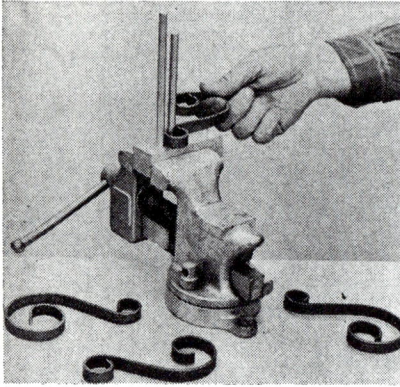

Steel flats are bent in jig made by inserting two rods in steel block, spaced apart to accept the metal as shown.

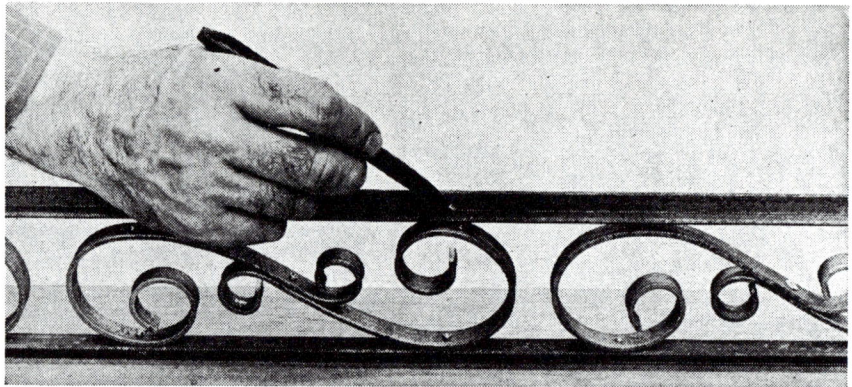

Scrolls were drilled first here; it's best to clamp the assembly and drill through the angle and scroll at the same time to assure alignment of holes.

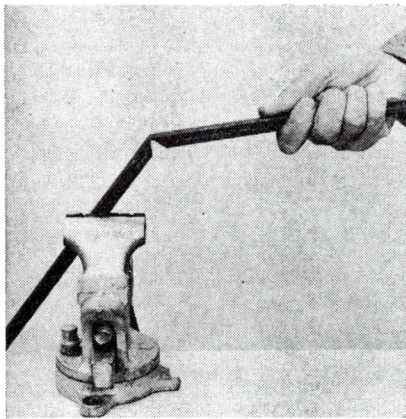

Angles for top and bottom of table frame are notched and bent. They should be positioned flat in vise, bent.

Blind rivets are used to assemble the scrolls to the angles, thus eliminating the need for welding and clamping.

Longer rivets are required to attach legs to the scrolls, because diameter of legs is more than thickness of flats.

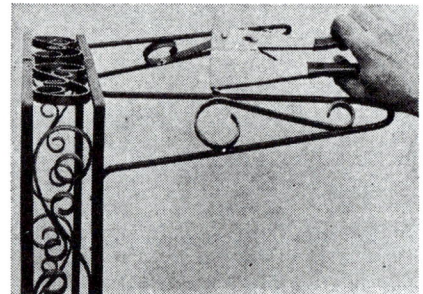

The upper and lower table frames are made from ½-inch angle, notched and bent as shown. The joint is located on one of the long sides of the frame, and is joined by using a short length of steel flat, and four rivets.

Legs are bent from 5/16 or 3/8-inch diameter rod. Use a piece of rod longer than required and grip it at the center in the vise. Bend the other end around to create the hair-pin shape, then cut off the excess.

The scrolls can be drilled first, then the locations of the holes marked on the angles, or the assembly can be clamped and holes drilled through the angles and scrolls at the same time. The latter method is more accurate in aligning the holes for the rivets.

When attaching the legs to the angle frames, longer rivets will be required. Note that the rivets may project slightly above the angle frame in which the glass sets. Peen these rivets down, or use strips of felt or rubber on the angle to support the glass above the rivets.

Wire-brush the metal and paint it flat white, flat black or a color to match your decor.

RUSTIC CONVENIENCE TABLE

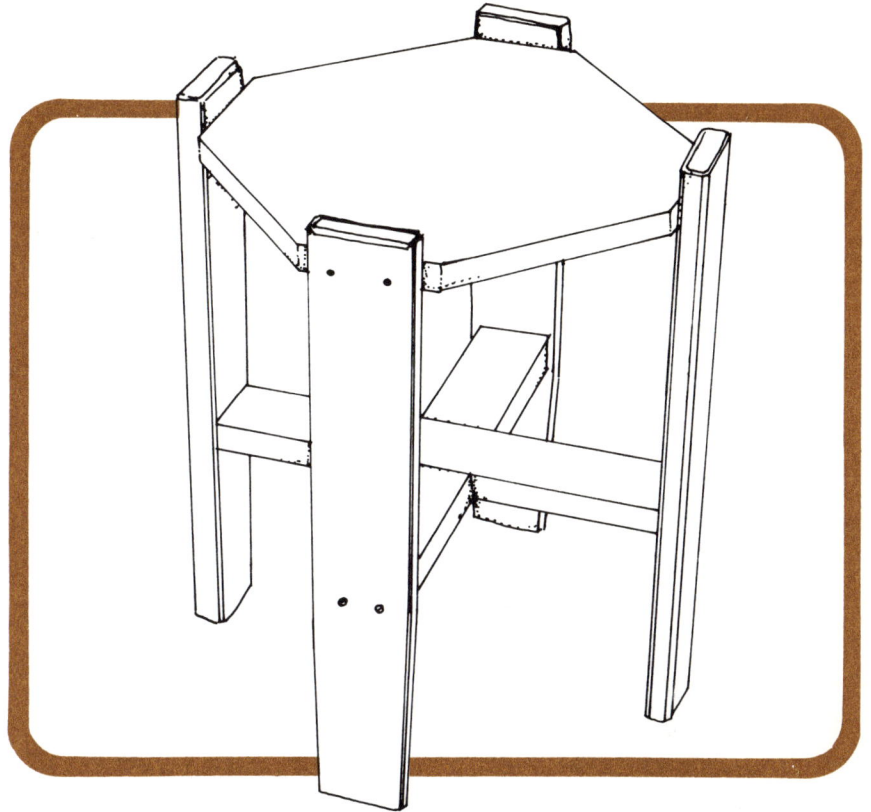

Small enough so it is easily moved for use where needed, this versatile table is also sturdy enough to support a large flower pot. The one shown was made of mahogany, but pine will do if you prefer. Also, if you make a few in redwood, you will find them very useful for patio entertaining.

Cut the top to shape with a handsaw, keeping just a bit outside the line so you can finish by using sandpaper. Make the legs next, trimming stock down to a 3-inch width. You can remove much of the material from the double taper at the base end with a saw, but it's best to do the actual sizing to the line with a plane. Attach the legs with glue and finishing nails. For outdoor use, you may wish to use round-head screws.

Next, cut the pieces for the cross-brace and make the layout for the half-lap. To shape the joint, use a backsaw to make a series of parallel cuts halfway through the stock, then remove the waste material by working with a sharp chisel and a mallet. To gauge depth when working with the saw, clamp a wood block to the tool to control the cut. Put glue in the joint and clamp until set; then place in position between the table legs and secure with either nails or screws.

Top edges of the legs may be chamfered with either a file or a block plane.

Finish with a coat of penetrating sealer and wax, stain and varnish, or paint.

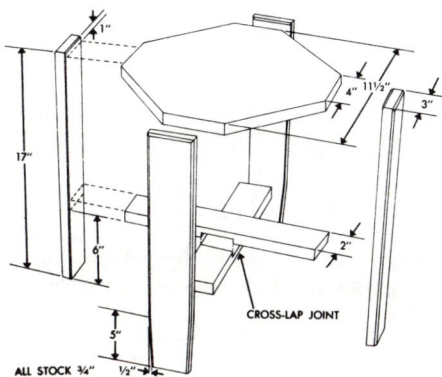

CROSS-LAP JOINT

ALL STOCK ¾" ½"

EIGHTEENTH CENTURY CANDLE TABLE

While its original function was to support a candle for illumination, in a modern home this attractive table can be used for an indoor plant, to display a figurine or any of another dozen uses.

The column is a simple between-centers turning, and should be a straight-grained hardwood. The remainder of the table can be clear white pine as is this example. If you cannot find a single pine board 14 inches wide for the top you will have to edge-glue narrower stock; use dowels to reinforce the joint. Veneered plywood also could be used, with the edge taped, but you then cannot "distress" the edges.

Use a "soft" finish, staining one of the early American colors such as maple or nutmeg. One of the penetrating sealers will give a hand-rubbed appearance to the finished table.

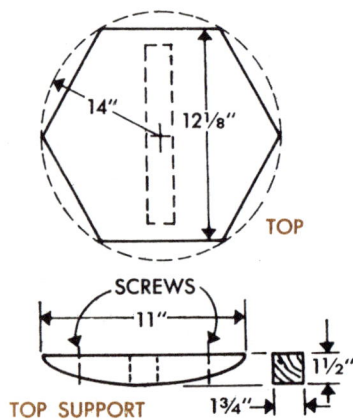

TOP

SCREWS

TOP SUPPORT

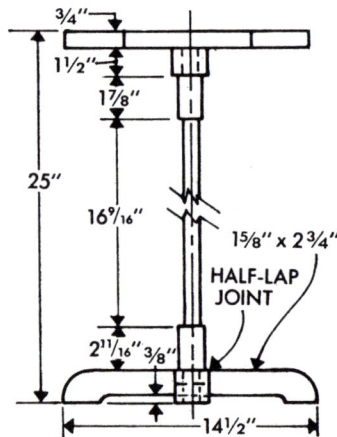

HALF-LAP JOINT

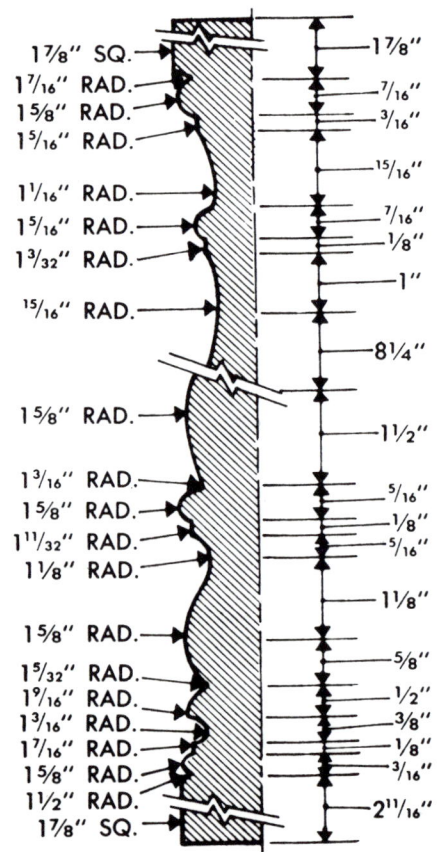

DANISH-INSPIRED END TABLE

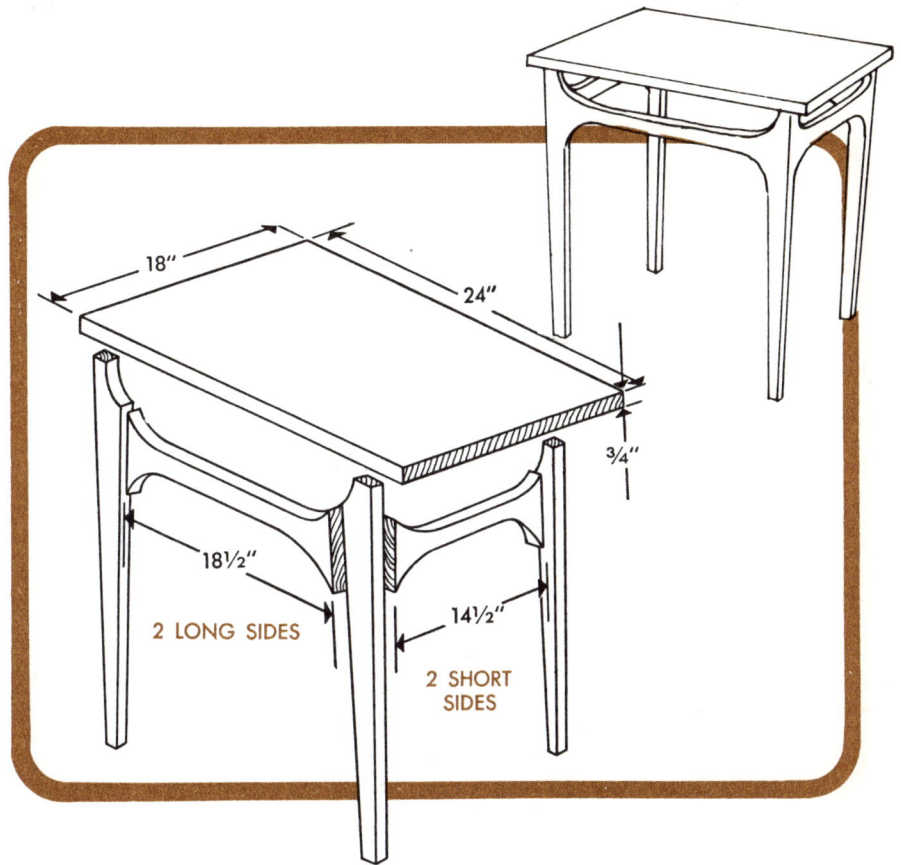

18" 24" 3/4"

18½"

2 LONG SIDES

14½"

2 SHORT SIDES

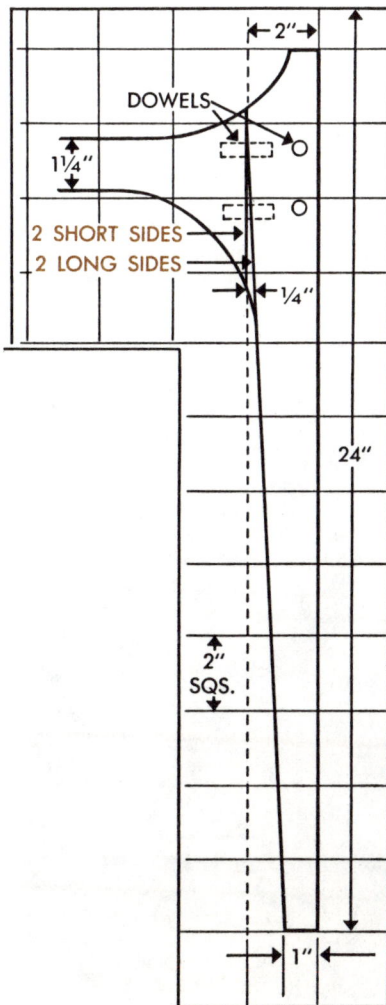

2"
DOWELS
1¼"
2 SHORT SIDES
2 LONG SIDES
¼"
24"
2" SQS.
1"

Simplicity of design and ease of building are the charms of this little table. Four legs, four stretchers and a top, and you have a table. Although a bandsaw was used to cut out the original, a jig or even a coping saw could be used. The grace of this modern design will go well with almost any style furniture.

Dowel and glue the top up from several lengths of walnut, alternating heartwood to sapwood so there will be no warping. All stock is ¾-inch thick. After the glue has set, square the edges of the top with a table saw or by using a rasp and sandpaper. Enlarge the squared drawing and make patterns for both sets of stretchers and the legs. Note that the short pair of stretchers are cut to fit the straight sides of the legs, while the long stretchers are cut to match the tapered sides of the legs. Cut all pieces to shape, and sand to remove saw marks. Using a doweling jig or doweling points, mark and drill holes in all four stretchers and legs. When doweling the short stretchers into the narrow portion of the legs, drill only to a depth of ½ inch. Place glue in the holes and dowel the pieces together, using a band-clamp, or a rope tourniquet to pull the assembly tight. After the glue on the leg assembly was set, drill dowel holes in the top of the legs, and mark the dowel holes on the underside of the top. These also should be blind holes only ½ inch deep to avoid drilling completely through the top. Glue and dowel the top in place holding it with a heavy weight until the glue sets.

Sand the table smooth, and apply a coat of walnut stain-filler followed by an oil finish.

HEXAGON END TABLE

One method of cutting spline grooves is to hold work against beveled fence, with parallel block to assure accuracy.

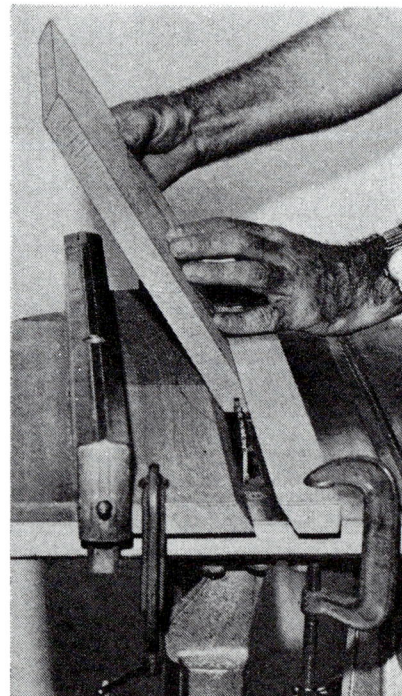

Number 2 common pine shelving is used to construct this unusual hexagon end table, but hardwood or hardwood plywood also could be used. Also, a minor change in the design of the door panels will give the table a modern, Mediterranean or period look, to suit personal preferences in styling.

For this model, two 12-foot lengths of 1 x 12 provided all the lumber required. The stock should be selected for small, tight knots. Cut four pieces of shelving to 23-inch lengths and two 21½ inches long. Dowel and edge-glue as indicated. Lay out the hexagon for the top and bottom and for the subbottom. The 21½ inches is sufficient to allow waste from which to cut the legs. The sides of the hexagons are cut first, the waste saved for the blocks to which the legs are fastened. Cut the corners of the hexagon at 30 degrees and these waste pieces are salvaged for the legs.

Next, cut six pieces 2 x 9¾ inches and cut the ends at 30 degrees. These pieces are attached to the underside of the top to form a sub-top. Attach them with glue and flathead wood screws. Cut the four sides to 15 inches, ripping at 30 degrees to a width of 10½ inches. Check the sides of the hexagons to make sure yours do not vary from the given dimensions, and cut the sides to a matching width. Groove them for the splines.

The legs are cut to the shape shown, then grooved for splines that can be 1/8-inch plywood or hardboard.

Assemble the sides of the table to the top and bottom, driving finishing nails through the sides into the subtop and bottom, and also using glue. Cut the leg-attaching blocks to size and glue and screw them to the underside of the bottom as indicated. Glue the splined leg members together and to the attaching blocks.

The doors are assembled from stiles and rails around a raised panel. The panel is cut to a net size of 7¼ x 11¾ inches. If you use pine, select material so knots are positioned the same, as shown in the one photo.

Hang the doors with hardware of your choice, as previously described. On the model shown, hinges were hammered copper H-L style with matching door pulls. Magnetic latches were used to minimize problems.

Stain or finish to suit the design you choose. Be sure to sand all surfaces smooth before applying finishes. If plywood is used, glue veneer tape to all edges.

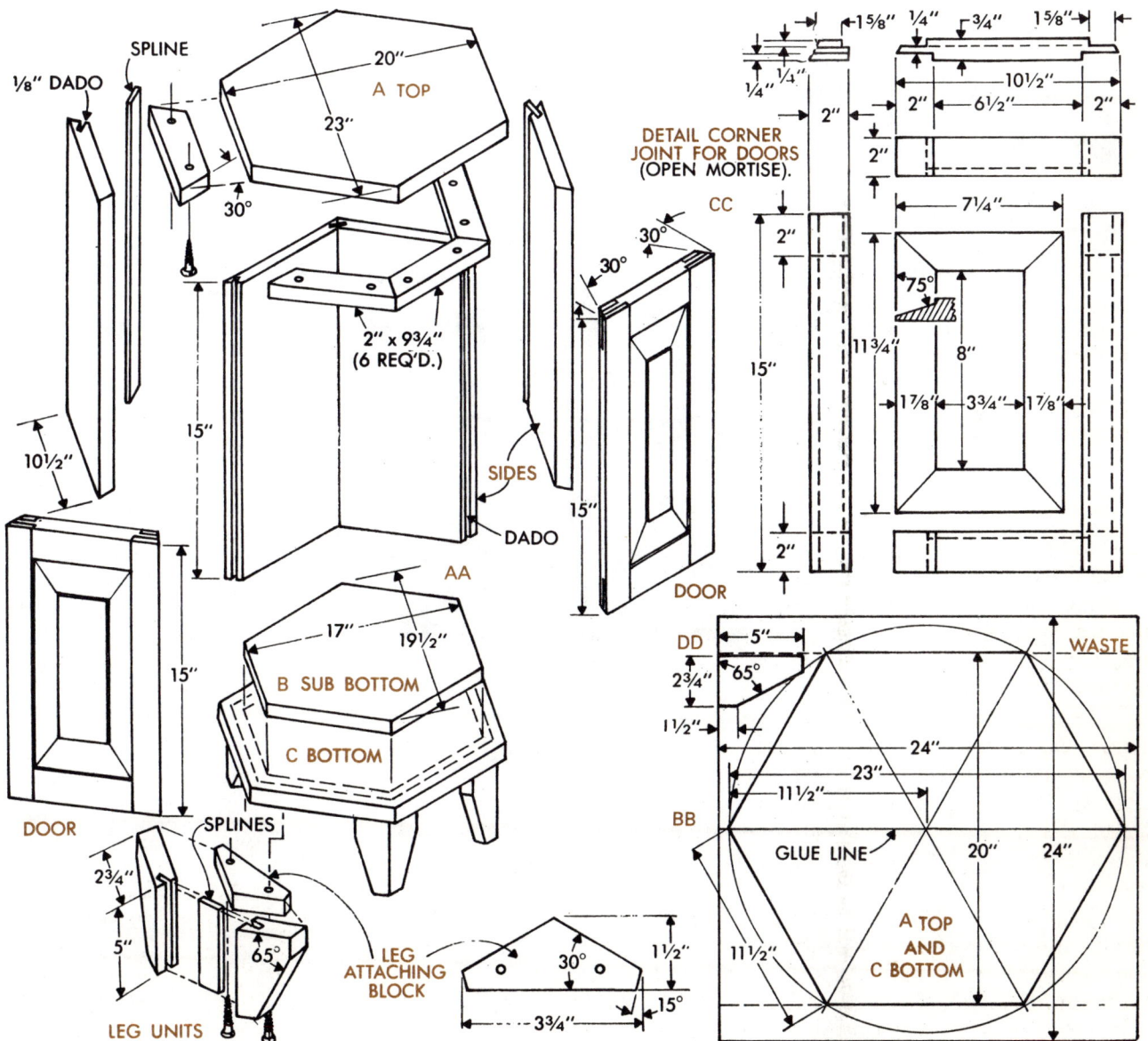

SPLINE

⅛" DADO

A TOP
20"
23"
30"

2" x 9¾"
(6 REQ'D.)

15"

10½"

15"

SIDES

DADO

DETAIL CORNER JOINT FOR DOORS (OPEN MORTISE).

CC

30°

30°

15"

DOOR

DOOR

15"

AA

17"
19½"

B SUB BOTTOM

C BOTTOM

SPLINES

2¾"

5"

65°

LEG ATTACHING BLOCK

LEG UNITS

1½"
30°
15°
3¾"

1⅝" ¼" ¾" 1⅝"

¼"

¼"

2"

2"
6½"
2"
10½"

2"

7¼"

2"

75°

11¾"

8"

1⅞" 3¾" 1⅞"

2"

DD
5"

2¾"
65°

1½"

BB

11½"

WASTE

24"

23"

11½"

GLUE LINE

20"   24"

A TOP AND C BOTTOM

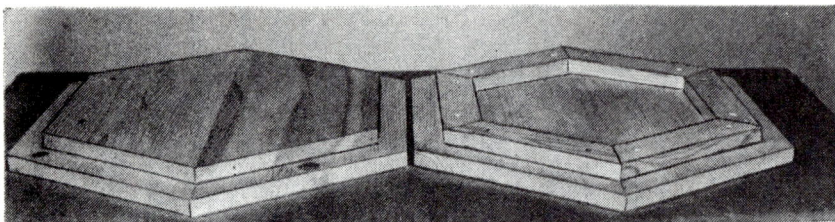

Bottom is two solid hexagons; top is one solid hexagon with framing for second; inner shape as indicated.

Spline grooves in legs are cut with the same setup used for cutting grooves in sides. Jig is safe and accurate.

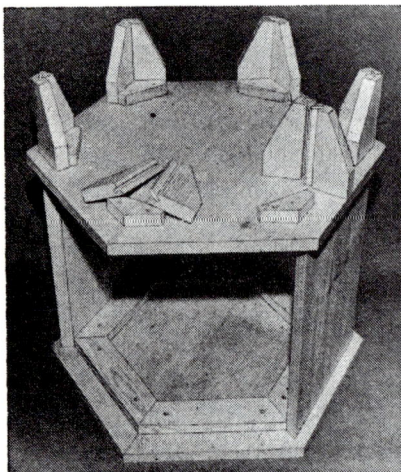

Inverted assembly shows how sides fit against upper framing. Legs are two pieces splined together, glued in place.

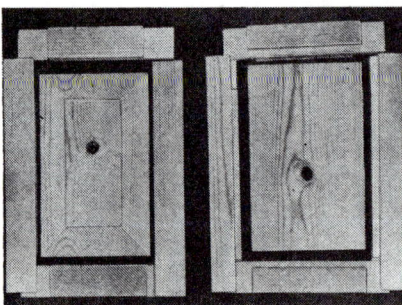

Table is completely assembled here, except for doors. No. 2 pine was used here, hardwood also could be used. Rails and stiles of doors are joined by a through mortise-and-tenon.

Raised panels on doors are cut as shown; first cut is made at right angles, then bevel cut is made.

Photo at left shows front (left) and back (right) of door before assembling stiles and rails around center bevel panels.

GATE-LEG TABLE

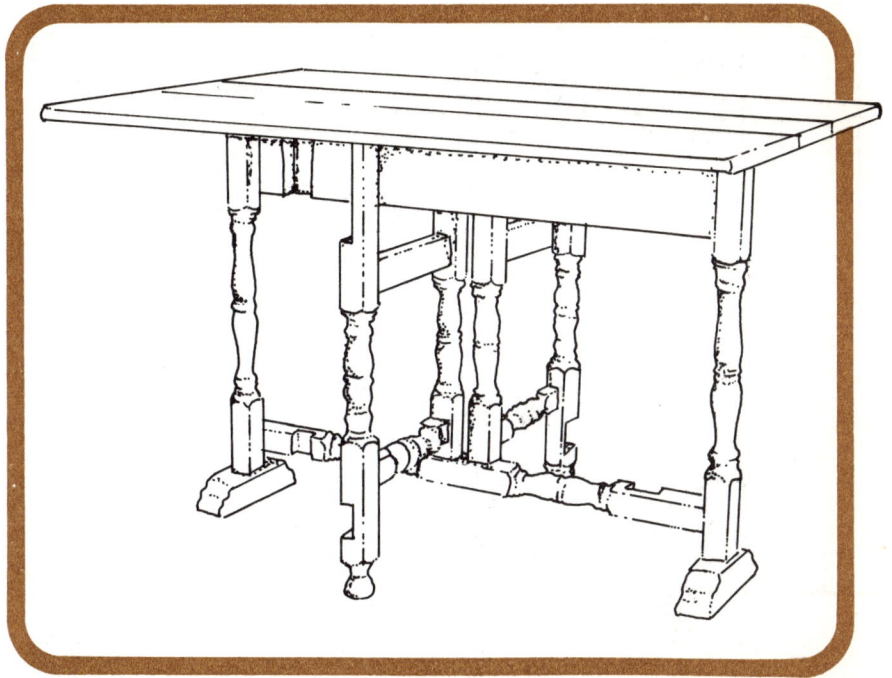

Swinging the gate legs on this table permits varying the width of the top from 6½ to 17 to 27½ inches, all with the length of 43 inches. Designed to be a space saver back in colonial days, it will do the same today in a small home or an apartment where space is at a premium.

There is no question that you will have to have a lathe to make this table, and with all the turnings required you will spend a lot of enjoyable hours at the business end of turning chisels. All the turnings are made from 2-inch-square stock, and the light cross-hatching on the drawings indicates the portions of the turnings that stay in the square. Note that pivoting leg F is a section of leg D, the outboard leg of the gate. The marked arrows on the pattern of D indicate the part that is F. Two each are required of legs B, D and F, with two stretchers E needed, one for each gate leg. Only one main stretcher C is required. Note that each half of this stretcher is the same, except that the 1 x 2-inch notches face the opposite way.

Two trestle feet are required, and they should be of good straight-grained stock, and the mortise and tenon between the leg and foot should be a tight fit.

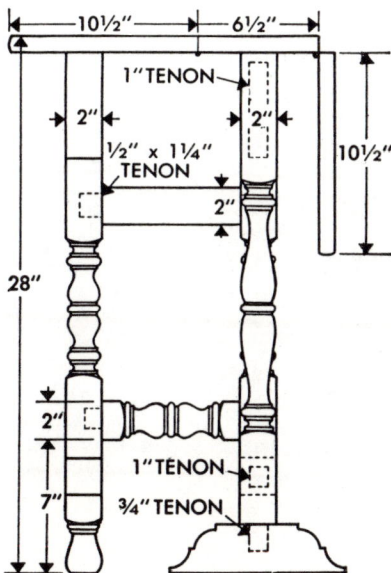

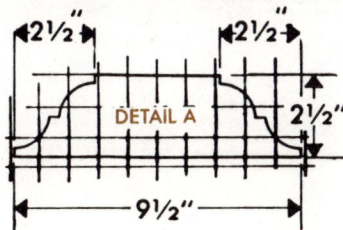

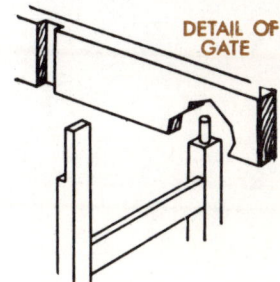

DETAIL A

DETAIL OF GATE

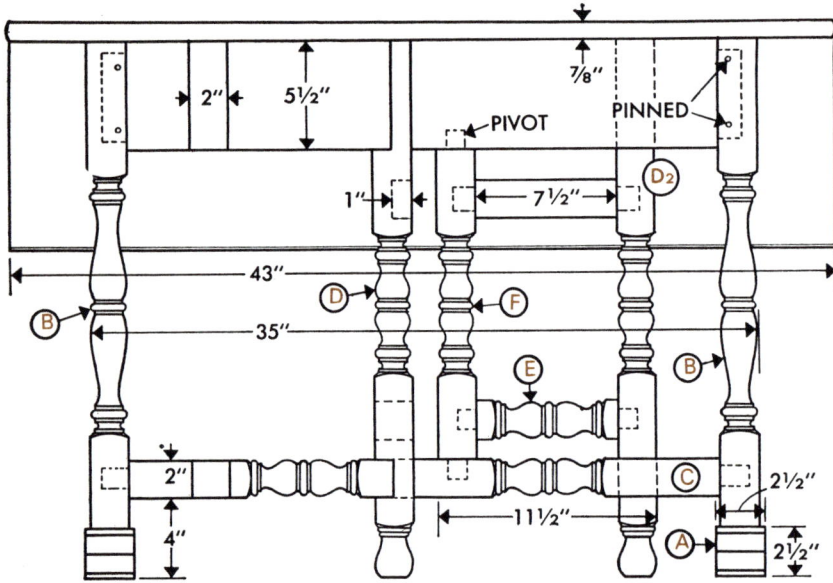

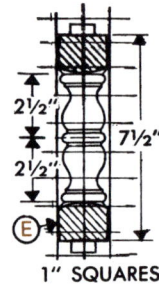

E — 1" SQUARES

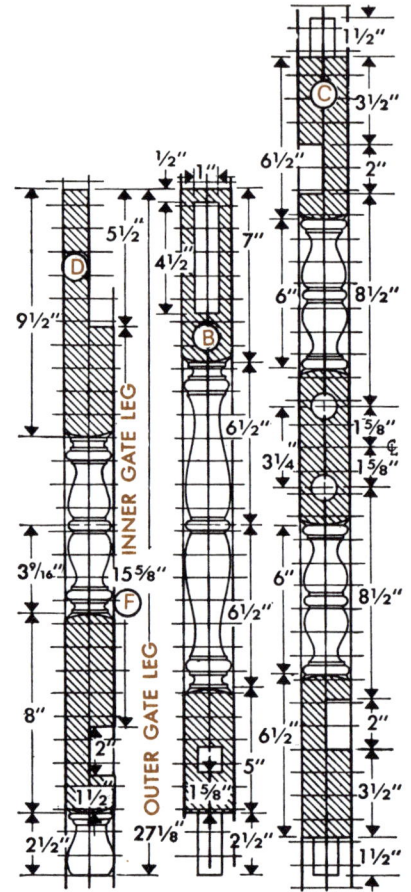

MAPLE HARVEST TABLE

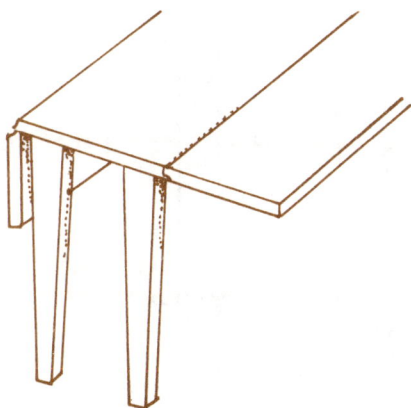

Classic simplicity in the design of this charming table makes it equally at home for casual family meals or completely formal dinners. Its name can be traced back to the time when extra help was required during the harvest season, and additional table space was needed to feed the workers. The harvest table evolved as a unit that took up a minimum of space when not in use, and a maximum of tabletop area when the leaves were raised.

If solid stock is used you will have to edge-glue several strips to create a panel large enough for the top, and one for each of the leaves. Plywood can be used, but the machined edges of the top and leaves will show when the leaves are down, and this might be objectionable. Doweling and gluing a strip of hardwood along two edges of the top, and one edge of each leaf would provide an edge for cutting the rule (drop-leaf) joint.

Start construction by making the four legs. Note that they are straight for the upper 6 inches, then taper to 1½ inches at the bottom. Mortises are cut in two adjacent sides to accept tenons cut on the ends of the aprons. The quickest way to cut the mortises is with a mortising chisel in a drill press, but boring a line of holes, then cutting with a wood chisel will produce the same result. Note that the mortises join, and the ends of the tenons are mitered.

Apply glue to the tenons, then assemble the four legs and four aprons. Clamp the assembly, square it up, then let it stand until the glue sets up.

The top requires jointing on two edges, the leaves on one. Note the three steps shown in the drawing; this is the simple way to make a

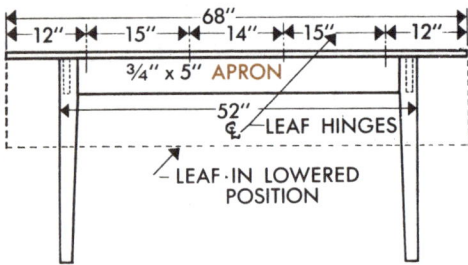

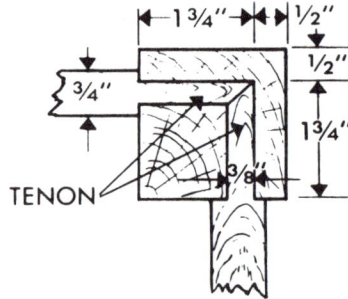

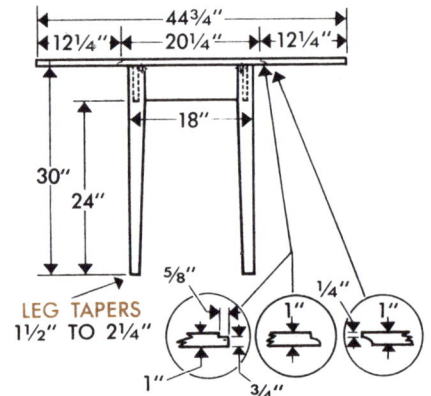

drop-leaf joint, and a molding head in a table saw, or a portable router can be used to form the two different profiles of the joint.

The center lines of the hinge leaves are indicated in the drawing. Four hinges are used on each leaf, as indicated, and two drop-leaf supports also are required. An 8 or 10-inch support should be adequate.

The top can be attached to the aprons in several ways. One way is to use glue blocks. The blocks are screwed and glued to the inside of each apron, but only screws are used through the block into the underside of the top. The screw holes should be slightly oversize. This permits the tabletop to expand and contract with heat and humidity changes without breaking any joints. If the top is held tight with glue, it quite possibly will buckle or warp.

The finish is up to the builder, and also will be influenced by the kind of wood used. Be sure to sand all surfaces absolutely smooth before applying stain and finish. The final step is to tap metal glides to the bottom of each leg.

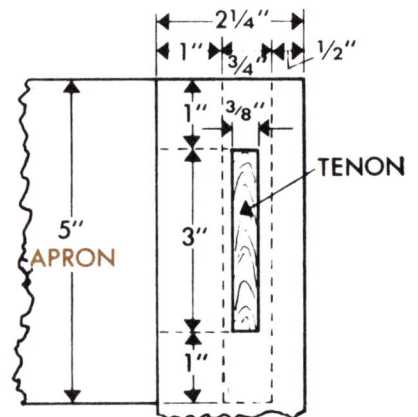

OCTAGONAL LAMP TABLE

In colonial days the only method of room illumination was by candle or lantern, which made lamp tables an absolute necessity. Every living room had one or more of these tables, and besides being designed for utility, quite a few of them are finely designed pieces of furniture. The octagonal table shown is a good example of these qualities.

The table is Queen Anne in style and dates from 1690 to 1700, a period when such styling was much in vogue on both sides of the Atlantic.

The table is made of pine and maple, these woods customarily being used in Plymouth, Massachusetts, from which the table came. As with most pieces of colonial furniture, any native wood, hard or soft, can be used, the choice of lumber for the original being dictated by the trees growing in the area in which the table was built.

The octagonal top will have to be edge-glued from narrow pieces of stock, or a piece of veneered plywood can be used. The edges will have to be taped to create the appearance of solid lumber.

The legs should be turned from hardwood, unless you are a skillful wood turner, as soft wood will not machine as well as hardwood. Mortises are cut into the square portion of each leg, at top and bottom, to accept tenons shaped on the ends of the apron and stretcher members. Dowel pins then are driven into holes drilled through from the outside of the legs, so they will show in the final construction. Note that the dowels are positioned so that on adjacent faces one is high, the other low, to assure that they are clear of each other.

Plywood can be used for the aprons, but applying veneer tape will be tricky on the short edges next to the curved portions. The stretchers should be solid stock, if there is any chance that feet will wear them down, as has happened on the original. As an option, a shelf can be installed over the stretchers to provide space for magazines or books, to make the table more suitable to contemporary needs.

Use an antique stain to give the table the proper look, and if you want to make the table a reproduction of an antique, you can distress it by beating it with chains, sanding the various parts to simulate the wear and nicking it to create the effect of age.

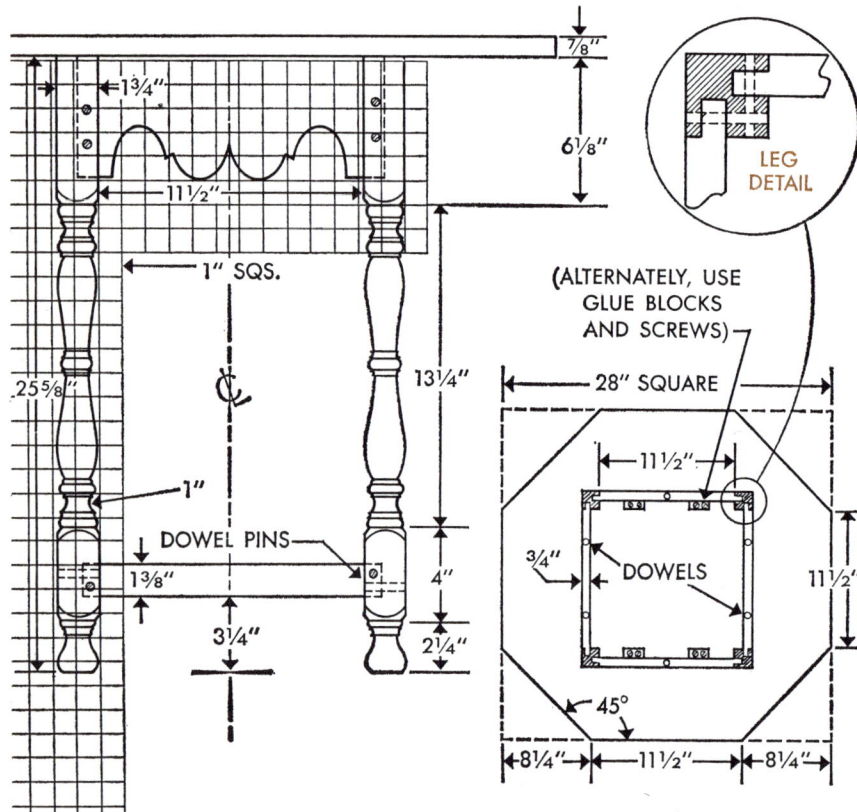

PICNIC TABLE

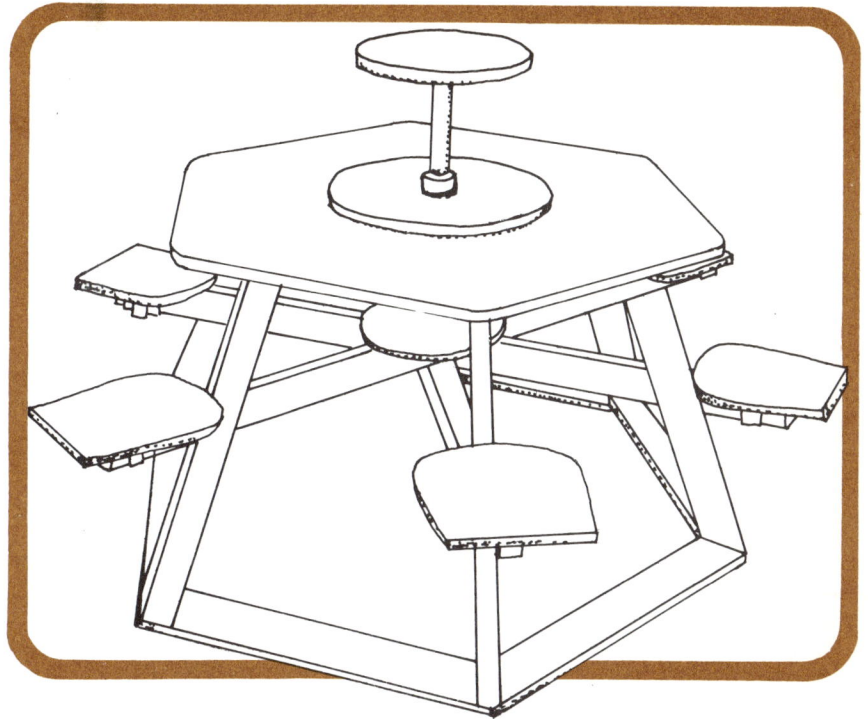

Use accuracy when making the third-lap joint, a big compass to lay out the top. Scribe a circle with a 24-inch radius, adjust the compass slightly and strike off six equal spaces on the circle. Draw lines through these points and the center of the circle, extending them to the edge of the plywood. Now, join points A, B, C, etc., to create the hexagon.

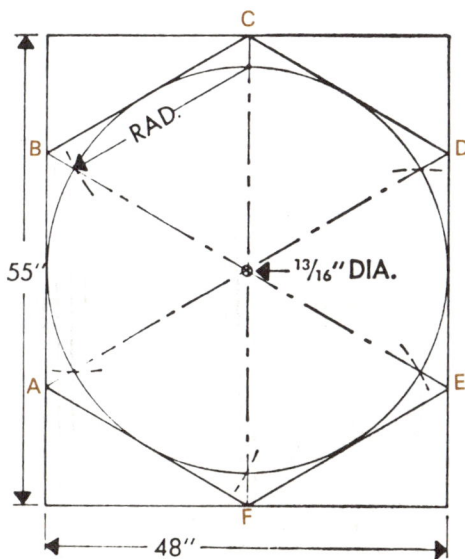

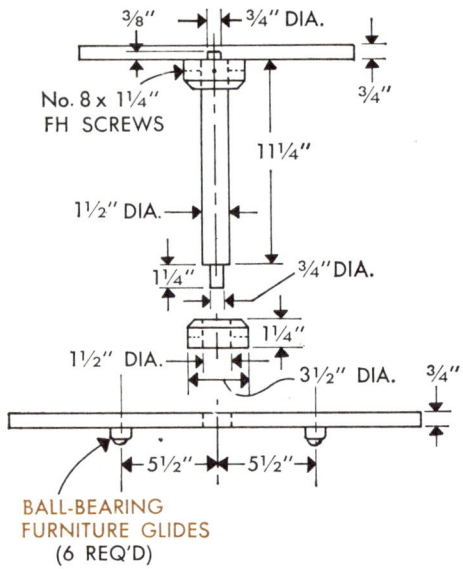

3/8"   3/4" DIA.

No. 8 x 1 1/4"
FH SCREWS

3/4"

11 1/4"

1 1/2" DIA.

1 1/4"

3/4" DIA.

1 1/4"

1 1/2" DIA.

3 1/2" DIA.

3/4"

5 1/2"   5 1/2"

BALL-BEARING
FURNITURE GLIDES
(6 REQ'D)

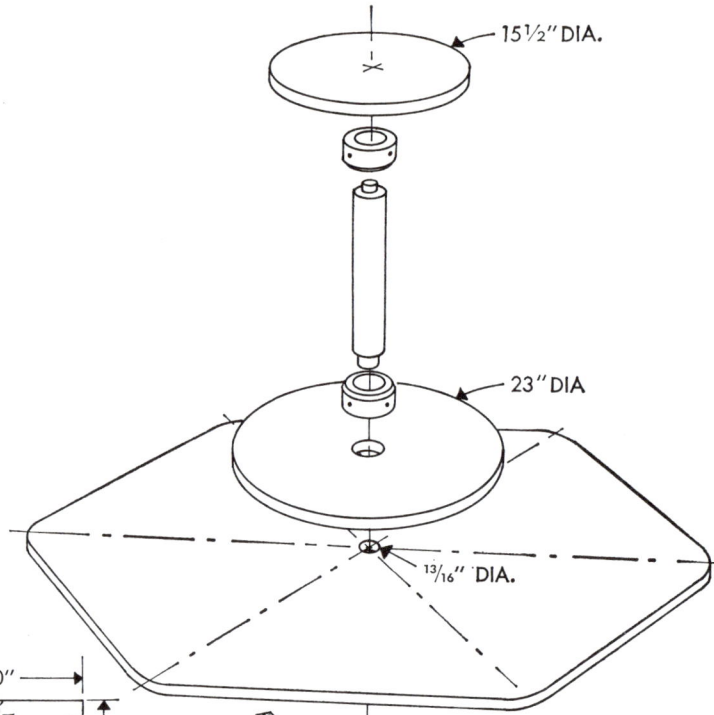

15 1/2" DIA.

23" DIA.

13/16" DIA.

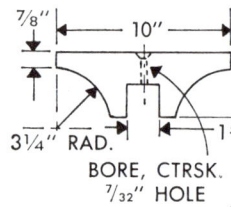

7/8"   10"

3 1/2"

3 1/4" RAD.   1 5/8"

BORE, CTRSK.
7/32" HOLE

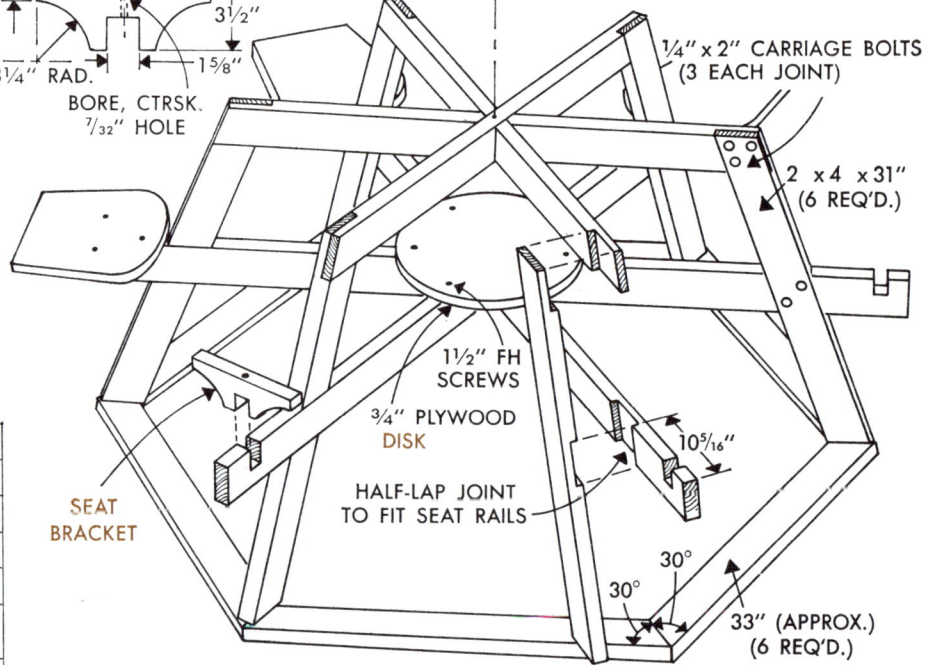

1/4" x 2" CARRIAGE BOLTS
(3 EACH JOINT)

2 x 4 x 31"
(6 REQ'D.)

1 1/2" FH
SCREWS

3/4" PLYWOOD
DISK

10 5/16"

SEAT
BRACKET

HALF-LAP JOINT
TO FIT SEAT RAILS

30°

30°

33" (APPROX.)
(6 REQ'D.)

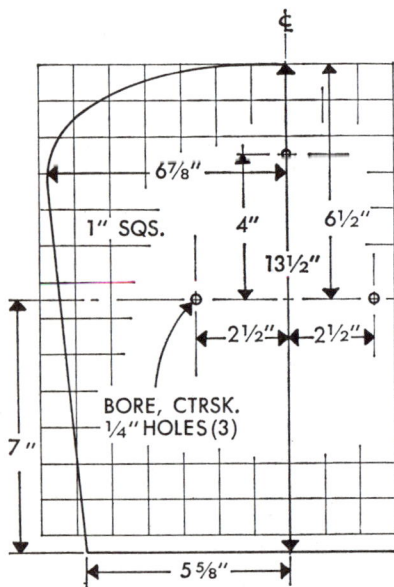

¢

6 7/8"

1" SQS.

4"

6 1/2"

13 1/2"

2 1/2"   2 1/2"

BORE, CTRSK.
1/4" HOLES (3)

7"

5 5/8"

21″

70°   (3 REQ'D)

8″ RAD.

2½″   (3 REQ'D)

36″

29″   17¼″   70°

33″

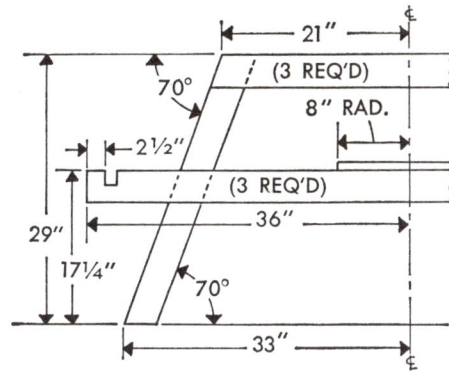

DETAILS OF THIRD-LAP CENTER JOINT

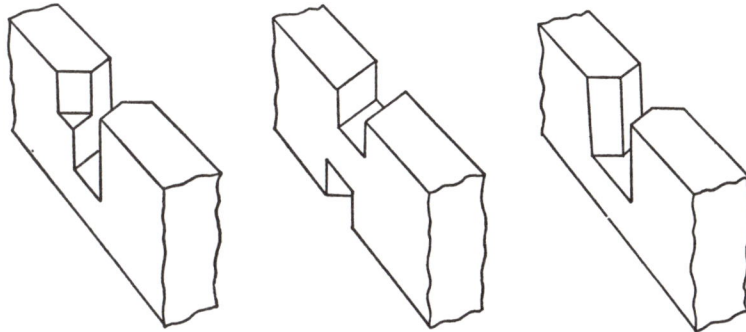

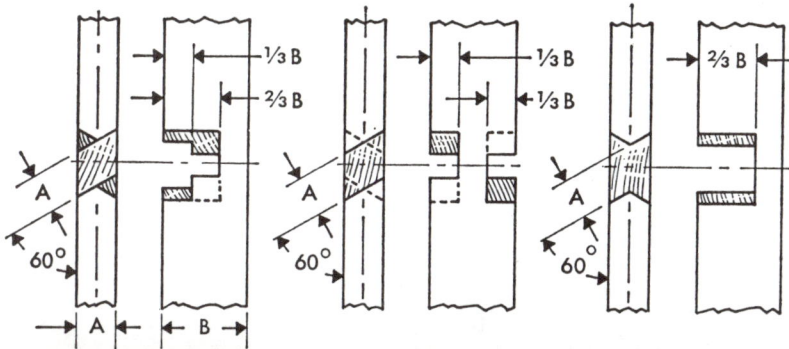

⅓ B   ⅔ B   ⅓ B   ⅓ B   ⅔ B

A   A   A

60°   60°   60°

A   B

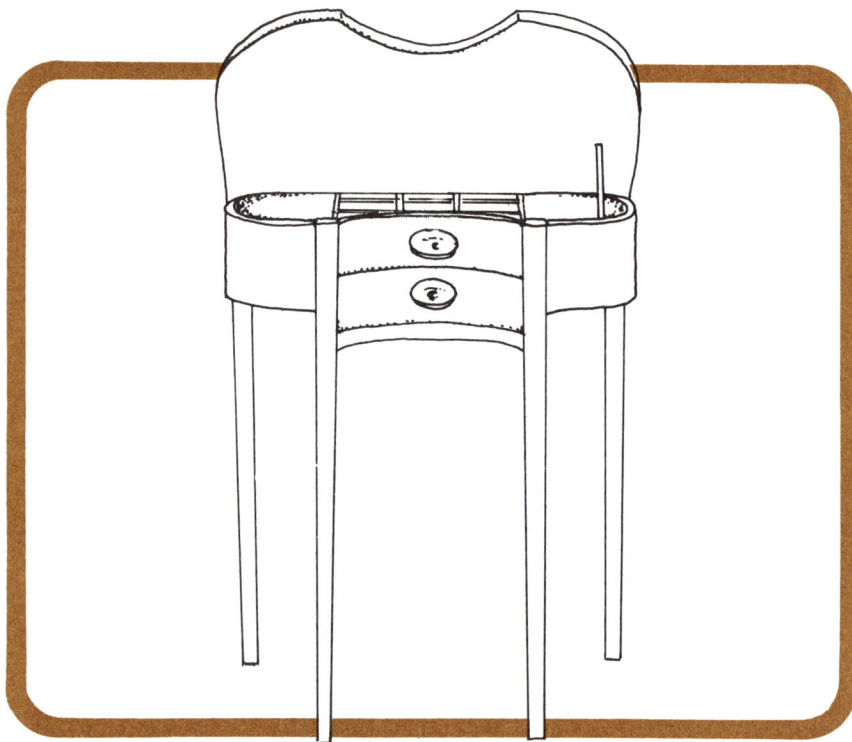

SHERATON SEWING TABLE

Truly elegance in mahogany, this dainty Sheraton sewing table is from the American Wing of the Metropolitan Museum of Art—a gift of Mrs. Russell Sage—1909.

To start construction of the table, cut the legs to the shape shown, starting the tapers on all four sides 6¼-inches from the upper ends. The back legs are notched to accept the sides, the front legs are solid.

Cut the two sides as one piece, 32 inches long with a ¼ x ¼-inch rabbet on the bottom inside edge, and make saw kerfs ½ inch apart to within 1/16 inch of the surface, 9½ inches on either side of the center line.

When cut apart at the center line, the separate sides will be somewhat longer than required. Make a full-sized drawing of the top view and place it on a flat wooden work surface. Over this, place waxed paper and position the kerfed pieces to form the curved side, holding them in place with small wooden blocks nailed to the work surface. When the sides conform to the curves of the drawing, fill the kerfs with glue and let dry overnight. (You may wish to cover the inner surfaces of the kerfed sides with veneer for appearances.)

Cut the back to the T-shape shown, and rabbet the lower edges to accept the compartment bottoms, letting the upper rabbet extend through the stock to form a dado. Dado for the two vertical partitions and fit a ¼ x ¼-inch strip 2¾ inches down from the upper edge to support the bottom of the center compartment.

Cut the two front-to-back partitions to size and from your fullsize drawing, lay out and cut the bottoms for the two side compartments.

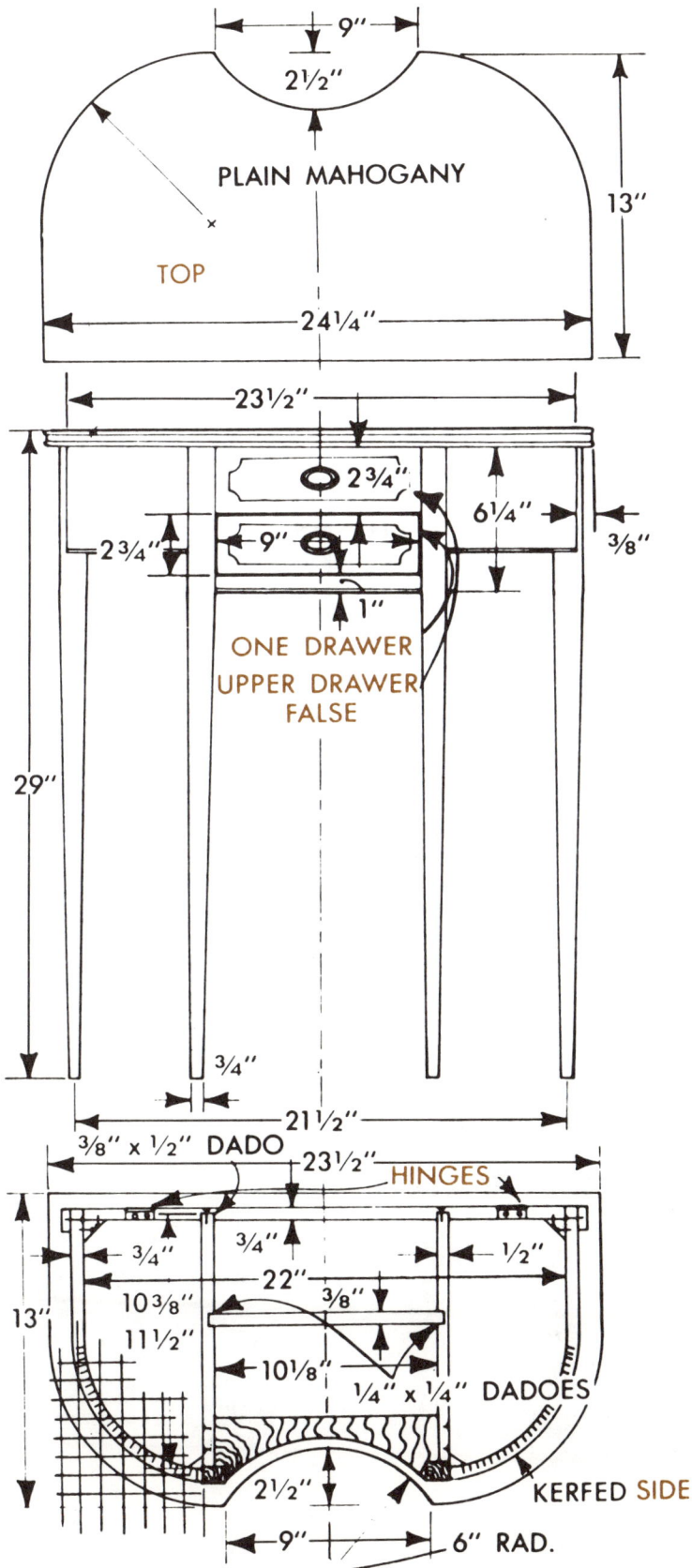

9"

2½"

PLAIN MAHOGANY

13"

TOP

24¼"

23½"

2¾"

6¼"

2¾"

9"

3/8"

1"

ONE DRAWER
UPPER DRAWER
FALSE

29"

¾"

21½"

3/8" x ½" DADO

23½"

HINGES

¾"

¾"

½"

13"

10⅜"

22"

3/8"

11½"

10⅛"

¼" x ¼" DADOES

KERFED SIDE

2½"

9"

6" RAD.

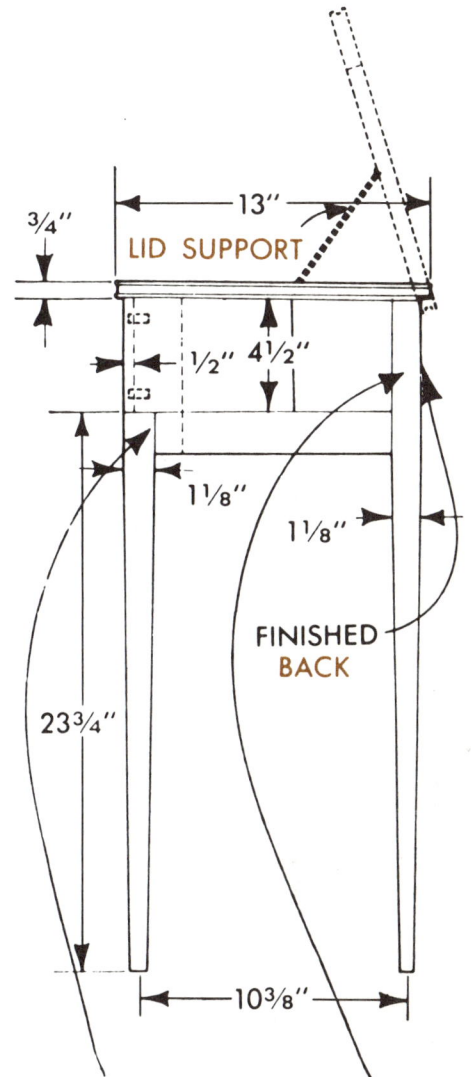

¾"

13"

LID SUPPORT

½"   4½"

1⅛"

1⅛"

FINISHED
BACK

23¾"

10⅜"

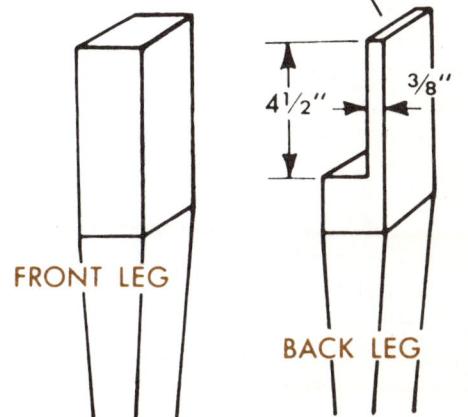

4½"

3/8"

FRONT LEG

BACK LEG

Be sure to allow for the ¼-inch projections on all sides to fit in the rabbets and dados.

When the glue has dried on the kerfed side pieces, remove them from the jigs and place on your full-size drawing. Cut the back ends to fit flush with the back of the table.

For ease of construction, assemble the table upside down on the full-size drawing. Join the back and sides with finishing nails through the sides into the back, then fasten the back legs with screws from inside. Glue blocks fastened to the sides and back strengthen the joint.

Cut the bottoms for the false-drawer compartment and the shelf on which the drawer rests, and fit them into the rabbets in the partitions. Slide the assembly into place and fasten to the back with glue and finishing nails. Attach the front legs and reinforce the corners created by the partitions, leg-corners and sides with glue blocks. Glue in the bottoms of the side compartments (a few brads will help). Now the assembly is strong enough to stand up and be checked to be sure all legs are equal length.

Cut the curved front blocks from glued-up plywood or solid stock. (Note the drawer block is cut to 8-7/8 inches to fit between the front legs.) The bottom facing block is 1 inch thick and the drawer and top blocks are 2¾ inches thick. The top and facing blocks have notches to accept the legs, and the drawer block has notches for the drawer sides.

Assemble the drawer using ½-inch stock for the sides and back, and a ¼-inch bottom in dadoes ¼ inch up from the lower edges of the sides. A notch cut in the bottom edge of the drawer back allows the drawer to travel on the guide strip as shown.

Cut the table top to shape and fasten in place with mortised butt hinges. Because of the curved front surface of the drawers, you will probably have to reshape hardware to fit. Cut a scrap of stock to the contour of the curve for a jig, take the handles off the screw eyes of the drawer pulls and bend the plates into the curve. Reshape the handles to fit. The original table was dark mahogany, but you may wish to use a lighter stain to match existing furniture.

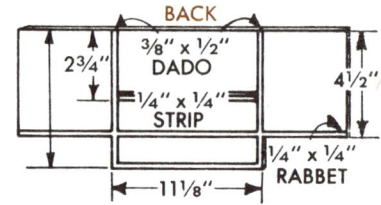

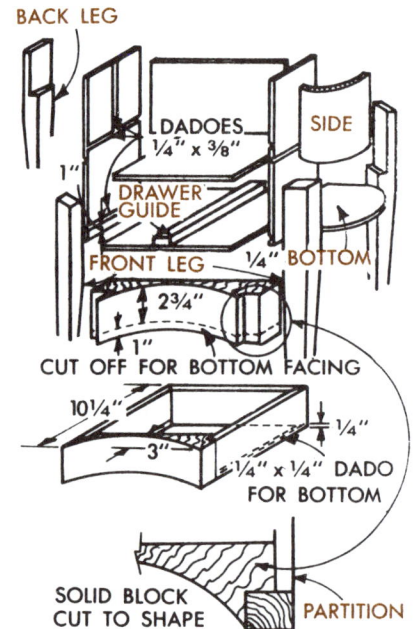

SPANISH TABLE AND CHAIRS

231

Black leather upholstery, decorative brass tacks, black wrought-iron scrolls, and beautiful oak wood combine with oak-grained plastic laminate and foam-rubber padding to produce this elegant Spanish dining table and chair set. The table and chairs not only complement any Spanish or Mediterranean decor, but will bring many comments when it's discovered you made them yourself.

THE TABLE

Begin construction of the table by gluing up the top. Using contact cement, fasten a 4 x 8-foot sheet of plastic laminate to a sheet of ¾-inch fir plywood. Use one of the new oak patterns in a natural or "suede" finish. Cut the glued-up top in half to make two 4 x 4-foot pieces. Turn these as shown, to make the grain run crossway. Cut off the 18-inch leaves, then cut off all pieces to make them 40 inches wide as indicated. Cut off the corners on the dotted line. Shape the edge molding and cut to the lengths needed. Finish the molding before it is glued and screwed in place.

Enlarge the squared drawings for the table legs. The curved pieces can be cut from a 2 x 6 if marked out as shown. To assure an accurate fit of all pieces, enlarge the leg-frame pattern onto a piece of brown wrapping paper and cut and fit pieces to match. Cut the top edges of the legs on a 10 degree angle to allow for the outward splay of the legs. Glue and dowel the leg-frame pieces together. Stain and finish the assembled frames.

Position the table top upside down on a smooth, flat surface (without the leaves) and install the table extension slides and catch.

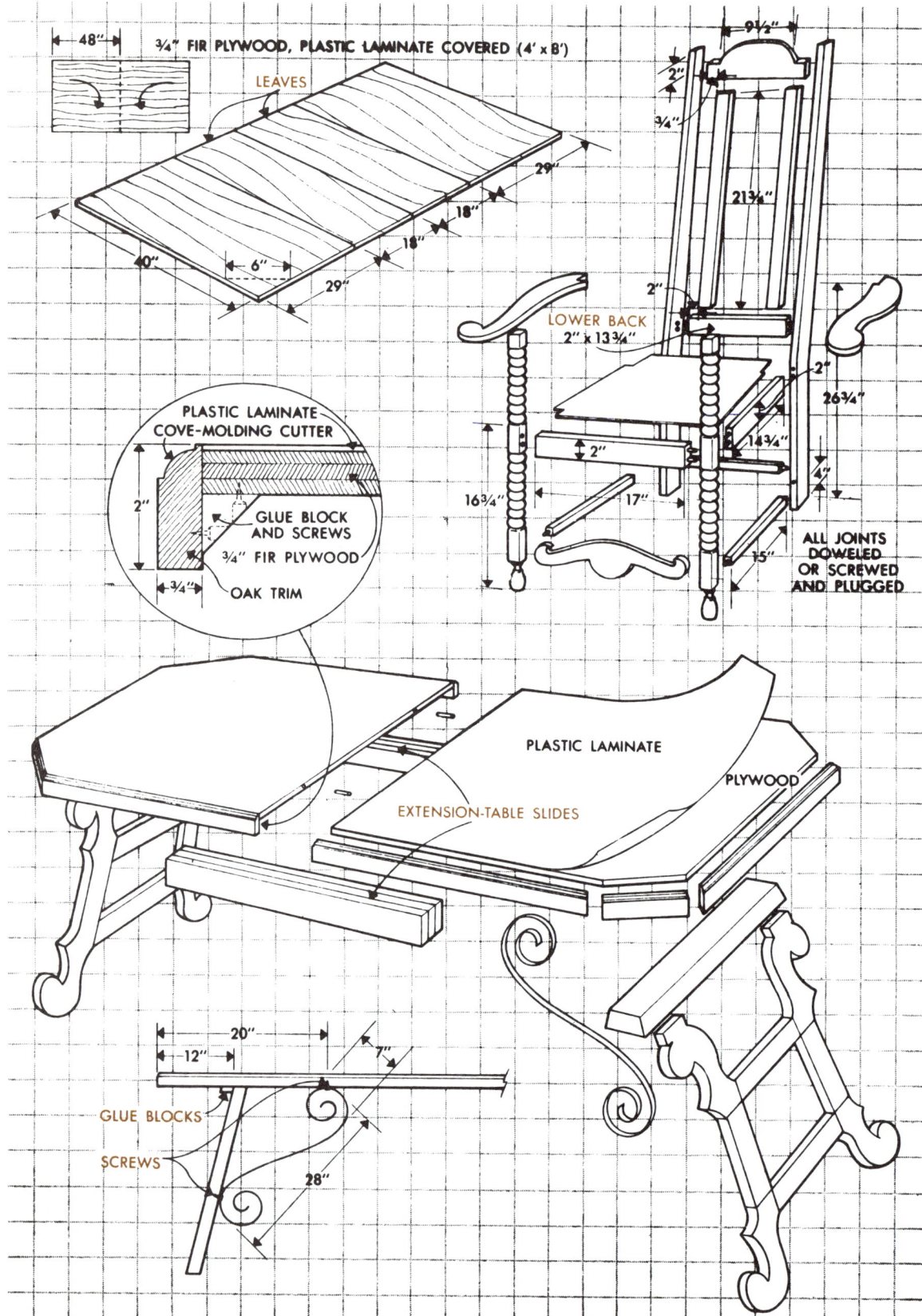

48"

¾" FIR PLYWOOD, PLASTIC LAMINATE COVERED (4' x 8')

LEAVES

29"

18"

18"

18"

29"

40"

6"

9½"

2"

¾"

21¾"

2"

LOWER BACK
2" x 13¾"

2"

26¾"

14¾"

2"

16¾"

17"

4"

15"

ALL JOINTS
DOWELED
OR SCREWED
AND PLUGGED

PLASTIC LAMINATE
COVE-MOLDING CUTTER

2"

GLUE BLOCK
AND SCREWS

¾" FIR PLYWOOD

¾"

OAK TRIM

PLASTIC LAMINATE

PLYWOOD

EXTENSION-TABLE SLIDES

20"

12"

7"

GLUE BLOCKS

SCREWS

28"

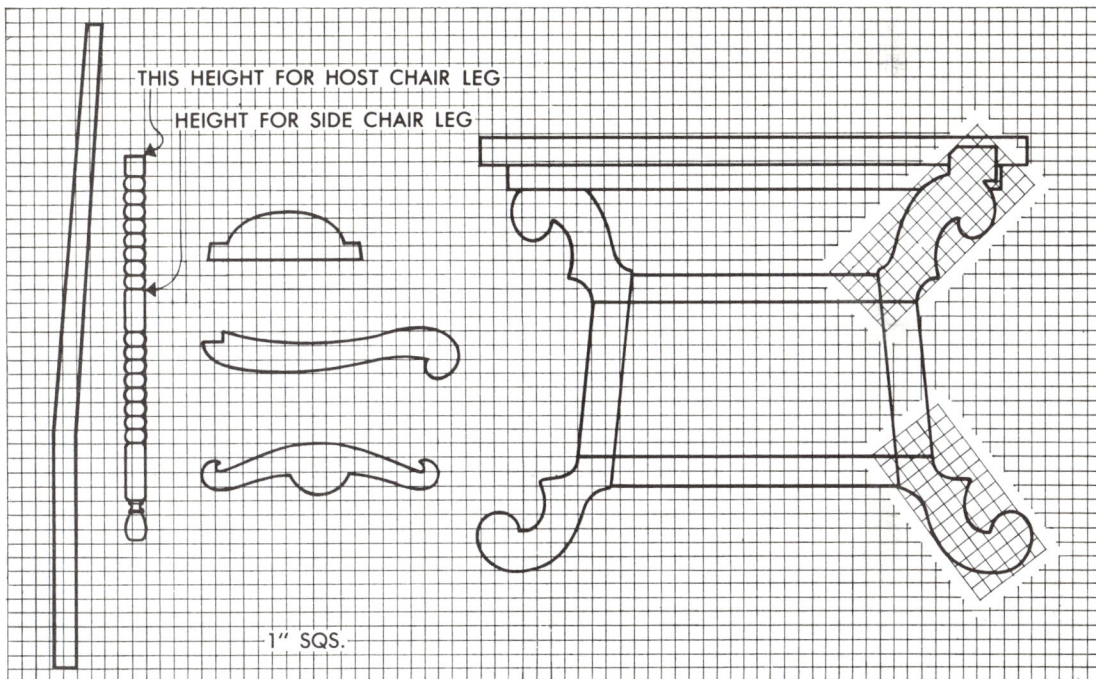

THIS HEIGHT FOR HOST CHAIR LEG
HEIGHT FOR SIDE CHAIR LEG

1" SQS.

Glue and screw the leg frames in place, bracing the legs with wrought-iron scrolls screwed to the table top and the frames. If you don't have the facilities for working wrought iron, have a local welder make up the scrolls according to the pattern.

Turn the table over, fit the leaves and drill for the aligning dowel pins.

Extension table slides and two 18" leaves extend length of table to 94" for company. Width of 40".

Wrought-iron scrolls brace table legs. Leg frames are held in place with screws and angled glue blocks.

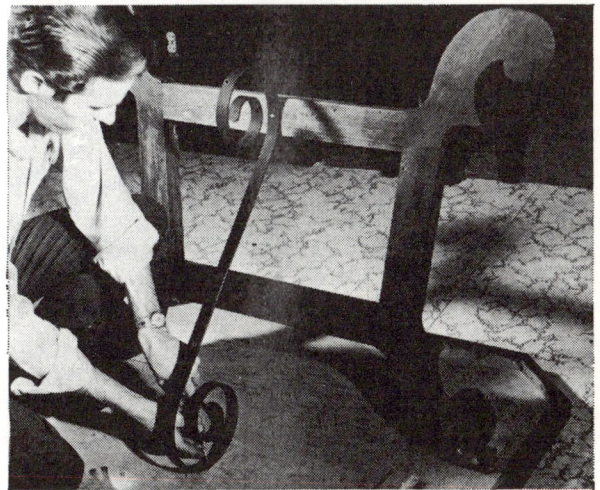

Front legs for chair are lathe-turned. Legs on host and hostess chairs are longer to support arms as shown.

Joints in chair are either 3/8" dowels or screws, depending on location. Doweling jig assures accuracy.

Plug cutter cuts plugs of oak to match chair wood. Plugs are driven in to cover screws, sanded flush.

After fastening back legs to top stretcher, legs are clamped to bend them into shape, screwed in place.

Band clamps apply even pressure to bring parts of chair together. Bar clamps equalize pressure.

Foam rubber padding is fitted between side and top and bottom of stretchers of chair back, flush with back of chair.

THE CHAIRS

Begin construction of the chairs by enlarging the squared drawings for the turned legs, the back legs, top stretcher, arms and the lower front stretcher. Turn the front legs; the host and hostess chairs' front legs are extended to fasten to their arms. The side-chair front legs are cut off at seat height. Cut out the top stretcher, lower front stretcher and the back legs, as well as the remaining stretchers. Fasten the top stretcher and the lower back stretchers to one of the rear legs. Fasten the other leg to the top stretcher using countersunk screws; apply clamps, bring the leg down and fasten to the lower stretcher, producing the bent back assembly for the chair. Use glue and counter-

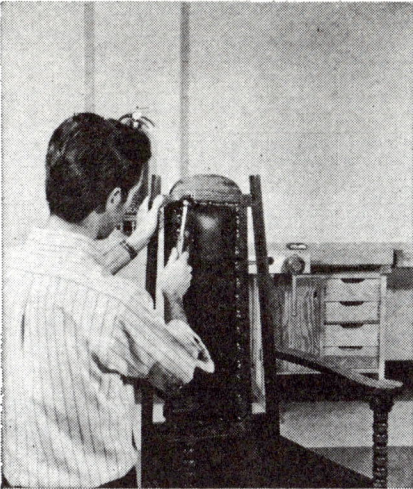

Vinyl upholstery material or leather is wrapped around a piece of corrugated cardboard, then tacked in place.

Material is pulled tight, edges folded over and tacked to chair front. Pulling the vinyl taut rounds foam padding.

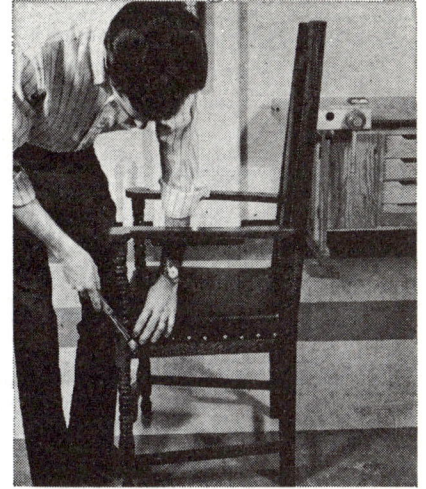

Chair seat is covered with 1½" rubber padding. Upholstery material is pulled down around edges, tacked.

bored screws covered with oak plugs for these joints. Fasten the remaining chair parts together using dowels and glue. Band clamps will draw the pieces together but use two bar clamps across the seat to keep the chair from twisting out of square. Sand, stain and finish the chair to match the table.

Cut a ¼-inch plywood seat and install with screws. Cut 1½-inch foam padding to fit over the seat and in the opening in the back of the chair. Fit the padding in the opening flush with the back of the chair. Fold leather or vinyl upholstery material over a piece of corrugated cardboard and tack it into place on the back of the chair, using decorative brass tacks. Cut material to fit over the protruding padding on the front of the chair and tack in place, pulling tautly to make the padding edges rounded. Cut upholstery material for the chair seat. Fold over and tack around the seat to the stretchers, pulling out wrinkles.

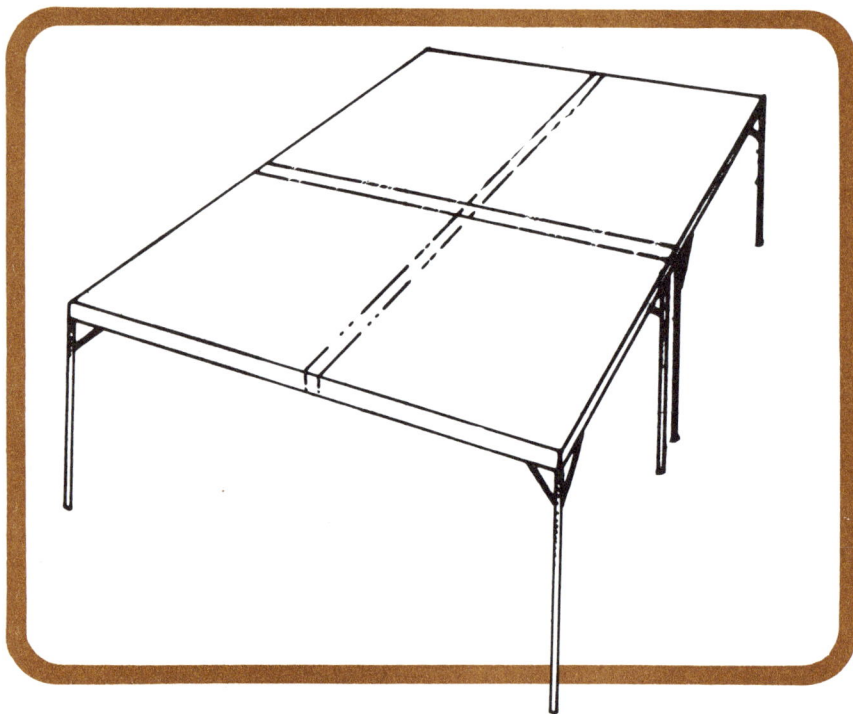

TABLE-TENNIS TABLE

This "ping-pong" table will provide the family with many hours of enjoyment, and if equipped with folding legs, can easily be folded up and moved from the recreation room out onto the patio for out-door playing, or stored until needed again. For ease of construction and storage, the table is built in two parts, each consisting of a frame, top and four legs. The two separate sections are simply bolted to-gether to form a larger playing surface.

To construct the table, cut 1 x 3-inch solid stock to the proper length for the top frames, as shown in the drawing, and fasten to-gether with glue and screws. Attach the two 4 x 5-foot panels to the frames with glue and 1-inch finishing nails spaced 4 inches apart along all framing members. Avoid nailing closer than 3/8 inch from the edges and set the nail heads flush with the surface.

Turn the table sections over and fasten the collapsible legs with wood screws to framing and wood shims as shown. Locate and drill holes for fastening the table sections together.

To finish the surface and framing members use a coat of primer and a coat of flat green enamel.

Fasten the table sections together with 2-inch carriage bolts. Then apply ¾-inch wide, white, plastic tape along edges and one cen-ter of table, cutting tape where the table sections join.

If you make your own legs, turn the table sections over, locate and drill holes for fastening the legs in place and also holes for fasten-ing the sections together. Hold the legs firm and square in the corners, drill through the legs, and fasten with 3-inch carriage bolts. For quick assembly and disassembly of the table you might wish to use wing nuts.

MATERIALS LIST

Table Tops:	Hardboard (Masonite, Tempered Duolux) 3/16"x4'x5' (2)
Leg Shims:	1"x3"x8" solid stock (8)
Framing Members:	1"x3"x5' solid stock (4)
Framing Members:	1"x3"x4'-4½" solid stock (6)
Line Marker:	White plastic tape, ¾"x37' (1)
Section Fasteners:	Carriage bolts ¼"x2" (2)
Leg Fasteners:	Carriage bolts ¼"x3" (16)
Table Legs:	2"x2"x4'-4½" solid stock (8) OR: collapsible legs 29¼" (2 sets)

TABLE TOP 4'6" x 5' MASONITE
3/16" TEMPERED DUOLUX

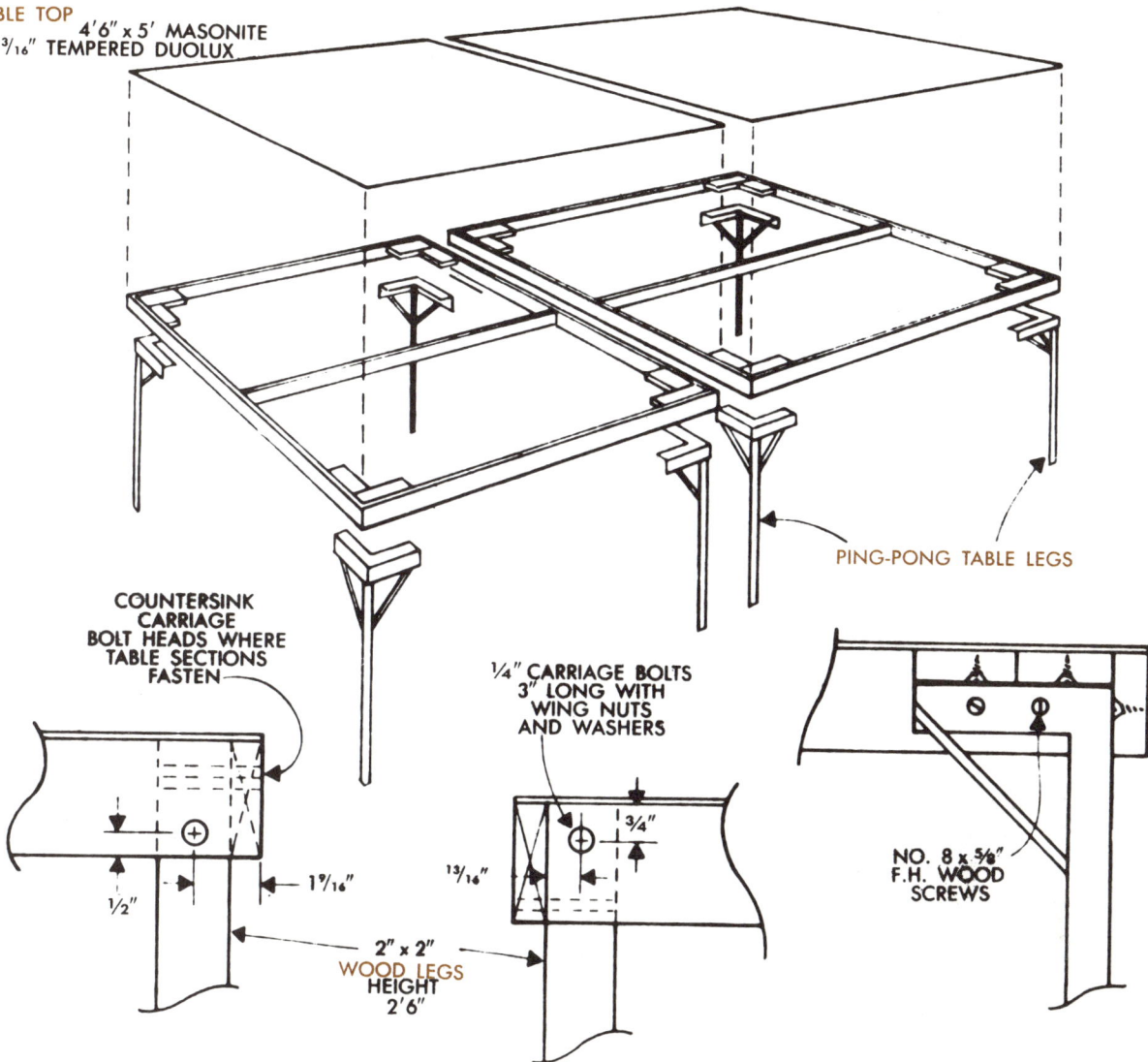

PING-PONG TABLE LEGS

COUNTERSINK CARRIAGE BOLT HEADS WHERE TABLE SECTIONS FASTEN

1/4" CARRIAGE BOLTS 3" LONG WITH WING NUTS AND WASHERS

NO. 8 x 5/8" F.H. WOOD SCREWS

1/2"   1 9/16"

13/16"   3/4"

2" x 2" WOOD LEGS HEIGHT 2'6"

First step in assembling table is fastening the frames together. Frames are straight-grained, solid stock.

Hardboard panels are glued and nailed in place. Two sections are bolted together to form completed table.

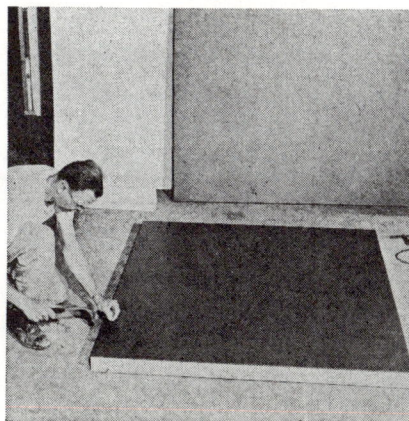

For shop-made legs, holes are drilled through legs and frames. Legs are held in place with carriage bolts.

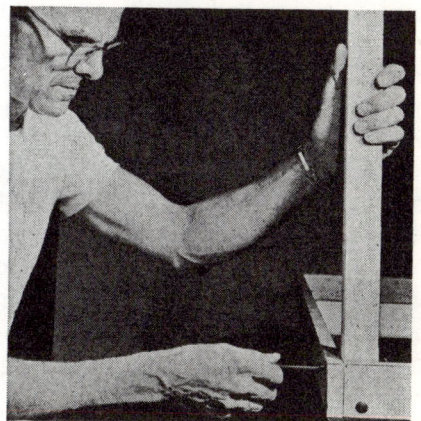

VITRINE

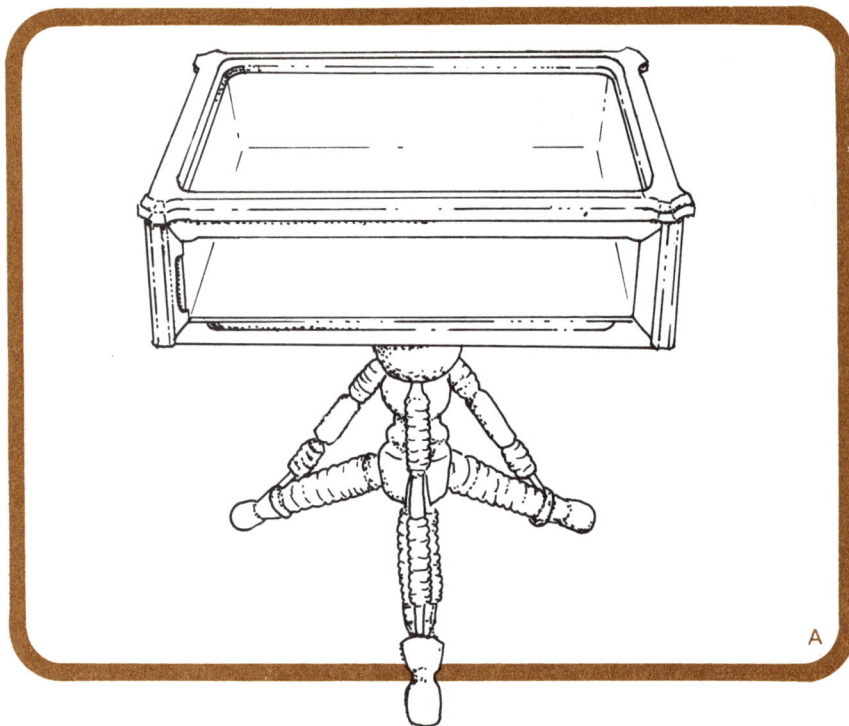

The word "vitrine" is of French origin, and it means a glass showcase for displaying souvenirs, trophies and the like. The top, and at least three of the sides, are glass, while the bottom is solid, usually covered with velvet. The back, generally the non-glass "side" also can be covered with fabric.

The rectangular table consists of four legs, with frames between. The glass fits in grooves in the top and bottom rail, and in the legs. After making the legs, and the rails, assemble the table "dry," to check for·fit, and to accurately determine the sizes of the pieces of glass required. The glass should be at least 1/16 inch shorter in length and width than the frame will accept, to allow for expansion and contraction with humidity changes.

Assemble two units of two legs and two long rails, inserting the glass during assembly. When the glue is dry, join these two assemblies with the shorter rails, again inserting glass during assembly. You may need help for the latter operation, and to square it up. The top is made separately, fitted with glass and hinged.

The smaller table consists of four separate frames, joined at their mitered corners. The top, again, is made separately and hinged to the case. The top projects ½ inch on all four sides.

The table shown was mounted on the column of an antique piano stool. The plans show how to make a reproduction of the column. Assembly is a little tricky, in that the brace turnings must be inserted in the short legs, then both fitted into the holes in the heavier column. Because this table rotates, glass is used on all four sides.

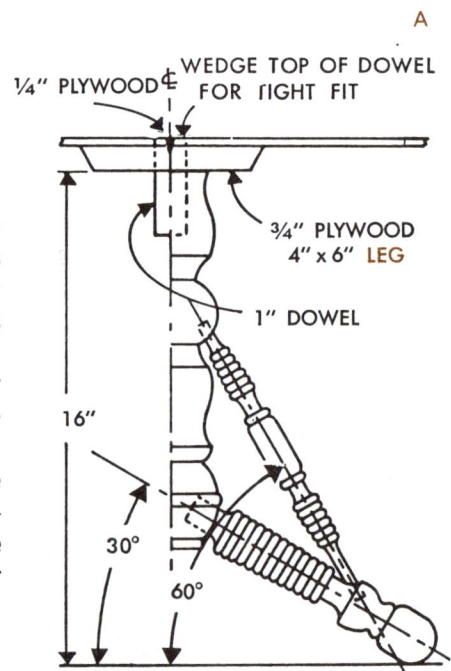

A

¼" PLYWOOD WEDGE TOP OF DOWEL FOR TIGHT FIT
¾" PLYWOOD 4" x 6" LEG
1" DOWEL
16"
30°
60°

TABLES

B

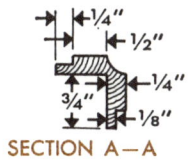

A

¼″
½″
¾″
¼″
⅛″

SECTION A—A

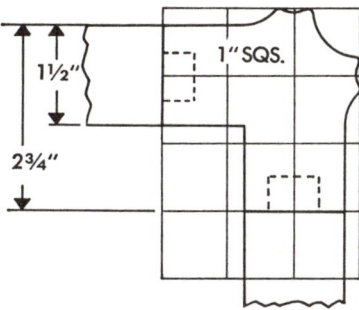

1″ SQS.

1½″

2¾″

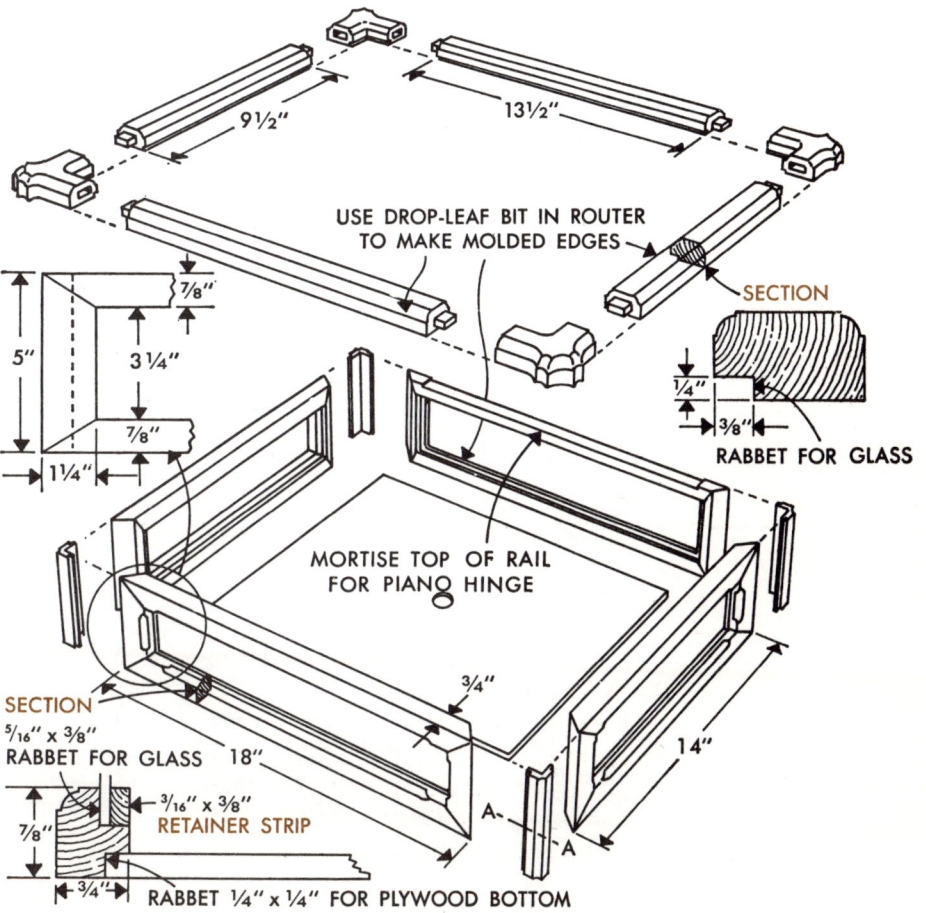

9½″

13½″

USE DROP-LEAF BIT IN ROUTER
TO MAKE MOLDED EDGES

SECTION

¼″
⅜″

RABBET FOR GLASS

7/8″

5″

3¼″

7/8″

1¼″

MORTISE TOP OF RAIL
FOR PIANO HINGE

¾″

14″

SECTION

5/16″ x ⅜″
RABBET FOR GLASS   18″

7/8″

3/16″ x ⅜″
RETAINER STRIP

¾″

RABBET ¼″ x ¼″ FOR PLYWOOD BOTTOM

A

A

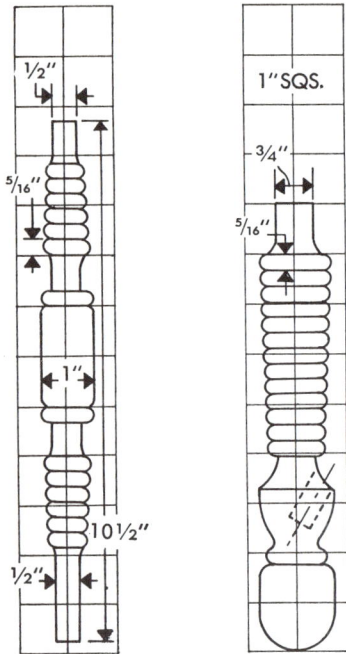

1/2"

5/16"

1"

10½"

1/2"

1"SQS.

3/4"

5/16"

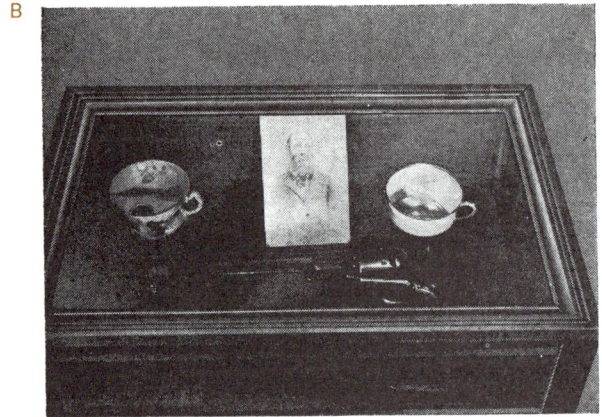

B

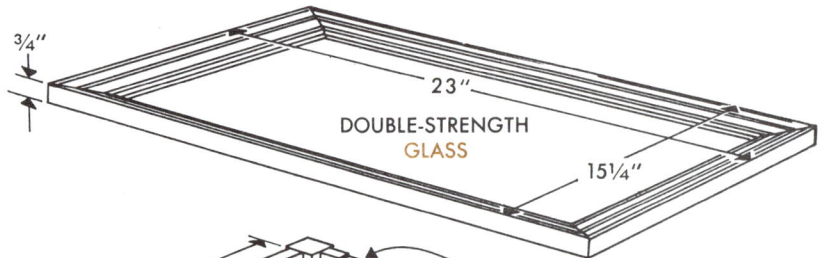

3/4"

23"

DOUBLE-STRENGTH
GLASS

15¼"

A

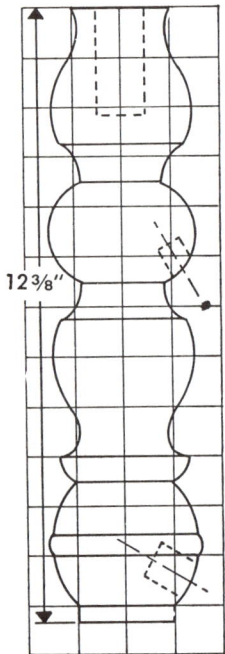

12⅜"

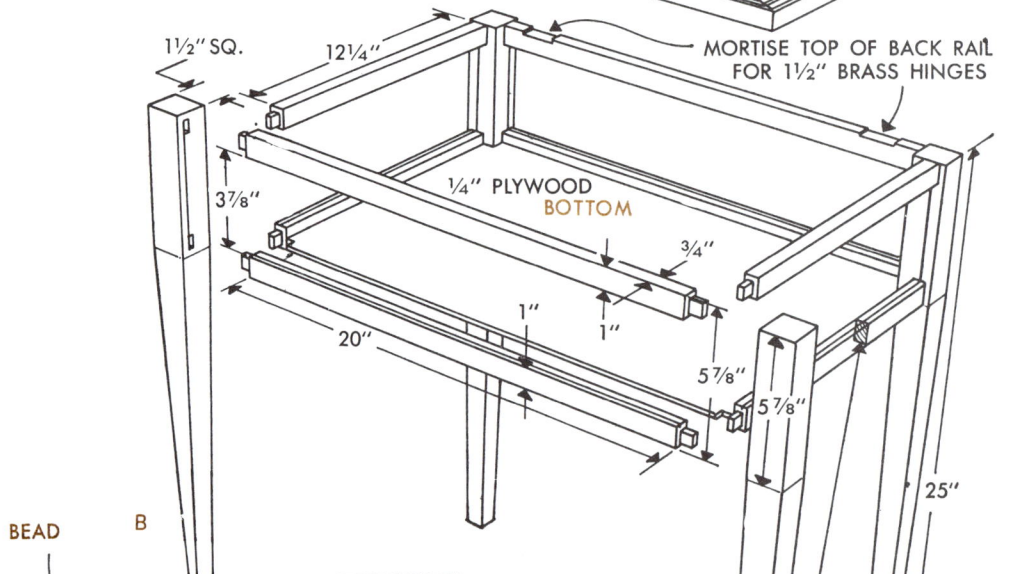

1½" SQ.

12¼"

MORTISE TOP OF BACK RAIL
FOR 1½" BRASS HINGES

3⅞"

¼" PLYWOOD
BOTTOM

3/4"

20"

1"

1"

5⅞"

5⅞"

25"

BEAD

B

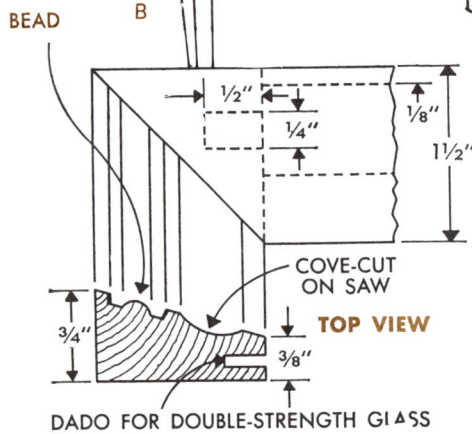

1/2"

1/4"

1/8"

1½"

COVE-CUT
ON SAW

3/4"

TOP VIEW

3/8"

DADO FOR DOUBLE-STRENGTH GLASS

SECTION

BOTTOM

1/8" DADO FOR
GLASS

3/8"

1/4"

BOTTOM
RAIL

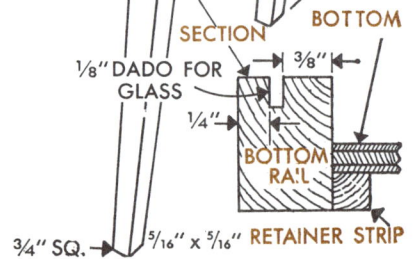

3/4" SQ.

5/16" x 5/16"

RETAINER STRIP

ROLL-TOP TRASH BIN

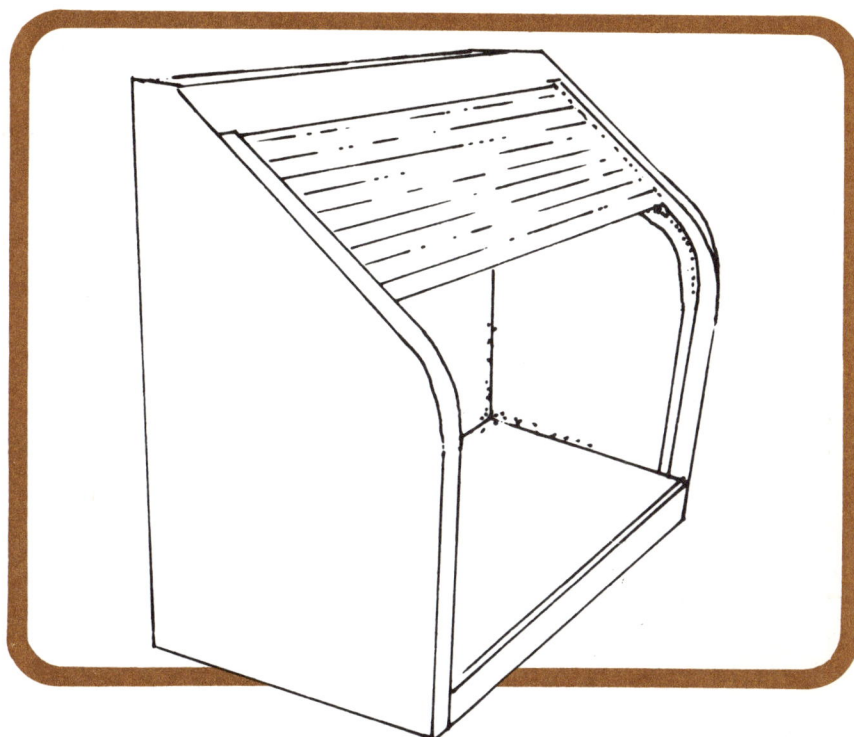

When assembling the slats for the tambour door, be sure to keep them square, so the door will work easily.

Designed to hide unsightly trash cans and prevent wandering dogs from knocking them over, this bin also would be ideal as storage for firewood for a fireplace, keeping it dry and ready to burn.

A space-saving feature of this trash bin is the vertical-sliding tambour door. This provides full access to the cans, yet requires no swing-space, as would a hinged door, so the bin can be placed adjacent to a wall, house door or between shrubs with no worry of damage or interference. The dimensions given are for a bin that will accommodate medium size containers; if yours are larger or smaller, change the measurements to suit.

Start construction by making the floor from four lengths of 2 x 4 and a piece of exterior-grade ¾-inch plywood. Use waterproof glue and nails for the assembly.

The ends are made next, from exterior-grade plywood, and strips are attached to form the tracks for the door. The outside strip is kerfed to permit bending it around the curve, as indicated, with an 8-inch radius. If your curve is slightly rough from the saw cuts, use contact adhesive to fit a strip of plastic laminate the full length of the groove to provide a smooth surface.

The door is made of strips, as profiled, with rabbets cut in diagonally-opposite corners, and the corners rounded as shown. These strips will overlap to keep out the rain and weather, and move easily as they pass around the curve. Light canvas and contact adhesive can be used to join the strips, or lengths of plastic webbing can be stapled to the strips to create the tambour door.

The assembled door is slipped into the track at the back of the

TAMBOUR DOOR
IS ASSEMBLED FROM
3/4" x 1 1/2" x 45" STRIPS

SECTION OF
STRIP KERFED
TO PERMIT
BENDING

3" RAD.
1 3/4"
1/2" x 3/4"

8" RAD.

1/4"
PLYWOOD
BACK

7/8"

7/8"
DOOR
STOP
7/8"

3/4" x 3/4"
1 3/4"

THIS SECTION
REMOVABLE TO INSERT
DOOR

42"

24"

12"

3/4" PLYWOOD
ENDS AND FLOOR

45 1/2"
3 1/2"

1 1/2"

23 3/4"

3/4"

1 1/2"

RABBET
1/4" x 1/4"

22" FROM
BOTTOM

8"

3/4"

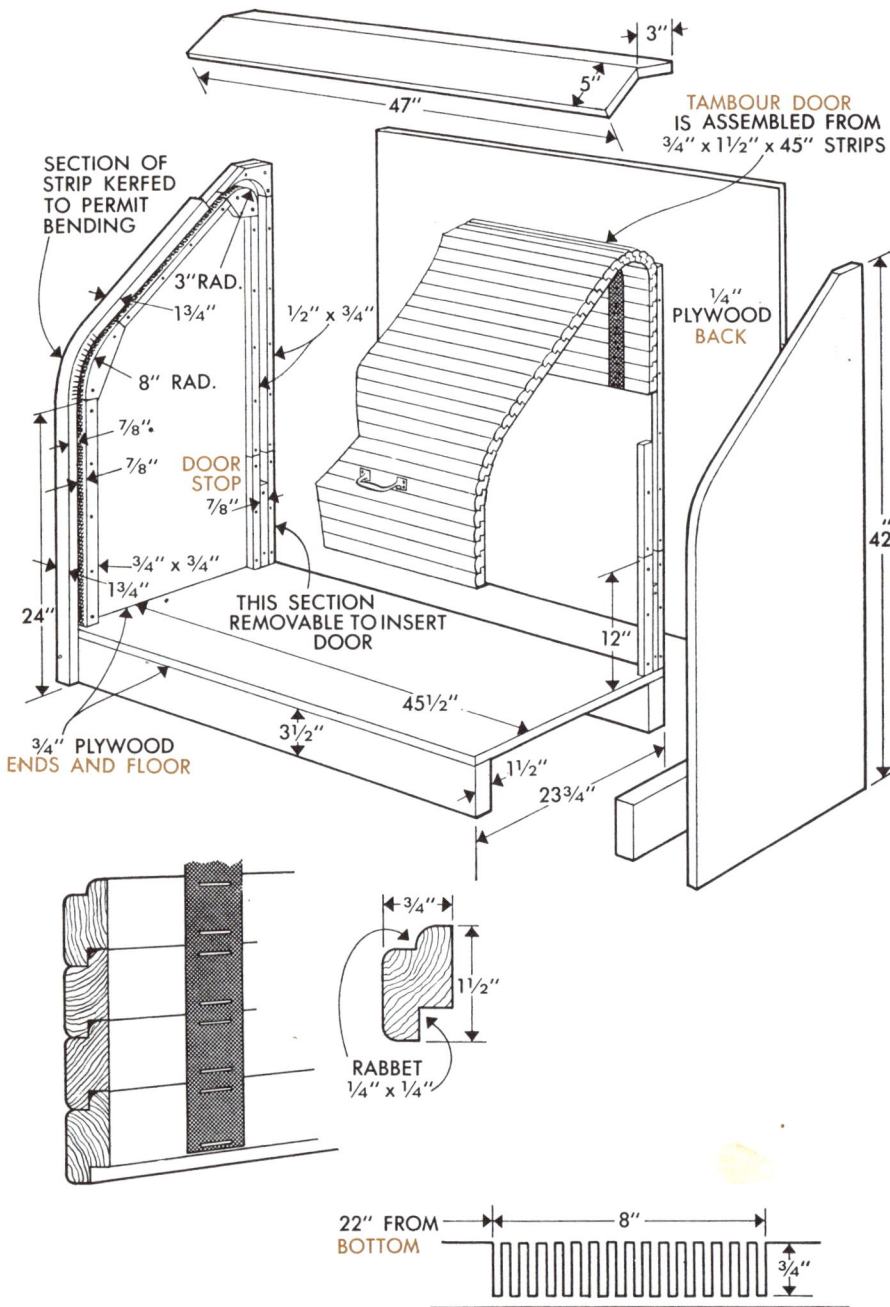

Heavy handles are attached about the
sixth strip to permit easy lifting of the
door without stooping.

bin by removing a 12-inch length of the outside strip. A strip at the
center of the slot provides a stop to prevent the door dropping all the
way down. About 30 strips are required depending on the size of the
bin. Paint the finished unit to match the house and set it on bricks or
concrete blocks.

THREE-TIERED SERVING TRAY

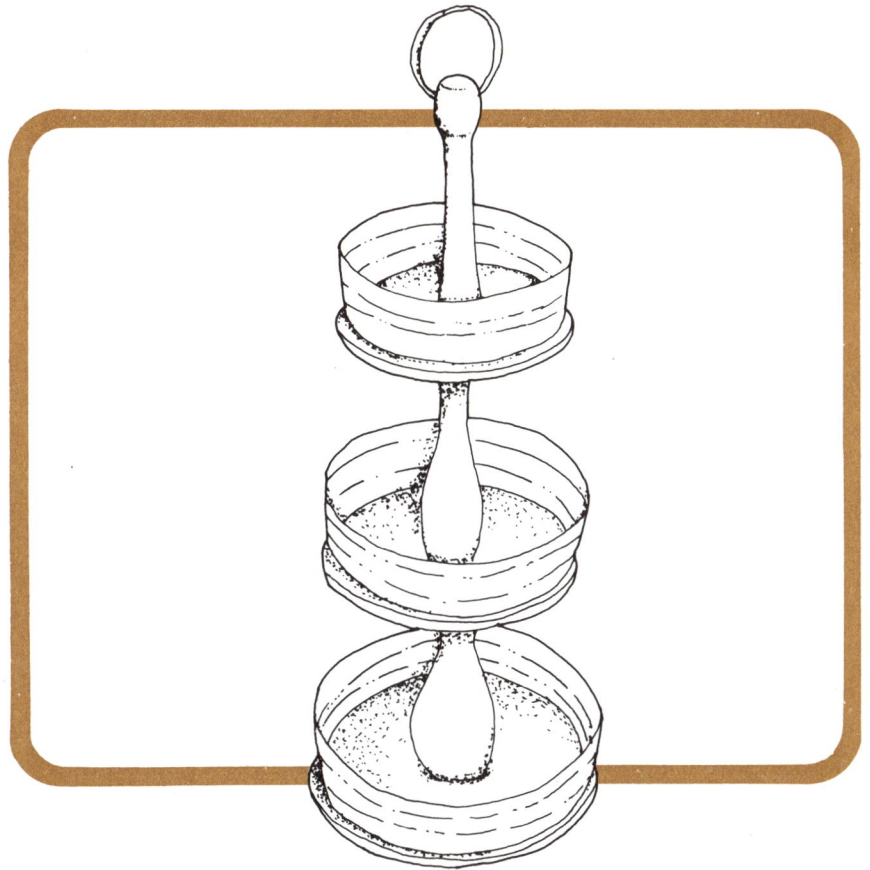

Each tier, or bowl, is glued-up from rings cut from solid stock, and fitted with a disk to create a bottom.

Attractive as a centerpiece, practical for serving party snacks, and a real fun lathe project, this serving tray can be made of any hardwood. Early American fans can turn it from clear, straightgrained pine.

Each of the three trays, or bowls, is assembled from three rings of wood plus a disk for the bottom. Two of the rings are ¾-inch thick, while the other ring and bottom are ½-inch stock. Turning, smoothing and rounding the upper edge will, of course, reduce the overall height.

When gluing up the rings and bottom be generous with the glue and clamp the assembly firmly; use plenty of clamps. Any glue that is squeezed out will be removed during turning.

The first step is to turn a disk on the faceplate, of a diameter slightly smaller than that of the finished tray. This disk is left on the faceplate and the tray blanks are fastened to it with a No. 10 or 12 screw. The centers of the trays will have been marked when the circles are scribed to make the disks for the bottoms.

Make the rough cuts at slow speed, then run the lathe faster for the finishing cuts. Keep in mind that only the single screw is holding the work on the faceplate.

Holes in the top and bottom trays should present no problems, but the center tray has an opening large enough to permit it to slide down over the column to fit the shoulder. Bore the larger hole with a big bit, hole saw or fly cutter. It can be slightly undersize, and fitted to the shoulder by sanding the column above the shoulder until you get a firm push fit.

The upper end of the column is turned as a separate piece and fastened to the lower column with a dowel. The ring in the top is a 2-inch chrome-plated ring of the type used for loose-leaf binders, and available at stationery stores.

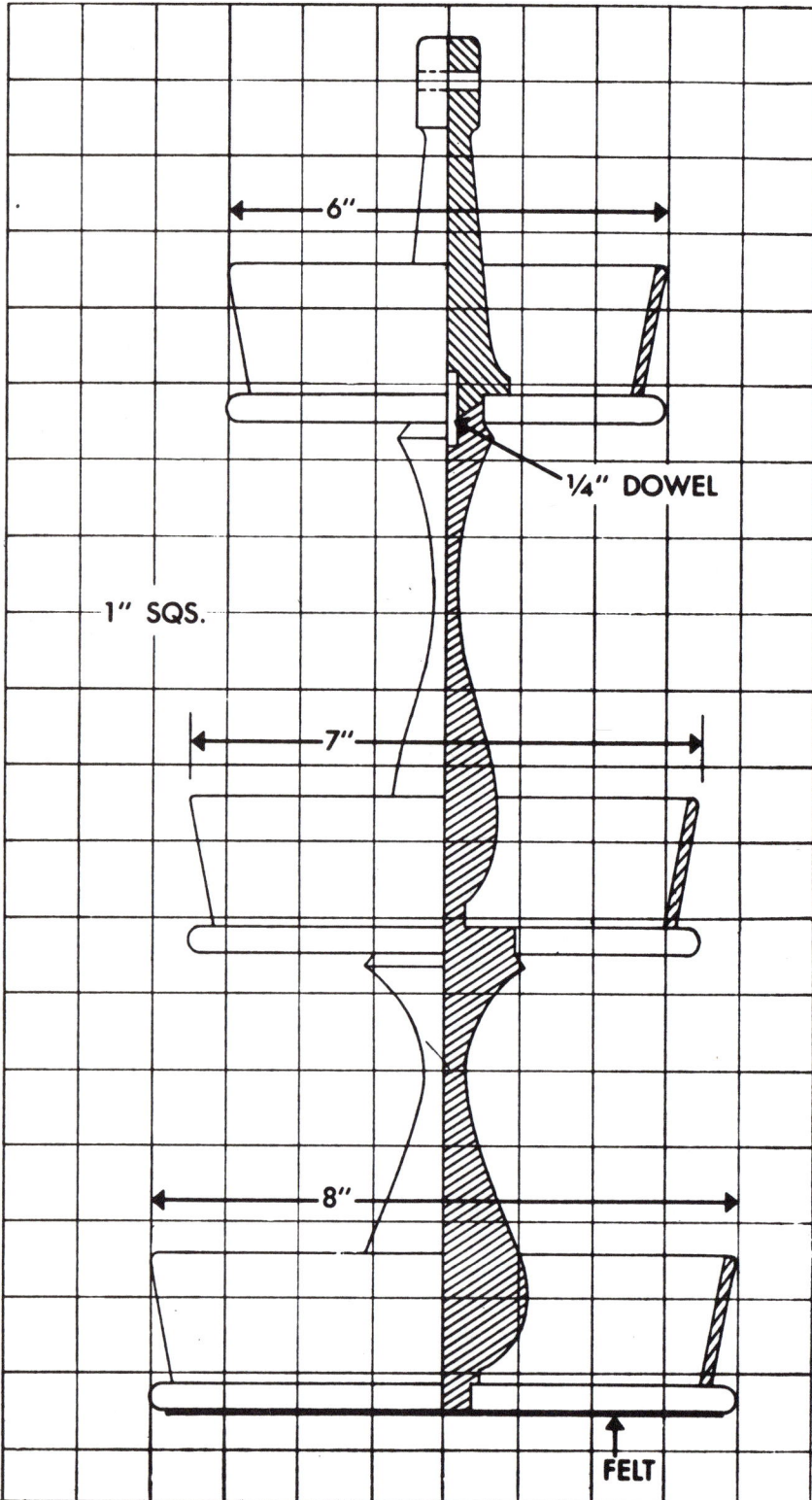

6"

¼" DOWEL

1" SQS.

7"

8"

FELT

Use plenty of glue on the rings and disk, and apply enough clamps to hold assembly firmly.

When turning the trays, first turn and leave on the faceplate a disk slightly smaller than the diameter of the finished bowls. Attach the tray with a screw.

The column is turned in two sections, is a between-centers operation. You don't have to stick to the profile shown, but remember to turn the shoulders to accept the three trays.

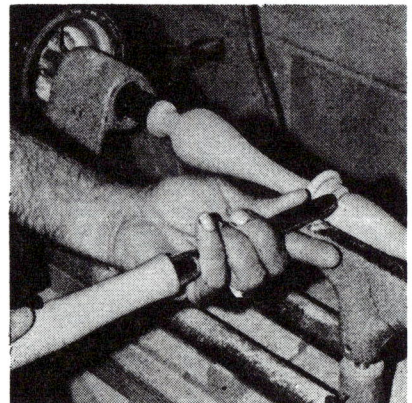

The hole in the center of the middle tray is cut with a flycutter or large bit. The hole must be a size that will slide over the top of the column and fit snugly.

It may be necessary to fit the center tray to the column by trying, slightly enlarging, then trying again until it just fits snugly. Best bet is to drill a hole in a scrap piece.

There are six parts, including the steel ring used for a handle. Three trays, two sections of column. Finish and stain to suit your decor.

EARLY AMERICAN SPOON TRAY

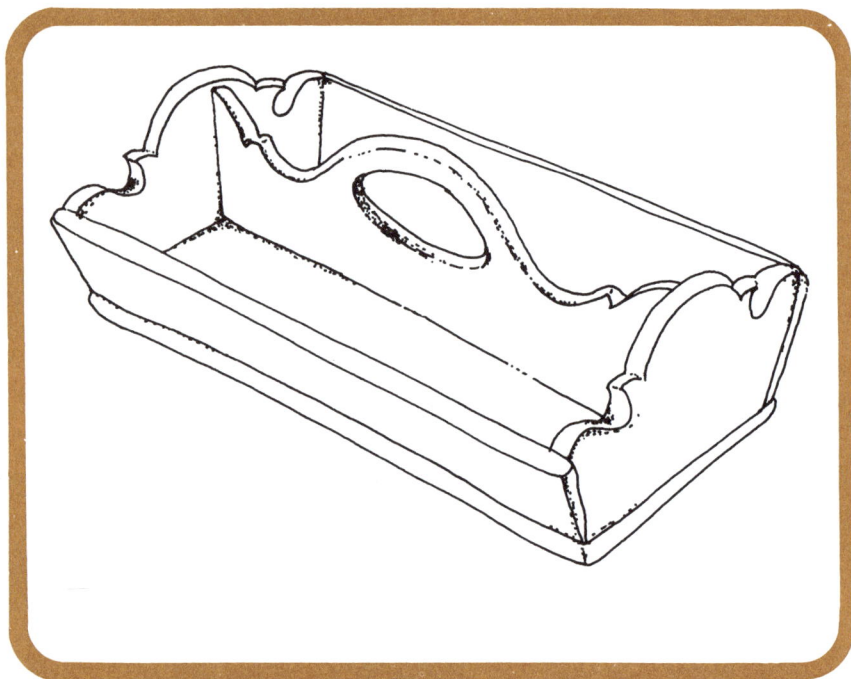

In the Colonial era spoon trays were used for what the name implies, storage of the family silverware (usually pewterware or some inexpensive metal). Today reproductions are used for everything from holding sewing supplies and collecting the day's mail to serving cookies and crackers.

This tray is a "fun" project. The only tricky part is planing the 60-degree angle on the lower edges of the sides. This can be a trial-and-error operation, so make shallow cuts and check the angle frequently to make sure it will fit snugly against the bottom when the sides are held against the ends of the tray.

Cut the bottom from one piece; this may require edge-gluing narrow stock. Make a pattern for the ends, and the partition-handle, by enlarging the squared drawings. Make the straight cuts with a handsaw, then cut the curved, scrolled portions with a scroll or jig saw. Slightly round the edges of all pieces to create a "worn" look (except for the lower edges of the sides), then glue and brad the various pieces together.

Sand all surfaces smooth, then finish with an antique color of stain. Follow this with several coats of well-rubbed clear lacquer, or apply a penetrating-oil finish that will produce a "hand-rubbed" look.

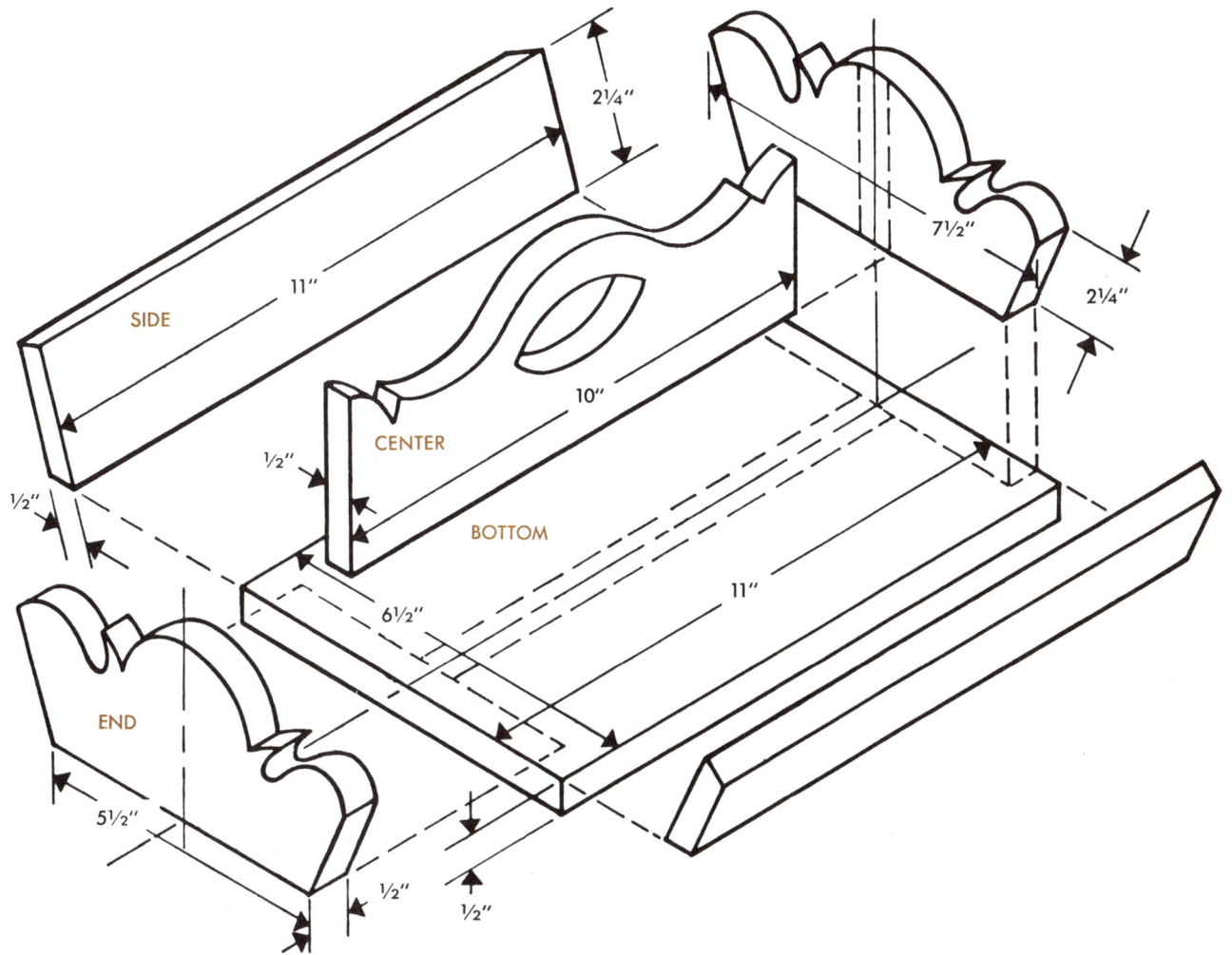

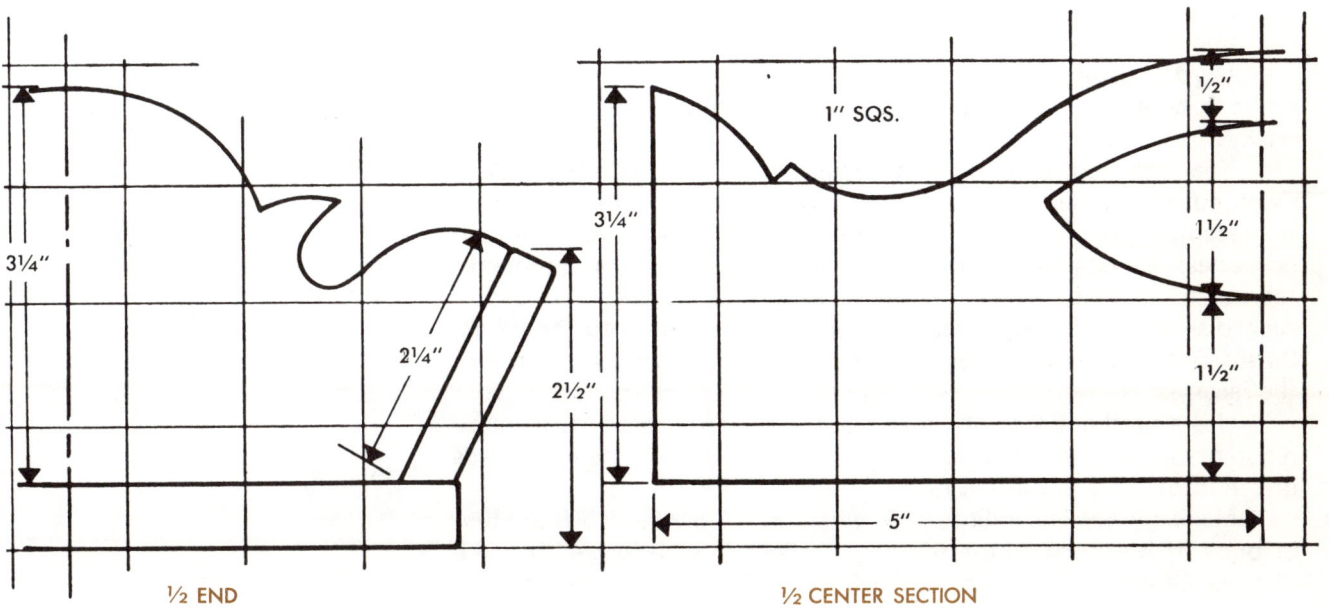

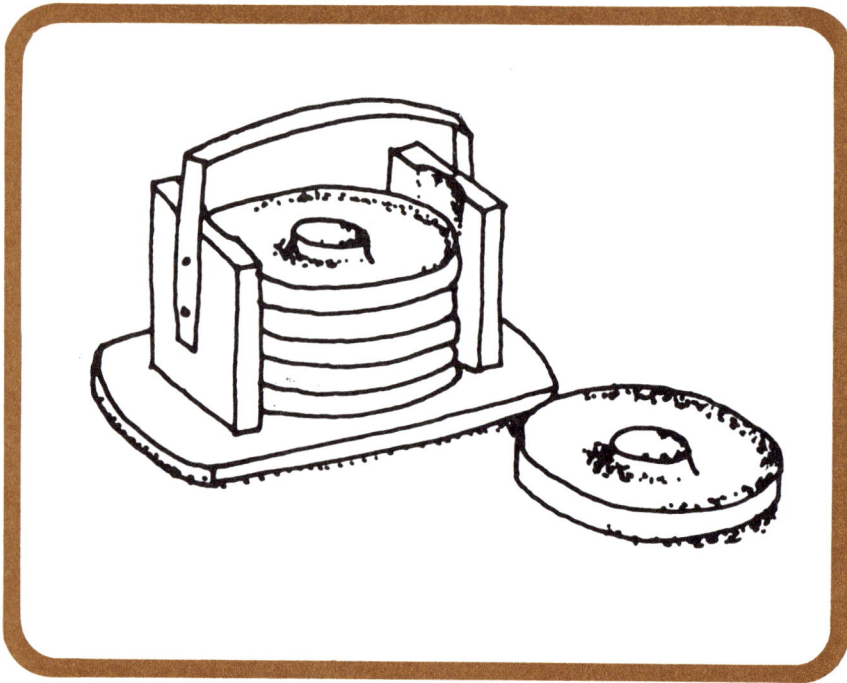

STACKABLE SNACK TRAYS

For those who like to entertain with a flair, this attractive set of snack trays will firmly hold a glass and still have room for something to munch on.

For the craftsman, it's a nice exercise in faceplate turning. The set can be turned from any hardwood that does not readily tear and split, such as black walnut and Philippine mahogany (lauan). Select a wood that will be compatible with the furnishings in the room where the set will be used. The wood used for the storage holder should be the same as for the trays.

If you have never done faceplate turning before, be prepared to waste a couple of turning blocks; faceplate turning can be a little tricky.

The first step is to make an auxiliary faceplate. This is a disk of wood cut slightly larger than the diameter of the faceplate. Screw it to the faceplate, then turn it to a diameter of exactly 8 inches. Drill small holes near the edge to accept brads or small finishing nails. Cut blanks for the trays about ¼ inch larger than the finished diameter. Center each disk on the auxiliary faceplate and tap the nails into the block. Be sure none will be in an area to be cut away by the chisel, then turn the recesses.

Use a urethane varnish or lacquer to provide a water and alcohol-resistant finish. Finish the bottoms of the trays, place them on brads driven into board; finish the tops.

Make the rack as indicated. The handle is 1/8 x ¾-inch aluminum or brass. If it is bent so the top part is about ½ inch longer than the distance between the sides of the rack a graceful curve will result.

1½"
8" DIA.
7" RAD.
6"
4⅛" RAD.
2⅝"
¾"

¼" ¼" 2¼" ¼" ¼"
½" ⅜" ¾"

GLASS HOLDER
8"
7½"
SNACK HOLDER

⅛" x ¾" ALUMINUM STRIP
½" RH SCREWS BOTH SIDES
5¼"
7¾"
7"
1¾" #6 SCREWS
¾"
14"

⅛" x ¾" ALUMINUM STRIP
6"
ALL TRAYS
¾"
1½"
1½"
1"
9"

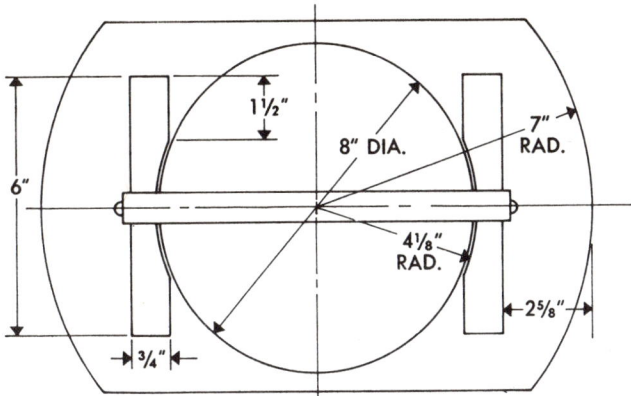

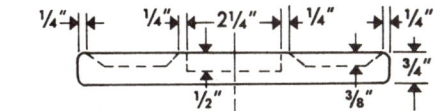

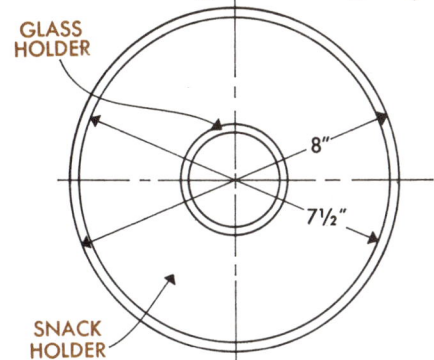

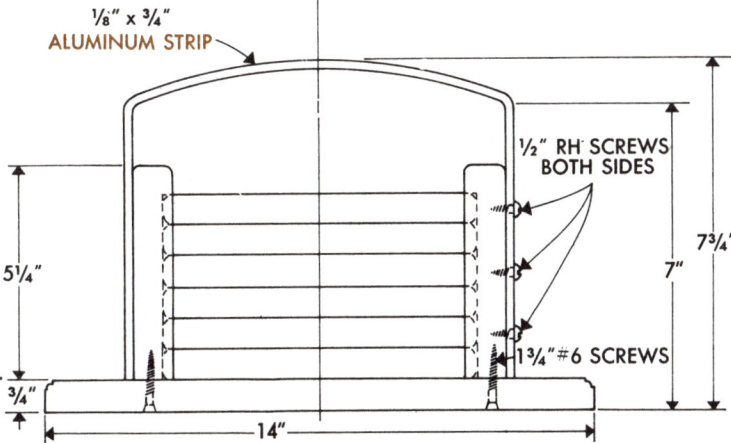

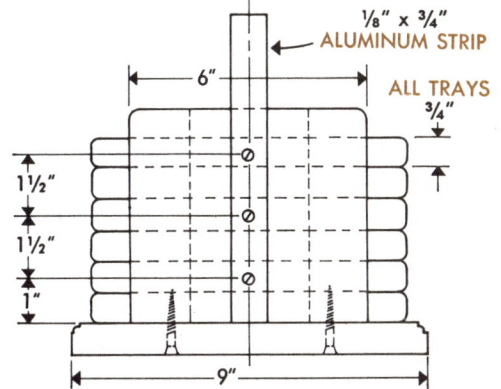

Attach the handle with roundhead brass or aluminum screws; the metal should match that of the handle.

Wood disk is screwed to faceplate, turning square fastened to it with aid of nails in holes in edge.

Block is centered on wooden disk as closely as possible, then nails are driven into block to hold it.

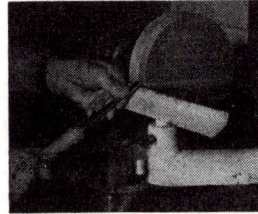

Lathe is run at 900 to 1000 rpm, stock is rounded to exact diameter of tray with square-nose chisel.

Section through center of tray; recess for snacks is 3/8" deep, depression for glass is ½" deep.

Finished trays are supported on 1" brads driven into board, which permits finishing both sides without marring.

Inside surfaces of side pieces that hold trays have concave profiles that match shape of trays. Saw or rasp to shape.

EARLY AMERICAN TOWEL HOLDER

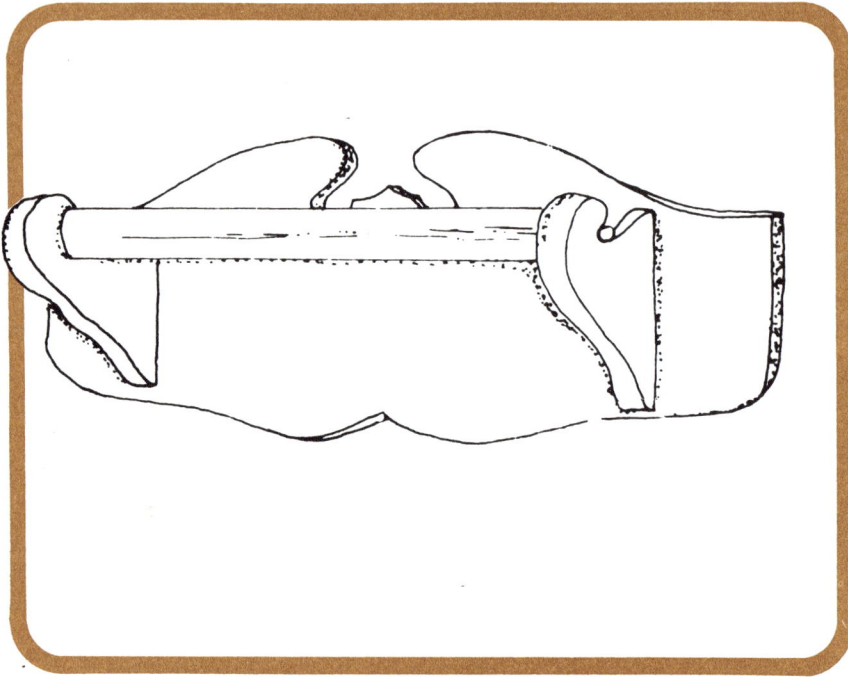

Here's a simple, one-evening project that requires only hand tools, and the result is an attractive, very practical item for the kitchen with colonial decor.

Make a pattern for the back and sides by enlarging the squared drawing. Mark the patterns on straight-grained ½-inch stock; you can use thicker material if that is all you have in the shop. Use a jig or band saw to cut out the parts. Locate and drill the pilot holes for the screws that attach the projecting sides to the back. Sand all parts smooth and "break" all sharp edges. Use glue and screws to attach the sides to the back.

The roller for the towel is a length of 1-inch dowel. Drill in each end for a ¼-inch dowel that is 1½ inches long. These smaller dowels should project ¾ inch, which means the larger dowel is drilled ¾ inch deep in each end. Glue the smaller dowels in place.

Wipe off any excess glue, stain the parts any desired colonial color and finish with satin varnish.

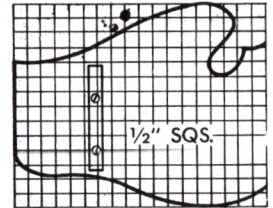

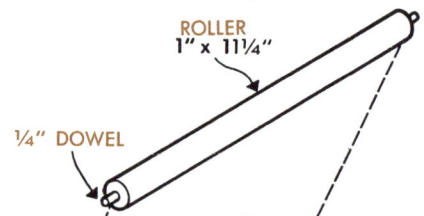

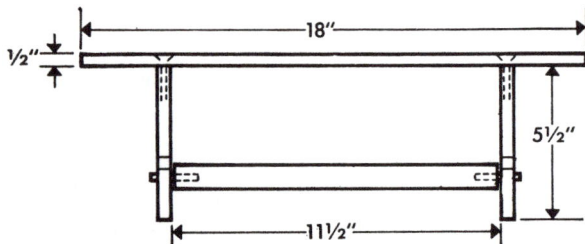

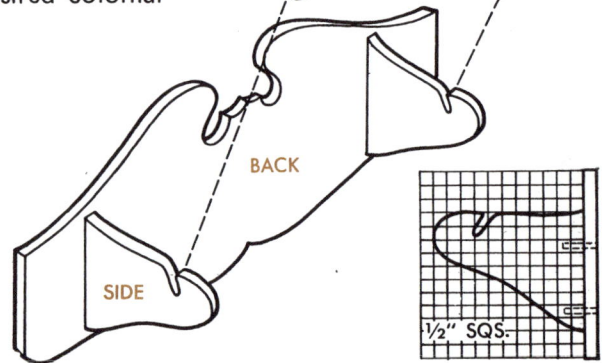

½" SQS.

ROLLER
1" x 11¼"

¼" DOWEL

BACK

SIDE

½" SQS.

18"

½"

5½"

11½"

256

T

U V

W